CATHOLIC
WATERSHED

To the love of my life,
Catherine O'Connell-Cahill

and to the priests
of the Archdiocese of Chicago

and in memory
of Sister Suzanne Zuercher, OSB

CATHOLIC WATERSHED

The Chicago Ordination Class of 1969 and How They Helped Change the Church

Michael P. Cahill

Foreword by Martin E. Marty

CATHOLIC WATERSHED
The Chicago Ordination Class of 1969
and How They Helped Change the Church
by Michael P. Cahill
Foreword by Martin E. Marty

Edited by Gregory F. Augustine Pierce
Cover, text design, and typesetting by Patricia A. Lynch, Harvest Graphics
Cover photo by Bigstock

Published by In Extenso Press
Distributed exclusively by ACTA Publications, 4848 N. Clark Street,
Chicago, IL 60640, (800) 397-2282, www.actapublications.com

Library of Congress Catalog Number: 2014947948
Paperback ISBN: 978-0-87946-994-8
Printed in the United States of America by Total Printing Systems
Year 25 24 23 22 21 20 19 18 17 16 15
Printing 15 14 13 12 1110 9 8 7 6 5 4

♻ Text printed on 30% post-consumer recycled paper

Contents

FOREWORD

The titles of two other fine books on American Catholicism signal situations of the Church that frame the story in this book. The first, by Steven M. Avella, deals with Chicago: *This Confident Church: Catholic Leadership and Life in Chicago, 1940-1965* (Simon and Schuster, 2004). The second, equally to the point, is Peter Steinfels' *A People Adrift: The Crisis of the Roman Catholic Church in America* (Notre Dame, 1993), which focuses on the turn-of-the-millennium decades. What happened between 1965 and 2003 to prompt talk of "confidence" followed so soon by "drift"?

Michael P. Cahill, aware of the big American Catholic picture, sensibly chooses to provide a close-up on the formation, career, and retirement of a generation of priests in a particular archdiocese. Through the eyes of six well-chosen representatives of the ordination class of 1969 in Chicago, men with whom he spent considerable amounts of time and to whom he brought a ready ear and a faithful recorder, Cahill provides a window on the larger Catholic scene at a time of drastic change. This priestly generation was graced or doomed (or both) to live through the transitions of that period, to be buffeted by changes which occurred largely beyond their control, and to take measured control where they were called and assigned to serve, chiefly in parishes.

"Change" is the key term in this account of what happened to these six men, whose world-and-church we get to know quite well. They entered the priesthood eager to participate in changes promised by the Second Vatican Council (1962 to 1965) and by cultural circumstances that occurred during their formative years. All of them have recently completed or are finishing up their active ministry, with the eagerness of their younger years at times dulled in the era of "drift" after the "confidence" came to be in shorter supply. As I read the many references to changes that Cahill chronicles so accurately and vividly, I thought of an observation by Richard Hooker, an Anglican divine in an earlier age: "All change is inconveniencing, including change from worse to better."

The book may at first be unsatisfying to one cohort of potential readers, leftover "triumphalists" who yearn for a nostalgic visit back to the simpler days of confident church life under authoritarian leaders who served or were being served by vast numbers of laity who took orders (and yet, I hasten to add, also often experienced grace and community). The Catholic laity were never mere Mass-attending serfs but full-bodied groups of people whose church life readers can appraise through the eyes of the class of 1969. Latter-day triumphalists no longer trumpet victories, but many of them have now regathered and are taking refuge in reactionary circles to celebrate recalled liturgies and reined-in laity. Cahill, recounting how post-Vatican II reforms were in the air in 1969, speaks of the latter-day "reform of the reform" that now attracts some priests—but none of the six we are tracking on the pages that follow.

The members of the class of 1969 whom we meet here are faithful to the Council, but they cannot be starry-eyed. They may be moved by Christian hope, but not by standard-brand optimism. The book reveals them to be sad when their efforts are discounted but mature and faithful when their multi-faceted careers allow them to reflect the light of the Gospel, even when the general culture and much church-culture does not share that light.

This foreword is about them and author Cahill, and not about me, a mere foreworder. So I'll climb on stage for only a moment and then head for the wings. On my daily walks I often pass what had been the little Gothic gem that was for so many years Quigley Preparatory Seminary High School, where members of this class in the late 1950s and early 1960s were surrounded by an astounding 1,300-some fellow teenage aspirants to the priesthood (see Chapter Two). They were highly visible in downtown Chicago in the days of the "Confident Church," but the students are now long gone, replaced by archdiocesan staffers in what is now the archdiocesan chancery offices.

Back then Quigley seemed remote and forbidding to Lutherans like me and fellow citizens of many faiths or none. Today, though we see quite literally thousands of citizens on our walks near or past the chancery and then Holy Name Cathedral, we see no cassocks, no habits of religious sisters, no Catholic insignia. (Be advised or forewarned, however: There may soon be some cassocked young priests who have reverted to clerical uniforms as part of their "reform of the reform.")

What went wrong to produce the post-confident and now-apparently-adrift Catholic Church (at least pending the intervention of the new Pope Francis)? The answer is not simple, and Cahill chooses to provide the reader with data and stories that can inspire a variety of partial answers to such questions. He devotes particular attention to three Cardinal Archbishops (Cody, Bernardin, and George), who were or are—at least in the eyes of these six veteran priests—in one case bad, in one case good, and in one case still receiving mixed marks. The author pays attention to and rewards with compliments many effective priests and laypeople. It is refreshing to me that he is not moved by ideology or an impulse further to polarize a divided Church. I know of no higher compliment to pay to a book like this one than to say that it provides a dispassionate, close-up, intimate, patient, and often revealing picture of part of the Church in action—in, yes, a time of change. Get acquainted now with members of the ordination class of 1969, as I did, and I am confident that you will be as rewarded as I have been.

Martin E. Marty
Fairfax M. Cone Distinguished
Service Professor Emeritus
The University of Chicago

INTRODUCTION

As teenagers making the decision to enter the high school seminary for the Church of Chicago in the late 1950s, Mike Ahlstrom, Larry Duris, Bob Heidenreich, Tom Libera, Ed Upton, and Bill Zavaski had no idea what lay in store for them. In a few short years, the hierarchically ordered, stable, rule-bound institution that had ready answers for everything would undergo a radical transformation. This sea change in the life of the Church would define their life and ministry. To a man, they embraced the renewal called for by the Second Vatican Council and implemented it across the archdiocese. Although at times troubled by the reaction against their ministry that they have had to endure mostly in the later years of their priesthoods, these priests cherish the lives they have led. Considering themselves blessed to have lived in interesting, not to say revolutionary, times in the life of the Church, they have chosen to tell the real stories of their remarkable adventures as Chicago—and American—priests in the pages that follow.

These six men were ordained as Roman Catholic priests for the Archdiocese of Chicago as part of the class of 1969. They have lived in three distinct periods of American Catholic history. Born in the midst of World War II just prior to the baby boom generation, they grew up in the pre-Vatican II Church, where they learned that the Church and its teachings and practices did not change. Then, in the middle of their seminary careers, the Second Vatican Council turned upside down their previous experience of an unchanging Church. To be sure, Vatican II did not penetrate all corners of the Church simultaneously, as these men's early experiences at Chicago's major seminary would demonstrate, but even hidebound seminary life changed drastically over time because of the Council. Launched into priesthood just after Vatican II, these men attempted to live out the spirit of that Council as Catholic priests on the front lines of Church life—that is to say, in parishes. Some twenty-plus years into their priestly ministry, their theology and pastoral practice came under increasing scrutiny in what became the third major period of their priesthood, not so much from people in the pews as from an increasingly conservative Church hierarchy in both the United States and Rome, and from a new generation of seminarians and priests. As background, then, a review of their three eras will put the story of these six priests in some context.

The Catholic Church of the grandparents and parents of the class of 1969 differed in some important respects from the Church the men themselves grew up in. Most of their grandparents arrived here from distant shores—Ireland, Poland, Lithuania—to discover an immigrant Church that often found itself on the defensive as its people attempted to assimilate into the American way of life while at the same time maintaining old world traditions. Often the victim of anti-Catholic prejudice, the Church—really, the parish—served as the most important institution in the lives of many in this generation born just before the turn of the century and living in Catholic ghettos. Priests, usually the most educated people in the parish, lived as men set apart, ruling their parishes with an iron hand, exhorting their people to "pray, pay, and obey" without question. Most parishioners accepted these strictures without complaint, both because their poor or working-class families needed discipline and authority to guide them and because the Church gave them so much. It provided identity in an often hostile world. It acted as not only the religious but the social center of their lives. It kept them focused on the "straight and narrow" as regards the many temptations of urban immigrant life: alcohol, lust, and greed. It offered spiritual consolation for difficult lives but also support to ease the tensions of social mobility. It served as a bridge between the old world and the new even as its magnificent churches provided a sense of beauty, mystery, peace, and dignity. In a world where the only constant was change, the Church alone offered continuity with the past and with timeless religious truths.

One generation later, the parents of these six men were raising their children in a Church that in many ways had changed from that of their parents, but in its essentials had not. The Church continued to be formalistic, separatist, and ethnically grounded, but it slowly became less an immigrant and more an American Church. Two of the six priests under consideration here had immigrant parents, but four had parents born in the United States. The Church of the 1930s through 1950s went from being defensive to one on the offense, growing in confidence in its efforts to convince White Anglo-Saxon Protestant (WASP) America that one could be fully American and fully Catholic. Pastors built Catholic schools across the country that featured the inscription "For God and Country" over the front doors. Women religious, universally called "the good nuns," taught children both an unquestioning loyalty to the Church and patriotism for the country. Brick and mortar bishops organized and centralized Catholic life by building a Catholic infrastructure of hospitals, universities, seminaries, cemeteries, and social service agencies that paralleled and rivaled those built by public and other private institutions. After World War II, the GI Bill helped to send thousands of young Catholics to college on the way to joining the ranks of the middle class. Church movements that anticipated the Second Vatican Council made their way into Catholic life, taking shape in groups such as the Christian Family Movement, the Catholic Interracial Council, and the Catholic Youth Organization.

For most Catholics, however, the Church in the era in which these six priests grew up remained more similar to than different from that of their grandparents. It was still a rule-bound, top-down institution where Father ran the parish, Sister or Brother ran the school, and Church teaching clearly delineated right from wrong. Most Catholics still lived their lives enveloped by the ethos of the parish, obediently attending Mass, receiving the sacraments, following Catholic ratings regarding which movies to attend, and avoiding much contact with non-Catholics, except perhaps at work. The Church taught them—through its priests, sisters, and brothers—not only that Church teaching and practice did not change but that it in fact could not change.

With the advent of the Second Vatican Council in 1962, the belief in an unchanging Church quickly crumbled. It was in this era of Vatican II, a time of radical change in the country but also in the Church, that these six priests completed their seminary training and spent the first quarter century of their priesthood ministering to the Church of Chicago. No one has done a better job of articulating the major events and issues that defined the changing American Church of the 1960s than Mark Massa, SJ, in his insightful history, *The American Catholic Revolution: How the '60s Changed the Church Forever*.[1] Massa described national events that transformed Church thinking and practice as regards liturgy, moral theology, authority and obedience, and social justice, to name a few. Massa brilliantly explained how a Church that seemingly would not and could not change did exactly that. At the Council, *Sacrosanctum Concilium* (Constitution on the Sacred Liturgy) led to a transformation of the Mass. The priest turned and faced the people; he and the people prayed the Mass in the vernacular; the priest gave a homily—a reflection on the scriptures of the day—rather than a sermon; the whole congregation took part in the prayers and music; and, eventually, laypersons entered into the "full, conscious, and active participation" called for by the Council by proclaiming the scriptures and distributing Communion at Mass.

In 1968, just three years after the closing of the Council, during a time when more and more Catholics in America and elsewhere had begun to question the reasons for Church teaching particularly as regards morality and sexuality, Pope Paul VI promulgated *Humanae Vitae*, which reaffirmed the Church's opposition to artificial birth control. The Pope made the decision despite the opposite recommendation of an international committee his predecessor had convened to study the issue. Many Catholics, from moral theologians to married couples struggling with the size of their families, questioned the teaching, both for its content, which seemed implausible, and because Paul VI had overridden the committee. Catholics, meanwhile, long accustomed to performing works of charity and mercy, heard from Jesuit Fathers Daniel and Philip Berrigan and their *confreres* of the Catonsville Nine, who had gone so far as to burn draft records in their protest of the Vietnam War, that becoming fully Catholic and fully American was not enough if it meant one could not live out Gospel values in the pursuit of social justice.

During this Vatican II era of the American Church, the six priests from the class of 1969—like their colleagues throughout the country —worked to transform parish liturgies, increase lay involvement in ministry, engage in honest dialogue with parishioners about difficult aspects of Church teaching, and advance the work of social justice. To be sure, naysayers existed who criticized the changes in the Church, but they were in a distinct minority in the parishes where these men served (perhaps partly due to the priests' leadership). Just as important, the leadership of the American Church supported the efforts of men such as those from the class of '69.

Nothing symbolized the ascendancy of the Vatican II era of the American Church for that class more than the years they spent under the leadership of Cardinal Joseph Bernardin, not only because of his supportive pastoral style in running the Chicago archdiocese but because of his national leadership among the U.S. bishops. Under Bernardin, these priests continued, as Larry Duris puts it, to "ride the wave" of Vatican II.

During the latter years of Bernardin's tenure, however, a strong counter-movement had begun to gain strength: the "reform of the reform," as some called it. By the early '90s, Pope John Paul II had served as Pope for almost 15 years. Over this stretch, he appointed bishops who often cast a more critical eye on the style of ministry personified by the work of priests such as those from the class of '69. Priests had become, in the eyes of critics, too close to the people and in their efforts to dialogue with the world had lost the objectivity necessary to teach, govern, and to confront sin. Vatican II-era Catholics—and their priests—had become too enamored of and too enmeshed with the culture, it was charged, and this hindered their ability to proclaim Christ as Lord to that culture. The roles of priest and laity, the argument goes, had become confused and an appalling informality had crept into liturgical celebrations.

Under Pope Benedict XVI, criticism of the implementation of the Council era became more explicit, especially in the area of liturgy. For example, a new translation of the Roman Missal recently brought in a literal translation of the Latin prayers to replace language that had been crafted to be understandable to people in the pews. While some pronounced the new language majestic and beautiful, many others—both priests and lay Catholics—found it unintelligible. In the Vatican,

Benedict sometimes celebrated Mass with his back to the people, facing the altar, and allowed a return to the use of the Latin rite (but only as the extraordinary, not the ordinary, language of the Mass).

Finally, the clerical sexual abuse scandal surfaced, precipitating even more criticism of priests, this time from the right, the left, and those in between.

The last 20-plus years of their priesthoods, then, caused these men to turn more deeply toward friendship and prayer in order to cope with both the criticism they faced and the disagreements they had with Church traditionalists as they continued to minister to the people of their parishes.

Here is their story.

Michael Cahill
Chicago, Illinois

....

1. Mark S. Massa, SJ, *The American Catholic Revolution: How the '60s Changed the Church Forever* (New York: Oxford University Press, 2010).

PROLOGUE
Ordination Day

On Wednesday May 14, 1969, at nine o'clock in the morning, 35 young men processed up the center aisle of the Chapel of the Immaculate Conception at St. Mary of the Lake Seminary in Mundelein, Illinois. The choir and people who gathered 600 strong in the packed chapel sang out the entrance song with full voice:

> *God of our Fathers, God everliving;*
> *Our faith unites us, we are your people.*
> *Come, all creation, make this day holy;*
> *Worship earth's master, we are his people.*
> *Thanks must be given to God Almighty;*
> *He is our shepherd, we are his people.*
> *God lives within us, unworthy sinners,*
> *Praise his great mercy; we are his people.*
> *Lord of the harvests, Light of the nations,*
> *Life-giving Spirit, we are your people.*[1]

The lyrics of the song, consciously chosen by members of the ordination class of 1969, spoke much about the spirit, theology, and pastoral mind-set of this group of seminarians preparing for the biggest moment of their young lives: their ordination to the priesthood of the Archdiocese of Chicago. The phrases "God lives within us," "Praise his great mercy," and "Light of the nations" reflected their belief in a present, forgiving, and guiding God. The repeated phrase, "we are your people," pointed to the focus of their ministry—the people of God— and their stance that "we" meant priest and people together.

The class of 1969 made this point explicitly in their ordination Mass booklet: "The words we will hear in this ceremony are quite clear in saying it is we, the people of God, who propose these candidates to the Archbishop…so that from now on they may be his fellow workers in serving the people of God."[2]

While the words of the entrance song and ordination booklet expressed the hopes and ideals of the class for "serving the people of God," the realities of both the universal and local Church looked quite different from those lofty ideals. Headlines appearing between April 10 and May 16 in the *New World*, the Catholic newspaper of the Archdiocese of Chicago, indicated some of the tensions these new priests would encounter at the universal level, especially in regard to the Church's teachings about sexuality:

- Pope Accuses Dissident Catholics of "Crucifying" the Church
- U.S. Bishops Urged to Face Challenge of Authority
- Celibacy Changes Desired Say Polled Clerics
- British Theologian Argues for Pill
- Brooklyn Priests Consider Themselves Free to Marry
- Priests Asked to Help Pick New Bishops
- Revised Ordinary of Mass Offers Variety: Ends Rigid Uniformity[3]

Such news stories testified not only to a Church changing rapidly in the aftermath of the Second Vatican Council, which Pope John XXIII had convened from 1962 to 1965, but also to the contentiousness touched off by the Council. Locally, too, John Cody's appointment as archbishop of Chicago in 1965 had led to innovations both substantive and stylistic that had brought him some praise, but also fierce criticism. Much of the latter came from his clergy, especially from the newly organized Association of Chicago Priests, founded in 1966, which challenged Cody on pastoral appointments and diocesan administration.[4]

Not only had members of the class of 1969 found themselves in the midst of changes that they could not control, but they had also instigated a major change of their own in their training. The seminary ordained men as transitional deacons in the spring, one year before their ordination to the priesthood. Traditionally, the new deacons would simply resume their last year of studies at the seminary after their diaconate ordination. The class of 1969, however, persuaded the seminary rector, Jack Gorman ('52) [the year of ordination for each Chicago priest mentioned will appear in parentheses following the first mention of his name in each chapter], to allow six months of parish apostolate work as part of their diaconate. Class leaders believed that their training must involve actual work with the people of God in addition to their academic, theological, and, as some of them would say, overly theoretical training at Mundelein.

As these 35 deacons walked up the aisle of the chapel on that May morning of 1969, they could not have but noticed two more changes, these to the ritual itself. First, of course, in keeping with the directives of the Second Vatican Council, concluded just four years earlier, Cody presided over Mass in the vernacular, English. Second, the Council had called for a completely new ordination rite containing significant revisions. Mundelein Seminary celebrated this new rite for the first time in 1969. The Introduction to the Mass booklet for the day explains:

> *The meaning of the various parts of the rite has been made more clear. The ordination itself takes place after the Gospel. The address of the Archbishop to the people and those to be ordained is the homily of this Mass. Then, there is (1) the interrogation of the candidates, (2) the promise of obedience to the bishop, (3) the litany of the saints, (4) the imposition of hands and the prayer of consecration, (5) the anointing of hands, and finally (6) the conferral of the paten with the bread and the chalice with the wine mixed with water.*

"This revised rite of Ordination to the Priesthood," the writer of the booklet noted, foreshadowing much of his class' belief about and attitude toward the laity, "is intended to help us participate in today's liturgy more intelligently and more actively."[5]

When the opening procession and prayers had ended, the congregation could at last take their seats for the first reading from 2 Corinthians 4:1-2, 5-7, referred to in Church circles as "Earthen Vessels." The fifth and seventh verses capture the heart of the passage.

It is not ourselves we preach, but Christ Jesus as Lord, and ourselves as your servants for Jesus' sake.... This treasure we possess in earthen vessels, to make it clear that its surpassing power comes from God and not from us.[6]

Perhaps this reading lingered in the subconscious of the new Father Edward Upton in the hour after the ordination Mass had concluded. Immediately after the ceremony, in what was a long-standing tradition at the seminary, the newly ordained stationed themselves in alphabetical order around the statue of the Immaculate Conception in front of the chapel to give their first blessings to family and friends. Seminarians had long ago nicknamed it the "DIME" statue because below the sculpture of the Virgin Mary sat four of the Old Testament prophets, Daniel, Isaiah, Moses, and Ezekiel. Upton stood between Father Ray Tillrock and his friend since high school seminary days, Father Bill Zavaski.

After finishing his blessings, Upton headed toward the cafeteria to attend the luncheon for families of the newly ordained. On the way there, he encountered a stranger.

Some lady came up to me. I had no idea who she was. She said, "Father, can I have your blessing?" Then it really clicked. This is the change. That people whom you don't know now have a right to ask you to do something. That little moment I remember more than the whole thing. It helped me focus that it's a different world now. I have a responsibility to not just who I know, but even strangers. I can't just say, "I've got to go have lunch, sorry, dear." So it's funny how that little thing just clicked in my mind.

Upton recalled the joy of the day. "My mother had rheumatic

heart disease when she was a child," he remembers, "so she had a damaged heart valve which they couldn't in those days correct. She had been in and out of the hospital, so it was really nice that she was able to be alive and be there, because she died a year later." An only child, Upton came from a small extended family and had a smaller contingent present at the ordination than many of his classmates. His encounter with the stranger on the way to lunch had clearly pointed to a future with expanded connections and responsibilities.

....

After the conclusion of the first reading, the Liturgy of the Word continued with the Alleluia and the Gospel, John 15:9-17. Verses 12-13, in particular, set forth a clear mission:

> *This is my commandment:*
> *Love one another*
> *As I have loved you.*
> *There is no greater love than this:*
> *To lay down one's life for one's friends.*

Father Tom Libera remembered the moment not long after Cody had proclaimed that Gospel, when the community prayed the Litany of the Saints over the seminarians. "You're prostrate on the floor in front of everybody at the altar," he recalls, "so that's a very dramatic moment of giving yourself over." He reflected on his struggles to arrive at that point of giving himself to a life of priesthood, asking himself at times, "Am I willing to go through another year? Do I really want to pursue a path that will not take me into marriage? There were moments where you had to be tested and say which scale was going to win out." In his recollections about ordination day, Libera lingered on those he loved, both present and absent, who had helped bring him to his moment of decision. "I remember my mother," he begins. "My dad had died already, but she and some relatives and friends were there— my brother, uncles, and aunts." Libera also treasured that many friends attended from his time doing summer work on the West Side of Chicago at St. Frances Cabrini Parish. "There were a number of us," Libera says, referring now to his classmates, "who were involved in summer apostolic work in the inner city. That fueled that you were going to be able to make a contribution."

....

The Rite of Ordination began after the reading of the Gospel. The deacon of the Mass called forth the candidates who each responded, "I am ready and willing." Of course, the process that had led them to this moment had not been so simple. "Leading up to that," Father Bob Heidenreich reflects, "there were all sorts of questions: Am I doing the right thing?" Heidenreich recalled that seven men from the class who had already been ordained as transitional deacons had left the seminary before priestly ordination. "That heightened the question," Heidenreich says, "what's wrong with them…or with me?" He also remembered questions arising in his own mind at the time of the class' diaconate ordination a year earlier.

> We were going up to the altar to sign our pledge of celibacy. I remember talking to whoever it was in front of me in line saying that it doesn't really make too much difference because—now this is the '60s—the promise of celibacy is going to be done away with in the not too distant future.

Heidenreich's disappointments about classmates leaving and his questions about celibacy, however, actually strengthened his vocation to priestly ministry. Referring to his departed classmates, he comments, "They realized they could do in the Church what they wanted to without being ordained. We were at the beginning of the insight into what are now the different lay ministries present in parishes. The insight these guys had was valid. The thing I liked—and maybe this is ego—is that the priest was core to this happening."

> Most of the images of pastors we had were dominant people that ordered people around and controlled everything. But I had this

image of what if it was somebody that could enable people like
my classmates and say, hey, that's a great idea, why can't we
do this, and wouldn't that lead to a vibrant parish life and to
even more people getting involved in Church in a meaningful
way.... It's ironic because this image was very much influenced
by my classmates, the ones ordained and the ones who weren't
ordained.

Parish life as a deacon in the months leading up to ordination day had only served to reinforce Heidenreich's nascent ideas about ministry. "The thing that got me to that ordination more than anything," he says, "was my experience as a deacon at Holy Ghost Parish in South Holland. It was just the ordinary things of parish life like standing out in front of church and getting to know the younger people. I started to see the building blocks of community, people who had some ability to minister, who had insight about what the Church could be, who were generous, and who liked a lot of fun. So when I said yes, I want to be ordained," he notes, reflecting back on his own "I am ready and willing" response in the Ordination Rite, "it was in a very proactive Church where you formed community as the basis for everything you do. That's what I've done and it was by God's grace. I've thought of this often, that I could've gone to Rome and applied for laicization based on what I said in line going to sign the [celibacy] document. But I never gave that much thought because this is where I knew I should be."

....

After Archbishop Cody had examined the candidates, the Rite of Ordination continued with the Promise of Obedience. Each candidate knelt in turn before the archbishop who clasped his hands around the joined hands of the candidate. "Do you promise me and my successors obedience and respect?" Cody asked. Each seminarian replied, "I do." In 1969, however, the ordination class, like many young people throughout the country in and out of the Church, found themselves questioning the real meaning of the concepts of obedience and authority. When Father Larry Duris thought back to ordination day, one of his first memories had to do with a potential protest. "It was the first time," he recalls, "they had Andy Frain [a local security company] ushers up there to fend off protesters." Project Equality, a non-profit group dedicated to advancing racial equality in the workplace, had picketed several events at which Cody had appeared due to his opposition to the group.[7] "The word was out," Duris continues, "that they were going to appear. We didn't have anyone protesting the fact that we were all male. That would come later. But they had Andy Frain ushers at the door." Although the protest never materialized, Duris well understood the commotion surrounding the possibility of it as a marker of the signs of the times. "That was fine with us," he says, speaking for his classmates about the anticipated protest.

Push for change within the seminary mirrored the social change occurring in society. "Everything happened in 1968," Duris recalls, "King was killed, Bobby [Kennedy] was killed. You had riots that summer, the police riot here. Richard Milhous [Nixon] was elected. *Humanae Vitae.*" Duris says of his classmates, "We looked at change in the Church like it couldn't happen fast enough." Duris had no love for the old seminary.

The old model we experienced, you locked people up for six years...two years of philosophy and four years of theology, away from the world, almost literally. You were still hopefully at the end of this a human being of sorts. Then you're thrown into a parish setting and expected to be effective with people. And you had the culture shift and the Church shift. When we were ordained, Father was no longer God in the way he had been. The way of looking at women was changing. Some of the cultural paradigms were falling apart. We were moving into a different world.

Duris thought back fondly to the attempt of Msgr. Jack Gorman to address the changes the class faced. Gorman had taught them at Quigley, the high school seminary, and had moved with them to teach at Niles, the college seminary. He had then become rector of Mundelein Seminary midway through their first year of theology. Just before the class signed their celibacy papers prior to their diaconate ordination in 1968—"as we said, signing away our sexuality"—Gorman addressed the class. According to Duris, he said:

> *I have high regard for you guys. When I was ordained in '52 we had locked up in our minds what priesthood was. My vision has changed since then. But it seemed clear cut what was expected. You guys are coming in where it's more fluid in terms of what ministerial priesthood is in relation to other ministries. And all kinds of people are leaving ministry. It's like you're trying to get through this revolving door and there's a bigger crowd rushing out the other way. So I have high respect for you.*

....

At the end of the short prayer following the promise of obedience, Cody knelt at his seat and the congregation joined him on their knees. The candidates prostrated themselves on the marble floor and began to listen intently as the whole community present prayed over them, invoking in song the names of the Church's heroes and heroines and asking for their prayers in the great Litany of the Saints. Following the Litany, the candidates stood and prepared for the actual moment of ordination: the laying on of hands. One by one each candidate would kneel before the archbishop, who would place his hands on the candidate's head and pray over him. Then, in a grand show of presbyteral fraternity and unity, a large number of the priests of the Archdiocese of Chicago, most of whom, due to lack of space, had waited outside the chapel, processed in and joined their archbishop in laying their hands on the candidates. As soon as they completed their part in the ritual, the assembled clergy walked back outside to continue socializing. "One of the big moments visually," Father Mike Ahlstrom recalls, "is when you lay prostrate on the floor during the Litany. That's a very dramatic moment. Everybody takes pictures. I can remember thinking, 'This is a hard floor. I wish they would get over with this thing.'"

> *Yet there was a sense that all these people were praying for us, all the saints were interceding for us. Then the big moment*

of ordination. I remember going up to Archbishop Cody and kneeling. He pressed down hard. I thought, he wants to make sure he's really ordaining us. Not that it was painful, but you knew you had hands laid on you.

Ahlstrom's ability to focus on the liturgical moment at hand foreshadowed his lifelong love of liturgy. "We had picked our own music," he remembers. "One song was 'My God is a Rock.' It rocked."[8] Ahlstrom had been deeply involved in the ordination Mass planning because he served as the seminary's liturgical master of ceremonies, in charge of coordinating services in assistance to the priests celebrating them.

Because of the new rites coming out after Vatican II, I had revamped the whole system. I was telling Msgr. Gorman beforehand, "This is what you do." He said, "I won't worry, you'll be up there to help me." I said, "No, if you don't mind, I'd like to get ordained."

Like his classmates, Ahlstrom reflected on the tradition of first blessings, but he recalled some wistfully. "I blessed a number of friends that did not go on to ordination," he notes. "Some were the ones I was closest to. There was a group of ten of us that was today what you'd call a basic Christian community. Of the ten, only four of us were ordained." What affected Ahlstrom even more than his classmates' seminary departures "was watching some of the faculty leave the priesthood. My spiritual director left just before I was ordained." Ahlstrom had, in addition, invited the director of the deacon program, Father Bob Doherty ('56), to concelebrate his first Mass. "He turned down my request," Ahlstrom says. "I couldn't understand it because at the ordination he was on the Archbishop's left. I found out that immediately after the ordination he married the first woman faculty member of Mundelein. That probably set back women faculty for a while!"

Ahlstrom's vivid memories of ordination day notwithstanding, his mother's comments a few days later made an even more lasting impact. "She said," Ahlstrom fondly recalled, "'Don't think I'm going to call you Father.' I said, 'You better not, I'm your son.' Then she said, which put me in my place, 'You better take out the garbage. We've got company coming over. You're still part of the family.' While she was very proud of me, she reminded me of who I am: 'Don't think you're above anybody.'"

....

The Ordination Rite continued with Cody's prayer over the newly ordained and then the Investiture of the Stole and Chasuble, the liturgical vestments worn by the priest when presiding at Mass, followed by the Anointing of Hands. Next, the entire assembly prayed "Veni, Creator Spiritus," or "Come, Holy Spirit," and the archbishop presented each of the newly ordained with bread on a paten and wine and water in the chalice. When Cody gave the Kiss of Peace to his new clergy, the assembled priests, gathered outside the chapel, once more processed in to join the archbishop in offering peace. "I'll never forget," chortles Father Bill Zavaski, "some woman in the crowd, when the priests started lining up, yelled out real loud 'Not again!' It was classic because the kiss of peace took forever." Grief, however, stood side by side with humor. "It was very painful," Zavaski laments over classmates who had left the seminary prior to priesthood ordination. "It never made me think twice about wanting to be ordained. I was totally focused on that. But these were your friends, and it was tough to see them go."

Not even the departure of his classmates, however, could cancel out the optimism, excitement, and joy that Zavaski felt on ordination day.

> It was cloudy and cold at the beginning of the day, with a lot of anxiety about the whole process. Then it was like a Camelot scene. Right after ordination the sun broke through. It was a glorious day. I was so excited about being ordained a priest. It was something you've been working on for twelve years. We sang "Moon River" on the steps. I think everybody remembers that. That was our class song.

....

After the newly ordained filed out of the chapel at the conclusion of the over three-hour liturgy on their way to the DIME statue to give first blessings, the ushers handed each member of the congregation a holy card commemorating the event.[9] The back of the card listed the 37 members of the class of 1969, including two from other dioceses not ordained at Mundelein. Underneath appeared "James Kelly 1943-1968," a classmate who had died during the third year of theology, along with a simple prayer: "Please pray for him and us." For the front of the card, the class had chosen a quote from Teilhard de Chardin (1881-1955), the Jesuit mystic and theologian. Chardin's theology had included many controversial ideas that drew both the Jesuits' and the Vatican's ire. As late as 1962, seven years after his death, the Holy Office denounced his books for being dangerous to the faith, especially for youth. The young class of 1969 nevertheless chose the quote from Chardin, because it encapsulated their passion as they began their new ministry as priests to share fully in the human condition.

> *To the extent of my power*
> *Because*
> *I am a priest*
> *I wish from now on*
> *To become conscious of all*
> *That the world loves*
> *Pursues and suffers....*
> *I want to become*
> *More widely human than any*
> *Of the*
> *World's servants.*[10]

Soon they would get their chance to serve the Chicago archdiocese. For now, however, they stood around the DIME statue and blessed their fathers, mothers, grandparents, siblings, uncles, aunts, nephews, nieces, cousins, friends, and also parishioners from their apostolate, deacon, and home parishes. Once finished with first blessings, they headed to the cafeteria with their closest family members to dine, while the remainder of the congregation and the priests who had come up for the day wandered off to the gymnasium, where the class had provided a catered lunch.

....

1. *Ordination to the Order of Priest*, Mass booklet for Class of 1969 Ordination, May 14, 1969. Ordination text by International Committee on English in the Liturgy, Inc., 1969. Entrance Song: Richard Wojcik (text), "God of Our Fathers," American Catholic Press, Oak Park, IL, 2.
2. Ibid., Introduction.
3. *The New World*, April 10 through May 16, 1969.
4. Cody's relationship with the ACP is best covered in Charles Dahm, *Power and Authority in the Catholic Church: Cardinal Cody in Chicago* (Notre Dame, IN: University of Notre Dame Press, 1981).
5. *Ordination to the Order of Priest*, May 14, 1969.
6. *The New American Bible* (New York: Catholic Book Publishing Co., 1970), 213-214.
7. For more on Project Equality, see letter to the editor from Chicago political activist Don Rose in *The American Prospect*, vol. 11, 2000.
8. "My God is a Rock," a black spiritual arranged by Richard Wojcik, was the third Communion sung song at the Ordination Mass. *Ordination to the Order of Priest*, May 14, 1969, 20.
9. Mass Card of the Class of 1969, given by Father Michael Ahlstrom.
10. The quote is from a letter Chardin wrote to his cousin Marguerite Teilhard on October 7, 1915. The information on the Vatican denunciation is from *Warning Considering the Writings of Father Teilhard de Chardin*, Sacred Congregation of the Holy Office, June 30, 1962.

PART I

TRAINING GROUND

CHAPTER 1

GROWING UP
The Roots of the Call to Priesthood

Born during World War II, the members of the class of 1969 grew up in a post-war world of economic boom, national unity, relative social cohesion, tremendous population growth, and Catholic confidence. Wages rose, marriages lasted, family sizes grew, crime rates dropped. Women gave birth to "baby boomers" all over the country, but Catholic mothers led the way, so much so that the Catholic population of the U.S. doubled from 1940 to 1960, while the Catholic percentage of the population rose from 19 to 23 percent. This rise was not primarily because of immigration, which had fueled Catholic numbers earlier, much as it has done today.

While most U.S. Catholics still lived in urban centers, the move to suburbia had begun. Catholics added rapidly to their infrastructure of churches, schools, universities, hospitals, and social service agencies, while at the same time increasing their influence in labor unions and local politics. And the number of men entering the Church's seminaries began to grow apace.[1]

The composition of the eventual ordination class of '69 also intimated change. To be sure, the class consisted only of Caucasians and, needless to say, males. While about 40 percent of the men had surnames indicating an Irish heritage, the number would have approached or even exceeded 90 percent earlier in the century. The growing number of seminarians of German, Polish, Slovak, Lithuanian, or other European ancestry reflected a trend that had been growing for years. While some seminarians had parents who had emigrated from those countries, many more of their parents hailed from Chicago or, in a few cases, other parts of the United States, and some of them could trace their Chicago heritage back three or four generations or more.

Not only was this class more "American," it was also more suburban. Almost half the class had families living in the suburbs; they came from Skokie, Melrose Park, Evanston, Niles, Winnetka, LaGrange, Evergreen Park, Oak Park, and as far out as Waukegan. Even those families still living in the city now tended to live in neighborhoods farther from the downtown district known as the Loop. Less likely now to come from working-class neighborhoods such as Bridgeport on the near South Side or West Town on the near North Side, more of the men came from middle-class enclaves such as Beverly on the far Southwest Side or Portage Park on the far Northwest Side.[2]

....

Ed Upton grew up in St. Helena of the Cross Parish on the South Side of Chicago, a then brand new middle-class parish that was a white ethnic melting pot. Neighborhood life for Catholic kids like Ed revolved largely around the parish. As was true for many of his classmates, parish life for Ed tended to center more around the nuns than the priests. In grade school Ed helped the School Sisters of Notre Dame with various projects; with their encouragement, he became an altar server and eventually took on the coveted post of "the kid in charge of the servers." Looking back, he says of the parish, "It was my second home."

Upton recalled that the nuns created "a mini-convent in the classroom. You had a holy water fountain at the door, a crucifix in the room. In May you had a rosary bulletin board. That was their world." The sometimes-heard stereotypes of nuns' meanness and incessant corporal punishment did not mesh with his experience. "They would yell," he admits, "or occasionally whack a kid, but they weren't terrorists. They were good women. They were young, so they hadn't grown cynical."

The priests of the parish supported the kids, especially at report card time. "But in those days," Upton explains, "the priests were not around a lot. Quite honestly, it was the nuns who were more influential." St. Helena's priests, however, did bring Upton face to face with the issue of excessive drinking. Serving as emcee in 1957 for the first Easter Vigil to be held in the evening, Upton found himself astonished. There was never a practice for the extensive liturgy. "I think the three priests were half smashed. I'm saying, 'This doesn't make sense. They don't know what the heck they're doing.' As a kid, it would never have dawned on me that the priests might have an alcohol problem. But the associate, if he had the first Mass of the day, you'd go to the rectory half the time to wake him up. I had a feeling he was out late at night, but we were told, 'Father was so busy he had to be tired.'"

Upton's experiences with the priests and nuns of St. Helena reinforced in him both the strong sensitivity and the pragmatic realism he had first developed living with his parents. Upton and his parents, Edward and Margaret, moved into St. Helena's in 1948 when Ed was 5, two years after Msgr. Henry McGuire ('06) founded the parish and named it after his sister Helena. The family's mostly Catholic neighbors—aside from the Episcopalian/Jewish couple on the corner—came from Irish, Croatian, and Italian roots. But all were second generation or later Americans; none spoke anything but English. Upton himself came from Irish and English stock. His paternal grandmother arrived from Ireland in the 1880s. She married Ed's grandfather, but only after he became a Catholic. "Probably against his will," Ed suspects.

Upton's family story contains many clues to what would become his personality and his world outlook. His maternal grandparents had five children but quickly gave them up for adoption. Ed's mom, born in Brooklyn, was adopted by a woman from Vermont and never learned what happened to her birth family. She attended boarding school until her adoptive mother died. After that she moved to Chicago to live with an uncle, an unhappy situation for the girl. Her new family made it clear they did not like her. "It was like Cinderella," says Upton. "She was the ugly duckling—they didn't treat her well. So at 18 she got the hell out of there and was on her own. So, though she is completely Irish, there's part of that South Side Irish hype that she didn't buy into."

As for what his dad did for a living, Ed says bluntly, "He and his brother fought. That was their first occupation. It was constant. My uncle was 10 years older. My dad resented being treated like the younger brother. He did the books and my uncle did sales in an auto sales store."

The family went through a major transformation during Upton's childhood, one infused with faith. His father suffered from alcoholism. "There aren't any priests," he jokes ironically, "that came from alcoholic families. But my dad got sober and went into recovery when I was in second grade. That was a conversion for him. He became very faithful to AA and to his religious practice in a deeper way. He was public about the change and how his faith was important to it. It wasn't just stopping drinking, but AA. It was a strong piety." Upton also experienced deep piety from his mother.

> I use this example: My mother went to the Little Flower Novena at church to get my father sober. She was convinced that that did it. It didn't hurt that she told him she was going to the chancery office to divorce him if he didn't change. But religiously it was clear to her that what happened to my dad was a direct result of prayer. I was seven. What sticks in your mind is the cause and effect. Now, the threat of a trip to the chancery may have had a secondary effect—but there was strong, unquestioning religiosity in the family.

The idea of priesthood first entered Upton's mind sometime in grade school. He built altars and played priest, as many Catholic boys did. His religious life at home featured ordinary Catholic piety: no meat on Friday, Mass every Sunday, the occasional rosary. The family had an appreciation for the comic, however, even in supposedly pious moments. Upton's dad invariably said the rosary in the Irish brogue he had learned at his mother's feet, so when Upton and his mom would hear the suddenly Irish tones emerging from his father at "Holy Mary, Mother of God," they would both start laughing. "Half the time we never finished the rosary," Upton says, grinning.

No one advanced the idea of him going to Quigley Preparatory Seminary, the high school seminary, either at home or at school, but once he decided on Quigley, everyone supported his decision, even though it involved an hour-long ride each way through the city on the elevated train. "My mother must have been half hysterical," says Upton, "but I realized later she never spoke up. Whatever her own fears, she didn't say, 'You can't do that.'"

The one story Upton tells about his "call" is not about Upton at all; it's a story about his parents' attitude toward a couple they knew well who had married outside the Church. The details, however, speak volumes about what has helped to form Upton's attitudes as a man and a priest. His mother clearly told the pair: "I'm praying for you that you get this straightened out."

"But even though there was this problem you better address or you'll go to hell," Upton points out, "there was never any negativity or exclusion. It never affected the way my mom dealt with the couple."

> *I didn't realize the distinctions being made. You think about this stuff later. It was a formative lesson that you accept people. Yeah, there's a problem. But that's separate. You don't judge or condemn them. They're your friends, your family—no matter what the situation. That's an attitude I hope I still have that comes from my parents.*

....

Larry Duris' childhood journey epitomized the post-World War II movement of Chicago's Catholics from ethnic neighborhood parishes in Chicago to melting pot parishes in the suburbs. Larry's mom, born in Czechoslovakia, grew up in the now-closed Sacred Heart Parish on the West Side. Larry's family, which included his parents and three brothers and a sister all younger than him, moved from Little Village, then a Slovak/Bohemian enclave and today a Mexican neighborhood on Chicago's West Side, to the town of Cicero just west of Chicago. Next they moved to Skokie, a then-booming suburb just north of Chicago.

The move to Skokie—and St. Peter's Parish—took place in 1952, right before Duris entered fourth grade. His father worked as a steamfitter, and he built a house basically by himself over the course of a year. When the family moved in, 19,000 people lived in Skokie. Another 41,000 people had made the trek by 1959. "It was the fastest growing suburb in the country for years," Duris says.

The move to modern suburbia did not diminish the faith of the Duris family. They continued to place church and faith at the core of what they were about. Duris' father belonged to the Men's Club, his mother became an officer in the Women's Club, and Larry joined the parish Boy Scout troop. Although Skokie had a large Jewish population, including about one third of the people on Duris' block, he had little contact with his Jewish counterparts largely because his life centered on St. Peter's, so much so that when Larry's parents and his brother died years later, he had them buried in the parish cemetery attached to the church.

Although the commitment to parish life remained strong, the Duris family believed in the melting pot mentality as far as ethnicity was concerned. "My folks both knew Slovak. I commented, 'I wish you would've taught us,' because another language as a kid would've encouraged me to take on other languages," Duris laments. "But they wanted their kids to be fully Americanized, to make sure we didn't have an accent."

Duris' parents' involvement in the Christian Family Movement (CFM) further symbolized the family's entrance into a more Americanized Church. Msgr. Reynold Hillenbrand ('29), a German-American Chicago priest, had helped to start CFM, along with a host of other Catholic action groups, in Chicago during the period in which he led the major seminary at St. Mary of the Lake Seminary in Mundelein, Illinois. He believed that Catholics should reflect and act in the world on the basis of their Catholic Christianity. The Catholic Action model that included CFM had its members meet as groups—or in CFM's case, as groups of couples—to "observe, judge, and act." Larry remembers hating meeting nights because he and his brother had to stay in the back bedroom. "Hearing all the laughter, however," he recalls, "was a great imprint that, gee, these are good, happy people."

Duris' peers played the major role in his early decision to move toward priesthood.

We had SVDs [Society of the Divine Word priests] from Techny, Illinois, who would help out with Masses. They would do altar boy retreats at their huge seminary in the far suburbs north of

Chicago, and I went in sixth, seventh, and eighth grade. What they were doing was recruiting, but we loved being away for a weekend.

The "we" included Duris' best friend Charles Schmitt. By eighth grade, he and Charles had to decide whether to attend Quigley or the SVD seminary in East Troy, Wisconsin. "I went to Quigley because he went to Quigley," Duris recalls, "and he went to Quigley because I did."

Duris felt he had a vocation, but it remained unclear exactly what that meant. "I went to Quigley," he explains, "because, yeah, I wanted to be a priest. You couldn't go there if you didn't." But the teenager had a lot on his mind. He had considered teaching and social work. He played the piano and organ but hadn't started early enough to make that a career. Duris also loved architecture but had little aptitude for math and engineering. "At 14," he says, "I didn't even know *what* I was, let alone *who* I was." What he did know was that eleven young men from St. Peter's would attend Quigley in the fall of 1957, part of the hordes of young men who entered the seminary in Chicago and across the nation in the post-war period. At the time, peer reinforcement sufficed. When Larry told his parents he wanted to attend Quigley, "they were surprised," he remembers. "Looking back, that was a real good thing. It showed me there certainly weren't any family expectations that I become a priest."

....

Unlike the Duris family, who moved from the old ethnic neighborhood into the suburban melting pot, the Zavaski family stayed put. Technically they lived in the suburbs, but in actuality it was a small town more than 20 miles north of Chicago called Waukegan, which contained within its boundaries several ethnic enclaves. The Zavaskis lived in St. Bartholomew Parish, a Lithuanian national parish where everybody seemed to know everybody. "The Church was a very central part of our lives," Bill Zavaski says. "There was not that much else to do, so if the Church had activities, then that's what we were involved in." The "we" included Bill's parents, second generation Americans of

Lithuanian descent, Bill, and his younger brother.

Bill remembered life in Waukegan as being very simple, a place where no one locked their doors. The close-knit ties even included the fact that Bill's mom's brother had married his dad's sister. Each family ended up producing two boys, one of whom would become a priest—Bill's cousin joined the Carmelite order. In one sense, the two boys' vocations seemed unusual because no one in their family had chosen religious life in the generation preceding them. But Zavaski feels that fact could mislead. "In Waukegan, a lot of girls went to the convent," he says, "and there were John Kuzinskas ('52) and Joe Gilbert ('54) in the priesthood. So for a little parish, we did have a number of vocations.

"My mother," he remembers with affection, "was very much involved in the parish; she did not drive, so my father had to drive her everywhere. She took care of the nuns and sponsored new immigrants that were coming during the '50s and '60s from Lithuania." Mrs. Zavaski's work with immigrants at St. Bart's led Father Kuzinskas, who grew up in and later served at St. Bart's as pastor, to tell Bill years later, "Your mother was my hero." Zavaski felt similarly toward Kuzinskas. "Father John," he says, "was a real example."

> John loved being a priest; he was happy. At my parish, the priests when I was growing up were not the happiest of people. The pastor was a crotchety old grouch, very unhappy. I remember saying, "Boy, if I ever became pastor of this place, I'd change it." Well, I went back.

Although now closed, St. Bart's remains close to Zavaski's heart. He eventually achieved his life goal of serving there as pastor. A picture of the church, rectory, and school hangs on his wall.

For Zavaski, who knew he wanted to be a priest by the time he entered third grade, encouragement for his vocation came not from priests—except Kuzinskas—but from the Sisters of St. Casimir. "The nuns," he exclaims, "were the real vocation directors and recruiters." When it came time for him to make a decision about attending high school, "Sister said, 'You could go to Quigley,'" Zavaski recalls.

Influence on a priest's vocation also comes in more indirect ways.

Zavaski recalls his parents as being always supportive once he made his decision. At that time, there still existed in the culture of ethnic neighborhoods the mystique and honor of the priesthood.

My mother and father were married for 13 years before they had me, so I was like the firstborn child who needed to be dedicated to God. For them, being a priest was the highest vocation. In my mind, it was one of the most significant things that you could do.

"I thought," Zavaski admits, "everybody would listen and do what you tell them. You walk around in processions with beautiful robes on, and they give you incense." Over time, Bill's views would change significantly. But that would come later. For now, his parents, Father John Kuzinskas, and the Sisters of St. Casimir had planted the seed.

....

Tom Libera grew up the eldest of three boys in what he described as a "traditional middle-city parish" located in the heart of the Northwest Side's Irving Park neighborhood. Immaculate Heart of Mary (IHM) had a heavy Polish and Polish American concentration—Tom himself came from Polish stock—although it was technically a territorial parish that served any Catholic within its boundaries, rather than a national parish designed to serve a particular nationality. The Sisters of Nazareth staffed the school, where each class attended daily Mass together and also sat together for Sunday Mass. An altar server, Libera served at the Sorrowful Mother Novena, which was conducted in both Polish and English.

Religious life loomed large in Libera's family. Both of Tom's parents had sisters who were nuns. His maternal aunt had joined the School Sisters of Notre Dame and spent most of her career teaching in Wisconsin. "We didn't have a car at the time," he remembers, "so it was a treat to take the train to Madison or Milwaukee." His father's sister, a Felician, worked in California and Oklahoma, returning to the Felician motherhouse, still on Peterson Avenue in Chicago just three miles north of IHM, for vacations. Libera also recalled a distant cousin who served as a missionary priest. "You had that atmosphere within the family," he says, "of pride and deference to those individuals."

The religious influence extended into the Libera home as well. Tom remembered saying the rosary as a family, praying at the foot of the bed, watching his mom go off to pray novenas, and looking at holy pictures that adorned the walls. "Religion," he says, "was part of the rhythm of every day."

Like Upton, Duris, and Zavaski, Libera had respect for the priests in his life but saw them as having influence from a distance. The more personal encouragement for his vocation seemed again to come from the nuns, peers, and family.

One event in particular shaped Libera's young life and his eventual vocation. "My dad was a postal carrier," he explains. "He got sick with cancer when I was in sixth grade. He died when I was in seventh grade. That was a quiet trauma." The loss led Tom to feel different from his classmates, most of whom then had a mother and father at home. "At my dad's funeral," he recollects, "the kids are looking at me. I didn't think they treated me any different afterward. It's more interior, how I felt about myself, my position in the class. That sense of losing him and feeling different," he notes, "overlaid itself with the thought of going to Quigley. The next year I decided to do that. It's hard to say why. I keep comparing it to a glove and the hand. At some point you put it on, and it seems to fit."

Libera, however, had doubts, particularly about his introversion. It helped that a number of IHM boys already attended Quigley and that two friends from his class planned to enroll. Reflecting about the roots of his vocation, Tom grew briefly quiet, before saying, "It was this is the road you take. We'll see how it works out. If there was any struggle, it was over being able to make friends." Libera could hide in the woodwork, but he persevered. "I'm going to proceed," he thought, "and do whatever it takes to keep on going to Quigley."

For that to happen and be sustained, however, Libera's mother had to change her life. "Initially she was a stay-at-home mom," he remembers, "which would have been typical of those times. Even a postal worker was able to make it. That allowed her to be involved in the parish. She had, after my dad died, to shift gears and go back to work." She waitressed, worked in an office, and then landed a job downtown with the Defense Department, which allowed her to continue to take public transportation. Eventually her job moved to an office near O'Hare Airport and, Tom says, "We had to get a car. She had to adapt to that and somehow take care of us, too," he recalls gratefully. "I could never appreciate all she had to go through at that time."

....

The contrast between Mike Ahlstrom's upbringing and the strong Catholic family life of his classmates couldn't be starker. For starters, Mike learned his Hail Mary and Our Father not from his parents, but from his older brother. But things soon changed for the brother. "He went to Loyola Academy in 1951-52," Ahlstrom says, "and was excited about space exploration."

> *This Jesuit made fun of him in front of the whole class. He said, "Man is not meant to go to the moon. There will never be space exploration." My brother got turned off. By the time he finished Loyola Academy, he announced that he was no longer Catholic. He never practiced any religion after that.*

In addition to his brother's departure from the Church, Mike also had to contend with his parents' ambivalence. His father, raised Lutheran, practiced no religion at all. His mother, an Irish Catholic, went to Mass, according to Ahlstrom, "more often than not," but hadn't received the sacraments in his lifetime. "We weren't," he notes, "the typical strong Catholic family portrayed back in the '40s or '50s." His mom had attended Catholic schools, even though she had to quit after the sixth grade. Ahlstrom's dad, in addition, left high school before earning his diploma. The incomplete nature of his parents' educations fueled a pervasive lack of confidence about academia that Ahlstrom struggled with for years in the seminary. "I came from an unusual family," he concludes, "in terms of what the stereotypical family of a priest would be."

The Ahlstrom family lived in Our Lady of Mercy Parish in the Albany Park neighborhood on Chicago's Northwest Side, but Mike attended Hibbard, a public school. Like the Duris family, when Ahl-strom turned 9 his family moved to the suburbs—Evanston, just north of Chicago, where Ahlstrom attended St. Athanasius School. He dis-liked the routine of a Catholic grade school of the 1950s: uniforms, the prayer bell going off every half hour, and, especially, going to Mass. "We had to go to Mass on the first Friday of every month," he remem-bers. "I always got sick. If you looked at me as a sixth grader, you'd say this kid is never going to go anywhere with the Catholic faith." Given his family history, this was hardly surprising.

During the seventh grade, Ahlstrom attended an event that for-ever changed his life: an altar boy retreat held at the seminary of the missionary priests from the Society of the Divine Word (SVDs) in the northern suburb of Techny, Illinois. The SVDs often spoke to seventh- and eighth-grade boys to recruit them for the order. Ahlstrom had protested attending the retreat on apparently solid grounds: "I was not an altar boy," he explains, "because I was afraid I couldn't learn Latin." But Father Jack Crosby ('52), an associate at St. Athanasius, insisted that Ahlstrom go. So he did. Against all odds, before he had even fin-ished the retreat, he knew beyond any doubt that he wanted to become a Catholic priest. From that time forward, his desire never wavered. "There was a sense of the holy," Mike recalls, "of the sacred."

> We had talks by different priests. A seminarian took a group of
> us and showed us the grounds. In those days they wore cassocks.
> I was impressed. Something clicked. I call it the Holy Spirit. I fell
> in love with the whole thing. To this day when I go to Techny, it
> smells holy. That chapel takes me back to when I was in seventh
> grade and it captured me. I don't go to Techny often, but when
> I do, I always say a prayer of thanksgiving in the chapel. This is
> where the birth of my vocation took place.

Despite the impression left by the SVDs, Ahlstrom knew from the start that his interest was in parish priesthood, not in the mis-sionary life. So when Jack Crosby took a group of eighth graders to visit Quigley the following school year, Mike decided that he wanted to attend the high school seminary. "My parents," he says unsurprisingly, "weren't very thrilled with the idea. My mother thought to be a priest was a strange way to live. My dad was quite upset; but he told my mom, not me. I found out from her years later the grief he gave her. So even though I didn't receive any encouragement to go to Quigley, that's where I went."

Father Crosby became a hero to Ahlstrom. He put Mike and the other St. A's boys who attended Quigley to work at the parish counting money from Sunday collections and answering phones and the doorbell. At last, Ahlstrom found himself fully invested in the life of the local church. For him, unlike his classmates, it was a priest and not the sisters who made the difference.

Ahlstrom had the least deeply imbued Catholic upbringing of his five classmates. Yet by the time they entered Quigley, he had the most unwavering sense of priestly vocation. How did that happen? Reflecting on his unlikely path to priesthood, Mike is clear: "It's the work of the Holy Spirit, because no human factor can explain why I became a priest. God called me. I never had any doubt while I was in seminary or since I was ordained."

....

Bob Heidenreich grew up a normal neighborhood guy on the working-class streets of the North Side of Chicago. Even when he decided to go into the seminary, a normal neighborhood guy was still what he wanted to be. Bob never thought of himself as set apart, as special, as having a corner on holiness. He wanted none of those things. Not because he was overly humble, but because they just weren't him and never would be.

Neither of Heidenreich's parents—both German immigrants—ever finished grade school, and neither was afraid of the hard work it took to pay the bills and feed their two sons. His dad ran his own butcher shop, rising before dawn to get down to the old Fulton Street Market on the near West Side to buy beef to deliver to restaurants. Bob's mom worked as a maid in downtown hotels. When Bob was 11, his father bought a restaurant in Chicago's Ravenswood neighborhood, near where the family lived. For years afterward, the restaurant ate up the family's energy and time. Bob ended up working there, typing up menus on a Smith-Corona portable typewriter. Although his mom usually made it home for dinner, his dad seldom did. "I would never get into the restaurant business," Bob says. "It is totally consuming. If my dad wasn't there, my mom was. We didn't see much of my dad. It was unfortunate when he died. I was 20 and thought he was the dumbest man in the world; I became 21 and realized how he had grown."

The family lived in St. Andrew's Parish, where Bob's mother attended Mass every week and worried about her husband, who resolutely stayed away from church. Although Heidenreich described his family's piety as ordinary at best, they did go out of their way to maintain strong ties with their relatives in Germany, where Bob's mother's sister served as a hospital nun. "My mother came over to the U.S. in the 1920s," he says. "In those times you didn't ever expect to go back. She always wrote to her sister. After the war, you could send things once a month to Germany. She would put a package together, from cookies and non-perishable food to clothes and tablecloths." Heidenreich met his aunt for the first time at his ordination; her order had paid her way to come. This prompted his mom to realize she could travel to Germany, which she began doing shortly thereafter. With her encouragement, almost 30 years after the Heidenreichs had started sending their post-war packages, Heidenreich accompanied his mother for his first trip to Germany. "People remembered her help," he reflects. "It chokes me up even now."

Ever since, Heidenreich has remained close to his German relatives. Now involved in a project with five Catholic dioceses in northwest Germany, he has had many opportunities to visit with both sides of his family. When Bob first visited his mother's town in the mid-1970s, he couldn't even find it on the map. At the end of that visit, while driving away, his mom said to him, "Now you know why I left." He described a picture of his mom and her siblings as children, in which they had clearly tried to dress up for the photo. "The kids had no shoes—no shoes," he recalls. "So there was a reason people left."

When eighth grade arrived, a nun at St. Andrew's asked the boys which of them wanted to take the admission test for Quigley. Raising his hand to get recognition, Heidenreich soon learned recognition had nothing to do with it, and that much hard work lay ahead. He described his grade school academic career as "not stellar." He had to take remedial classes over the summer to get into Quigley. "The nuns," he recalls, "had me staying after school—I thought it was punishment. But I was successful because the nuns tutored me." Time and again in the stories of the young lives of these men from the class of '69, religious women not only encouraged them to consider priesthood but made it possible for them to succeed and grow in their vocation.

In Heidenreich's story, priests played an important part as well. "I don't know why," he maintains, "but I wanted to be a server at St. Andrew's." Priests at the parish had included such standouts as Jack Gorman ('52), John Enright ('53), and Ed Hughes ('51). "Those guys did something exceptional, but it's taken for granted now—they stood outside at the back of church after Mass." Kids like Bob hung around and got to know them. As it turned out, Gorman would follow Heidenreich throughout his seminary career: teaching him Latin at Quigley, psychology at Niles College seminary, and serving as rector of the major seminary in Mundelein. "If I have a father in priesthood," Heidenrich explains, "it's Jack Gorman. I don't know if Jack would be aware of that. But that's who I trace my priestly lineage back to."

Just before Heidenreich graduated from eighth grade at St. Andrew's, the family moved two parishes north to St. Matthias, the German parish in the Lincoln Square neighborhood. He got to know people by serving Mass and hanging around on front porches. "It was a normal growing up," he says. "It wasn't like I hung around with seminarians. I wanted to be a normal person who happened to be a priest." He noted that the term used for diocesan priests is "secular," as opposed to the term "religious," which is used to describe order priests. The description fits him. "I always considered myself secular," he says. "I don't know if I ever wanted to be holy. That was not part of my game plan." Bob wanted to be a normal guy who worked hard and served, and who was not above hanging out, whether on the front porch or in the back of church.

....

1. Charles R. Morris, *American Catholic: The Saints and Sinners Who Built America's Most Powerful Church* (New York: Random House, 1997), 221-224.
2. Information on ethnic and geographic backgrounds of class of 1969 members is from *The New World*, May 9, 1969.

CHAPTER 2

EXPANDING HORIZONS
The High School Seminary

When Ed Upton entered the doors of Quigley Preparatory Seminary as a 14-year-old in the fall of 1957, he could not possibly have imagined the ways in which the institution would change him and his new classmates.

Upton recalled with appreciation how his parents, especially his mother, held a generally open and tolerant attitude—but with an important exception. "I must say," he admits, "there were limits to that, especially if you were dark-skinned." Chicago's South Side remains highly segregated even today, and in the 1950s neighbors watched neighborhood boundaries—viaducts, railroad crossings, opposite sides of major thoroughfares—like hawks. "It was more my father," Ed continues. "I think back to 55th Street. There was a clear line, and he would be incensed that black kids had crossed that line. They didn't belong there, in his opinion."

Once at Quigley, Upton found himself confronting his parents' prejudices, telling them, "You're just wrong. You don't know what you're talking about."

"Maybe it was out of rebellion," he speculates now, "that you wanted to stand against your parents and say we have to accept black people on the South Side, which was not, in the '50s, a popular point of view in Chicago. That tolerant attitude came from Quigley. The faculty kept drilling that into us." An African American priest, Father Roland Lambert ('49), for example, gave a talk to the Young Christian Students group that opened Upton's eyes. "I never realized that people were dis-

criminated against. They were hurt, and it had never dawned on me."
Ed also encountered African-American students in school for the first
time in his life.

Upton also reflects on the diversity he encountered while taking
the train to and from school and to visit new friends.

> *I had to take the Halsted Street bus to 79th, change to 63rd, and
> get on the "L" at 14 years old. You rode with black people. And
> Quigley opened you up. There were people from the North Side
> there; you got mixed up with people from all over. You talk about
> Bill Zavaski and me. I took the train all the way to Waukegan to
> visit him. We visited Bob Heidenreich on the North Side. So, at a
> young age, you got to different parts of the city.*

Quigley Prep plucked Ed Upton and his classmates out of the
small worlds of parish and neighborhood in which they had grown
up, dropping them into the center of the sprawling, diverse, and very
Catholic metropolis that was the Archdiocese of Chicago.

....

For generations of Catholic boys who took their faith seriously, Archbishop Quigley Preparatory Seminary stood not only in reality as a
beautiful Gothic building adorning the Near North Side of Chicago,
but also in their minds as a dream about what their futures might
hold. Over 400 boys entered the doors of Quigley as freshmen in 1957.
Gradually those numbers diminished as the eventual ordination class
of 1969 made its way through four years of Quigley, two years of college seminary at the then brand new Niles Campus, and finally six
years of philosophy and theology at the major seminary in Mundelein,
Illinois, where 35 of them were ordained in May of 1969.

Named for Archbishop James Quigley, who led Chicago's Catholics from 1903 until 1915, and built by his successor, Cardinal George
Mundelein, Quigley Preparatory Seminary opened for classes in the
fall of 1918. Even today, Quigley—now the Archbishop Quigley Pastoral Center, or chancery, for the archdiocese since the closing of the

high-school seminary in 2007—on the corner of Rush and Chestnut Streets, impresses the passerby with its great gothic spires and statues of saints gazing down toward the street. Undoubtedly, Quigley's most impressive feature to this day remains its Chapel of St. James. The chapel's famous stained glass windows mark its true greatness. The designers used over 630,000 pieces of glass and included, according to the architectural historian Denis McNamara, "Art Nouveau inspired golden yellows, oranges and pinks…to create a vibrant, fiery glow."[1]

Tom Libera recalls his first trip to the chapel: "This was a whole other world to go into. *Salve Regina* was a powerful hymn to have within that chapel."

When Ed Upton, Mike Ahlstrom, Larry Duris, Bill Zavaski, Bob Heidenreich, and Tom Libera entered Quigley as first-year students in the fall of 1957, their sense of entering a "whole other world" extended beyond even the magnificence of the physically imposing chapel and Gothic buildings. For one thing, Quigley, the largest high school seminary in the country, conducted school on Saturdays, giving students Thursdays off. This was to keep the students away from others their own age (especially girls) on Saturdays. The seminary required its students to take Latin, Greek, and another foreign language. Seminarians studied Plato, St. Paul, St. Augustine, Cicero, Virgil, and Shakespeare. In short, they received a classical education. Extracurricular activities included both interscholastic and intramural sports, glee club, orchestra, and school plays.[2] *Le Petit Seminaire* and *The Candle*, the school yearbook and newspaper, helped to produce many writers over the years. The mandatory religious program included daily morning Mass, prayers throughout the day, Benediction of the Blessed Sacrament once a week, days of recollection at the end of each quarter, and daily time for meditation. Seminarians could also join the Beadsmen, who prayed the rosary daily after school; the Sacristans, who served all the liturgical ceremonies; the Mission Society, which raised money for the foreign missions; the Catechists, who taught religion to students at nearby St. Joseph's grammar school; as well as various choirs.[3]

One other factor added to the sense of awe, if not intimidation, experienced by the new Quigley students starting their minor seminary careers in the fall of 1957: the sheer numbers of students. "I was absolutely petrified going into the city," Bill Zavaski recalls. "My graduating class in grammar school had 14 kids. I go to Quigley—Quigley had 400 guys in the first-year class." Enrollment had grown so much that by 1957 over 1,300 seminarians attended Quigley at the same time. Zavaski and his classmates actually numbered 421, at that time the second highest enrollment ever for a freshman class at Quigley.[4]

This growth forced the seminary to devise a short-term solution to the overcrowding. They purchased the Ogden Public School not far from Quigley, which came to be called the Annex. But there was a problem. According to the commemorative book *That We May Have Priests*, "the building was a veritable fire trap."[5] Over 600 seminarians, Larry Duris remembers, attended the Annex.

> *Inside was all wood, including the support timbers. The building was sagging inside. My sophomore year, December 2nd, [was the] Our Lady of the Angels fire. Ninety-two kids, three nuns [killed]. Before that week was out, the fire department stationed a fireman in the Annex the entire school day, every day. Speculation was that if a fire got started in the basement, maybe 30 of the 600 of us would get out alive.*

The leaders of the archdiocese could clearly see the need for major changes to the high school seminary system by the fall of 1957. For the 14-year-olds entering Quigley that autumn, however, their concerns had far more to do with adjusting to the architecture, history, programs, and sheer numbers of an institution venerable to most, but brand new to them.

....

For the six men being followed here, attending Quigley brought its share of difficulties. Some struggled more, some less; some earlier, some later. But Bill Zavaski took the prize for the most difficult beginning, not only in his first year, but on his very first day. "I got lost going home," he recalls. "It was very traumatic, but it was also really funny. I took the train in with a couple of other guys from Waukegan that morning. After the first day of school, I couldn't find these guys any-where. I had no idea where I was. I ended up going to the South Side and Jackson Park instead of north to Howard Street." The experience left such an imprint on Bill that he later wrote an essay about it that appeared in *Le Petit Seminaire* during his third year, excerpted here:

> *After what seemed like only a few hours, someone from the rear of the train yelled, "Jackson Park, last stop, Jackson Park, everybody out." Thinking that I had finally reached my destination, I inquired as to where I could board the North Shore, going to Waukegan. To my surprise, I found that the North Shore Line happened to run on the other side of town, at the other end of the line! With pulse barely beating and heart hardly pounding, I got in the nearest train going North. Within a few minutes, I was at long last heading in the right direction.*
>
> *At last I had reached my long lost terminus, Howard Street. Sick to my stomach and scared stiff, I got off the "L." In a short while, I saw the familiar green and red colors of the North Shore, a prairie schooner on wheels. Without bothering to ask what the first stop was, I got in and sank into the first vacant seat.*
>
> *As we sped out of the station the conductor came up to me and took my ticket. Then as we began traveling in unfamiliar territory, I asked the conductor if we were near Waukegan. "Waukegan?" he said. "This is a Mundelein train and the first stop we make is Knollwood."*
>
> *What a nightmare! First to Jackson Park, then Howard, now to Knollwood and…? Well, the conductor let me off at the first stop and with a smile on his jolly face he shouted, "Good luck." He left me off in the middle of nowhere and pulled away. But there in the distance I saw hope—a small building about three blocks away…. It was a telephone booth. I was safe…if only I could remember our number.[6]*

Zavaski looks back on the day with bemusement. "There was a phone strike at the time," he remembers. "I saw a pay phone, but it was for emergencies only. I pleaded with the operator that I was lost."

She let him make the call. But when his family picked him up, Bill acknowledges today, still with a shudder, "They almost decided, 'This is goofy—he's not going back again.'" He is thankful they finally relented. To add, literally, injury to insult, just when Zavaski began to get over the initial shock of navigating the crowded school and the big city, he broke his leg. He survived taking the train downtown, cast and all, figuring the remaining years at Quigley could only get better.

....

Ed Upton also remembers his early days at Quigley as daunting. "It was so big," he says, "that I got out of there after school. I was not a big athlete." His parents reinforced that habit because of their worry about Ed returning home after dark. Even so, Upton's days started early and ended late. He arose at 6 a.m. for 6:30 daily Mass, came back home for breakfast (the Communion fast then required no food from midnight on), and boarded the bus at 7:10 to get to Quigley. "You'd have your classes," Ed concludes, "and then take the bus at 3:30 and get home at 4:30-5. It was a long day for a kid."

Upton recalled that the overabundance of students prompted a pair of responses from the faculty. On the one hand, they ran a very strict operation. "You could only walk from the 'L' on certain streets," Ed recalls. "Rush Street was considered slums—if they caught you, that was a demerit; you could even get expelled. They'd say, 'We don't need you,' and kick people out."

On the other hand, faculty did not get to know the students. Because they taught so many classes, "They barely knew your name. One of the things was the faculty didn't seem to care about us," Upton says, "whereas later it was, 'How can we help you? What can we do for you?' There was none of that. It was: 'If you don't like it, go. Too bad.' There was absolutely no sympathy."

This lack of knowledge about the students caused funny as well as painful events to occur. Upton relishes telling the story of the seminarian from the neighborhood near Midway Airport who ran the candy store outside the gym.

*All of a sudden this kid disappeared. He was stealing money
from the candy store and taking a helicopter home from Meigs
Field to Midway and wearing a Quigley jacket. Finally the guy
from the helicopter company called Quigley: "We have one of
your students flying home every night. We were wondering
where he's getting all the money." They probably said it's coming
in quarters and dollar bills.*

Despite the seemingly uncaring faculty, Upton persevered at
Quigley. "The measure was I was happy," he says. "It was a place I belonged." Over time, some of the students grew to hate chapel or other
aspects of the daily regimen. Ed Upton never did.

....

Mike Ahlstrom's early difficulties at Quigley had little to do with transportation, school size, or discipline. His major concern had to do with
his family's lack of religious practice and what effect it might have on
him in relation to his fellow seminarians. "I had this impression," Ahlstrom says, "that all Quigley seminarians were going to be super holy
people and maybe I wouldn't fit in because I wasn't holy enough and I
didn't come from a holy family. I realized quickly that the others were
no different than anybody else and, if anything, I was more serious
than they were." Mike settled into first-year life at Quigley relatively well, but then that seriousness, an illness, and academic problems
combined to turn his second year into a disaster. "My sophomore year,"
he recollects, "was one of my worst years ever. I had pneumonia and
missed a lot of school. Being 15 years old—and we were supposed to
be chaste—the whole celibacy thing was very confusing and upsetting
for me. I was overly scrupulous. If I had not gone to Quigley, with the
struggles I had in accepting my sexuality, I would've said celibacy is
impossible. I don't think I would have ever become a priest."

To make matters worse, Ahlstrom also struggled with school-
work. "I was a classic underachiever," he reflects. "My first-year Latin prof said, 'Your marks are so low I don't think you'll ever make it
to priesthood.'" In sophomore year Mike began to fail his classes. "I

flunked everything," he says, "and was on the verge of being expelled. Father Jack Crosby ('52) came to the rescue and told the rector, 'This is a good kid.' So I was allowed to repeat sophomore year. I consider my failure a Paschal mystery of good coming out of bad. The best thing that happened to me was that I had to repeat that year."

Repeating not only moved Ahlstrom into the ordination class of 1969, but he also began to learn something about himself during that year. "I took an adult I.Q. test," he recalls, "which tested in five verbal and five non-verbal areas." He scored a "non-functional" 16th percentile on one of the non-verbal tests, but scored over 99 percent on the verbal tests. He now refers to himself as a dreamer and a creative person. "My mind," he says, "was always in another place than where it was supposed to be. In those days, academics were largely a question of memorization. There wasn't a lot of room for creativity and the things I was good at." So Ahlstrom learned to memorize, but he also began to understand that his intelligence was not lacking; rather, it was of another sort.

....

Larry Duris recalled his endeavors to develop a sense of self as he confronted adolescent insecurities at Quigley. "Initially it's overwhelming," he says. "There were 1,400 of us down there. I was very much an introvert. I wasn't a jock and was very defensive about that. I was a musician and was very defensive about that as well." So much so that when Msgr. Charles Meter ('36) held auditions for the chorale, Duris purposely sang off key so Meter wouldn't select him, because Larry didn't want classmates labeling him as part of the singing group, often looked down upon by the competitive jocks. Eventually Larry did join both the glee club and the orchestra, but tests and grades consistently haunted him. He remembered that others gave him more credit than he gave himself when it came to academics. "As a kid," he admits, he had "maybe not the strongest self-image." But over the course of his four years at Quigley, a myriad of experiences and relationships would significantly change Larry Duris' sense of self.

....

Like Mike Ahlstrom, Tom Libera had to repeat a year at Quigley—in his case, third year. And like Larry Duris, Libera's introversion made it difficult for him to make connections in the new, large, and overwhelming world of Quigley Preparatory Seminary. Tom recalls that his early struggles had little to do with his vocation per se. "It was more about adapting," he says, "being able to make friends. I could hide in the woodwork." Almost literally: "Way up on the top floor of the library," he says, "it's like a loft section." Libera remembered stealing away there with the complete bound volumes of the Jesuit Missionaries of North America. His introversion also made him sensitive to how seminarians treated those who might be considered different. "One fellow came from Poland," he says. "He was still learning the language, and the people in the class were supportive of him."

During his third year, Libera faced what he called his own "biggest test." "I was not studying well," he recalls. "I failed Greek and a few other things. So I had to repeat the year." He asked himself how much he wanted priesthood. "If you do," he recalls thinking, "then this is what you have to do." Tom dreaded breaking the news to his mom, but he found her supportive when he did. So he committed himself to improving academically, and in his second try at third year ended up being named a "beadle." (The top two students in each classroom earned the respective titles of prefect and beadle, taking charge of monitoring classroom discipline, handing back graded papers, etc.) Having survived this ordeal, Libera continued to trudge the road toward graduation, with his eyes fixed on the long-term goal of priesthood. Along with Mike Ahlstrom, Tom Libera feels thankful, looking back on the experience of having to repeat a year, that it landed him in the ordination class of 1969.

....

By the time Bob Heidenreich entered the doors of Quigley, the nuns at St. Andrew's had helped to transform him from an at-best average student to an excellent one, so much so that he served as prefect for part of his time at Quigley. His obstacle at Quigley was friendships, not academics. Bob, as noted earlier, had developed close ties to his neighborhood friends. "The structure of Quigley," he remembers, "was that we went to school on Saturdays and we were off on Thursdays. That forced you to hang around with a different crowd." Bob Heidenreich would eventually develop friendships with his Quigley classmates, but without losing his identity as a normal neighborhood guy who just happened to want to be a priest.

....

Time and again when asked what about Quigley Preparatory Seminary helped them overcome the various problems they each encountered adjusting to high school life, the six classmates spoke of the same three things: the sense of expanded horizons, the opportunity to develop great friendships, and the example of priest faculty members.

Larry Duris spoke of experiencing a real, though limited, diversity. "What was good about Quigley?" Duris asks rhetorically. "Racially it was really off balance, but so was everything in the Church and most everything in society. There were not many blacks."

> But you had people from the whole metropolitan area you ended up becoming friends with—you didn't ask where someone lived before you became a friend. It broadened your perspective of the world. Different lifestyles, different communities. I looked at my siblings. My brother under me, Jim, was like Columbus. I took him on a dry run of his prom the night before, and he still got hopelessly lost with the girl, God love him. But his world was Skokie, Evanston, and the far North Side of Chicago; same with my sister, a lot narrower than mine.

For Duris and his classmates, the entire city and suburbs of Chicago became their world. In an attempt both to encourage seminarians to socialize together and to make sure they did not do so with anyone else—particularly girls—parishes, with the unofficial endorsement of Quigley, took turns sponsoring monthly "mission parties" for groups of Quigley students on Wednesday nights, the night before the seminarians' day off on Thursday. The effort to protect the young men from the outside world had the ironic effect of allowing them, in their travels to the parties, to see almost every kind of neighborhood in the diocese. For a small fee, "You'd play cards and have something [nonalcoholic] to drink," Bill Zavaski recalls, "and then the monies they raised were given to the missions." Ahlstrom says that the parties were about the only social life the seminary allowed them, so much so that when his Quigley class celebrated its 50th anniversary in 2011, one of the lay alumni hosted a mission party for them the following day.

In addition to the mission parties, service projects offered another opportunity for the class to turn their horizons outward during their days at Quigley. St. Joseph's Parish stands just a few blocks from Quigley and long had large numbers of poor residents. Quigley seminarians would volunteer on their free Thursdays to teach catechism to the grade school students from the public school. Teachers dismissed the Catholic students early so they could walk to St. Joe's. "We were told to wear our cassocks for safety," recalls Larry Duris. "You saw a whole different side of life."

....

In addition to the sense of expanded horizons that Quigley life opened up, the men also talk today about how the high school seminary started up the lifelong friendships they made with classmates including among the six of them, other ordained members of the class—those still in the priesthood and those who have left, and those who left the seminary somewhere along the journey. "One of the things I prayed about every day," Bill Zavaski remembers about his first year, "was that I would develop a really good group of friends that would help me get through school." Zavaski, overwhelmed by Quigley's size and unable to participate in many extracurricular activities because of his long trip back to Waukegan every afternoon, worried about his ability to develop good friends. But when the mission parties began, he began to stay overnight at classmates' homes in order to attend. "Quigley was the beginning of developing some key relationships in my life," he says.

For Larry Duris, the unique schedule of attending school on Saturday and having Thursdays off changed his world of friends. "It worked real well," he comments, "in disconnecting you from your grammar school peers." On the other hand, it brought the eleven Quigley men from St. Peter's together. "On Thursdays," he asks, "what else were you going to do? We'd end up at the 8:15 Mass and afterwards go to the coffee shop across the street and chew the fat for an hour. When I look back now, those Thursday Masses and breakfasts were Church for me."

The class got to know one another during their first year in high school on the basis of the alphabet, because the administration assigned first-year students to classes that way. Ed Upton, for example, met his friend of 53 years, Bill Zavaski, through the alphabetical system.

Upton also remembered the tension that surfaced—and remained—between his class and the class ahead of him. When Niles College opened in the fall of 1961, it enrolled two classes from Quigley. The last group of men who spent the traditional high school seminary term of five years (rather than four) at Quigley, who became the ordination class of 1968, and the first four-year graduates of Quigley, the ordination class of 1969, graduated Quigley together in the spring of 1961. "Their class controlled all the graduation stuff," Upton says, "so there was not a happy spirit. We got cut out of everything." Suffice it to say that seminary life could produce not only lifelong friends, but also longstanding resentments.

....

The six young Quigley men made few significant connections with the faculty, but those they did forge had long-term effects. The sheer number of students attending Quigley—more than 1,300 by the late 1950s—necessitated a very authoritarian and formal approach to classroom instruction; as Ed Upton noted, most faculty members didn't even know his name. Exceptions to this highly controlled hierarchical model, on the other hand, began to emerge over the men's four years at Quigley, as certain faculty members began to engage the seminarians in ways both more creative and more personal. Faculty members from the ordination class of 1952, in particular, began to establish connections with the class of 1969 that would last throughout their priestly careers.

Ed Upton remembered mostly the rule rather than the exceptions. When asked if any priests at Quigley made him want to follow in their footsteps, he said no. "There were," he continues, "a couple of jerks. One priest tried to have a reign of terror and frighten people. If you weren't prepared, he would belittle you." Upton also recounted the tale of a student who was expelled for clandestinely correcting his friend's homework paper; he was betrayed by the lead that fell from his pencil, which was spotted by a faculty member who theatrically cried out, "Freeze!" and dropped to the floor to retrieve it as evidence. Upton does concede that Quigley had hired a mostly young faculty and that, despite the problems encountered, most of them treated the seminarians with respect. "There was never," he maintains, "a kid that got hit."

Echoing Upton's ambivalence about the faculty, Mike Ahlstrom recalled again the humiliation of his Latin teacher telling him he would probably not make it to ordination. "I certainly did not have any feeling of affirmation from the faculty," he maintains.

By third year, however, Ahlstrom began for the first time to gain some academic self-confidence. He credits the change to then Father John Fahey ('49). "He was one of my heroes," Ahlstrom says. "He was teaching us about the new approach to Scripture and was light years ahead. He helped me begin to believe I had something to say." His academic struggles improved to the extent that he won one of five spots offered to students to publish a literary essay in the yearbook.[7] He recalled one other faculty member of note: Father Stan Rudcki ('53), who taught history, religion, and music. "He was," Ahlstrom says, "one of the last of the universal minds. He and Fahey excited me."

Larry Duris mentions the same two men who so impressed Ahlstrom: Rudcki and Fahey. Duris told the story of how his third-year English class went from hating to loving Fahey overnight.

> *First day, before class was over, I don't know how many demerits he had given out. A couple of people were smart-mouthing. He laid down the law of what he was expecting. We walked out of that class thinking, how did we get this ass? We are doomed.*
> *By the end of the week, however, we loved him. I learned more English in that one year than the other three years combined.*

We had high respect for him because he pushed us. We had to do a typewritten theme every week; it was due on Saturdays. He'd have them back on Monday, all read and corrected with comments despite his being at a parish where he had confessions Saturday night and two Masses on Sunday. He would spend time after school. He became a mentor.

Bill Zavaski noticed that many of the best faculty members at Quigley hailed from the ordination class of 1952. He mentioned the rapport he felt with Fathers Jack Gorman, Bill Flaherty, and Marty Winters. (Zavaski's boyhood hero, Father John Kuzinskas, also hailed from this class.) "Our class has always had," Zavaski says, "great respect for the class of '52."

Larry Duris recalled how one member of that class added to an already exciting fourth year at Quigley. Reports about the approaching Vatican Council called for by Pope John XXIII filled the air, with rumors of a possible change to the Mass being said in English. Duris' class, in addition, would soon after graduation embark on the adventure of opening a new college seminary. The United States, meanwhile, faced the imminent question of whether voters would elect the first Catholic president. That topic occupied Father Marty "Red" Winters' social studies class for the entire fall of 1960. "We did not open the book," Duris says, "until after November 8, election day."

It was the Kennedy/Nixon campaign. It was politics every day. We enjoyed that. On Election Day at the end of class, Winters said, "I'm confident."
Then he said, "This is close."
Then he said, "You never can tell."
Lastly, he said, "Gentlemen, I have one favor. If it looks about midnight like it's not going well, if a few of you would be so kind as to come down and see me off the Michigan Avenue Bridge." And we just roared.

Faculty members such as Winters and the other men from '52 personified the excitement of the times. "People talked about the spirit of the Chicago presbyterate," Duris says. "That image was appealing. Ministry can be a very cold, stony, impersonal kind of thing. It wasn't that at Quigley."

....

Quigley Preparatory Seminary celebrated its 100th anniversary in 2005. But in 2007, Cardinal Francis George made the decision to close the high school seminary, citing declining numbers of young men advancing to the college seminary.

Looking back, members of the class of 1969 appreciated the opportunities that a Quigley academic education provided. "We have classmates from Quigley," Bob Heidenreich explains with clear pride, "who are very successful in the world. It laid a great liberal arts foundation." Larry Duris agrees. "They claimed at one time," he maintains, comparing Quigley to Chicago's perhaps most well-known Catholic high school, "that it was a toss-up between Quigley and St. Ignatius over which was the best Catholic high school in the city." (Actually, as late as 1999, *U.S. News and World Report* listed Quigley as one of the top 100 high schools in the country.)[8]

Tom Libera lost his grammar school and high school on the same day when Immaculate Heart of Mary appeared with Quigley on the list of archdiocesan schools to be closed. "It was a sad day," says Libera. "Quigley closing was not a good thing for Chicago, in the sense that contributions could have been added to that stream of good leadership."

Libera's sense of loss served not only to underscore how much Quigley meant to so many of the seminarians who had trained there, but also to contrast how much the Church had changed since the heady days of 1961, when Tom and his classmates graduated from Quigley. In 2007, just over 200 students attended Quigley, continuing a long-term decline since the 1960s, when 1,300 students walked the halls.

The year 1961, however, had ushered in a hopeful new beginning for the archdiocesan seminary system. For one thing, John F. Kennedy had just begun his first term as the first Catholic president in U.S. history. Locally, Albert Meyer, who had become Archbishop of Chicago in September of 1958 and would play a prominent role in the Second Vatican Council, engineered a major change in the seminary system, with the announcement of plans to open in the fall of 1961 both Quigley South (a second Chicago high school seminary, which eventually closed its doors in 1990) and Niles College, which eventually moved to the lakeshore campus of Loyola University of Chicago and was renamed St. Joseph's College Seminary in 1994. Cardinal Meyer would send most of the teachers from the ordination class of '52 who were serving at Quigley on to Niles, which meant that they would begin their careers as college professors at the same time the class of '69 entered the college seminary.

Meanwhile, as both the fourth- and fifth-year men prepared to graduate from Quigley in 1961 and move on to become the first two classes at the new college seminary, they posed for graduation pictures. The fifth-year students—the eventual ordination class of 1968—wore the traditional cassocks for their photographs. Not so the class of 1969, the first to break with this Quigley custom. They wore suits and ties, an unmistakable foreshadowing of the profound change that lay just over the horizon.

....

1. Denis R. McNamara, *Heavenly City: The Architectural Tradition of Catholic Chicago* (Chicago: Liturgy Training Publications, 2005), 9.
2. *Le Petit Seminaire* (1955), 98-99, 160-161, 170-171, 174-175, 186-187.
3. *Le Petit Seminaire* (1955), 78-80, 86-89, 230-231.
4. Memorandum: "Percentage Remaining in Seminary Each Year," September 1967, Archdiocesan Archives of Chicago (AAC).
5. *That We May Have Priests* [a book celebrating the opening of Quigley South and Niles College], 9.
6. William Zavasky, "Thank you Mr. Bell," in *Le Petit Seminaire* (1960), 97.
7. Michael Ahlstrom, "Education in America" in *Le Petit Seminaire* (1960), 117.
8. *U.S. News and World Report*, January 18, 1999.

CHAPTER 3

A NEW SEMINARY
FOR NEW TIMES
Niles College

During their two years at Niles College, the class of 1969 experienced an almost dual world. On the one hand, they lived under a severe though gradually moderating monastic spiritual discipline. On the other, they played a key role in an important experiment in seminary education that would offer them heretofore unprecedented freedom. The six men being followed here agreed on these two points but not necessarily about whether or not the faculty had, if you will, a method to their madness. While Bill Zavaski says, "I don't think they knew what they wanted to do," Tom Libera and Ed Upton saw a plan on the part of the faculty to prepare their class to challenge the status quo when they would arrive at Mundelein, where the rector, Msgr. Malachy Foley ('31), held tightly to the existing seminary model. "I suspect the administration was experimenting with what would be the best way to prepare us for Mundelein," says Tom Libera. Ed Upton concurred:

They realized that Mundelein had to change. It was so isolated and Mal Foley was just out of it. So they deliberately set out to create a new kind of seminary which had much more, for those days, student responsibility. There was a student government. You could talk to the faculty; there was more personal freedom. I think they felt if you do this here, when people go to Mundelein they will react—which is what happened.

After some contentious public debate, the Combined Board of St. Hedwig's Orphanage at Harlem and Touhy Avenues in near north suburban Niles, Illinois decided on February 17, 1960, to allow the Archdiocese of Chicago to take over their campus. The orphanage, run by the Felician Sisters, would send its children elsewhere, and the buildings would house 268 college seminarians starting in the fall of 1961, when the Niles Campus of St. Mary of the Lake Seminary would open. (Later the archdiocese would shorten the name to Niles College. In 1968, Niles would affiliate with Loyola University of Chicago.)[1]

The quickly rising number of seminarians and the limited space of both Quigley, the high school seminary, and the major seminary in Mundelein, Illinois prompted the creation of a junior college component of the seminary system. In the early 1950s, the first-year classes at Quigley had averaged about 235 seminarians. The ordination classes of 1968 and 1969, who entered high school in 1956 and 1957, started Quigley with classes of 441 and 421 students, respectively.[2] Soon thereafter, with the opening of Quigley South in 1961, combined first-year enrollment at the two Quigleys would soar to over 600 boys who thought they wanted to become priests.

....

The spirit of the many changes taking place in the Catholic Church during the early 1960s would eventually make its way into the life of the new college seminary. First, however, the seminarians would have to confront the old Church.

Shortly after their arrival, they received a copy of perhaps the greatest symbol of the unchanging and uniform seminary system: the Rule. Officially entitled "St. Mary of the Lake Seminary Junior College Department Guide," the Rule contained 34 pages of instructions, schedules, and penalties that regulated virtually every area of a seminarian's life. The Rule proper began with the listing of the Class Day Schedule. That schedule follows:

Class Day Schedule

5:40	Rising
6:05	Morning Prayers, Meditation
6:30	Mass, Thanksgiving
7:15	Breakfast, Short Recreation
8:00	Chapel Visit – Study Period
9:00	Optional Class Time
9:55	First Class Period
10:50	Second Class Period
11:40	Short Recreation
12:00	Noon Day Prayer
12:15	Lunch, Short Recreation
1:20	End of Short Recreation – Chapel Visit
1:30	Third Class Period
2:25	Fourth Class Period
3:15	Long Recreation
5:00	End of Long Recreation
5:20	Spiritual Reading or Conference
5:45	Rosary, Angelus in private
6:00	Dinner, Short Recreation
7:15	Chapel Visit – Study Period
8:50	Short Recreation
9:00	Points for Meditation and Night Prayer
10:00	Lights Out[3]

Seminarians also discovered in the Rule a dizzying array of regulations. Although not an exhaustive survey of the precepts, the following examples will provide a flavor of the discipline involved in seminary life. The Rule required total silence during study periods, in the residence halls at all times, and during the Great Silence, which commenced after night prayers and ended the following morning after Mass.[4] Seminarians could never enter a neighbor's room, could not have televisions or radios in their rooms, and had to have any books, newspapers, or magazines they wanted to read approved by seminary authorities.[5] Students could leave the grounds only with explicit permission, and the administration granted that sparingly, for example permitting only a one-day absence at the death of a grandparent to attend the funeral. The Rule also admonished the young men to keep their contact with lay staff to a minimum. The seminary did not allow visitors and reserved the right to open all student mail, while dictating the dress expected of a seminarian. Students wore cassocks, Roman collars, and surplices for all liturgies.[6] It is interesting that the Rule was least strict when it came to smoking, permitting it outside any time during recreation.[7] Any violation of any one of these and other rules, depending on the severity of the infraction, could result in immediate expulsion from the seminary.

"We were freshmen in college," Bill Zavaski says, "and were treated like children." Zavaski especially found the combination of close quarters and absolute silence ironic. The seminary had transformed the former orphanage into several dorms, each housing twelve seminarians in small un-roofed cubicles seven by nine feet. "We were living in cubicles," he says. "But we had to have this grand silence. You're living right next door to somebody and you can't talk to them. That was crazy."

"It was more old seminary than new," Ed Upton recalls. "You couldn't even call home."

....

The change that would soon reach the new college seminary mirrored the change sweeping through the Church of Chicago on many fronts during the late 1950s and early 1960s. Priests were taking on new leadership roles in the fight for civil rights; they were embracing an entirely new theology of working with laypeople; and, at least since 1958 with their new archbishop, Albert Meyer, whom Rome elevated to the College of Cardinals in 1959, they had increasingly begun voicing their honest opinions and asking for his support for new initiatives. Each of these developments would soon significantly affect the class of 1969.

When Meyer had arrived in Chicago in 1958, he had toured the archdiocese with his Urban Affairs director Father (later Msgr.) Jack Egan ('43) and consulted about race relations with the chaplain of the

Catholic Interracial Council, Father (later Msgr.) Dan Cantwell ('39). Meyer subsequently allowed Egan to draft a statement in his name in 1959 to the President's Commission on Civil Rights urging greater action to facilitate integrated housing in the country.[8] Meyer's leadership in this area eventually led to an ecumenical National Conference on Religion and Race in January of 1963 and to the U.S. bishops issuing a pastoral letter on race relations in September of that year.

Leadership also emerged from the ranks of the Catholic clergy on the issue of religion and race in Chicago. Father Bill Hogan ('52), assistant at St. Raphael Parish in the Englewood neighborhood of Chicago, wrote Meyer in July 1961, encouraging his support for priests' participation in wade-ins taking place in an effort to integrate Rainbow Beach in the South Shore neighborhood on the South Side. Hogan informed Meyer that Mildred Fentress, a black Catholic, had taken her son and daughter, both of whom attended Catholic high schools, to the beach, unaware of the ban of custom on blacks. While there, a crowd of white teenage boys began to throw objects at them. Although a policeman rescued the Fentresses, he warned them not to return to the all-white beach. Mildred Fentress then wrote a letter to the newspapers; several groups, including the Catholic Interracial Council (CIC), began using what they called "wade-ins" to protest the beach's segregation. The CIC asked that priests attend as observers, and many had attended the first wade-in. "The presence of the clergy," Hogan assured Meyer, "was extremely effective.... The wade-ins will go [on] every Saturday and Sunday until Fall. My only hope is that you would not frown on the presence of a few Priests as observers."[9]

Other clergymen, meanwhile, complained to Meyer about the continuing use of Latin in the Church. Father Gerard Weber ('43) wrote the archbishop to tell him about administering the last rites to a dying infant. "The wonderful, powerful, beautiful prayers of the Church," he lamented, "brought no consolation to the people present. When I prayed, it was in a language utterly foreign to them. In so many instances of this sort, the use of Latin hurts our missionary efforts."[10] The very fact that priests could voice their opinions candidly to their archbishop indicated the openness and mutual respect that existed between them.

Of all the issues confronting the Church, however, none would hold more importance for the class of '69 than the proper vocation of the laity and the clergy's role in encouraging that vocation. On September 19 and 20, 1961, days before the opening of the Niles campus, the archdiocese held its annual Clergy Conference on the topic of "The Layman in the Apostolate." Father John Krump ('54), a respected member of the Chicago clergy, gave a talk entitled "The Theology of the Layman's Vocation" that presented what would become the working theology of the class of 1969.

Krump claimed that priests must help to move the laity to take more responsibility for the work of the Church. Surveying the activities that clergy and laity had already embarked upon together in Chicago and across the country, he focused on groups such as the Catholic Interracial Council (CIC), the Christian Family Movement (CFM), the Young Christian Students (YCS), and the Cana Conference. Because of these groups, Krump argued, pastors had noticed greater participation of the laity in Mass, more lay teachers in schools, and more lay volunteers teaching catechism. More Catholics, it is important to note, had begun to recognize their role in working for a just social, political, and economic order.

As for the role of the clergy, Krump stated, "The priest must make an act of faith in the layman. When the Church treats the laity like children, they became indifferent to the Church's faith and life." He therefore called for a "listening and learning" priesthood, insisting that without priest and people looking honestly at life together, the clergy would fail in its efforts to train the laity to "put shoes on the Gospel and make it walk around."[11]

....

Over a very brief period of living and studying at Niles College, both the faculty and students began to embrace the spirit of change they saw and heard about across the archdiocese. Free of the history and tradition of either Quigley, founded in 1917, or the major seminary at Mundelein, which opened in 1921, those living on the Niles campus entered into a collaboration that led to the re-creation of seminary life.

"I even put on a thing with one of my classmates called the Mass of the Future," says Mike Ahlstrom. Father Marty Winters ('52) performed the role of celebrant for this "Mass." "It wasn't a real Mass," Ahlstrom recalls, "but we had songs in English and 'Communion' under both forms—the bread and the wine—and very futuristic thinking."

From the point of view of Father (later Msgr.) Eugene Lyons ('42), the new seminary's rector, as well as the faculty, nothing epitomized change more than their ongoing discussions of whether and how to modify seminary discipline in regards to the Rule. At an October 20, 1961, faculty meeting, during a discussion of penalties for violation of the Rule, Lyons agreed to explain to students later that "little things are little things. Forget about them and become a good seminarian."[12] At an October 30 meeting, the faculty discussed the merits of students' complaints that they had too much scheduled study time and under what circumstances the faculty might permit them to venture off campus.[13] By a June 8, 1962, meeting held at the close of Niles' first school year, the faculty had begun considering whether to permit talking in the residence halls. Some suggested that faculty and students needed to spend more time interacting by eating with one another.[14]

In the fall of 1962, the once uniform life of the seminarians underwent even further and more significant long-lasting changes. On December 3, faculty members met and agreed that students would have longer rec periods, would be allowed to venture off campus during them on limited nearby streets, and could stay up one hour later on evenings before a day off.[15] By April 1963, the faculty had relaxed the rule of silence to the extent that it now applied only during study periods, in the library, and during the Great Silence overnight. Seminarians could now finally talk to each other in the residence halls. Change had indeed come to the college seminary.[16]

As the Niles campus adjusted to this somewhat looser environment, students showed growing signs of restlessness. In his rector's log for April 10, 1962, Lyons had noted that Father Chris Melone ('52) had caught a student watching the *Late Late Show* at 12:30 a.m. during the Great Silence. This led Lyons to make a visit to the rec hall, where he discovered nine seminarians watching a hockey game.[17]

When seminarians returned from their Christmas break on January 3, 1963, they found an announcement posted from Lyons: The rector deplored their conduct on the night before they had left for break. "The faculty and student body," Lyons chided, "apparently don't agree. We keep trying to treat you as adults and you keep insisting that you are not adults. At the moment you are winning the argument hands down." Despite bumps in the road, however, seminarians and their faculty seemed delighted with the changes in seminary life.

The late Father Andrew Greeley ('54) has referred to many young Catholics of this time, including seminarians, as the "New Breed."[19] "We looked on ourselves as pioneers," Bob Heidenreich says, echoing Greeley, "not only because of starting this new system at Niles but because we had another vision of how we would minister as Church. We were the new breed looking to change things. Niles fit right into that because it was a new way of addressing reality."

When reflecting today on the "new" aspects of seminary life at Niles, members of the ordination class of 1969 focus most on three areas: the development of peer friendships, the spirit of collaboration with the faculty, and the increasing concentration on involvement with the Church and world outside the seminary walls.

As the rules slowly loosened up at Niles, and as the faculty encouraged collaboration through activities such as the Board of Prefects, the literary magazine *Compendium*, and school plays, it became easier for the seminarians to build friendships. As a member of the Board of Prefects, Ed Upton found himself getting to know fellow students through discussions about changing the seminary. "You could," he explains, "have a conversation about the Rule: 'Could we take a walk outside the grounds?'"

The tight living arrangements, especially in the second year when the administration allowed talking in the residence halls, also contributed to the development of friendships. "We lived in those crazy cubicles," Upton says, "but they never bothered us. We didn't know any different."

Bill Zavaski has emphasized the importance of the friends he made when he attended Quigley, especially during his difficult freshman year. His first year at Niles turned out to be far more traumatic, and he remains grateful that friends, old and new, reached out to him then as well. The rector's log for January 8-14, 1962, contains this simple and somber entry. "The mother of a first-year man, William Zavaski, was buried this morning. Father Lyons…took eight of the seminarians to the Mass and to the cemetery."[20]

"My major crisis of faith," Zavaski recalls, "happened when my mother died. She was not sick at all. I was told in November that she had what they thought was pleurisy. It was lung cancer. She was dead by January." Zavaski remembered clearly his friends rallying around him.

> *There were several classmates who I spent time with who were supportive those two years, like Bill Keating and Bob Petrusiak—those are two who have left. Eddie [Upton] was very supportive, Mike Ahlstrom, Bob Heidenreich. I was angry for the whole time at Niles. After she died, it was very painful. Part of it was—I can still remember this and I speak to this at funerals today, too, with kids who lose their parents—I had all these lovely people who kept saying, 'This is God's will.' You hear that all the time. People are trying to be very nice. Well, I hated God. She was 50, not sick. November to January. It was awful. She died a terrible death. Terrible. I was so mad. So mad. But you live with those things. I kept on praying for friends to be supportive to help me get through this thing. That was a key thing for me, having a support group of friends.*

Along with deepening friendships, members of the class of '69 happily discovered over time that the faculty at Niles desired a level of collaboration with them that they had rarely experienced at Quigley and couldn't imagine existing at Mundelein, based on what they had heard from major seminarians studying there. One change, for example, took the form of an increased confidence in the use of psychology in seminary affairs. Father Lyons asked and received permission for Niles faculty member Father (later Msgr. and then Bishop) John Gorman ('52) to earn an advanced degree in psychology. Gorman's studies led him to champion healthier faculty/student relations at Niles.

The Niles faculty invited these 18- and 19-year-old seminarians into a world they had never known before, where their professors began to treat them like adults. "I loved Niles," says Mike Ahlstrom. "The rector, Gene Lyons, was a rather progressive thinker. The faculty encouraged us to think. You could debate things. You could go to a prof's room and say, 'Hey, I want to ask you some questions. I need to talk about this.' The faculty respected us, and we respected them. They were trying to stimulate us."

This approach of friendly collaboration came at a crucial time for Bob Heidenreich. While in second year, his father died. His mother, concerned about raising Bob's teenage brother alone and, not being a businesswoman, having given up the family restaurant, convinced him over Easter break to leave the seminary. When he called the rector to tell him, Lyons asked him to return early Sunday evening, before the other seminarians returned to campus. "'You won't have to stay, but I want to see you,'" Heidenreich recalls Lyons telling him. When he arrived for the meeting, Lyons gently encouraged him. "You're doing great," he remembers Lyons saying, "and chances are that if you leave now, you won't finish college, and you could make it. But more than that, you could be a good priest. I'd like you to think twice about this."

"So I went home and I did," Heidenreich states simply. He later found out that his uncle stepped in to help his mom financially. His eyes welled up when he told this story and, when he said that this is what family is all about, he was clearly referring not only to his extended family but also to Father Eugene Lyons.

For Ed Upton, the newness of the enterprise for both seminarians and faculty made a huge difference.

> It was all of their first time teaching college. So they were
> learning themselves, which was the best part in retrospect. What
> you remember is, "Hey, we can build something new. We're
> learning; you're learning." That attitude was a great attitude
> for a young person to develop. It wasn't like at Quigley, or later
> when we first went to Mundelein: "We have all the answers.
> You learn them, and then you will have all the answers." There
> was a much more collegial spirit before that word became really
> commonplace. And that was the real learning for me.

That spirit of collegiality, Upton says, permitted faculty and students to build a new type of seminary.

> *A theme in my own life is that Niles was brand new. It was the first year. Gene Lyons would say, "We are going to create a new seminary. What you guys do is going to perdure." We're creating a new tradition, but it was the "we." Not just the rector, not just the faculty, but together we're creating something that never was here before. For 18-year-old kids that's very exciting. That stayed with us for our whole life, because we were always at the beginning of something brand new.*

The brand new event that would most color the lives of the class of 1969 began during their time at Niles: the Second Vatican Council. In addition to the Council itself, the progressive activities of Chicago Church leaders, clerical and lay, as well as the Church's national focus on civil rights, all indirectly worked their way into the life of the college seminary. The faculty encouraged the students, through speakers at days of recollection, involvement in apostolates, and writing for the seminary's literary magazine, to expand their horizons beyond the walls of the seminary to the Church and world outside.

"You got a flavor," Bill Zavaski recalls, "that something about the Church was changing. Bits and pieces came from the faculty because they were engaged in local parishes and were very young and excited about what was happening in the Church."

Tom Libera offered an example: "As liturgy developed at Niles, we weren't just going to do Mass the old way. Whatever new was going to be allowed, we would have the advantage of doing it." Libera also recalled Cardinal Meyer's growing role at the Council and the excitement of "one of our own being one of the top guys."

When Meyer issued his report on the first session of the Vatican Council at the Clergy Conference of Chicago held on March 6, 1963, his statement that the Council had three main objectives—pastoral, missionary, and ecumenical—underlined the increasing outward focus of the Church that the Niles faculty had begun to impress upon their seminarians.[21]

On December 3, 1961, the faculty invited their first outside visitor to speak to the seminarians for their Sunday Day of Recollection. Father George Kane ('51), a priest of the archdiocese, spoke on his work in "Negro" parishes in Chicago. The rector's log for the week states that "all the questions were about work among Negroes."[22] One week later, another Chicago priest, Father (later Msgr.) Leo Mahon ('51) gave the Day of Recollection. Mahon exhorted the students to love Christ and the Church, insisting that the Church cannot ordain a bachelor who is not in love and that love was, in the end, what matured a person. Mahon also commented on how quickly and constantly the world was changing. "There is an old saying," he related, as he urged the seminarians to become relevant to the modern world, "'The Church moves slowly but with wisdom.' I agree with the wisdom part, but there is no excuse for moving slowly."[23]

One month to the day after Mahon's talk, almost as if in response to it, the rector and Father Stan Rudcki ('53) went to the Town Hall at the Village of Niles to join with other ministers to prevent a threatened disturbance because an African-American had moved into the village.[24]

Even more important, in terms of focusing seminarians' attention outside the campus walls, is the fact that the faculty began to encourage the seminarians to get involved in what became known as summer urban apostolates. Initially these involved work in either the Hispanic or African-American communities. Seminarians could volunteer to take the parish census at St. Bernard's in Englewood, for example, or to work with Father Bill Hogan doing community organizing at another Englewood parish, St. Raphael. Other choices included attending meetings of Caballeros de San Juan at Holy Cross Parish in Woodlawn with Father Leo Mahon as part of what was then called the Cardinal's Committee on the Spanish Speaking; working at the Catholic social service center on the Near West Side, Marillac House; or running a day camp at St. Agatha's in the West Side North Lawndale neighborhood.[25] St. Agatha's also took part in a tutoring experiment during the school year run by Sister M. Hildegarde, BVM and Father Dan Mallette ('57), an assistant at the parish, in which 58 Niles seminarians took a bus to the parish twice a week to tutor 160 grammar and high school students.[26]

The faculty at Niles also encouraged the seminarians to think and to express themselves by permitting the Student Board of Prefects to publish *Compendium: A Journal of Thought and Opinion* six times a year in order to "present opinions on controversial issues."[27] Surprised that any seminary would allow, much less encourage, them to engage in controversy, the students took full advantage, writing about such topics as the emerging laity and student councils in seminaries.[28] Larry Duris contributed an article entitled "Toward a Philosophy of Seminary Education" in which he tried—interestingly, given the culture of the Niles campus—to explicate the balance necessary between "discipline and freedom of thought" in a seminary curriculum. Bob Heidenreich penned an essay with the provocative title "A Baptized Communism," dealing with the need for an active laity. "We need someone," he wrote, "who'll be a Catholic worker, someone who is not afraid to roll up his white sleeves and pick up a shovel to help dig out the buried Negro. The Church needs a Catholic layman whose actions have made him an example to the community as a good neighbor because he's a good Catholic."[29]

The increased freedom enjoyed by the Niles seminarians seemed bound to cause a reaction when they matriculated to Mundelein Seminary at the end of their second year. Evidence of this type of reaction came in a letter from an unnamed member of the ordination class of 1968, who had just spent his first few months at Mundelein after finishing up at Niles the previous May. Father Lyons published the letter in the Niles bulletin on November 16, 1962. The seminarian praised the spiritual direction and confessions at Niles in comparison to Mundelein. "The atmosphere here," he added, "seems more impersonal and cool than at Niles." He also expressed gratitude that at Niles a student could make an appointment with a professor or the rector at any time, a practice not allowed at Mundelein. Although Mundelein seemed more religious to him, he lamented the fact that no student council existed there.[30]

Seminarians were not the only ones reacting to the differences between Niles and Mundelein. In his rector's log for April 1, 1963, Lyons expressed discouragement about relations with Msgr. Mal Foley, the rector at Mundelein. "We have been in operations for one and a half years," Lyons wrote. "The communication with Mundelein has been practically nil. Last year we had no basketball game [between the students] because we were not invited. Letters to the rector get no response. If this keeps up, I think we should give up trying."[31]

At the end of the same year, on December 10, Lyons confided to his faculty in a letter that Father Dick Wojcik ('49), a diocesan priest and professor of music at Mundelein, had visited him to share his anxiety about growing tension between the Niles and Mundelein faculties, especially the latter's long-serving Jesuits. Wojcik complained that a student had quoted a Niles faculty member as saying the years at Mundelein were a waste of time. Mundelein's Jesuits had gotten wind of the comment, with predictable reactions. After urging restraint in what had become an "explosive situation," Lyons advised his faculty not to discuss Mundelein with any other priests of the diocese.[32]

These glimpses of the situation clearly indicate that a great deal of tension existed between the institutions and, by extension, that such tension would greatly color the transition from Niles to Mundelein for the class of 1969.

....

1. The negotiations between the Felician Sisters and the archdiocese caused quite a stir. The *Polish Daily Zgoda* published a front-page story under the headline "Possibility of Losing a Polonia Post." No ethnic league in Chicago had more strength than the Polish League. But the Felician Sisters needed help, between running the increasingly crowded St. Andrew's old people's home right next door to St. Hedwig's and continuing to staff Good Counsel High School on the Northwest Side of the city. Only 150 orphans remained at the huge Niles facility, and Angel Guardian Orphanage and Maryville Academy had plenty of room to take them in. The Board insisted that archdiocesan officials make proper and respectful communication of this decision to Polish pastors, the Polish Roman Catholic Union, the Polish National Alliance, and several other Polish groups. See Memorandum of meeting of the Combined Board of St. Hedwig's Orphanage, 2/17/1960, AAC. See also *Polish Daily Zgoda*, 12/4/1959. For enrollment numbers at Niles, see Enrollment Statistics, First Year Quigley through Ordination, September 8, 1964, AAC.

2. Memorandum: "Percentage Remaining in Seminary Each Year," September 1967, AAC.
3. *St. Mary of the Lake Seminary Junior College Department Guide* (The Rule), 7.
4. Ibid., 21-34.
5. Ibid.
6. Ibid. Quote from page 32.
7. Ibid. Smoking rules, 29.
8. Steven M. Avella, "Cardinal Meyer and the Era of Confidence" in Ellen Skerrett, Edward R. Kantowicz, and Steven M. Avella, *Catholicism, Chicago Style* (Chicago, Loyola University Press, 1993), 120-121.
9. William E. Hogan to Cardinal Meyer, July 17, 1961, AAC.
10. Gerard Weber to Meyer, N.D, AAC.
11. John M. Krump, "Theology of the Layman's Vocation." Talk given at Clergy Conference of Chicago, September 19-20, 1961, AAC.
12. Minutes of Niles Faculty Meeting, October 20, 1961, AAC.
13. Minutes of Niles Faculty Meeting, October 30, 1961, AAC.
14. Minutes of Niles Faculty Meeting, June 8, 1962, AAC.
15. Minutes of Niles Faculty Meeting, December 3, 1962, AAC.
16. Special Note from the Rector to the Students and Faculty, April 21, 1963, AAC.
17. *Rector's Log Book (RLB)*, April 10, 1962, AAC.
18. Announcement Posted January 3, 1963, AAC.
19. Andrew M. Greeley, "The New Breed," *America*, May 23, 1964.
20. *RLB*, January 8-14, 1962, AAC.
21. Report of Cardinal Meyer to Clergy Conference of Chicago, March 6, 1963, AAC.
22. *RLB*, December 7, 1961, AAC.
23. *RLB*, December 10, 1961, AAC.
24. *RLB*, January 10, 1962, AAC.
25. Notice: Volunteer Opportunities in Chicago's Urban Apostolate, AAC.
26. "Seminary Students Help Lawndale Youth," *The New World*, May 31, 1963.
27. Minutes of Board of Prefects, April 4, 1963, AAC.
28. *Compendium: A Journal of Student Thought and Opinion*, vol. 2, #2, December, 1962.
29. Ibid., vol. 2, #5, 34-36 and 38-39.
30. Unnamed student to Lyons, published in Niles Campus Bulletin, November 16, 1962, AAC.
31. *RLB*, April 1, 1963, AAC.

32. Lyons to priest faculty, December 10, 1963, AAC.

CHAPTER 4

PROTECTED FROM "THE WORLD"
St. Mary of the Lake Seminary

The assassination of President John Fitzgerald Kennedy remains vivid in the memories of six men who were studying at St. Mary of the Lake Seminary in the Chicago suburb of Mundelein at the time, but not for reasons shared by the vast majority of other Americans. Even a half-century later, these men recall the days of Kennedy's death and funeral with resentment and indeed outrage toward those who then led Chicago's major seminary.

On Friday November 22, 1963, Lee Harvey Oswald assassinated Kennedy, the 35th President of the United States and the first Catholic ever to hold that office. For days afterward, the nation expressed its shock and sorrow in a myriad of public ways, culminating on Monday, November 25, with the President's funeral Mass and burial. Americans sat glued to their television sets over the weekend. On Monday, many schools—both public and parochial—closed for the funeral; others allowed students to watch the ceremonies on television, effectively turning the day into a sad but important civics lesson.

Except at Mundelein Seminary of the Archdiocese of Chicago.

Three months before the assassination, the ordination class of 1969 being followed here, having completed their two years of junior college at the rapidly changing Niles Campus the previous spring, had arrived at Mundelein, as the major seminary is commonly called to this day. Here they quickly learned that Mundelein, governed by an unchanging Rule dictating virtually every aspect of seminary life and conduct, had apparently been frozen in place for years. Come November 22, two students were walking down the main road of the seminary. "Somebody driving through stopped and said, 'President Kennedy has just been shot,'" recalls Larry Duris. The seminarians ran back to the building and told Father Ed Fitzgerald ('40), Dean of Formation and Disciplinarian, who had up to then not heard about the tragedy. The bell rang, signaling that it was time to go in for a study period before class. Twenty minutes later, Duris says, the bell rang again.

> *Fitz goes out into the corridor and shouts, "Oh, the President is dead. The President is dead. Pray for the President. Go back to your rooms." Then the bell rings for class. We had a test, philosophy, and God save him, the prof insisted we take the test. Well, nobody—people left the paper blank. They were stunned. Across the hall the other philosophy professor had been doing syllogisms that morning, and he happened to be using the initials JFK for the syllogisms. He comes in, doesn't say a word about what has just happened, says a prayer in Latin, and then erases all the JFK's on the board and puts in LBJ's, and then proceeds to go on like nothing [had happened]. I guess this is supposed to be macho, or strength, or detachment. Or stupidity. I think that's what it is.*

"It was," Bill Zavaski says, "the most historic thing that happened in this country in my life and we were not told. We weren't allowed to watch TV. It was crazy."

"No radio, no nothing," Ed Upton reports. "We had [a student] play that Sunday night...when Broadway shut down, the whole world shut down. But Mundelein had to do its damn play."

By Saturday morning, the day after the tragic shooting, the administration budged slightly from its business-as-usual posture. "Next morning," Larry Duris recollects, "big concession: Ed Fitzgerald left his morning *Tribune* in the rec hall, one copy for 180 guys to glance at, just the front section." (The seminarians were usually not allowed to read the newspaper.) The newspaper contained only articles about the president's death; everything else had been scissored out. After Sunday had come and gone, with no mention of the President's death by any seminary official, even at Mass, the administration allowed the students to watch the funeral—the Mass only—on Monday. "It was extraordinary," Tom Libera says, "that Fitz actually brought a TV out of his room." The priest wheeled the 16-inch television into the rec hall for the occasion and wheeled it right back out again when the funeral was over. As Larry Duris remembered it, even this concession did not involve time off from classes. "The only reason [we had off]," Duris says, "was it happened on the Feast of St. Catherine, so there was no class that day."

"It was rather paralyzing, and one of the instincts was just to pray," Libera says. "It had to unscramble itself over that period of days that seemed like weeks." Eventually the students insisted on a memorial event to the late president. "I'll never forget," says Zavaski. "They took that famous cartoon of Lincoln [with his head in his hands by Bill Mauldin] and blew that up. That was the backdrop for the memorial." The men insisted that they got their real information on the tragedy only when they went home for Christmas. "My mom," Upton says, "had saved all the newspapers. I then realized what had happened in the world and how insane our seminary system was. You were upset with Kennedy's death, but you didn't realize the impact it had had on the nation. There was no newspaper, no way to experience that. Then you realize," he says, referring to the Rule at Mundelein, "this is just nutso."

....

Seminarians at Mundelein back then arose at 5:35 a.m. and spent five hours in study, four hours in class, and three hours in prayer five days a week. The students could not have radios, newspapers, or novels, and while the philosophy students (those in their last two years of college, all of whom majored in philosophy) went home for the summers, the major theologians (those in the four-year theological graduate program leading to ordination) spent them at the Villa, a summer camp in Wisconsin owned by the archdiocese. Seminarians conducted their affairs in English except for classes, which their teachers, who were all Jesuits at the time, taught in Latin.

In 1936, near the end of his tenure as archbishop, Cardinal George Mundelein, who had planned and built the pristine 1,000-acre campus in 1921 and for whom both the seminary and the town in which it is situated are named, had decided on a bold change for his seminary. He named 31-year-old Father (later Msgr.) Reynold Hillenbrand ('29) rector. [1] Over the next eight years, Hillenbrand changed much of the focus of seminary life, concentrating his efforts on training seminarians in social and liturgical reforms that not only presaged the Second Vatican Council but also created a cadre of over 500 priests with a reputation for progressive activism rooted in the concept of the Church being the Mystical Body of Christ in the world. Although having little direct impact on academics, which the Jesuit teachers at the seminary controlled, Hillenbrand himself taught courses in liturgy and papal social thought and brought speakers to Mundelein such as Dorothy Day from the Catholic Worker movement and Catholic leaders involved in race relations and the labor movement.

By 1944, however, as tensions with the Jesuits and with Cardinal Samuel Stritch, who had taken over as archbishop when Mundelein died in 1939, boiled to the surface over Hillenbrand's liturgical reforms, Stritch replaced him with Father (later Msgr.) Malachy Foley ('31). Foley dismissed most of Hillenbrand's hand-picked diocesan formation faculty and eliminated his programs to the extent that what Hillenbrand had made unique about the seminary soon disappeared.[2] Foley served as rector for over 20 years. As innovative as Hillenbrand had made seminary life, Foley made it dull. He maintained an aging core of Jesuits to teach academics, insisted on the unchanging discipline of the Rule, and allowed no outside information about the changes occurring in the Church and society to upset the staid routine of seminary life. Ironically, however, the priests Hillenbrand had trained in the 1930s and 1940s, and those ordained in the 1950s, who had learned their craft in parishes under the mentoring eyes of "Hilly's men," would eventually pressure even Mal Foley's seminary to change.

....

Albert Meyer, appointed to succeed Cardinal Stritch as Archbishop of Chicago in 1958, found Chicago bustling with lay and clerical activism that priests such as Hillenbrand had encouraged in areas such as ecumenism, race relations, liturgy, and labor issues; Meyer would soon take the lead on these issues. He made a point to visit the campus during a break in the Second Vatican Council on September 6, 1963, just after the class of 1969 had arrived, to preside at the annual Mass of the Holy Spirit to kick off the school year. During his homily, he discussed the Council's desire for *"aggiornamento"* or "bringing up to date" the life of the Church.[3] In a letter 13 days later to the whole archdiocese, he quoted Pope John XXIII: "Now is the hour of the laity!"[4]

Meyer's commitment extended especially to race relations. In March of 1964, he raised the question with his priests: "Should one's color or creed disqualify him from purchasing or renting a home?"[5] Meyer worked hard with recalcitrant pastors to persuade them to accept all children in their schools, regardless of race or creed. What can be forgotten looking back almost 50 years is the courage it took for Cardinal Meyer to stand up against racism so confidently because many—perhaps a majority—of his flock felt uncomfortable with, if not overtly hostile to his efforts.[6]

Many of his priests and more activist laity, however, thought he should move even faster on this and other issues. A talk given by Father Leo Mahon ('51) at a clergy conference held at Niles College in April 1964 titled "What is a Priest?" best exemplified the intense concentration of Chicago's priests on their role in reinvigorating the life of the laity. One hundred fifty-five priests from 83 parishes attended. Mahon offered some rather radical images for priesthood. "The priest," he said, "is a catalyst of change; a creator, not just a functionary; a thought provoker to inspire search; a revolutionary, not a modernizer; an innovator, not a renovator; a discoverer, not an administrator; a man of divine, not merely ecclesiological, faith; a creator of Liturgy, not just a performer."[7] Mahon's words, intended to provoke, no doubt had their intended effect.

Members of the class of 1969, however, would find when they got to Mundelein in 1963 that Meyer's efforts to bring the life of the Chicago Church "up to date" had not extended to include his major seminary.

Joining 89 other classmates, Ed Upton, Larry Duris, Bill Zavaski, Bob Heidenreich, Tom Libera, and Mike Ahlstrom arrived in the fall of 1963 for their first year at Mundelein Seminary. Seminarians over the years used various nicknames for the major seminary, such as the Big House or Candy Mountain, or the one most popular in 1963, the Enchanted Forest. Over 370 seminarians attended Mundelein that year, counting all those in the two years of philosophy and four years of theology that made up the major seminary program.[8] But the huge numbers masked a growing problem. On the one hand, seminary enrollment on the whole had grown substantially throughout the early 1960s, especially at the high school level with the opening of the second Quigley on the South Side in 1961. This led to more students feeding into Niles and then to Mundelein. The average number of priests ordained for the Archdiocese of Chicago, which had stayed at a steady 36 to 38 from 1937 thru 1957,[9] had ballooned to 44 in 1965 and 49 in 1966.[10] But even with increasing total numbers at Mundelein, the percentages of men staying in the seminary all the way through to ordination had begun to decline, and the trickle of men leaving the priesthood after ordination would soon become a flood.

For the class of 1969, the numbers broke down as follows. Four hundred nineteen boys entered Quigley in the fall of 1957. Of those, 190, or 45%, graduated in the spring of 1961. One hundred sixty two of those graduates attended Niles, and 95, or 23% of the original high school class, started at Mundelein in the fall of 1963.[11] But only 10% of that original class made it to ordination (while for the just noted classes of 1965 and 1966, 15% of their Quigley freshmen had done so).[12]

It didn't take long for the men of the class of 1969, from the day they entered Mundelein, to discover that their relationship with the faculty at the major seminary would in no way resemble the growing give-and-take and mutual respect that they had experienced with the Niles faculty. The men met a bus at the Prudential Plaza building downtown that would take them up to Mundelein, a journey then of about two hours. When they arrived, they could not take their bags to their rooms or even visit them. Instead, they placed the bags in the rec hall and met the Dean of Formation responsible for discipline, Father Ed Fitzgerald, in the chapel. "Fitz would call out names," Ed Upton recalls, "and you'd say, 'Present,' and he'd give you your room number. Then you'd go to the rec hall, get your suitcases, bring them to your room, and begin to set the room up. So Denny O'Connell, whichever you're supposed to say, 'Here' or 'Present,' said the opposite. That stopped the whole thing. 'What are you doing?' Fitz said to him, 'Are you being a smart aleck? Are you being disobedient?' It was like, oh, this is BS. This is not going to be happy."

Former priest Bill O'Shea ('67) wrote an article for the Associated Press on February 18, 1974, which was syndicated to several newspapers throughout the country, in which he recalled his first meeting with Fitz, quoting his opening speech.

> *"Everybody wants to know what God's will is for his life. Now that you are here, you know what his will is for you. It is the rule of the seminary. You are to maintain silence at all times in the corridors and in your rooms. You are to study and pray without communicating with the man next door." Then old Fitz threw in the clincher, the rationale behind all that silence: "You will be alone in your room with Jesus. He will guide you and form you into a priest." For two years we thought he must be right, and our own impulses to mix with each other and the rest of the world must be wrong. Our spiritual directors taught us to imagine Jesus as an obedient servant who wanted us to be meek and unquestioning. But we did not buy this passive Jesus for long.* [13]

As the class of 1969 began to live daily life at Msgr. Mal Foley's Mundelein Seminary, they felt a certain shock, especially after their two years at the still strict but quickly changing Niles campus, where challenging academic courses and dialogue with the formation faculty had slowly become the norm. Here, both the academics and discipline appeared to exist in a time warp. "Mundelein was just pathetic," Bill Zavaski says, "because we had all those Jesuits that were beyond hope." Ed Upton recalls, "Everything was in Latin and they would just read these silly notes. They couldn't care less." Mike Ahlstrom tells of the widely held opinion that the Jesuits, having assigned their best men to their own seminaries and the second best to their universities, sent the leftovers to Mundelein.

Of these six members of the class of '69, Mike Ahlstrom has by far the most to say about the defects in the academic system at Mundelein. "We took chemistry," he says, "and the guy handed out World War II comic books about how they made bombs. You weren't encouraged to think." As for the Philosophy of Education class, "We didn't have the textbook," he remarks, "and the prof just got up and read to us from the book. Then one of the guys found the textbook in the library, kept a page ahead of him, and kept raising his hand and saying, 'What about this?'"

"Guys would start asking him questions," Ed Upton also recalls, "just to drive him crazy. He never figured out how they could figure it out." The Jesuits were not allowed to fraternize with the students. If a student wanted to talk to a professor outside of class, he had to get permission from the diocesan prefect of discipline. But the Jesuits did reign supreme in their individual classrooms. "If you asked questions in class," Ahlstrom says, "you got in trouble. One guy got into an argument. The prof took away his book, which meant he got Ds."

> You really were discouraged from thinking at Mundelein. I
> had no respect for anybody who taught me in my junior and
> senior year of college, because there was no stimulus. It was
> memorization, and if you could repeat the definitions you got
> a good mark. Everybody that thought outside the box was an
> adversary. It wasn't philosophy; it was indoctrination.

When a new Dean of Studies at the seminary finally required professors to teach class in English, the change provided comic relief for Larry Duris and Ed Upton. "We had this guy," Upton says, referring to one of the Jesuit faculty members, "who was still teaching in Latin. Larry and I said to the Dean, 'He's still teaching in Latin but don't tell him we said so.' The next day, of course, he calls on me first and Duris second, so the dean had gone and immediately told him we were complaining about him. We still laugh at this."

Upton did not find all of the Jesuits' practices so amusing. In the years before Pope Paul VI promulgated the encyclical *Humanae Vitae*, which reaffirmed the Church's opposition to artificial birth control, moral theologians including Mundelein's Father John Dedek ('55) offered possible reasons for informed dissent from the teaching. Tom Hickey, a seminarian from the class of 1970, brought up the topic in another class and, as Upton recalled, almost got expelled for raising the issue. Bob Heidenreich remembered a similar situation occurring during the first year of theology. Seminarians had begun to learn, in large part through reading the Jesuit weekly magazine *America* on their own, about the documents of the Second Vatican Council, which had just finished meeting in Rome. Because the Jesuits published *America*, it was one of the few periodicals the administration allowed students to read. The Jesuit professor of apologetics would advance arguments in class against heresies, and students had to give the proper reply in defending the faith. "Somebody got up," Heidenreich says, "and quoted from the Council's schema on religious liberty."

> *The professor says, "Now where did you get that gobbly stuff?"*
> *"Well, this is a quote from the Vatican document."*
> *"It's not true. Throw it away."*
> *"But it was in* America *magazine."*
> *"Don't believe everything you read in there."*

If academics at Mundelein dismayed the class of 1969 during their time in philosophy, the system of discipline presided over by Mal Foley and Ed Fitzgerald proved that diocesan priests could cause them as much consternation as the Jesuits. Larry Duris recalled an early meeting with Fitzgerald. "We had gone through two years of Niles," he says, "and the spirit was different. We got there and heard, 'I don't want you to even come to my office for six months. You guys know nothing.' He was—arrrrgh—fanning the flames."

> *The bell rang at 5:40 a.m. and you had 20 minutes to get to chapel, morning meditation, Mass. Over to breakfast and then*

back to chapel for a visit. Then a short study period, classes,
back to chapel, lunch, and a short rec period which was basically
a smoking period. That's how most of us winded up becoming
smokers. What else were you going to do for 20 minutes? Back
to class and then long rec from 3 to 5 p.m. You could only use
the gym every other day because philosophy students had gym
one day, theology the other. You weren't supposed to talk to each
other lest you get corrupted by the older men. Lights out at 9:45.
What drove you nuts was the day was broken up into all these
little segments.

The administration, in addition to the tight schedule, also placed severe limits on communication, especially with the so-called outside world. "You were told basically to stay away from people," Duris recalls. "There was even something in the rulebook that if you were to run into a layperson on the grounds, you were to politely excuse yourself."

Ed Upton remembered the absurdities of dealing with Mal Foley. "There were efforts," Upton says, recounting a typical conversation with the rector, "to get Mal to do stuff."

> *"Monsignor, could we have a pop machine?"*
> *"Son, you've got the refreshing pine trees. What do you need*
> *a pop machine for?"*
> *"Could we have a more family atmosphere and talk in the*
> *residence hall?"*
> *"Well, son, we do your laundry."*

Upton also resented what he regarded as Foley's outdated and unchristian racial attitudes. He recalled an insulting incident between Foley and an African-American seminarian from, as Upton says, "probably the wealthiest parish on the South Side, but it was beginning to change racially. Mal said something along the lines of, 'Whose house does your mother clean?'"

These kinds of incidents in the seminary made Upton sensitive to what he saw as the uses and misuses of authority throughout his priestly career. "It was a closed system," Ed says, reflecting on the seminary under Foley, "totally authoritarian. They are the boss and they have the answers." When it came to "bosses," Bill Zavaski focused his attention on Fitz. "My God," Zavaski exclaims, "this was the '60s. Wild things were happening and he couldn't figure us out. Mundelein was a totally rigid system. Two students were supposedly expelled because they walked around the lake. We were living like monks, and people were constantly fighting Fitz."

But despite problems that outraged his classmates, Zavaski had—and has—a soft spot in his heart for Mundelein Seminary.

I loved Mundelein. Classmates thought I was weird, but I had my own room, my own bathroom, and three square meals a day. I didn't have that at home because my mother had died. My father was living with my mother's mother and my brother, and it was very painful, so I was happier at school than at home. They all thought there was something wrong because I loved it. They all hated it. When I was growing up we used to take rides to Mundelein and look at the grounds. I remember my dad telling me that he was at the first Eucharistic Congress there. I survived it because at that time they did musicals, and that's when I got into theater. It was a healthy diversion because if you were involved in theater, you got to leave your room at night to go to rehearsal; you got out of living like a monk. We had great times. Jack Wall ('68) and Wayne Prist ('67) were my first directors. We were able to live at Mundelein in a party atmosphere, only we never told the administration that we were living in a party atmosphere.

At last cracks began to appear in the once-ironclad enforcement of the Rule. "In a moment of weakness," Larry Duris recounts, "Mal Foley in our senior year gave Fitzgerald permission to give anyone he wanted unlimited lights out. The nice thing was, it was the first time in the day when you could make a decision: Am I going to stay up or go to bed?"

At first allowed to go home only for Christmas, by second year the class of 1969 could also go home for Easter. This glacial pace of change only encouraged what Tom Libera referred to as "mini-rebel-lions," mostly but not exclusively carried out in secret. He recalled the seminarian organist who mingled strains of "We Shall Overcome" with church music during a service in the chapel.

Ed Upton remembered a spontaneous chapel sit-in that he missed out on, much to his chagrin, as well as covert smuggling operations. One seminarian who visited the city on Thursdays to see an orthodontist would return bearing a secret copy of *Time* magazine; his buddies would pass the magazine around hidden in their cassocks. "There was also a group that used to go out at night," Upton says. "We called ourselves the raiders. I don't know how we got called the raiders, but we'd sneak out of our rooms at 12:00 a.m. We'd go to the Ivanhoe Inn [a tavern]."

Upton went on to explain creative ways around seminary smoking restrictions, which forbid the students from smoking anytime except during rec periods and any place except outside the buildings. "They did have a reign of terror. The last night of first philosophy," he says, "I decided I was going to smoke in my room. I opened the window of the bathroom. I'm lying on the bathroom floor. I'm totally uncomfortable just to have the cigarette. I'm convinced Fitz could see the light and would come down; it was so crazy."

Bill Zavaski recalled his fear over another rule. "You weren't supposed to talk," he says. "You could not have another guy in your room. That was absolutely verboten. I'll never forget when Jack Wall walked in my room one day. I just about died. I thought, oh my God, they're going to throw me out. "

Zavaski next mentioned what became an iconic incident for the entire class. "It was October 19th," he says, "the Feast of the North American Martyrs, and guys were caught outside when they shouldn't have been outside." The Catholic Church celebrates the martyrdom of eight canonized Jesuit missionaries serving in Canada who were caught in the midst of the war between the Iroquois and Huron tribes in the 1640s. Seminarians caught breaking the Rule on their feast day feared the seminary equivalent of martyrdom: immediate expulsion. Bob Heidenreich saw the events of that day as a clear harbinger of change. "I'll tell you exactly the time," he says, "we knew it was changing":

It was a memorable day. We were in second philosophy in the fall of 1964. It was the Feast of the North American Martyrs. We had been granted a concession. On Saturday night you could leave your lights on in your room as late as you wanted to read. Of course nothing else changed. You still had to get up for Morning Prayer at 5:30. One of the guys had snuck over to the deacon rec hall where there was a pay telephone, the only telephone on campus, and had called Bill's [restaurant] and had gotten pizza orders. There were parties in different guys' rooms. This guy had arranged to meet the delivery guy in back of the handball courts, which were these big structures you couldn't see behind. You could wait in the weeds there. So he delivered this pizza along with two or three big Coke bottles. This guy is sneaking back in the house and who does he meet at the side door but Ed Fitzgerald, who says, "Go to the chapel and pray." The young man said, "I was toast. I knew it. I'm out of here, on the train. How am I going to tell my parents?" He's kneeling in the chapel. Meanwhile, Fitz is going around and listening at doors. So into the chapel come two other guys. "Well, at least there are three of us." Three more guys wandered in and then a few more. Finally, this one guy came in wearing a wetsuit with flippers and a diving mask—he had been going around scaring people. That's when the guy with the pizzas knew that things were going to be okay. Fitz said, "Just go to bed." So that's when the handwriting was on the wall that things were going to change.

Faced with a massive breakdown in the Rule—men outside the building and in each other's rooms eating and drinking—Fitzgerald couldn't expel them all. As months went by, perhaps emboldened by their Martyrs Day experience, the seminarians' rebellions against seminary discipline grew more serious, culminating with a boycott of the annual opening school retreat at the beginning of first theology in the fall of 1965. "They brought in a guy who was just awful," says Ed Upton. "So all of a sudden people didn't go to the retreat. Half the chapel was empty. They didn't know what to do. This had never happened before. It was our little civil disobedience." By this time, the conflict between the students and faculty had reached a head.

"The faculty was worried about us," Bob Heidenreich explains. "We were called the new breed and we were out to change things, and we were told that nothing ever changes in the Church." But, in fact, nothing at Mundelein seemed the same, and the increasing absurdity—not to mention tension—of the discrepancy in expectations and behaviors between the students and the authorities meant that something would soon have to give.

"We really knew it was crazy," Ed Upton says. "That's why I go out of my mind when people want to go back to the old Church."

> *The old seminary sucked. It was not a good thing; it did not help people grow. So don't give me this crap about going back. The old ways ended because they were terrible, awful. I remember a younger priest saying, "We should go back to the old way." I said, "Oh yeah? Then you give me the car keys, buster. Give me the stereo in your room. Give me your money." No, the old ways sucked. You can put that in the book. It wasn't healthy. And that's why it changed.*

....

As hard as seminary authorities tried to keep outside influences from penetrating the campus and culture of St. Mary of the Lake, they found it increasingly difficult. One issue that proved intractable for them—and that may have had more to do with the changes that would eventually come to the major seminary than any other—was what to do with the philosophy students over the summer. The seminarians in the four years of theology had to spend their summers at the Villa, a camp owned by the archdiocese in Eagle River, Wisconsin, to prevent contact with the outside world. The Villa, however, had limited space, and so philosophy students returned home for the summer to work. Mundelein did sponsor summer apostolate programs for some of them, housing them at Angel Guardian Orphanage and at Maryville Academy, homes for orphaned children. Other seminarians in philosophy set up their own summer live-in apostolate programs such as at Precious Blood Parish on the West Side, or they joined existing summer programs for laypeople and members of religious orders, such as at St. Frances Cabrini Parish. "As philosophers," Bill Zavaski remembers, "we had more privileges than those poor souls at Eagle River. We could drive a car, go out drinking. They couldn't leave the Villa."

As the members of the class worked together in summer ministries and came into contact with laypeople involved in those ministries, memories of their two relatively loose years of study at the Niles campus resurfaced. This inevitably brought them into conflict with authorities when in the fall they returned to the strict Rule of Mundelein Seminary. "Since you've had these experiences out on the street," Tom Libera says, referencing his own summers at St. Frances Cabrini Parish, "then going back into a closed environment at Mundelein, that naturally caused some tension. 'We should be out there' versus 'You need to be in here.'"

"After my first summer living on the West Side at Precious Blood," Larry Duris recalls, "we said to our rebellious selves, 'We're coming back next year. Villa is stupid. We're not going to Villa.' We weren't quite sure how to do this and still get ordained."

Having tasted ministry through their summer apostolates, the class of 1969 sought the opportunity to experience more. Near the end of the summer of 1964, wanting to receive permission to spend their day off on Thursdays in parishes, they decided on a novel approach, bypassing the seminary rector completely and writing a letter directly to Cardinal Meyer. Duris reflected on the audacity it took to send it, but also on the fear that it would come to Mal Foley's attention that he and his classmates had stepped outside the chain of command. "Talk about arrogant!" Duris reports. "We figured we're not going to ask Foley or Fitz about this because you won't get anywhere."

Instead, the class went right to the Cardinal, describing the glories of their apostolate and asking for permission to come on Thursdays, their day off, to continue their ministry. "We got a letter of response from Meyer," Duris recalls, "that he referred it to Foley and of course it's addressed to me because in the signing of the thing the group decided to go alphabetical, the chickens. So my name is the first name." Even before receiving Meyer's reply, and wondering whether Foley had gotten wind of the letter, Duris had gotten a call from Foley. It turned out Foley had called because a conference of archdiocesan Catholic school principals needed an organist to play up at Mundelein. "It was so funny," Duris says, "when I went up there because I could smell how conflicted he was because here I was this insubordinate but these nuns were saying, 'Your seminarian is so wonderful,' and 'We're so happy.' They probably saved my vocation for Chicago." It turns out that Foley knew about the letter to the Cardinal, but he ignored it.

By the time the class of 1969 had entered first theology in the fall of 1965, it had become increasingly clear to the leaders of the Archdiocese of Chicago that the old regime at Mundelein Seminary had not been able to shield seminarians from the momentous upheavals taking place in both the Church and the world. Tensions between faculty and the students, whether over academics, discipline, or the role of apostolates, had reached a boiling point. Again it seemed something would soon have to give.

....

During the late summer and early autumn of 1965, two not unrelated events took place that would soon turn the environment at Mundelein Seminary upside down. First, on August 24, John Cody—whom the Pope had appointed Archbishop of Chicago on June 16 in the wake of the death of Cardinal Meyer—took the reins after a solemn installation ceremony held at Holy Name Cathedral. "Cody comes in," Larry Duris recalls. "I don't know that anybody could do this today, move that quickly. We were delighted. Cody had his first meeting with the faculty in September. A couple weeks later we had two meetings with him. At each one he announced rule changes."

But Cody saved his biggest announcement until October 5, when he appointed Father Jack Gorman ('52) to be Vice-Rector of Mundelein Seminary and also named him a monsignor. Gorman had served on the faculties of both Quigley and Niles when the class of 1969 studied in those respective seminaries. Larry Duris remembered vividly the lunch held to announce Gorman's appointment to the students. "We walked into the lunchroom," Duris says, "and there's a big faculty table and there's Jack Gorman. Like a bunch of old ladies, we're all abuzz before the grace started. We had speculated, 'There's the new rector. Why the heck else would he be here?' At the end of the luncheon," Duris recalls, "Cody gets up to talk. 'It's customary for the Archbishop to bring a gift,' he says. 'I brought a gift for you: your new Vice-Rector.' The place went wild. Everybody knew," Duris maintains, "what that meant." Shortly before Christmas, Cody informed Mal Foley that he had appointed him pastor of St. Bride's Parish on the South Side. Gorman would take over as rector after the break. Gorman remembers driving Foley to St. Bride's on Christmas Eve 1965, describing the ride as "sorrowful."

For the members of the class of 1969, however, Gorman's arrival signaled joy, not sorrow. Bob Heidenreich stressed the radical difference between the way Foley—who had treated them like children— and Gorman talked to students. "It was typical," Heidenreich reflects, "for Gorman to say, 'Now men, you are mature adults. I expect you to act like that.'"

Bill Zavaski remembered the excitement his class felt because Gorman belonged to the class of 1952, so many of whom—Gorman included—had taught them at Quigley and Niles under circumstances they vastly preferred to those at Mundelein under Foley. Gorman, in particular, exuded empathy towards seminarians and creativity about seminary education. "We were there," Zavaski says, referring to the start of the Gorman era at Mundelein, "when everything changed. It changed from being a monastery to being an open place."

"We had the biggest investment," Larry Duris says, referring to his class, "when Jack Gorman came in. We had three and a half more years [to go before ordination]."

"The climate there was literally about to explode," Gorman recalls. "When I walked in, the first two or three classes—'66, '67, and '68—just wanted to get out of there."

But the class of 1969 bought into Gorman's ideas and applauded his moves. "He had to deal with some faculty who were very resistant," Duris says, "and to bring on new people, people that would hopefully not leave ministry. He was excellent in dealing with Cody."

Cody kept close tabs on him. Cody liked to meddle and micro-manage. He'd say: "Monsignor Gorman, nothing is too small to give me a call about." When Cody would hear a rumor, he'd get on the phone: "What's this I hear?" The rumor mill was flying in the diocese with especially the older baron pastors who were saying, "What in heaven's name is going on in the major seminary?" But Gorman was able to say: "You're the Archbishop, I'm the rector. You want me to do this job."

Gorman also had to confront his brother priests, in addition to Cody, to explain changes in the seminary. Diocesan priests made an annual retreat at the retreat house on the grounds of Mundelein. "Every Wednesday I would take one formation and one academic guy," Gorman says, "and go to the retreat house, where there were always 35-40 priests":

First hour was explaining what we're doing and why we're doing the changes in the academic and formation training of the priests. The second hour was their reaction, which Bob Doherty used to say was vomiting, because they were comparing it, of course, to the formation and the academics they had, what they knew. It was wild, absolutely wild. The third hour was wonderful.

During that third hour, Gorman would ask for the priests' blessing. Eventually, most—but not all—of them would support Gorman and his new vision of what a major seminary should look like. For those who remained opposed, Gorman found a staunch ally in Cody. "Cardinal Cody," Gorman says, "received all kinds of concern from the priests about the changes in the seminary." Gorman describes Cody's response as being tremendous. "He protected us against the clergy," Gorman recalls gratefully. "He said, 'I'm in charge.'"

Ed Upton concurred with his classmates about the beginning Gorman had made. "I was ecstatic," he says, "as was the group of people I hung around with. If there were unhappy people, they dared not say anything. But I don't think anybody was happy with the old system or wanted Mal to stay. Everybody liked Jack." Upton fondly remembered a story of Gorman's personal touch that has remained with him throughout his priesthood. "It was," he says, "the beginning of second theology. He called the house. I was in a panic." Gorman wanted Upton to serve as a prefect. Prefects at Mundelein were second theology students who lived with and mentored the younger philosophy students in their cams (dorms).

> *That was very powerful—that was the first time an authority figure had singled me out and asked me to do something. There were 12 or 14 of us in the group of prefects. We met every week. It was an opportunity to talk about what was going on in your life and, secondly, to try to do the same thing with the cam [short for the Italian "camerata," which is derived from the Spanish "comrade," referring to a dormitory but signifying the working or friendship group that existed among the men in that dorm]. That was a shift from fussing with all those little rules. It was at a deeper level personally, and that carried me through the rest of the seminary. It was the first time I'd seen myself as a leader. It's not a big thing, but when you're 24, it was significant.*

The heart of the changes that Msgr. Gorman brought to St. Mary of the Lake involved implementing at the seminary level the modifications in liturgy and theology that the recently concluded Second Vatican Council had called for in its various documents. This meant not only alterations in discipline and academics and an increasing focus on apostolates outside the seminary grounds, but also a metamorphosis in the culture and ambiance of seminary life. Gorman took over the reins of Mundelein while studying for a doctorate in psychology. He melded the insights he had learned about the human person and the importance of small groups with his attempts to bring the seminary into line with the mandates of the council. "Vatican II said that the seminary is supposed to be more pastoral," Gorman says, "so the idea was to get parish priests who knew what they were talking about to help the guys who were going to become parish priests, rather than the training we got, which was only academic and had no contact with the world, never mind the parish. We gradually got some of the best parish priests in the diocese."

> *I wanted to change the seminary so the climate was no longer controlled by fear, because that's clearly how we were trained— you didn't dare break a rule or all hell would break loose. That is ridiculous for men who by this time would have been married and taking responsible jobs in the world. So we opened up; freedom was a big thing. The idea of: if you live according to the Gospel it's a life of responsible freedom, not fear. That's part of the criticism we get from some people looking back, saying, you screwed up the whole seminary system. I don't think we did. The idea was helping the guys live in the kind of world you're going to live in. I said, "You have to internalize your faith and the way you understand your mission. It can't be just what they tell you in seminary—this structure is going to go." The whole story of Jesus in the Gospel is about relationships. I said, "That's what pastoral ministry is: relationships. You're supposed to be good at that, but to be good at that you have to know yourself and be able to communicate effectively out of love. Your job, first of all, is to become a man, then a Christian, and then a priest."*

One of the first areas to change was liturgy and, in particular, language. Both Mass and classes eventually changed from Latin to English. As liturgical changes took center stage at Mundelein, the library took on greater significance. No longer so constrained as to what they could read, seminarians began to expand their horizons. "*National Catholic Reporter* began publication," Upton says, "so we were able to read what was going on at the Council."

"We were grabbing up books," Larry Duris concurs, "in tune to what was going on with Vatican II." When the Vatican published the actual documents from the Council, the seminary made them available for seminarians to read.

Over time, the system of formation and discipline also began to adjust, especially when Gorman removed Ed Fitzgerald as Dean of

Formation. The annual seminary catalogue for 1966-1967, Gorman's second year as rector, reflects some of the changes. Gorman and his faculty included previously unheard-of language: "The rules recognize the freedom and initiative of the seminarians as basic human and Christian prerogatives," the catalogue reads, "not as concessions or permissions."[14]

Language like this was music to the ears of the class of '69. "What really changed was the formation," Bob Heidenreich recollects.

Gorman brought in Fathers George Kane ('51), Ray Wicklander ('63), and Bob Doherty ('56) as new formation faculty members. Under them, seminary life relaxed a bit, some said a bit too much. "Even cars were allowed after a while," Tom Libera remembers.

"You could leave the grounds," Ed Upton adds. "You could go off campus on Thursdays and go into town. You could talk in the building, stay up after 10:00 p.m., have a radio, read a newspaper, read a novel. You could bring different furniture into your room. It all sounds so silly."

At times, of course, seminarians abused their new freedoms, particularly the newly earned right to spend Thursdays off campus. Apparently too many of them had wandered into Emil's, a local watering hole. "I can still remember the (second) Thursday," Bill Zavaski says. "Jack Gorman said, 'You can take off but you can't go to Emil's,' because 600 guys had gone to Emil's that first Thursday. So you couldn't go to Emil's," he bemusedly recalls, "because the regulars couldn't get a drink."

Gorman has acknowledged the occasional abuse of the new freedoms, but he defends them as absolutely necessary to producing mature priests capable of making their own decisions.

In place of Foley's stone wall, Gorman introduced mandatory open forums held every Sunday after Mass where students could express their concerns about seminary life. The sessions provided a release valve to ease the tensions the community experienced as it adjusted to the changes, which were still too few and too slow for most of the class of 1969.

As turbulent as things got at Mundelein, Gorman felt the same respect for the class of 1969 that they clearly did for him. "The guys in '69," Gorman says, "came with tremendous ideas and questions. They were questioning everything. They had the foundation of both the formation they got at Niles and the new stuff by that time bubbling out of Vatican II. They had a confidence, they were bright—the guys who stayed and those who left. When they came to Mundelein, they came with a fresh expectation that was developed at Niles. They weren't mad; they weren't hurt; they weren't angry. They came with an expectation not of the old but of the new. They were ready for change. Not only ready, but expecting it. It was like, 'What are you waiting for?'"

Under Gorman, student publications also took on a more open, honest, and critical point of view. To be sure, student writing had long tackled serious subjects at the seminary. *The Feehan Review*, published from 1963-1966, contained mostly pieces written under the watchful eye of the faculty. *The New Southwell*, published from 1961-1966 and its successor, *Mandala*, published from 1967-1968, however, operated under student auspices. Articles ranged from theological essays and political commentary to short stories and poetry.

For example, Bob Heidenreich wrote a short story for the January 1965 edition of *The New Southwell* entitled "Is Love the Answer?" The story concerned Simon, a seminarian, and Susanne, a coworker at a summer job. Simon struggles with his attraction to Susanne, even as he tries to answer her doubts about Jesus' real presence in the Eucharist. At first, Simon gives textbook answers, until he realizes she can't understand him. Then, he begins to speak of love.

> *"God Himself actually became a Man named Jesus Christ. Just like me. This took love. The Mass is filled with love.... This is a broken Body for me. Could all this love be in vain? And men all around, in every person, I can see Christ's love."*
>
> *Simon quit abruptly. He felt Susanne's presence.... Simon sought to feel her soft brown hair against his cheek. He sought to hold the warmth of her hand. He wanted to love Susanne. But panic froze him. Mumbling something about after lunch, he fled.*[15]

What is remarkable about the story is that the seminary authorities allowed it to be published at all. Permission for a student author to acknowledge a seminarian's sexuality and vocational struggles in a semi-public forum, even in a fictional account, was rare.

After Gorman arrived, a new edge appeared in the articles. Titles included "We Shall Overcome," "Vietnam: A Reconsideration," and "Celibacy of the Secular Priest."[16] An editorial in the January 1966 edition of *The New Southwell* titled "The Devalued Priesthood" exemplifies much of the new tone of the writing:

> *Our fear of getting trapped in the institutional church is*
> *understandable because every evil in the church has been pinned*
> *with the label—"institutional." Capriciousness, dumb-iron power*
> *wielded by cut-off men, fortress mentalities, manipulations and*
> *smothering of consciences, value systems that effectively rank*
> *things and buildings over people, fear and ignorance—all have*
> *come to be synonymous with the "institutional" church.*[17]

Other members of the class of 1969 contributed to the literary journals. In the same issue that "The Devalued Priesthood" appeared, Mike Ahlstrom authored "The Role of the Priest," an article delineating the different but complementary roles of the ministerial priesthood versus the priesthood of the faithful. Ahlstrom called for priests to call the laity to social action on behalf of the Gospel in the affairs of the world, so that priests could get off the front lines and return to focusing on the Word and sacraments.[18] In the winter 1968 issue of *Mandala*, Tom Libera penned a rather scholarly, yet pastorally centered, essay called "Some Social Dimensions of the Virtue of Hope."[19]

Although Msgr. Gorman received praise from his seminarians for the liturgical, extracurricular, and disciplinary changes rapidly remaking seminary life, academic changes posed a greater and lengthier problem for him. Gorman faced resistance from the Jesuit faculty, but by the 1968-1969 school year only seven Jesuits remained on the faculty out of 26 full-time teachers. Gorman had replaced Jesuits with mostly diocesan clergy, but also some religious order priests and sisters and even a lay woman and man.[20] "We then had," Larry Duris says, "faculty who were in tune to what was going on with Vatican II."

Although replacing the faculty required both time and patience, Gorman did not wait long to bring in noted speakers. For example, he invited the renowned German Jesuit theologian Karl Rahner to the seminary for a question/answer session. Rahner had exerted much influence at the Vatican Council and had authored numerous theological works. "It was neat to see one of these heroes in the flesh," Larry Duris says, "sitting on the stage in the auditorium and it's wintertime and his pants are high and above the socks there is his white long underwear." Rahner made even more of an impression with his humanity than he did with his theology. "He just looked," Duris says, "like a person you'd really want to get to know and hang out with."

Tom Libera also fondly remembered Rahner's visit. "It was big," he recalls, "for somebody to ask him, 'Can you explain the supernatural existential?' We were getting the stars coming through there."

As much as important speakers and new-blood faculty increased the level of excitement about change at Mundelein Seminary, at least some members of the class of 1969 saw value in both the old and the new approaches to seminary life. For Tom Libera, the tension between styles of seminary education, while at times uncomfortable, afforded him and his classmates a unique perspective on the Church. "That tension of the old and the new coming together," Libera notes, "certainly became an asset in the sense of being able to appreciate a few different mindsets that Catholics could have."

> We're eating up the new freedoms, but others feel a grief and loss and trying to sort that out. Most of us were more interested in the future than preserving the past. Even then, a few guys like Jim Kehoe ('70), who was a class behind us, were more traditional or conservative. When you talk to him you say, "Here's another part of the Church." You don't agree, but he's staking a perspective out that has value. You don't want to completely eliminate that. As a pastor I appreciate operating where you're going to be yourself, but you still have to relate to a broad spectrum of people if you're going to be successful or at least not do much harm.

Bob Heidenreich also appreciates the perspective that comes from spending about half of his seminary training under both the old and the new systems. Like Libera, Heidenreich says, "This gives us a unique perspective on the Church. We had—I don't know if the other guys would say this—the best of both systems. We saw what was good about devotions," Heidenreich admits, "yet we revolted at Mundelein, because that formation was initially really bad."

Just two short years after having arrived at a seemingly unchanging Mundelein Seminary, the class of 1969 had helped to initiate an ongoing live-in summer apostolate program that significantly altered the seminary's focus by pointing it outward—for the first time since the 1940s under Msgr. Hillenbrand—toward the parishes it was intended to serve. The Villa in Wisconsin was finally closed and the theology students all spent their summers in various ministries.

Msgr. Gorman and the class of 1969 collaborated in many other ways to extend seminary education beyond the walls of campus. Gorman instituted Clinical Pastoral Education (CPE) at Mundelein. CPE consisted of an intensive hospital ministry experience lasting six to eight weeks in which seminarians reviewed their ministerial encounters in a group setting with fellow seminarians of their own and other faith traditions, guided by a trained director. Members of the class, however, remained unsatisfied and began pushing for one more significant change: an intensive six-month diaconate internship that would involve their leaving campus for virtually the entire half-year after their diaconate ordination in order to immerse themselves in parish ministry. At the time, except for serving as deacons at Masses at the seminary or the nearby convent, the deacons received no pastoral training. "We wanted to have an internship," Mike Ahlstrom says, "because prior to 1968 you had academic and spiritual formation and no pastoral and not much human formation. You just got ordained and learned by the seat of your pants. We actually had come up with a program," Ahlstrom continues, "where we would be in a parish setting from June until Christmas and then come back to Mundelein to finish our academics."

Not everyone at Mundelein supported the new proposal. "That was the biggest question," Bishop Gorman says. "Were we putting too much emphasis on the pastoral over against diminishing the academic? So there was always tension between the academic faculty and the formation guys. Which was a healthy tension—I thought." So much so that Gorman brought the internship idea before the entire faculty. "On the faculty council," Larry Duris says, "a number of the academic faculty were against it."

> *They said, "How are they going to make up for lost time during the semester fourth year?" Basically, "How are you going to keep them on the farm? If they go to the parishes on weekends for fourth quarter they're not going to be studying." Blah, blah, blah. We politicked for that change with the promise that come January when we got back up to Mundelein, we wouldn't go roaming back to the parish. It passed. It wasn't certain that it was going to, but it passed.*

And so the experiment began. The class of 1969 became the first class in the history of St. Mary of the Lake Seminary to go out into the parishes of the archdiocese for a full-time, six-month internship as ordained deacons. On the one hand, the seminarians, for the most part, enjoyed the work, and many reported a new excitement about priesthood. Early on, on the other hand, faculty disputed the wisdom of the program. Academic faculty members, in particular, noticed that, despite their promise to the contrary, the men, after their return to Mundelein for the final semester, seemed to stay off campus and miss class frequently. Of the class promise not to desert Mundelein for parish life, Larry Duris simply says, "We lied. The faculty admitted later they knew we had lied."

"We came back for classes from January to June," Ed Upton remembers. "It was a nightmare, awful. We ended up going to the parishes half the time and were hardly at the seminary."

For at least one seminarian, another conflict arose over where the administration would assign him as a deacon. The subtext of this conflict had to do with race. "We were being interviewed," Larry Duris says, "about where we wanted to go for our deacon assignments. I said I wanted to go to a black parish. Bob Doherty was the dean of formation. In the conference," Duris recalls, "I was told, 'You've been very involved at Precious Blood for the past four years. Faculty is recommending that it would be good for you to do your diaconate in a white parish. They're concerned about you getting tunnel vision.'"

"I'm not quite sure," Larry continues, "back then where I got the balls. I said, 'There's a point to what you're saying. But if we're going to go there, we need to go that way for everyone. I've got classmates who either did no apostolate or did it in white communities. If you send them to a black or Hispanic parish so they don't get tunnel vision, I'll go to a white parish.' I actually said that."

Not only did Duris say it, but it worked to the extent that the seminary assigned him to a parish that was changing rapidly from white to black.

Despite the conflicts, over time the seminary powers decided to make the deacon internship an integral part of Mundelein's curriculum. The internship seemed a good way to address a serious—in fact, overwhelming but unaddressed—problem at Mundelein: students leaving the seminary in droves. Some of the departures came under the heading of normal attrition. After all, as previously noted, only 10 to 15 percent of Quigley High School freshmen eventually got ordained. But as the Church and world turned upside down in the 1960s, more seminarians made the choice to leave Mundelein. And the partings took on an air of mystery. "The first year several guys left," Bill Zavaski says. "We never talked—nobody told us. Packed up, gone. All of a sudden a room was empty."

The internship program—and the summer apostolates that preceded it—stopped the escalator long enough for seminarians to get a glimpse of what parish ministry might really be like. For some young men, the actual experience of ministry led them to seek another vocation. "A lot of guys never came back," Gorman remembers. "They got new experience. We didn't want them to define priesthood in terms of the seminary." Gorman would stress this when talking with his seminarians.

> *"You guys don't have a vocation to the seminary; you have*
> *a vocation to the parishioners." Some of those guys had a*
> *wonderful vocation to the seminary, but they got lost once they*
> *got ordained without all the school structures. Parish internship*
> *is a way of finding out.*

For the class of 1969, their parish experiences as deacons worked quite well to help them discover whether priesthood was for them. "If you look at the classes ordained in the '60s," Duris says, "you had many men leaving from that group."

> When you got to our class, it's significant. We lost nobody for the first five years. What we would attribute it to was that, starting with the Gorman years, we had more experience with apostolates and then the diaconate. We lost nine guys in deacon year. As they experienced ministry in a parish setting, what they had imagined this to be and what they were experiencing were two different things.

For Larry Duris and the other five men whose stories make up this narrative, however, their seminary parish assignments did not so much raise questions about their priestly vocations; rather, as the next chapter will explain in detail, they cemented them.

A single weekend just prior to their diaconate ordination also greatly encouraged the six men. Canon law required that the seminary sponsor retreats in the days leading up to ordination to both the diaconate and the priesthood—at Mundelein they were usually led by a clerical, often Jesuit retreat master. Under Msgr. Gorman, the deacon retreat, like so many other things, changed radically. The retreat committee of seminarians—itself an innovation—met with Deacon Director Father Bob Doherty and decided to invite Father Pete Shannon ('53) and a group of lay couples who led weekend Cursillo retreats, which focused on personal witness and sharing, to conduct the ordination retreat.[21] "This was a very powerful experience," Ed Upton recalls, "given by laypeople. I remember saying to myself, what are they going to say to us? We've always had theologians and all these big highfalutin Jesuits."

> This was a group of people that formed—I won't say an underground church—but an intentional Christian community with Pete Shannon. They had all been through Cursillo, so they were giving witness talks. What I remember was the sincerity

*and faith. One of the subthemes was how important priests, the
Church, and the parish were in their lives, and how important
Pete Shannon had been.*

Upton recalls that members of the retreat group said to the
priests-to-be, "Some priests aren't open, don't help us, and have pat answers, but you don't want to be a priest like that. You want to welcome
and help form laypeople, not just criticize them or say no."

"But that wasn't their main theme," Upton continues. "It was
their personal witness of faith. That was the first time I had thought
about the importance of priests."

> *It was absolutely wonderful. Everybody was excited. Impact is
> something that you only realize later, but it did have a long-
> lasting influence. It was not heady. It was the first retreat that
> had impact instead of just a bunch of talks going over your head.
> I don't think it would happen today. It was real and encouraging.
> I'll never forget that retreat.*

....

1. For more information on Cardinal Mundelein and his seminary see
   Edward R. Kantowicz, *Corporation Sole: Cardinal Mundelein and Chicago Catholicism* (Notre Dame, IN: University of Notre Dame Press,
   1983), 99-127.
2. Steven M. Avella, "Reynold Hillenbrand and Chicago Catholicism" in
   Skerrett et al, *Catholicism, Chicago Style*, 81-94.
3. Cardinal Albert Meyer's Homily at Missa de Spiritu Sancto, St. Mary of
   the Lake Seminary, September 6, 1963, AAC.
4. Meyer to Archdiocese of Chicago, September 19, 1963, AAC.
5. The Chicago Conference on Race and Religion, *Why the Three Major
   Faiths Oppose the Proposed Referendum on Open Occupancy Legisla-
   tion*, March 20, 1964, AAC.
6. See, for example, John McCarty to Meyer, April 23, 1964, AAC. Mc-
   Carty, a white parishioner from St. Simeon's in Bellwood, complained:
   "To bring in colored pupils and teachers not only would mean the beginning of the end of a successfully developing parish, but to almost
   destroy the chance of ever seeing the new Church paid for.... Many of

our parishioners, like myself, come from St. Mel's, Presentation, and Our Lady of Sorrows parishes, now ghost parishes. Integration is not what we wanted. The white population has run to the suburbs to permit their wives to walk the streets without fear of rape."

7. Summary of Talk by Father Leo Mahon, "What is A Priest?" at Clergy Conference, "The Catholic Church and the Negro," held at Niles Campus, April 13-16, 1964, AAC.
8. "Enrollment Statistics: First Year Quigley through Ordination," September 8, 1964, AAC.
9. "Memorandum to His Excellency The Most Reverend Albert G. Meyer," April, 1959, AAC.
10. "Percentage Remaining in the Seminary Each Year," September, 1967, AAC.
11. "Enrollment Statistics: First Year Quigley through Ordination," September 8, 1964, AAC.
12. "Percentage Remaining in the Seminary Each Year," September, 1967, AAC.
13. Bill O'Shea, "Former Priest's Class of '67," in *Independent*, February 18, 1974.
14. St. Mary of the Lake Seminary Catalogue, 1966-1967, AAC.
15. Bob Heidenreich, "Is Love the Answer?" in *The New Southwell*, #11, January, 1965.
16. "Celibacy of the Secular Priest," Cover Story in *The New Southwell*, #11, January, 1965. "We Shall Overcome," in *The New Southwell*, #8, March, 1964. "Killing God the Scholastic Way" and "Vietnam: A Reconsideration," in *The New Southwell*, vol 2:1, Autumn 1966.
17. Bill Carroll ('67) (ed.), "The Devalued Priesthood," in *The New Southwell*, #14, January, 1966.
18. Mike Ahlstrom, "The Role of the Priest," in *The New Southwell*, #14, January, 1966.
19. Albert Meyer, *The Spirit of Christian Unity*, Lenten Pastoral 1964, quoted in Thomas Libera, "Some Social Dimensions of the Virtue of Hope," in *Mandala*, Winter, 1968.
20. "Faculty of the Mundelein Campus," in St. Mary of the Lake Seminary Catalogue, 1966-1967, 1967-1968, 1968-1969, AAC.
21. Ivan J. Rohloff, *The Origins and Development of Cursillo* (1939-1973) (Dallas: National Ultreya Publications of the United States National Secretariat, 1976), 19.

CHAPTER 5

WHAT MADE THE DIFFERENCE
Apostolates and Diaconate

Seminary classroom training, no matter how effective, cannot begin to cover every situation that might arise in parish life. Bob Heidenreich discovered this fact one afternoon during his summer apostolate at St. Mark's Parish on Chicago's West Side. His fellow seminarian, serving with him at the parish, had always wanted a snake. Heidenreich and others chipped in to buy him not just any snake, but a boa constrictor. "This was the talk of the neighborhood," Bob says. "The teenagers wanted to see the boa constrictor eat a mouse." So Heidenreich ended up on the back of a teen's motorbike, roaring off to find a suitable rodent to offer up.

"I walk into this pet store," he remembers with glee, "and say, 'This might sound a little strange, but I'd like to buy a mouse.' The lady says, 'How big is your boa constrictor?'"

Carrying the mouse in its cardboard carton, back they went to the parish, where the snake's cage had been moved outside for the big event. Neighborhood kids had gathered in droves. Some intrepid soul grabbed the mouse and threw it into the cage. The mouse, seemingly unaware of its fate, traversed the cage, sniffed the snake, and returned unmolested to a far corner, where it marked out its territory by "peeing all over the bottom of the cage. The snake wouldn't go near him," says Heidenreich. The kids oohed and ahhed. And Bob Heidenreich discovered that the work of parish ministry was full of surprises.

Whatever the six members of the class of 1969 being followed here thought parish ministry might look like, they decided early on during their years at Mundelein that they had had enough of waiting to encounter it. As seminarians some of them simply began to create their own summer parish apostolates, and later, as they approached their ordination as deacons, they insisted that they needed an intensive six-month diaconate parish internship program to learn about parish ministry before becoming priests.

When they arrived at Mundelein Seminary, the class of '69 found that the administration offered only two options for summer apostolates: working at either Maryville or Angel Guardian Orphanages, which Mike Ahlstrom, Bob Heidenreich, and Bill Zavaski chose to do. Larry Duris and Ed Upton, meanwhile, put together their own apostolate at Chicago's inner-city Precious Blood Parish, while Tom Libera worked at nearby St. Frances Cabrini Parish. Later, based on the work of these young pioneers, seminary administrators would make Precious Blood an official seminary program. Once Mundelein finally began to encourage participation in summer apostolates, Zavaski joined his classmates at Precious Blood, while Heidenreich volunteered at St. Mark's Parish, temporary home of the boa constrictor.

Years later, when Cardinal Cody ordained them deacons in the spring of 1968, each of the six men began the diaconate parish internship they had fought to establish. Tom Libera continued his interest in the African-American Catholic community by serving at Our Lady of Solace Parish on Chicago's South Side. Larry Duris happily accepted an assignment to the racially changing Resurrection Parish on the city's West Side. Ed Upton, Bob Heidenreich, and Bill Zavaski all received assignments to suburban parishes: Upton to St. Celestine's in west suburban Elmwood Park, Heidenreich to Holy Ghost in south suburban South Holland, and Zavaski to St. Dismas in far north suburban Waukegan. Finally, Mike Ahlstrom spent his diaconate internship working at the college seminary, Niles College. For each of these men, despite the fact that some of them encountered skepticism from other seminarians and resistance from family members over their choice to work in the inner city, hands-on ministry became critical to strengthening and focusing their priestly vocations.

"A significant turning point for me," Larry Duris says, "was the Precious Blood apostolate. I had had it with Mundelein, the old system. But I got back from that first summer and said, 'I want to be a priest. Ministry is real.'" Father Bill Berghaus ('52), an assistant at Precious Blood, had asked Duris and six other seminarians from Mundelein to join him for an informal summer experiment in inner-city ministry that, for Larry, lasted parts of four summers.

Today a mainly Hispanic parish staffed by religious order priests as a mission of St. Malachy's Parish, Precious Blood, located at Congress and Western on Chicago's West Side, encompassed within its boundaries in 1964 two neighborhoods in one. Split into north and south by the huge Eisenhower expressway, the south side of the parish included mostly Catholics: Hispanics moving into the area as well as Italians holding out against racial change. North of the expressway stood the Rockwell Gardens public housing project, populated by almost exclusively African-Americans, most of whom were not Catholic.

"We worked mainly in Rockwell Gardens," Duris says. "That's what Berghaus was interested in, because the parish had no contact with that project, and the expressway isolated the buildings. It was like crossing the Alps psychologically." The seven seminarians made the crossing, canvassing 1400 apartments over the course of their summers at Precious Blood, inviting the residents to take part in the life of the parish. They ran Bible studies and day camps, trained adults for baptism in the Rite of Christian Initiation for Adults (RCIA), gathered teens together for activities, and even worked with the projects' building councils to improve maintenance and security at Rockwell Gardens.

Because the seminary had no direct sponsorship of the program, Berghaus could—and did—improvise. He had Larry and a fellow seminarian move into the projects for a few weeks. And he frequently asked the seminarians a question they had not heard since their days at Niles: what do you think? After the first two summers—and after the changes at Mundelein had begun under Msgr. Gorman—the seminary began sponsoring the parish apostolates and assigned Father Chris Melone

('52) to spend summers at Precious Blood as director of formation. Melone gathered the seminarians three mornings a week to reflect on their experiences of ministry in the parish, which fostered a sense of camaraderie among them. At the height of the program, 13 seminarians worked at the parish at the same time.

Precious Blood remained a mainstay of the apostolate program for years, training scores of seminarians for inner-city ministry, including the white man who would become the controversial and highly effective pastor of St. Sabina Parish in Chicago's South Side African-American community, Father Michael Pfleger ('75). Not all seminarians, however, showed interest in working in poorer, minority parishes. From some of them, Duris heard disdain. "I caught," he says, "that down in this part of town, this really isn't Church."

> It's social work. Real Church happens in communities that are Catholic. There's less of that now, but for years when we talked about the personnel crisis, it was, "If we close all those damn parishes in the inner city, we wouldn't have a crisis." The judgment was that "Blacks won't become Catholic, so why even bother?" without looking more critically at why there aren't more African-Americans who are Catholic.

Many parents of seminarians also protested against their sons working in the inner city. Often parents who were either European immigrants or the children of immigrants from Catholic neighborhoods—where racial attitudes tended toward the unenlightened, to say the least—sometimes felt a mixture of fear (Is my son safe?), animosity (Why is he working with "them"?), and bewilderment (Are they even Catholic?) upon hearing of their son's decision to work with blacks. "A couple of guys that did black community work, their families almost disowned them," Duris says. Fortunately, he had a different experience when he returned home after the first seven-week summer program at Precious Blood officially ended. "I told my folks," Duris recalls, "'I'll find a job for the rest of the summer so I can take care of my fees for Mundelein.'"

The only thing I could find was selling some Catholic magazine in a territory that was changing racially. So people were in no mood to buy anything. The second or third day after trying to sell these things, I came home. My folks said, "We just asked you how it's going and you said okay. You lie. You look miserable. We were impressed with what was going on in your life down at Precious Blood and Rockwell Gardens. We'll cover your expenses. With our responsibilities we can't be down there working in the projects, but that's our way of being down there." So they said the next morning, "Get on the L; go back to priesthood." It still chokes me up.

And so, for three more summers, though still not ordained, Larry did "go back to priesthood" at Precious Blood. The experience profoundly changed him. "We were the ones," he says, "that were ministered to. We went down as these—this is the era of the Peace Corps—hot shot liberals who were going to save the world. I'm just glad we allowed ourselves to be taught by the folks. The faith of black people was a wonderful gift."

Duris says the experience made the difference for him in terms of his desire to become a priest. "It made the vocation question real," he insists. "It's a challenge to allow yourself to take a swim in someone else's gumbo and to get the smell on you." Larry Duris took the challenge and has no regrets. "If anyone asks what saved my vocation," he says, "even though it sounds disgustingly romantic, I say the folks at Precious Blood."

....

Bill Zavaski also had his eyes opened during his time at Precious Blood. "I had never worked in the black community before," he says. Zavaski's relatives, however, had their doubts about his serving in the inner city. "My family thought I was nuts," he recalls. "I'll never forget it; we invited our families to visit the convent where we were staying. The night before, there had been a riot between the Puerto Ricans from south of the Eisenhower Expressway clashing with African-Americans from the north of it. We ushered our families into the house to protect them."

Ambivalence best describes Bill's recollections of his Precious Blood days. "The riots were awful," he says. "People were just frantic. You could see the West Side burning, people running. We were working in the community, so in some sense they knew us, but it was still a little traumatic." In Bill Zavaski's case, continued ministry in the inner city was not in the cards. But he took valuable lessons with him from Precious Blood. "It certainly made me conscious," he acknowledges, "of ministry to the poor and just how the Church can be effective in it."

....

St. Frances Cabrini Church, now long closed, stood just south of the Eisenhower expressway at Sacramento Boulevard on Chicago's West Side, literally three quarters of a mile due west of Precious Blood. The neighborhood around Cabrini originally housed mostly Italians and Italian-Americans but by the late 1960s had begun to attract Hispanics and African-Americans. An Italian order of priests, the Scalabrini Fathers, still ran the parish. This fact made Cabrini an unlikely place for a diocesan seminarian to spend his apostolate. But because Mundelein Seminary did not administer these summer programs in their infancy, seminarians chose their own sites. Tom Libera ended up spending three summers there running summer day camps and teen clubs and also doing some work with gang members.

From the beginning, Tom found his time at Cabrini extraordinary; he noticed his horizons expanding and his connections with others, never easy for him, growing. "I was beginning to feel lonely," he recalls of his time at Mundelein. "There were maybe one or two friends. So getting involved with these other young people my age was a plus." The apostolate team included seminarians from Minneapolis, religious women, and several lay volunteers. Libera developed a sense of camaraderie at Cabrini. "I could test where I felt comfortable or didn't," he recalls, "but through it all be part of this supportive group. I got in contact with people from parts of the country that I wouldn't have touched in any other way. It was a cross-section of active Catholics asking what they were going to do with their lives. Cabrini helped me to come out of a shell and be able to do ministry." Tom has maintained lifelong friendships with several of the college-age volunteers he met during those summers.

Father Charles LaVerdi, then pastor of Cabrini, provided another sort of encouragement to Libera. "LaVerdi was the catalyst to bring people together," Tom recounts. "He would plan things on the spur of the moment, risking things and not knowing how he was going to finance them. He was my inspiration." Libera marveled at how LaVerdi operated with confidence in God's providence and people's goodness, despite working in a poor community with limited resources. "He would throw himself into what needed to be done," he says, "and motivate people."

In attempting to make a difference himself, Libera found himself drawn to the marches that Rev. Martin Luther King, Jr., was leading in favor of civil rights. He marched with King on both the Southwest and Northwest Sides, which brought its share of dangers. "You had to be alert," he remembers, "because you never know what could be hurled out of a group besides words. At one march Dr. King was hit by rocks and knocked at least to his knees, and then got right back up and kept going."

Parish living, too, brought tensions. "One summer we were staying in a classroom at the school," Libera says. "You'd have that almost surreal sight of seeing National Guard trucks going by at night trying to keep the peace." Despite the precariousness of the environment, or maybe because of it, Tom found the work invigorating. "There was a sense," he says, "of being at a cutting edge."

Unlike Larry Duris, who received unequivocal support from his parents regarding his work in the black community, Libera discovered that his apostolate surfaced conflicts in his family that reflected tensions in white-ethnic Catholic America as a whole. "My mother," he recollects, "was concerned. 'You shouldn't be there'—just all the questions of racism that were boiling to the top at that time." She particularly worried about his marching with King in Marquette Park on the city's Southwest Side. "But I went anyway," Tom says. "I recall feeling the tension, people sensing an invasion, a threat to one's area and property. Knowing that those marches were in neighborhoods with strong Catholic parish influence and that many of the people there were Catholics like us, trying to be followers of Jesus, made this rather ugly too."

Some members of Libera's family exhibited prejudice. Although his dad had died, Tom still saw his father's family regularly. "So they knew what I was doing," he says.

> *The presumption was that I was going to be "for the blacks" or whatever racial words people would use. There'd be some ribbing between me and a few of my uncles. It wasn't disrespectful, but certainly they had a South Side prejudice that wasn't uncommon. They'd let me know, "The people you're working with are trying to take from society what we're working hard to get, and they want it for free." That would be expected when we would get together.*

Living at Cabrini changed Tom Libera. So when it came time to determine a deacon assignment in 1968, he did not hesitate. "I didn't fight," he says, "moving into inner-city urban work."

....

Adventures with the reptile kingdom weren't the only surprises Bob Heidenreich experienced when he spent a summer at St. Mark Parish in the West Town neighborhood on the city's West Side. A second tale of the unexpected touched him. The racial makeup of the parish was changing from Polish and Polish-American to Hispanic. The parish St. Vincent DePaul Society, an organization dedicated to meeting the needs of the poor, asked Bob to join their meetings. "The Vincent de Paul guys would sit," he says, "and drink their beer and smoke their cigars. They weren't, I didn't think, too open to the Hispanics." He joined a member on a call to a home where they encountered a pregnant wife who already had four children. Their refrigerator had died; the husband had lost his job, and they had requested funds. "I presented the case with this guy at the next meeting," Heidenreich recalls.

The Vincent de Paul guys had a history with the family. They said, "This guy is an alcoholic. We saw him in the tavern. We're not giving him money." It just pissed me off.

I said, "Fine! I'm going to give them the money."

"We don't want you to."

"That's all right. You guys don't want to help."

Finally they said, "We'll pay for it."

A couple of weeks later I saw the man drunk in front of the tavern. They were right. I don't know if he ever got the fridge or if he just drank up the money. I was 22 and idealistic. I thought these Polish guys didn't like Hispanics, so they're being cruel. But they knew more about it than I did; they were nicer to me than I was to them. That was also the first time I saw that some families lived on the edge without money.

Bob Heidenreich's experiences at St. Mark's not only sensitized him to the needs of the poor, but they also offered a lesson in humility as well as an opportunity to recognize the wisdom of the ordinary people he would encounter in the parishes of the archdiocese.

....

For these six members of the class of 1969, the experience of working in summer apostolates only whetted their appetite for more chances to participate in hands-on ministry. The class, therefore, as noted, fought successfully to establish a six-month parish diaconate internship that took place for them between June and December of 1968. These six months consolidated for the men what the summer apostolates had begun: they grew more confident in their ability to serve as parish priests, and they looked forward with growing eagerness to the opportunity.

When Larry Duris arrived for his diaconate internship at Resurrection Parish in the Austin neighborhood of Chicago's West Side, he found a parish and neighborhood at the tail end of a period of vast change. White flight and an influx of black families were accelerating on a daily basis in the parish, about three and a half miles due west of Precious Blood. He could literally see the community changing right before his eyes. "You could see week by week the numbers diminishing," Duris says. "We cut the Mass schedule back two Masses."

Rectory living at Resurrection reflected the experience of the parish in two ways, illustrating two markedly different attitudes toward change. Father Frank Phelan ('40), the new pastor, had spent his entire priesthood in the black community. "He was a lifer," Duris says, "a real inspiration, full of energy. He wanted the place to be very involved in the community." Father Mike Rochford ('62), the associate, had also spent considerable time in African-American ministry. He became Larry's mentor and supervisor. Not everyone in the rectory, however, rejoiced over the parish's new focus. "The parish secretary," Duris says, "was one of those classic secretaries that ran that place—just ran the place."

> Res would get a newly ordained every year. She would give
> him orders: "You can't go into the front office area without a
> cassock. You polish Monsignor's shoes and take his clothes to
> the cleaners." She managed the bulletin. She was offended with
> the stuff we were putting in there—suddenly it's all about the
> community and black people and the Organization for a Better
> Austin (OBA), and "This is not the way we have done it." She
> could see what was happening under Phelan. He wasn't going to
> play the game. She was gone by the end of that year.

The secretary's efforts first to resist change and then to escape it exemplified the experience of many of the whites at the parish in the late 1960s. "Most whites that were still there were just waiting for the moving trucks, almost literally. There were, however, whole groups of whites," Duris recalls, "who were about successfully integrating the parish."

> There was a group that worked with OBA and a group that
> would go on night raids literally stealing for sale signs off front
> lawns, because one of the things being fought for was to get red
> lining legislation in. The real estate people were getting away
> with murder with their scare tactics. A changing neighborhood

in a place like Chicago is a ball field where everybody loses the
game. The Catholic Church is one of the very few institutions
that stayed through it.

In Austin, the Church not only stayed but strove to make a difference in the neighborhood. Phelan, Rochford, and Duris worked with
OBA, famed community organizer Saul Alinsky's West Side organization, to address the abuses of real estate agents and slumlords, which
had become increasingly common as the area's racial composition
changed.[1]

> *I went door-to-door to organize meetings to go after slumlords.*
> *Went down to court. Picketed their businesses. I was threatened*
> *by a couple slumlords' goons: "Next time we see you in here,*
> *you're going to get shot." These guys would play poker with their*
> *slum property deeds. We'd finally get 20 people from the building*
> *to court to raise hell. The ass appears and says, "I don't own that*
> *building anymore." So you start from scratch.*

Victories seemed few and far between. "OBA lost the battle,"
Duris laments, "but prevented a number of people from being totally
screwed." Working at Resurrection as a deacon, meanwhile, only confirmed what ministering at Precious Blood had begun to convince Larry Duris of: that he wanted to serve as a priest in the black community.

....

Bill Zavaski, Mike Ahlstrom, and Bob Heidenreich's diaconate intern-
ships provided them with the opportunity to learn central components
of successful priestly ministry, especially the importance of closeness
between a priest and his people.

Assigned to St. Dismas Parish in his hometown of Waukegan,
Zavaski quickly got involved with one of his pastor Pat Hunter's ('36)
best innovations: base communities. Since 1962, the Archdiocese of
Chicago had run a mission in San Miguelito Parish in Panama. Under
the leadership of Father Leo Mahon ('51), the parish, like many in Lat-

in America, had organized itself into small groups—base communities —to strengthen ties and confront issues facing the parish and neighborhood.[2] Progressive pastors in Chicago such as Hunter experimented with the practice in their parishes. "Hunter was very open-minded," Zavaski says. "These small Christian communities were a good learning experience as far as making Church a real personal thing."

Mike Ahlstrom ended up serving as a deacon back at the college seminary, working mostly on retreats and living with the seminarians in the aforementioned cubicles. "A lot of it was just being present to the students," Ahlstrom says, "and listening and sharing. Because the Council had just happened, all these changes were coming out—we had Mass in English, the notion of collegiality. And these guys were very idealistic, open to change. The '60s was a highly experimental time. I had my creative juices in gear, bringing a little inspiration to what I hoped would be our future priests." Early on in his work at Niles, Ahlstrom helped to conduct the freshman retreat. "Here I am," he says, still incredulous, "leading a retreat for seminarians. With what an underachiever I had been, I said, 'Wow, look how far I've come.'"

When Bob Heidenreich arrived at Holy Ghost Parish in South Holland for his diaconate assignment in June 1968, he found a surprising mentor: the people of the parish. "I experienced what was this special gift," he fondly remembers, "of getting to know a number of the adults, and forming a community." Heidenreich learned from the people that "priesthood is being a father to a group of Catholics who are normal people and want to make a difference in this world. I found that both exhilarating and challenging. And at that point I was pretty sure that that's what I wanted to do."

When Cardinal Cody ordained these classmates as deacons in the spring of 1968, a great deal of turmoil roiled both the church and the country and would continue to do so. Some parishioners still fought the changes in the Church brought on by the Second Vatican Council; others thought change hadn't gone far enough. On the national scene, Rev. Martin Luther King, Jr., had been murdered in April, leading to riots in major cities including Chicago, and Bobby Kennedy was killed in June; the beatings of protestors by police at the Democratic Convention in Chicago in late August had also riveted the nation.

Ed Upton was glad to be at St. Celestine's, a middle class Italian and Italian-American enclave in Elmwood Park. "The city was a tinderbox," he explains. He lived in the rectory with the two assistants, Fathers Bill (Willy) Shields ('52) and John Price ('66), both progressive sorts. The pastor, Father Phil Neenan ('36), lived in a house across the street and frequently kept to himself.

Feeling dim relief about ministering in the suburbs did not mean Ed had lost his social conscience. Early on he began writing a weekly article in the bulletin for the parishioners' reflection. "I cringe to think I did this," Upton recalls ruefully. "There was this big story about a Presbyterian pastor in Chicago who was inviting the Blackstone Rangers into his church. I wrote in the bulletin about what a good thing I thought that was."

Soon after the parish published the article, Upton noticed people complaining, but not to him. They took their concerns, instead, to Neenan. Ed paid close attention, studying the way the pastor navigated the thorny situation. "What I realized," he says, "was the pastor got a lot of flak. I didn't get anything. He didn't yell at me. He just said, 'You ought to think more carefully about what you're writing.' He brokered it."

> I had thought that he was a putzy old guy, but he protected
> me. "Out of stupidity and immaturity" is probably how he
> defended me, but it was what a leader does. He was pretty good
> at that. He taught me to be careful. But he also showed me what
> leadership was because since it was okay with him, they didn't go
> after me.

Upton also observed leadership in Bill Shields, his supervisor at Celestine's. Shields wanted to implement the reforms of the Vatican Council at the parish level, but knew he must take care in doing so, both with the pastor and parishioners. "Bill was always manipulating," Ed says. "He'd say, 'We have to talk to the pastor on Wednesday because if you talk to him on Friday he will have been with his classmates [on

Thursday, his day off] and they will have turned him around again.'"

Upton had helped to take a door-to-door parish census. "I about died," he says. "This was an Italian neighborhood. They're yelling, 'Why are they changing the catechism?' Being in seminary, you think these are wonderful ideas, but people are screaming about the awful changes. What I learned from Willy was we're going to keep brokering it, but we're going to move forward," he says. Ed also learned to appreciate the wily Shields' political savvy in parish life. One day Shields took Upton with him to visit the second grade at the parish school. Afterward Shields told the young deacon, "We have a parent meeting tonight. I wanted the kids to all go home and say Father Shields saw me today."

What worked—and what didn't—fascinated the pragmatic Upton. What he noticed in watching the interplay between pastor, assistants, and parishioners was that while ideology and theology may have mattered, both took a back seat in importance to relationships. "The thing I learned with Phil and Willy and John," Ed Upton remarks, "was when you're connected with people and you know them, you can do a lot." And he had begun to believe that he could "do" priesthood.

....

Mike Ahlstrom, Larry Duris, Bob Heidenreich, Tom Libera, Ed Upton, and Bill Zavaski all agreed that living in parishes, or in Ahlstrom's case, at Niles College, as deacons for six months cemented their vocations to the priesthood more than any other aspect of their seminary careers. The actual doing of ministry transcended what they had learned about priesthood in class. Whether occurring during summer apostolates or the diaconate internship they had fought so hard to create, moments of contact with parishioners' problems and hopes set these men on fire with passion for ministry. As the six men reluctantly returned to Mundelein in January for their final six months of classes, they could hardly wait for priesthood ordination so they could get back into "the trenches."

....

1. Alinsky had previously worked with the Chicago Church and Bishop Bernard Sheil ('10) in the Back of the Yards neighborhood in the late 1930s and again in the 1950s with Msgr. Jack Egan—with support from both Archbishops Stritch and Meyer—at parishes on both the Southwest and Northwest Sides. See Steven M. Avella, "Reynold Hillenbrand and Chicago Catholicism" and "The Rise and Fall of Bernard Sheil," both in *Catholicism: Chicago Style* (Chicago: Loyola University Press, 1993), 99, 122.
2. For more on the mission in San Miguelito, see Leo Mahon with Nancy Davis, *Fire Under My Feet: A Memoir of God's Power in Panama* (New York: Orbis Books, 2007).

PART II

YOUNG MEN ON A MISSION

CHAPTER 6

NEWLY ORDAINED
First Assignments

....

Having survived 12 years of seminary education, the men of the class of 1969 now readied themselves to embark upon their first assignments as parish priests. Hopeful and idealistic, feeling at least somewhat prepared thanks to the months of parish ministry they had successfully injected into the seminary curriculum, class members found themselves bumping into unpredictable and fascinating situations that challenged their youthful confidence.

First, however, they each enjoyed a brief moment of thanksgiving: celebrating their first Mass. Often referred to facetiously as "coronations," first Masses tended to be large-scale wedding-like events. Held in the home parishes of the newly ordained, they featured many priests concelebrating and a great parish-wide celebration afterwards that honored both the new priest and the parish itself for having successfully fostered a vocation. Two such events bear noting here, due to their long-term impact on the lives of Bob Heidenreich and Tom Libera.

Heidenreich's first Mass at St. Matthias Parish had traditional elements: an important priest to preach the homily—in this case the rector of Mundelein, Msgr. Jack Gorman ('52)—and a seminarian Master of Ceremonies from the parish to keep the event running smoothly, for which Bob chose fellow parishioner Dave O'Connell ('70). But the striking memory for Heidenreich had to do with his mother's sister coming from Germany. "Both my parents were born in Germany," Heidenreich says. "My mother's sister was a hospital nun, and her community paid for her to come with her nephew, my cousin. I had never met these people and they did not speak English, and at that time my German was nonexistent."

It was delightful to meet them. My mother realized that if her sister could come here, she could go there, which began a traveling back and forth. Eventually my mother said, "Bobby, you've got to come." Six or seven years after my ordination I started going to Germany and meeting all the relatives, an association I keep up till this day. And I work with all of the German priests now. [1]

Heidenreich for years has collaborated on behalf of the Archdiocese of Chicago with German diocesan priests in an effort to study the implementation of Vatican II in both countries. The connection never would have happened but for his aunt coming to his first Mass.

Tom Libera invited an Episcopal priest to be present in the sanctuary at his first Mass, an innovation that would have been unthinkable just a few years earlier, before the Second Vatican Council. But Libera also looked back to another memory that he considered almost more important than even his ordination. "A few days after ordination, I was in old St. Mary's Church on Van Buren and Wabash sitting in the congregation for an afternoon Mass. I remember feeling enveloped by this living body of Christ; that somehow I was part of them, and part of their world was going to be part of my world. It was wonderful having had the ordination," he recalls, "but this was like, 'You're really with the people.' This confirmed what I hoped would be the character of priesthood."

That was a powerful experience, one of those foundational moments you're thankful for. It had almost a luminosity to it. A few weeks ago I was reading stuff celebrating 50 years of Thomas Merton's spiritual awakening. He was in Louisville on that street corner and felt a unity with all the people there. That made an impact on him. There are some parallels there. That was a very affirming moment.

....

In May of 1969, Cardinal Cody assigned the 35 newly ordained priests to their first parishes. For a new parish priest, the first assignment tends to leave, for good or ill, a deep imprint that often significantly impacts his future ministry. The first assignments for the six priests under consideration here follow below:

- Father Mike Ahlstrom to Most Holy Redeemer in the southwest suburb of Evergreen Park
- Father Ed Upton to St. Alexander's in Palos Heights, also in the southwest suburbs
- Father Bob Heidenreich to St. Martha's in Morton Grove in the northwest suburbs
- Father Bill Zavaski to St. James in Arlington Heights, a suburb farther northwest
- Father Tom Libera to St. Ladislaus, a Polish national parish on the Northwest Side of Chicago
- Father Larry Duris to St. Ethelreda's on Chicago's Southwest Side

At these parishes, the young men would take on an assortment of challenges, among them the reality of adjusting to a new boss. Nothing caused as much consternation or joy as learning to live with and communicate with their new pastors, only some of whom embraced the changes wrought by the Second Vatican Council. Often the men ordained in 1969 found themselves driving the implementation of those changes. At other times, however, the demands of their parishioners pushed them to advocate for new ways that a parish could function. Social issues such as racial tensions also played a major role in the ministry of the young priests, as did coming face to face with illness and death in the parish. And during all this they had to decide whether and how they would maintain friendships with classmates they had relied on since they were teenagers. All in all, these first years as young associates would be for them a baptism by fire.

The very process of learning about his first assignment put Ed Upton into conflict with the relatively new archdiocesan Personnel Board. The confrontation exemplified new tensions that had begun to erupt in the formerly obedient relations between new priests and their superiors. "I get a call from the Board: 'Your assignment is St. Alexander's in Palos Heights,'" says Upton. "I said, 'I never heard of Palos Heights. Where is it?' He told me. I said, 'Who is the pastor?' He said, 'We can't tell you.'"

> Smart aleck that I was, I said, "If you can't tell me, I'm not going to say yes." He said, "We've given the Cardinal a name, but he gets very upset if that name gets out before he has announced it. I'll tell you but you can't tell anybody. It's Msgr. Cornelius McGillicuddy ('39)." That meant absolutely nothing to me. But I felt better that I had staked my integrity on not blindly doing what the institution had asked.

So Ed drove south to Palos Heights, where he would soon begin a battle of wills with his new pastor. "McGillicuddy," he admits, "I thought was so old. He was 55, but I thought he was older than God. It was like an Irish household. At times we wouldn't talk. There would be silence about what we were mad about. We both would know about it and then we'd get over it and go on. Those were rough times."

> We had started this young priests' caucus, which put together a list of parishes where young priests should not go. I can't imagine doing that today. He got incensed because we had listed his first pastor: "How can you do that?" We would have little tiffs.

Upton learned through trial and error to negotiate with McGillicuddy. Their biggest fight came over what would become a classic post-Vatican II parish battle: in one corner, the parish school, and in the other, the religious education or CCD (Confraternity of Christian Doctrine) program. "The parents who wanted to send their children to a Catholic school," Ed remembers, "couldn't get them in because it was filled. So people were putting their kids in religious ed. I thought religious ed people were second class. They were the 'publics.' They didn't care about their faith." Upton soon learned he was wrong.

> All of a sudden, I meet all these people who are dynamite. They're very dedicated to their faith, at Mass every Sunday. They were very concerned about religious ed. The Catholic school had 42 kids in a room.

As the new coordinator of religious education, Upton was by himself handling a program serving hundreds of children. Meanwhile the school principal began asking for funds to hire a school secretary. "You might not believe that they didn't have a secretary," Ed says, "but they didn't. I wanted to hire a DRE (Director of Religious Education). My argument was that's more important than a secretary. We had a huge fight. I shouldn't have, but I did it at a public meeting—I said, "We need a director of this program. We've got 500 kids."

At the time, the DRE job stood out as an innovation in parishes. "Often it was conflictual," says Upton, "because the DREs were not as subservient to the pastor as the school principals were. And McGillicuddy's classmates had had problems [with DREs]. Secondly, he was very cheap. He didn't want to spend the money. We fought about this back and forth."

Eventually a group of parishioners approached the pastor to weigh in on Ed's side. Upton recalls the pastor's response: "At first he said, 'It's a volunteer ministry, you don't pay people.' All that crap. But the people went to him and he changed. We were able to get a Providence nun as DRE who was from the same community as the school nuns. She was Irish—not foreign born, but she had the proper last name! McGillicuddy settled down then. That was a big accomplishment, because I was a strong believer in religious ed. It was clear the old model wasn't working. The religious ed families are not second-class citizens. They are as active as anybody."

Once Upton saw that his pastor could show flexibility after all, he suspected that he needed to question his own assumptions. He wound up discovering that McGillicuddy, who had worked for years as chaplain of the Sheil Catholic Center at Northwestern University, had theological views that often dovetailed nicely with his own. "At Northwestern," Ed says, "he had worked with kids and laypeople, so he was not threatened at all about parish councils and finance councils and actually encouraged those, so he had a liberal bent. He was a man of his times, but his theology was open." Ed Upton ended up becoming McGillicuddy's friend, a bond that lasted long after he had left St. Alexander's.

....

In dealing with parish conflicts between what was called the "old" and the "new" Church emerging out of the recent Vatican Council, many young associates butted heads with recalcitrant pastors set in their ways. Often these confrontations took place in ethnic parishes, which tended to hold on to traditions fiercely and embrace change slowly, if at all. So Tom Libera felt particularly lucky to discover quickly that his pastor supported him in his efforts to implement the changes of Vatican II. St. Ladislaus, a Polish parish on the Northwest Side of Chicago in the Portage Park neighborhood, took up a full square city block. Libera vividly remembers the Polish flavor of the forty hours devotion. Beginning and ending with solemn Mass on Friday night and Sunday morning respectively, the devotion drew hundreds of people. The Blessed Sacrament stood exposed on the altar for Eucharistic Adoration throughout the two-day event, and scores of priests visited from other parishes to hear confessions. "You got to see the Polish segment of Chicago priests," Libera explains. "There'd be 30 of them in our rectory. That's a thing of the past now."

The heavily ethnic flavor initially left Libera worrying about what it would be like to work with the first of the pastors he had at his first assignment, Father Clem Jagodzinski ('39). "That was his first pastorate," Libera says. Jagodzinski had worked for years as a chaplain at Alexian Brothers Hospital near DePaul University, and his experiences there, Libera believes, had moved him beyond the ethnic confines and concerns of the Polish league of priests. "He came into the pastorate,"

Libera continues, "with openness. When he would get together with his Polish confreres who were more entrenched in their ways, Clem would offer them an alternate way. He had a little influence on those fellows in terms of bringing them along in Vatican II."

Bill Zavaski had an even better experience with his first pastor than had Libera. When he arrived, full of excitement, at St. James in the northwest suburb of Arlington Heights in June of 1969, Zavaski says, "I didn't even know where Arlington Heights was. I knew they had a racetrack. The parish had about 2,500 families. They were saying Mass in three different places—we had a full house." Zavaski's initial enthusiasm turned into elation when he got to know the other priests assigned to the parish. "Ed Laramie ('33), the pastor," Zavaski recalls, "had a lot of appreciation for the changes in the Church. He started a parish council, a finance committee, a school board, a resource center; he hired one of the first DREs." Zavaski also thought highly of Ed Hughes ('51), one of Laramie's two associates. "A lot of Laramie's ideas," Zavaski says, "were from Hughes. He was a recovering alcoholic who owed his life to Laramie. He had gone to Guest House [a treatment facility for alcoholic priests], and Ed Laramie had supported him.[2] Laramie let us do whatever we wanted. Being in the midst of Vatican II, he never set restrictions on anything. He was incredibly great to work with. Some of my classmates did not have as good an experience as I had and were envious."

Not among the envious, Bob Heidenreich's assignment to St. Martha's Parish in the northwest suburb of Morton Grove was just what he'd been hoping for. "It's what I wanted," Heidenreich says, "a middle-class, working-class neighborhood. It was in the suburbs but not really suburban." In other words, the parish makeup seemed similar to the two Chicago parishes he'd grown up in, St. Andrew and St. Matthias. Bob had also heard good things about his new pastor, Father Bill Devereaux ('37). "Bill was somebody," Heidenreich recalls, "that believed the whole idea is that we're here to serve the people. He was very warm and welcoming." Dev, as Heidenreich called him, had even started a lay finance council, a real innovation for 1969.

Not everyone at St. Martha's, however, shared Heidenreich's enthusiasm for Dev's progressive views of ministry. As often happens in parishes experiencing leadership transitions, some of the old guard remained loyal to the former pastor's ways of operating. "The choir director was a good friend of the former pastor's," Heidenreich says, "so the first Christmas Dev said to me, 'We better meet with her, because if we don't, she's going to have all Latin music for the midnight Mass. We'll have a little Latin, but let's combine it with English.'" The priests met with the organist and came away satisfied; they had given her plenty of time to buy the music and train her choir. "Sure enough," says Heidenreich, "we start midnight Mass and the opening hymn was in English. But as soon as we got up to the altar, everything else was in Latin. What can you do? The three of us are on the altar and she's up in the choir loft. By the time Mass was over and I got back there, she was gone."

Throughout Heidenreich's priesthood, he has found himself drawn to appreciating how each generation of priests has passed on the craft of priesthood to the next generation. This core interest owed much of its early development to his first assignment at St. Martha's, where he soon began to feel a debt of gratitude to Bill Devereaux. As Heidenreich met others who knew Dev, they would describe what made him such a good priest. "He would go out with the kids when they were on recess," Heidenreich says of one such practice, "and walk around the block with them, hearing their confessions. And he'd help people, out of his own pocket." Dev also introduced Heidenreich to the joys of nightly cocktails before dinner. "That's where I picked up a lot of these priestly habits," Heidenreich says, laughing. "Every day we'd have a drink at 5 p.m." Dev used cocktail time not only for conviviality, but also for teaching lessons about priesthood.

Heidenreich recalls one lesson in particular. Dev was Irish-American and Heidenreich German-American. Heidenreich knew enough about ethnic rivalries in the Chicago Church to realize that the Irish and Germans did not always get along. He recalled one day when the pastor, then in his early 60s, showed him pictures of the priests who had been his own pastors.

Dev pointed out one of them, a German named Bill Shubridge (1896): "I'm going to tell you a story about Shubridge. One day he says to me, 'Bill, I'm happy to have you as my assistant, because when I was ordained, a very good priest, an Irishman, accepted me as a German and taught me everything I know about priesthood. I could never thank him enough. I want you to know that.'" I think back on that often. See, that's the way the Chicago presbyterate works. You don't learn how to be a priest in Mundelein Seminary. You learn it from these guys that are experts and know how to do it.

Because of that experience, Heidenreich now eschews the advice of some colleagues to avoid working with young priests. "A lot of guys my age," he notes, "say, 'Stay away from the newly ordained. They're so conservative. It's nothing but problems.' But it's also a way of passing on exactly what you're talking about in this book for the future."

It was Devereaux who taught Heidenreich that a chain existed linking one generation of parish priests to the next. What an Irish pastor had passed on to Shubridge, Shubridge passed on to Dev. Dev, in turn, taught Heidenreich, who has tried to transmit the spirit of the Chicago priesthood to the newly ordained under his care. Heidenreich traced much of the growth of his own abilities as a priest back to Dev and St. Martha's. "I learned how to form community," he says, "by being welcoming and going out of your way."

Heidenreich can still hear Devereaux talking to him more than 40 years later. "Last Sunday, I had a baptism. I didn't know the people, a younger family. It turns out they moved here from California six months ago. Afterward they invited me to the house. I wanted to balance my checkbook—nothing that had to be done. I said, 'I'll try to come.' I got to thinking," Heidenreich admits, "Devereaux would have said, 'Go. That's how you tie people in.' So I went over for 45 minutes, had a glass of wine, something to eat, listened to their stories, saw the family pictures. Little things like that, that's how you do it."

....

Larry Duris faced a radically different situation with his first pastor. St. Ethelreda Parish stood at 87th and Paulina on Chicago's Southwest Side in the Longwood Manor neighborhood. (Although the parish has since closed, the school remains open.) When he learned of the assignment, Duris says he thought, "Ethel who? It sounds like a disease." He had never heard of the place. His astonishment only increased when he learned that white Irish-Americans and not African-Americans made up the vast majority of parishioners at "Ethel's," as many South Siders called it. Having spent his seminary apostolate and diaconate in black parishes and feeling called to serve there in the future, Duris had requested that the Personnel Board send him to an African-American parish. The Board ignored his request.

Although racial change would soon dominate Duris' time at Ethel's, his immediate concern had to do with his new pastor, Father Ed Cronin ('42). Hoping for leadership, Duris found a hesitant man instead. "Ed was gracious, kind," Duris says, "but insecure. In addition to the parish changing, Father Willy Lahayne ('19), the emeritus, was living there. He intimidated Cronin. Willy was a gruff old Irishman. He had been pastor for 20 years. That wasn't good for Ed."

> Second year, I wanted to get a seminary deacon. I was like a
> stubborn kid and pushed. We got Erwin Friedl ('71). Part of it
> was my survival in the house, because at dinner, Lahayne would
> mention "Sister Mary Holy Water who made her vows in 1903,"
> blah, blah. Cronin would feed into that to keep Willy happy. We
> were always talking about the past. Once Erwin came, and then
> John Cain ('58) became a resident, we would occasionally bring
> up outrageous topics just to say them. I brought up condoms one
> night at dinner. I thought Cronin was going to die.

Duris came to understand his pastor's desire to keep the peace only when Cronin shared the story of his own first day at Ethel's, just months before Larry's arrival. "I found this out," Duris says, "one night after the second or third Manhattan before dinner when he'd loosen up. The Sunday before he got there, the guy I replaced, Charlie Kelly ('48), had preached on race." Kelly had chastised parishioners for participating in picketing Foster Park School, the local public school, because blacks had started to enroll there. "Well, people went at him after Mass. Kelly said, 'I'll be happy to talk with you. But I can't do it right now. I've got the next Mass. Come over Wednesday night.' They did come over Wednesday, 300 of them in the hall, and they called the press. Cronin moves in that day for his first day as pastor. His first doorbell, it's NBC news at 5 p.m.: 'Where's the big parish meeting?' It had Cronin traumatized." Over time, not only did Duris feel Cronin had failed to mentor him, but he became so worried about Cronin's health that he fervently urged him to take a week's vacation.

By the time young Father Mike Ahlstrom had spent a few weeks at St. Bernadette's in south suburban Evergreen Park at his first assignment, he already felt his youthful idealism beginning to wane. "It was culture shock," he says. "I was disillusioned quickly." Ahlstrom recalled three sources of that dissatisfaction: the people's racial attitudes, their complaints about the new liturgy, and his relationship with Father Morgan O'Brien ('29), the founding pastor of the parish. "The honeymoon did not last," Ahlstrom admits. "O'Brien was 40 years older than me, in his late 60s—about the age I am now, but I thought he was ancient. I told people, 'I don't think he's read a book since the day he left the seminary.' He didn't seem open to our ideas."

For months, fellow assistant Father John Hennessey ('67) and Ahlstrom worked in tandem, but in isolation from O'Brien. "After about a year and a half," Ahlstrom recounts, "I got in a huge, horrible fight with Morgan. He started out at supper. He said, 'If I was an assistant here, I'd walk out tomorrow.' I said, 'What are you talking about?' He said, 'You young guys talk about communication but you're full of it. You never communicate.' I said, 'Well, you don't give a damn.'"

> Then Hennessey came home and the three of us got in a fight. At one point Morgan got down on his knees. He said, "Do I have to beg you guys?" It finally hit us that he really does care. Our whole attitude turned around 180 degrees towards him. We had been isolated—us versus him. We stopped that. That fight was a conversion moment. We said we've got to do things differently. And he saw us reaching out to him. That built up trust and he started listening to us. We started listening to him as well, because he did have wisdom to share.

Ahlstrom says he grew to love and admire O'Brien, not least because he began to observe how well the pastor knew the people in his parish. "He hand-delivered the envelopes every year. He saw where everybody in the parish lived and kept track of the census. He would give me your address and tell me all about what you were like. He might not be up on the newest theology, but he had a sense that what we were doing was good for the people, and he trusted us." By the end, Ahlstrom says, O'Brien was telling other priests that he had the greatest assistants in the archdiocese.

"I stayed somewhat close to him after he retired," Ahlstrom says, still shaking his head at the memory of O'Brien falling to his knees in supplication. "I had a great affection for Morgan."

....

Sometimes inspired by—and other times in spite of—their pastors, these six young priests set about, as they called it, "building up the kingdom of God" by implementing the reforms of the recent Second Vatican Council in their respective parishes. For the most part, they moved forward with the unqualified support of their people. Bob Heidenreich treasured the growing awareness of the importance of sharing ministerial roles with the non-ordained. At St. Martha's he befriended Sister Luanne Wilhelm, a sister of the Living Word who went on to become DRE at Sacred Heart in Winnetka, where Heidenreich later served as pastor. The story of that friendship's beginnings captures the collaboration suddenly growing between ordained and non-ordained at the time. "There was a fire at Martha's," Heidenreich relates, "in the convent."

> I was in the rectory and the doorbell rings Sunday night about
> 8:30 p.m. It was one of the older nuns. She said, "Father, our
> convent is on fire. Do you think we could come over here?" I
> said, "Sure." There were seven nuns in the rectory, all still in their
> habits. Bill Devereaux comes home and sees fire trucks and hoses,
> and learns about the fire. It's now out, but the convent is still full
> of smoke. So Father Gerry Broccolo ('65) and I approach Bill. We

had two spare bedrooms…we also had a large living room and you could seal the doors. We said, "We have to ask the nuns to stay tonight." "Oh no, we can't do that." "Are you going to turn them out, put them up at a Holiday Inn?" "No, no." "Well?" "All right, all right." So they brought some bedding over. The three of us—we had a seminary deacon—and three of the nuns ended up in Gerry's room drinking at 11:00 p.m. They all smelled of smoke. During the conversation, the nuns wondered, "Why couldn't we be part of the staff?" "No reason. What do you want to do?"

As a result of that impromptu late-night session, Sr. Luanne went off to get trained as a Director of Religious Education, and the other two nuns began working on the music in church. "These were competent women," Heidenreich says, "who knew what they were doing. People from that assignment were big influences on my life, Luanne certainly. When I came in '69, it was like the old picture of Mundelein where the priests were the only ministers. By the time I left in '74, there were many ministries established in the parish. That was the beginning of where we are today. That's what I learned at Martha's."

At St. Alexander's, Ed Upton also began working with laypeople, focusing on religious education, strengthening the liturgy, and investing in the parish's teenagers. Because the pastor had started at the parish concurrently with Upton, things tended not to get stuck in the past. "It was terrific for a young guy," he says, "because the pastor couldn't say, 'We've always done it that way.' You really could move forward." And move forward Upton did. "We did home catechetics," he recalls. "We would go to people's houses and have discussions. I wrote all the lessons for the catechists to use. It was fun because we would meet every week with six couples who had a great way with kids. Then they would meet with the kids. I'm still friends with those people today."

Early on in his work with youth, however, Upton bumped into a conflict not of his own making regarding First Communions, which had broken out the month before he arrived. The previous associate and the school principal had decided that, instead of the second graders all receiving their Communions together at one Mass with a traditional procession, the students would simply sit with their parents at whatever Mass they normally attended and walk up with them to receive Communion. "Parents went out of their minds," Upton recalls. "They said, 'We will have our own practice. We will do it the way we want, and we don't care what you say.'"

Upton learned from this experience that dictating to laypeople was not the way to go about working for change in a parish. "'We'll have options next year,'" he recalls telling the parents. "'We'll have the procession or I'll do a home Mass or you can just sit in the pew with your kid on Sunday.' They loved options. It solved the fight. They were respected. It wasn't like we're going to do it only my way."

Working with people on home catechesis and First Communions, Upton found a unique way to bring both projects together. "I did home First Communions. Theologically," he admits, "it blows the notion of initiation into the parish community. But it was a way for people to have a Mass in their house. I would explain the Mass. People loved that, and some still talk about it. They'll say, 'You gave me First Communion in the house!'" It was one of the better things I ever did—a great way to get to know people in a small group. These were all people already connected to the large Church, already part of the community. So this was a way to make that large community smaller. I wouldn't do it today; since people aren't as connected with the larger Church, it would remain a private thing for my child at home. But these were people who already went to Church.

....

For Ed Upton, the spirit of experimentation even extended to his early homilies. "I'd ask at Mass," he says, "'Anybody got any questions?' And people would ask questions."

Experimentation loomed large for Bill Zavaski as well when his pastor Ed Laramie assigned him to take charge of liturgical renewal in the parish. Initially, things did not go exactly as planned. "I had this couple," Zavaski says, "that wanted to get married in the woods. 'We'll get you married in the woods,'" I said, "'No problem.' I'm thinking nothing of it. Anyway, the invitations went out, and Cardinal Cody found out and had his secretary call."

I'll never forget this Saturday afternoon. It was a week before the wedding. Ed Hughes picks up the phone. I hear Ed say, "Oh no, nobody would be that stupid to marry somebody in the woods. Not here. There's some mistake. I'm sure it's just a reception there." I'm thinking, oh God. He puts the phone down. The first thing he does is call, "Bill!" He knew it was me. We had to figure this out. So I married the couple in the chapel. Then they renewed their vows out in the woods, so we covered our bases."

For Zavaski, his experiences directing liturgies improved after that. "It was exciting," he says, "because the parish had not focused on liturgy. I ended up being the new guy developing liturgy teams, committees, boards. People realized they could be lectors and proclaim the Scriptures and loved it. We got into sacred dance, dramatic readings, picking different types of music. People believed that they were the Church. When you're in a parish, people get committed by inviting them to be part of ministry."

Zavaski learned firsthand about his people's willingness to respond to that invitation when, in suburban Arlington Heights of all places, one of the parish's families faced eviction. "A blind lady," Zavaski says, "with five kids, her kid rang the rectory doorbell and said they were throwing them out in the street."

She lived right down the block. I didn't know what to do. So I got up on Sunday and said, "We've got a lady in the neighborhood. She's going to be thrown out of her house. I need some help." Some people complained. But the majority was helpful. I had 20 people willing to take in her kids while she went to blind school. It was an incredible experience. I learned their generosity and goodness. Whenever I wanted something, I just asked. The blind woman led to us forming an organization called Volunteers Unlimited, a support group for families in trouble. But this was all their idea. I just said we've got to do something, and overnight there were people who just came.

At St. James Parish, often ahead of its time, shared ministry among the priests and laity on the 14-member staff became the norm, along with other innovations. "We had regular staff meetings," Zavaski says. More than anything else, however, as an extrovert, Zavaski enjoyed the day-to-day give and take with parishioners as they began to put their own talents to work. His next move was to invite the teens of the parish to put on a play. Once again, in the initial stages of his new project, he found himself in over his head. "Our first year was *Bye Bye Birdie*," Zavaski recalls. "That was traumatic. These kids here are talented, but problematic. They used to get in trouble. My lead got arrested three days before the show for vandalism." When an older parishioner volunteered to handle discipline issues, Zavaski relaxed. "The musical," he says, "was a real community builder here and it still is. It's been going on for 40 years." Zavaski brought a spirit of conviviality into his attempts to build an active faith community. He persuaded his fellow priests that they should hold parties for parishioners in the rectory. "They never did that before," Zavaski says. "People loved it. We started a social organizing committee also still going on 40 years later. I spent a lot of time in people's houses. Every night after we got through with a meeting, I would visit somebody's house and have a drink. Developing relationships with people was the big thing."

Like his classmates who worked to develop lay leadership and involvement, Mike Ahlstrom focused on the liturgy. Ahlstrom's love of liturgy led him to train with the Office for Worship, opened by the archdiocese in 1970 under Father Dan Coughlin ('60). There, Ahlstrom began to soak up the spirit of excitement then surrounding the liturgy. Armed with new ideas, he set out to persuade the people of St. Bernadette's of the value of the liturgical renewal called for by the recent Vatican Council. "John Hennessey and I," Ahlstrom recalls, "helped continue a program where we went block by block through the parish, inviting everybody to a host's house. We showed a filmstrip on the history of the Mass. Then we did a home Mass with guitar in an informal setting. For many people, that was a turning point. Before, they would say: 'I can't stand this new Mass.' By the end they were saying, 'This wasn't so bad.'"

We started one of the first liturgy teams in the archdiocese, which the Office for Worship used as a model, and we became a road show on how you plan liturgy. I heard negativity initially, but people's attitudes changed. We did a survey and two-thirds of the people approved of things like the greeting of peace. That taught me, don't go by stereotypes.

....

For Tom Libera, tensions at St. Ladislaus between groups of parishioners made encouraging lay ministry a challenge. Some of the longtime Polish American parishioners resisted change in the liturgy, but they always had the safety of the traditional Polish Mass. "For those who wanted that," he says, "that wasn't messed with." While respecting the "old," Tom put most of his energies into working with the "new," especially working with liturgies and in the school. He decided to expand his horizons, obtaining a certificate from Loyola University in counseling. But he found that at Ladislaus not many parishioners availed themselves of the opportunity for counseling. To talk about difficult personal things explicitly, outside of the confessional, would require a great adjustment in their thinking.

Libera soon found, however, to his great surprise, that a parishioner was calling him into a new ministry. "A woman named Gerry," he recalls, "kept bugging me. She was a divorced person." She wanted Libera to work with her on starting a ministry for the divorced and separated in the parish. "That issue had come up," Tom recalls, "in one of the cluster meetings of parishes where priests would get together. This was the beginning of the Church reaching out to the divorced and separated. Somehow I took a role."

Libera, reflecting on Gerry's request and on what he was hearing at the cluster meetings, at last worked with her to plan an information night at nearby St. Patrick's High School. It would focus "on just what the Church does say on divorce—tackling all these myths about being excommunicated and all those things that were really keeping people away."

You knew there was misinformation. So we advertised it in the area. Twenty minutes before we were going to start, people had already filled the library and were all the way down the stairs. Fortunately, we were able to move the event into the cafeteria. We wound up with 400 people. Incredible. There were parents of divorcees—it wasn't just the divorced and separated—so you knew there was a need that you were tapping.

A support group for divorced and separated Catholics soon evolved out of that packed meeting at St. Pat's. Shortly afterward, Libera made contact with a national retreat program for the divorced and separated known as Beginning Experience, modeled on the Cursillo movement. Tom and his local group developed a second retreat for people to attend as a follow-up. The group copyrighted that retreat and eventually gave the copyright to Beginning Experience. "The idea," Libera says, "was to try to move people through their own grief, reconnect them with their faith, and then get them into groups afterwards. I felt it was bringing people back just by giving them information that they were not excommunicated. That's misinformation. You can come to community. Don't stay away. You're welcome. You need us. We need you. But the one thing you wouldn't want them to do would be to walk away." People clearly appreciated that someone representing the Church had decided to walk with them through their suffering.

As Libera met with people in support groups and on weekend retreats, the issue of divorce and remarriage and the reception of Communion arose. "Even if you're not in a regular situation," he recalls telling people, "you still should be here; there are options." Some divorced people would work to annul their first marriage. Others did not wish to go that route. "If they didn't," Libera says, the next question was, "How would you work with them on an individual basis?" Tom often suggested people sit down with a priest and sort things out. "In the internal forum," he explains, using a Catholic term that refers to a private moment of spiritual direction, "some guys would be more flexible in how they worked with people."

The whole issue of Communion for divorced and remarried Catholics, in Libera's mind, needs a thorough reexamination. "The largest religious denomination in the United States is the Catholic Church," he says, "and the second largest are people who used to be active members of the Catholic Church, many of whom moved on because of the divorce and remarriage piece."

> You've got to get through barriers of alienation before people feel comfortable in the Church. We've got this legal way of expressing things in our western Church. The eastern Church, the Orthodox, has some wisdom in terms of allowing subsequent marriages with some penitential element and not getting caught up in annulments—which can be a ministry if people are willing to walk that route. But there're ways of allowing people to enter into relationships that don't have to be maneuvered through an annulment process to try to stay faithful to the tradition. There're other ways of honoring the tradition that are part of broader Christianity. I would try to look at that whole thing. There's more that could be done.

Tom Libera made some good friends in his work with the divorced and separated; he acknowledges, however, that although a few groups remain, the whole way that Catholics view marriage has changed. "There are other outlets for people who divorce, or they just make their own decisions. They don't have to deal with the stigma that they had in the past. But it was a hot ministry that went on for years after I went to another parish. It made me feel like I was making a unique contribution there."

....

For three of the classmates, all spending their first assignments on either the Southwest Side or in the southwest suburbs, one issue consistently challenged them in their relations with the laity: race. Unlike Larry Duris and Mike Ahlstrom, who had both spent most of their childhoods in the northern suburbs, Ed Upton, who hailed from the South Side, was not surprised by his parishioners' racial prejudice. Upton, it will be recalled, used to argue with his father about race, and he and many of his parishioners found themselves on opposite sides of the issue as well. "At Alexander's," he says, "the biggest resistance was the parish sharing program. Bishop Bill McManus ('39) started this idea of sharing between parishes. Larry Duris, at the time, was at Holy Cross Parish. I said to McGillicuddy, 'Why don't we share with them?' But you're talking about the South Side in 1970."

Holy Cross was a South Side African-American parish with much poverty. Frequently Upton heard some version of the following response when advocating that St. Alexander's participate in the sharing program: "Why are we sharing with those damn n - - - - - -?" Eventually he and the pastor at Alexander's decided on the path of least resistance. They mailed envelopes to parishioners so those who wanted to donate could do so quietly. Over time the parish sponsored some activities with their sharing parish. "It was not totally embraced," Ed recalls. "It was tolerated."

Upton came at least to understand his parishioners' perspective. Many of them had reluctantly fled South Side city parishes during the many years of rapid neighborhood racial change. Bitterness remained. "These were people who had lived in St. Sabina's, St. Dorothy's," he says. "They saw it as they had gotten pushed out. If not they, their parents." Many had hoped to re-create in Palos the parish-centered lives they had lived in their city neighborhoods. But they found it difficult to do so. "When I first got there," Ed explains, "the big thing was that at St. Sabina's they had had roller skating and dances and 'Can't we do that here?' People were trying to replicate the parish being the center of the community. At Alexander's, parish life wasn't going to be that, but they had hoped it would. Those days were gone. There really were no neighborhoods. We were in subdivisions. And there wasn't a single school that everyone attended."

While Upton says racial attitudes at the parish did not improve in his six years there, he did find significant improvement when he took the long view. After founding another parish not far from St. Alexander's in 1990, he encountered a changed landscape: the parish's biggest committee involves outreach to the poor. "The amount of time and effort that people want to give is incredible," he says. "That has been a shift. There's some of that bias still there, but there is a much better sense of—social justice probably is too strong a word because that's more transformative of systems and I don't know if we're there yet. But there is a great willingness to help people. We have a Catholic Charities subcommittee; they do 800 backpacks in the fall for kids, Easter baskets, and at Christmas the outpouring is terrific."

Upton reflected on what he learned at St. Alexander's about confronting racial attitudes. The Clergy Association in the area, including Upton, had signed a letter in the *Southtown Economist* newspaper supporting open housing for the southwest suburbs. He also preached on the issue. After hearing complaints, Ed Upton came to an important understanding. "Even having gotten them angry about open housing," he recalls, "in the end they don't walk away. People respected you if you were thoughtful. They might say, 'You're wrong. You're just a young stupid kid.' But they also thought, 'There's some truth to that.' If you try to articulate what the issues are, and connect it with Scripture, you don't need to make the conclusion for them. They know what your conclusion is. They get angry, but you're respecting them. So you stand for something without being ideological."

....

If race was an issue for Upton in Palos, it appeared to be *the* issue for Larry Duris on the Southwest Side. And having spent most of his life in a northern suburb, Duris, unlike Upton, felt shocked at the prejudice he found at St. Ethelreda, where so much appeared to revolve around the color of one's skin. He had arrived on the scene with great confidence. "I walk in," he remarks, "and say this is going to be fine because it's a changing parish. I know what it's like to be white, and I've worked in the black community the past five years." Very soon, however, he faced disillusionment. "I certainly knew nothing," he admits, "about the white South Side Irish Catholic community—I mean nothing." Larry would sit looking out his window in the evenings: "I remember my first summer," he says, "wondering if there's anyone for miles around that thinks or feels like I do." He persuaded pastor Ed Cronin to hire the parish's first DRE, but when she made changes in the school, "she became the whipping post for people," Duris recalls. "Of course we were doing this for 'them.'" The irony of this accusation was that the school had only ten black students out of an enrollment of over 600. As Duris puts it, "just a few specks of pepper."

Early on, Larry discovered that physical boundaries carried huge importance in the neighborhood. The parish went from 83rd to 91st Street north and south, about a mile long. The east/west boundaries went from Loomis to Damen, a distance of about three quarters of a mile. "When I got to Ethelreda's," Duris says, "Loomis to Ashland (a quarter of a mile east to west) was black from 83rd to 91st. The other side was all white. Maybe two black families. I was there two years and there was movement—and this constant whispering: 'Did you hear on Marshfield? Did you hear on Paulina?' Two or three times walking across Ashland, I had a parishioner driving by holler at me: 'What are you going over to that side for?' or, 'Make sure you defend us when you go over there.' I discovered," he reiterates, "I did not know the South Side Irish Catholic community."

Duris met families who had moved fairly short distances two or three times before ending up in St. Ethelreda. "I couldn't understand," he contends, "how, if they didn't want to live near black people, the first move wouldn't have been many miles away up to the North Side. But it was like the community almost moved together."

Racial tensions caused Larry to confront the negatives of the Catholic tradition of community-based parish living. "Our parishes," he says, "are our greatest strength and yet at times our greatest weakness." In other words, parishes are great communities for those who live in them, but God forbid the arrival of those who don't fit in.

Duris also discovered that some of the clergy in the area did not always stand on the side of racial justice. Father Francis Lawlor, an Augustinian priest who taught at St. Rita High School on the Southwest Side, had started block clubs in many South Side parishes, including Ethelreda's. The clubs usually denied that their express purpose was to refuse to sell homes to blacks, but Duris disagrees. "The duplicity of this 'We're not against blacks' was nonsense," he says. "It was the classic 'Keep them out' block clubs. When I got there, the first half dozen people who invited me over to their house and nuzzled up to me were Lawlorites. They tried to win me over, that they were the defenders of the parish." Lawlor himself developed quite a following and ended up getting elected alderman. Duris made one to-the-point comment about his fellow priest: "Jerk. Prime, in my humble opinion."

Despite the lack of nearby clerical role models, as a young priest Larry felt responsible to help shepherd his entire flock, and he therefore worked both to reach out to the parish's black newcomers and to address existing racial prejudice. "We had 10 black families coming to Mass," he says. "I tried to get them involved. How did one person put it so beautifully? 'Don't worry, we're not leaving, but we don't feel a need to be part of everything right now.' They were basically saying, 'We know you're not ignoring us and where you're at, even though we get the stares and the looks from others.'"

Attempting to confront such racist attitudes, however, came with its own repercussions for the staff. "When we did speak out," Duris recalls, "there were reactions. My second year, Deacon Erwin Friedl and I talked at all the Masses one Sunday because of what had happened the day before First Communion."

> A bunch of white kids at a teen party had gone after the party to 87th Street and beaten up a black kid and an Asian kid, had put them in the hospital. So we preached on race. Monday morning I go into the garage and the two fenders of my little Barracuda are smashed in. Friedl's old car, his windshield was gone. You could see the footprints. We were also having a real problem with vandalism, but people couldn't see it was the white teenagers sitting on the wall on Paulina. You talked to parents, and their kids could do no wrong. The only problem this community had was "them" across Ashland.

Larry Duris spent just over two years at Ethelreda. He considered asking for two one-year extensions so as to witness the birth of a "new" parish. But he was open to moving if a challenging assignment in the black community opened up. Soon enough, it would.

....

Although he eventually came to understand and respect the people at St. Bernadette's, Mike Ahlstrom, like Larry Duris, first reacted to the racial attitudes of some of his south suburban parishioners with shock. "I grew up a North Sider, then an Evanston North Shore liberal," he explains. "I was used to having black kids in school with me. I could not believe the open bigotry that I encountered in Evergreen Park. People had moved two or three times through changing neighborhoods and they were scared. I thought they didn't have any brains. If they wanted to run, why didn't they run way out instead of a mile? Each time they'd lose money on the value of their home, which is part of what brought on their anger."

Ahlstrom initially faced his shock by confronting parishioners directly about their racial attitudes. He found it difficult, however, to convey to the adults the message that racial prejudice was wrong, in part because the pastor, Morgan O'Brien, who hailed from Chicago's South Side, shared many of his parishioners' views.

The new musical group Up With People, which consisted almost solely of young adults, received Ahlstrom's permission to practice at Bernadette's for an upcoming concert in the Chicago area. "We were having lunch," Ahlstrom says of O'Brien, "and there was a big picture window looking out on the parking lot. This car came in. O'Brien said, 'Who are all those young people getting out of the car?' I said, 'Up With People.' Another car pulls up—more young people. 'What are they doing here?' I said, 'They're a church choir coming to practice.' 'Okay.' The next car pulls in. 'Uh-oh, there's a n - - - - - getting out of the car.' Then, 'The car is full of n - - - - - -. What are we going to do?'" As Mike shakes his head at the memory, he tells a countervailing story about the pastor. Catholic school kids had been harassing a black patient who parked near the school while visiting a doctor at Little Company of Mary Hospital. "O'Brien told those kids off: 'You have no right to talk to anyone like that.' So he knew deep down that is not the way he was supposed to be, but this was what spontaneously came out of him."

Over time, Ahlstrom's strategy for confronting the race issue changed substantially, although not consciously. "It changed," he says, "by the grace of God. I don't think I recognized this at the time, but I learned that part of priesthood is falling in love with people, and when you're in love with somebody, you accept them the way they are. You don't demand they change."

You hope they'll change, but you take them where they are and just love them. The irony was that's what opened them up to change. And it's a lot more fun loving people than fighting them. That doesn't mean that I changed my ideals. But I learned to challenge people in a loving instead of a confronting way. Instead of saying, "You people," I'd say, "We need to talk." So I grew, and I call that the grace of God.

By the time Mike Ahlstrom left Bernadette's at the end of his first assignment, he noticed subtle shifts in the attitudes of some parishioners: "One guy said, 'You know what I like about you, Mike? You totally disagree with me about those [blacks], but I respect you because you take me where I am, and you know I know I'm not right.' Because I accepted him, it opened him up to realize that he wasn't right with his bias."

....

Ed Upton and Bill Zavaski ended up learning the same lesson—that the important thing was first to care about their people—through meeting illness and death in their first parishes. Upton in particular found this side of parish ministry difficult to negotiate. "One thing I learned on CPE (Clinical Pastoral Education)," he recalls, "is when you grew up in an alcoholic family with a lot of fighting and conflict, my strategy was to walk away. I'm never comfortable in tense situations, so I want to walk away. And I never wanted to give pious platitudes. I've often felt that in those situations I have not been helpful because I don't want to say, 'It's God's will' or 'It's going to be all right.' I don't believe that. So oftentimes less is more: to be with people and let them express whatever they are trying to say." He struggled, however, with what to say in place of platitudes. "I realized that you don't need a lot of words," he explains. "When you've experienced death, you realize that the most helpful people are just people who are present. They don't do a lot of explanations." Ed Upton learned to apply this to his ministry as a whole. "The real takeaway is if people know that you care about them," he says, "you can go a long way. They will love you. If they think you don't care, or if you're distant, that's trouble, but if they know that you have a connection with them, people will accept your foibles. People tell me, 'You were great—the kids loved you.' I don't have a bloody clue what the heck I did or if it had any impact. But it was true that I did care about the kids, and that effort is what people remember."

Bill Zavaski too had shied away from hospital ministry, preferring the more active, upbeat side of parish life. A chaplain at a nearby hospital told him, however, that he must visit people in the hospital. "If you don't go," she said, "you will miss where you really will touch people's lives." He followed her advice, to learn that crises often create the strongest ties among parishioners and their priests. "We had a family that had a terrible automobile accident," Zavaski explains. "They were going to their oldest son's graduation at University of Illinois, and the two youngest children and the grandfather were killed. It was one of the most traumatic events we ever had here."

> I became very close to those people, just because I ran to the hospital to sit with them. The three of them were all buried from here at the same time. It was awful. They were two grade school kids. The kids in the school were devastated. Through painful experiences you develop some really close bonds with people. They shared their struggles with me. I guess I was one of them.

Any priest who humbly saw himself as one of his people fit the spirit of the times in the U.S. Church in the early '70s. For Bill Zavaski at least, being one with his people was not an abdication of leadership, but rather his chosen method and style of leading his people in faith. "I didn't put the collar on," he says, referring to the just-noted tragedy. "I still don't wear the collar. There's not that distance where I'm different than you. These were my friends. Developing relationships is a primary act of a parish priest, to feel that people are part of my family."

Working as new priests all across the archdiocese in their new parish assignments, members of the class of 1969 had to adjust to a strange new reality: For the first time in over 12 years, they didn't see each other every day. This raised questions all classmates face upon graduation, namely whether and how they would keep and strengthen the bonds they had forged at school.

Most priests in Chicago take Thursdays as their day off. Initially after ordination, these classmates traveled to one another's parishes to visit. But rectories left little room for privacy. Someone suggested the idea of buying a house for the class. When they met to discuss it, 16 members, nearly half the class, decided to purchase a house in Michigan City, Indiana. "Good thing. Great thing," Larry Duris says now. "It kept a group of us together."

The 16 who purchased the house included Ahlstrom, Duris, Heidenreich, Upton, and Zavaski. "We called it 'Pinion,'" Zavaski explains, "because it's a place of refuge, like under the bird's wing." Early on, the refuge included a fair amount of partying. "The first couple of years," Duris says, "the house was like a toy." "We were pretty wild," Zavaski concurs. "It was 1970. We were 26 years old. We'd get up there on Wednesday night and go to 3 or 4 a.m. and then sleep till 11. Our poor neighbors." Over time, the men used the house to host family events, staff meetings, and parish retreats for small groups. Primarily, however, Pinion served as a gathering place for the classmates. "We saw it as important," Duris says, "to have peer relationships; the *esprit de corps* was attractive." Tom Libera, although not part of Pinion, referred to it as "our home" and saw its value. "That was a way of holding people together," he says, while also mentioning the annual class Mass and dinner, "a place to acknowledge that we do appreciate and respect each other. There is a broad support among all of us for getting together that is part of the glue that kept us going."

The group sold the original house, building one in New Buffalo, Michigan in 2007. They spoke of Pinion with gratitude. "Of the Pinion group," Mike Ahlstrom recalls, "I'd been close to only one or two in seminary. That became a bond of new friends." "There's a bit of competition in the group," Bob Heidenreich admits, "but also a tremendous amount of support. It's been one of the best things for me." Zavaski agreed. "I love it. I bet every one of the people in the house feels that way. Our class has been very tight because of the house."

Fortified by their unity as a class, many sustained by their experiences at Pinion, these six members of the class of 1969 arrived at the end of their first assignments still enthusiastic about their priesthood. Although they had faced difficulties, they had begun to find a comfort level as priests. They found that they could indeed organize, lead, preach, counsel, and even learn to confront, directly or indirectly, some of the problematic aspects of parish life. As they prepared to move into their second assignments, one thing was crystal clear: To a man, they loved working with the laity. This would serve them well their entire lives.

···

1. For many years, Heidenreich has been involved in the *Crossing Over* project, a collaboration between the Archdiocese of Chicago and five dioceses in northwest Germany.
2. Opened in Michigan in 1956, Guest House is a nonprofit, charitable organization dedicated to the treatment of Catholic priests, deacons, brothers, seminarians and (since 1994) women religious with alcoholism, other chemical dependencies, and related problems. For men's treatment call 1-800-634-4155. For women's treatment, call 1-800-626-6910.

CHAPTER 7

MOVING TOWARD LEADERSHIP
A Variety of Assignments
....

By the time the priests from the class of 1969 had completed their first assignments, they had clearly moved beyond both their training days in seminary and the exhilaration and confusion of being the new priest on the job. As they took on their subsequent assignments, they often found that more was expected of them both in their parishes and, over time, in the archdiocese as a whole. Veteran priests now, they continued to learn from the people, but they also kept a closer eye on their pastors, for the simple reason that they knew that eventually the time would come for them to take the helm of a parish. If the lessons of their seminary training and their first assignments focused mainly on how to be an effective priest, during their subsequent assignments the men from the class of 1969 began to learn how to lead.

....

To lead, one must have seen leadership exercised well. And, for the most part, these young priests served under effective pastors. At times, however, they had to learn the hard way about how not to lead. After serving seven years at St. James in Arlington Heights, Bill Zavaski accepted an assignment to St. Zachary's in the northwest suburb of Des Plaines, the next town south and east. Zavaski found his new pastor to be a study in contradictions. On the one hand, he was generous. On the other, he tended toward a combative and at times flighty personal style that made him difficult to live with. "He was very kind and sensitive," Zavaski says, "good to people if they got in trouble."

But he told me after I was there two months that he was
extremely jealous of me. I was stunned. He could not understand
how I could get along with all these people. Evidently he was
more of an introvert. He had a tough time working with people.
I had this ease about connecting with people because I am an
extrovert. He was difficult because he loved to argue with people.
It was part of his Irish heritage, I guess.

Zavaski remembered a harrowing clash between the pastor and the parish's transitional deacon. "These two Irishmen," he says, "had this big fight one night."

The deacon came in late or left the door open or didn't put the
garbage out. The pastor would be upset if people left dishes in the
sink. That's just the way he was. I'm up at our house in Michigan
City. The deacon called me and said, "I just called him a f------
lunatic." I couldn't believe this. I said, "Get in the car and come
here right now." I wanted him out of there. I was petrified that
anyone would call the pastor this.

During a time when rules about the composition of altar bread were taken less seriously than they are today, the pastor also made a less than wise choice about bread to use for Holy Thursday. "He bought 100 dozen Parker House rolls," Zavaski recalls, laughing. "He consecrated all the Parker House rolls. We went through 50 dozen, but we couldn't put the remaining mounds of Eucharist back in the tabernacle. We had to find a room to put the Blessed Sacrament in and then try to use it. But the Parker House rolls got hard. Easter Sunday we're trying to get rid of the rolls. Our seminarian is holding up the Body of Christ. A guy took a bite of it and left the rest in his hand. He said, 'What do I do?' I said, 'Put it back. Give it to somebody later down the line.' What were you going to do?"

Ed Upton also struggled with a lack of leadership from his pastor when his second assignment took him to St. Fabian's in the blue-collar southwest suburb of Bridgeview. In his three years there, he learned what a difference the presence of a not so good pastor could make to parish life. "My pastor was a wonderful guy," Upton says. "But I learned absolutely nothing from him. He had no clue what he was doing. He didn't have a vision. He didn't lead the parish."

> *I never could figure out what he did all day. The parish had done a parish development project. At the third meeting of the steering committee, he starts asking questions. I'm saying to myself, "We did this at the last meeting." He had blacked out. He was totally smashed and didn't remember a thing. His drinking was dysfunctional. He'd come for religious ed—the nun would say, "You're drunk. Go back to the rectory."*

Much more fortunate, Tom Libera rejoiced at the chance to serve under the pastor of his second assignment, St. Eulalia's Parish, in the near western suburb of Maywood. Eulalia's encompassed the increasingly African-American Maywood and parts of Broadview, still predominantly white. Msgr. William Quinn ('41), who served as pastor there from 1967 until 1986, also directed the U.S. Bishops' Committee for Migrant Workers and had attended the Second Vatican Council as the U.S. bishops' liaison to the Latin American bishops. Trained at Mundelein by the noted Msgr. Reynold Hillenbrand ('29), Quinn spent a lifetime focused on social justice and the needs of the poor. He served as a mentor for many young priests, encouraging in different generations scholars such as Fathers Andrew Greeley ('54) and Robert Barron ('86) to pursue higher education. "It was a treasure," Libera notes, "to work with someone like that, with his vision of Vatican II. In a very gentle way, he was a great teacher who encouraged lay leadership."

> *People respected Bill Quinn. He wasn't temperamental or unapproachable. We opened up a chapel for the weekday Masses in a basement room of the school. Typically, we called it the Thomas More Gathering Room. It was characteristic of Quinn's spirit to name the room for a layperson who tried to live the faith out in the world with its complications.*

When Libera got the opportunity to become the chair of the independent Association of Chicago Priests (ACP), Quinn supported him. "He let me take the time away that I needed, at least two days a week," Libera remembers with gratitude. In a study in contrasts, for five days a week Libera lived and worked under the master of communication—Bill Quinn. The other two days, he labored at the ACP office and, as a later chapter will reveal, vainly attempted to dialogue with a leader who all but ignored him—Cardinal John Cody.

....

Although it took some of them a while to find their niche, eventually these six priests began to concentrate their efforts in specific ministries. Working in the areas of liturgy and sacraments, Catholic education, social justice, and training lay and clerical leaders in collaborative ministry would all prove important not only in and of themselves but also in terms of helping them one day lead parishes and run programs in the Archdiocese of Chicago.

When Mike Ahlstrom's term at St. Bernadette's ended in 1975, the Personnel Board assigned him to St. Gertrude's in Franklin Park. Ahlstrom, who had never so much as driven through Franklin Park, a blue-collar suburb west of the city, found that his early skepticism soon changed to excitement—so much so that he later claimed his experience at St. Gertrude's surpassed that of any of the other parishes at which he served as an associate. Mike got his "hands dirty" doing just about everything in the parish. "The parish was totally dead," he explains. "By the time I left there were 20 organizations. I started 16 of them: the pastoral council, ministries to the sick and the engaged, youth ministry and young adult ministry." Father—later Bishop—Jim Keleher ('58), then rector of Mundelein Seminary, took notice of Ahlstrom's success and began sending newly ordained priests to Gertrude's so Mike could mentor them. "I don't know how I did it all," Ahlstrom reflects. "I could never operate at that pace today." But at the time the young priest felt, as he says, "at the height of my energy."

Despite having a hand in developing so many parish activities, Ahlstrom, like most of his classmates, focused on one area in particular. While at Gertrude's, Ahlstrom spent parts of four summers at the University of Notre Dame, earning a master's degree in liturgy. He felt proudest of his work in the Rite of Christian Initiation for Adults (RCIA), a program that welcomes non-Catholics who wish to convert or be baptized as well as Catholics who had never received the sacraments of Eucharist, Reconciliation, or Confirmation as children and prepares them to receive those sacraments.

"I used to worry about content," Ahlstrom says about his involvement in RCIA. "I was giving them a mini-seminary course in theology and Scripture. It was the laypeople that said, 'Michael, stop worrying about that stuff. That's not what they need. They need to learn how we pray, how we do Church, how we belong to a parish.' Not that we didn't talk about Church teachings and Scripture, but it was put in a context. The lay ministers helped me learn what RCIA was all about. It isn't me giving instructions. It is parishioners working with me as a team welcoming people into the life of the Catholic Church." Once Ahlstrom came to this realization, he changed tactics. "I began by running it myself," he says, "but then I groomed people to take it over. I took a back seat so it would continue when I was no longer there."

After serving six years at St. Gertrude's, Mike Ahlstrom spent another six years at Mary Seat of Wisdom Parish in Park Ridge, an upper middle-class suburb just north of Chicago. He then transferred to Tom Libera's home parish, the working-class, multi-ethnic, but Polish-dominant enclave of Immaculate Heart of Mary. While at these parishes, Ahlstrom continued to focus on the laity and liturgy—especially RCIA, which he started at three different parishes—until the opportunity to take a pastorate presented itself.

....

Tom Libera discovered his niche at St. Eulalia's in the Christ Renews His Parish (CRHP) retreats. Held for men and women separately twice per year, these retreats, modeled on the Cursillo movement, invited people quite unused to sharing their personal journeys in faith to do just that, in order to inspire others making the retreat to reflect on the presence of God in their lives. "They were a wonderful way of forming people to do witness," Libera says, "something Catholics don't naturally do. They brought people together to form a whole generation of parish leadership."

Not surprisingly, Bill Zavaski quickly involved himself with the social aspects of parish life at St. Zachary's, including picnics, carnivals, and parties. "I was there three years," Zavaski says. "I developed relationships with three couples who have become my closest friends." But another area stood out because of its uniqueness: Catholic education. Most parishes in Chicago during the 1970s had a well-attended Catholic grade school. The children who attended religious education or CCD (Confraternity of Christian Doctrine) classes for instruction on a Saturday or Sunday for 90 minutes usually had parents who either couldn't afford the Catholic school tuition or who, in some—usually suburban—communities, thought the public schools provided a better education.

But religious education at Zachary's was different. "The school," Zavaski explains, "had a timeshare with the local public school. The students could go half a day to the public school and half a day to the Catholic school five days a week. It was the sweetest setup."

Half the class took their religious education and some other classes in the parish school in the morning. Then they would go to the local public school for science and subjects not offered in the Catholic school in the afternoon. The other half of the class did the reverse. The sharing of facilities was phenomenal. I've never seen that in any other parish.

"When the pastor left," Zavaski laments, "the new pastor decided that this setup wasn't smart. Honest to God, it was the smartest thing you could do." Later, when Zavaski became a pastor, he would continue to experiment with ways to pass on the faith to young Catholics.

....

After two years at the racially changing St. Ethelreda, Larry Duris in 1971 accepted an assignment to Holy Cross Parish on the Southeast Side of Chicago. Holy Cross stood in the urban Woodlawn neighborhood, just south of the University of Chicago. After staying up all night talking to his new pastor, Father Les Mollohan ('51), Duris took a drive through what would soon be his new community. "I'm going east on 65th Street," he recalls, "and it's a couple of vacant lots. The rest of the lots had buildings, but all but two were burned out. I said, 'What did I just say yes to?' It's 3 a.m. and it looks like Berlin or Dresden after the bombings during World War II. But I decided to go."

Larry clearly saw ministry in the African-American community as not only a conscious choice but also a lifelong one. "People are very sensitive to whether someone has unpacked their bags for the duration," he says, "rather than being someone who is just passing through. People will say at times about a white minister in a black parish, 'He never unpacked his bags.' What are they saying? Everything from physical fear that he never came to terms with, to not valuing the richness of the community, to this was never home for him."

For Duris, the commitment to immersing himself in the African-American community had its challenges. He told a harrowing story. "Got to know some families on Drexel Avenue," he says, "who were across the alley from the school."

One night got a phone call right after the 5:00 Saturday evening Mass. "Come down here. Something is wrong at Elva Mae's." So I ran down the block and upstairs to the second floor, and old lady Mama Kate, 70-something, is trying to get down the back stairs in the ice and snow. We get down to the first floor, back door is open and she's looking for her friend Elva Mae. She sensed something had gone terribly wrong. I looked through the kitchen and dining room and I see Elva Mae on the floor tied up. So I stuff Mama Kate in the pantry. I said, "Don't move until I come and get you." I go into the dining room and there's Elva Mae's head tied up. I go to pull this stuff off and suddenly my hands are all full of dried blood and the top of her head is gone. Shot in the head. Got to open the door for the police. I walk by the bedroom and there's a sheet with bullet holes with her husband under it. It was a nephew, would you believe, on drugs, looking for money. One or the other of them surprised him and he panicked. This helps you grow up.

Many people, including many of the white clergy, would have sought an immediate transfer after facing such violence. But Larry saw something beyond that violence when he witnessed people's response to the tragedy. "It was one of those blocks," he remarks, "where people looked out for each other. What set off the idea that something was wrong was that Elva Mae wasn't at bingo at Holy Cross that Saturday. Nobody had heard from her. The way people pulled together was amazing."

Duris' empathy with his parishioners' struggles led him to commit more deeply to ministry at Holy Cross, with a particular focus on the themes of liberation and social justice that resonated with his African-American congregation. He has long believed, for example, that the presence of Catholic schools in the black community is a great vehicle for justice. Holy Cross had more than 500 children attending its school, a large number for an African-American Catholic parish. The pastor had also hired one of the first black lay principals in the archdiocese. Many Catholics, clergy included, however, failed to see the value of such an approach. "There was a sense among some," Larry says, "that we were just doing social work in the black community. 'Why are we running schools with all these non-Catholic kids?' Our sense was that the school was a tool for evangelization and part of our preferential option for the poor. But that was challenged."

Duris' sense of the importance of justice in the Church for "the least of these" extended beyond school children. Over time, he invested heavily in community organizations because of his outrage at seeing the neighborhood's housing stock literally burn to the ground.

We were in the midst of the burn-down of Woodlawn. I don't believe in conspiracies, but I did believe that the University of Chicago had something to do with it. When you'd watch certain blocks, especially adjacent to 61st Street [near campus] disappear within a year's time, it looked systematic. There were times where there was a major fire once or twice a week: 12 flat, 18 flat, 24 flat. These big courtyard buildings were being torched.

The fires led Larry to join The Woodlawn Organization (TWO), which worked primarily on improving housing conditions, initially focusing its efforts on the University of Chicago, long rumored to have had a role in the "clearance" of Woodlawn. After the university reached a settlement with the community by agreeing to help build a new housing development, TWO turned its attention to calling slum-lords to task.

He also joined another community group, founded by Les Mol-lohan, the 65th Street Building Corporation, which consisted largely of Holy Cross parishioners attempting to rehab apartment buildings and "save" Woodlawn by offsetting the massive loss in housing stock due to slum landlords, lack of upkeep, abandonment, and fire. The corpora-tion successfully rehabbed six buildings during Duris' tenure. "Les and I babysat a building on Ingleside for about a month and a half," he says of an effort to prevent another burn-out, "before we could get funding to get security service. He and I took turns sleeping in this abandoned apartment building. No electricity. But we did have a phone installed. This is before cell phones. I never told my mother until years later."

Larry Duris enjoyed Holy Cross so much that at the end of his five-year term he applied for an extension. Circumstances intervened, however, and he ended up becoming a pastor instead.

....

Nearing the end of his five-year term at the working-class St. Martha's, Bob Heidenreich was living his dream of being a regular guy serv-ing regular laypeople. With several months left in his assignment at Martha's, however, he got a call from the Personnel Board asking him to transfer to St. Joseph Parish in the far northwest suburb of Liber-tyville. There, Heidenreich entered a whole new world. "This was not exactly blue-collar working class," he says. "There were great big man-sions. There were companies like Baxter up there and International Harvester, a lot of new homes, and people who were wealthy, but also very professional."

So Bob struggled in his early days in Libertyville. "St. Joe's was a whole different ballgame compared to Martha's," he explains. "I had known how to deal with those folks. So for the first year I was out of my league. I don't think I did well. I felt threatened by the people. If they don't like what you're doing, they tell you."

Despite his early difficulties at St. Joe's, however, Heidenreich's time there proved most fruitful. "In a sense it prepared me for coming to Sacred Heart as pastor," he says, "because I learned a number of lessons from some very smart people, CEOs."

> *I started learning how to act with more sophisticated people. I'm still learning. The challenge that I got from those people was I can't get up and shoot from the top of my head. I had to think things through. I learned an awful lot of organizational skills. If you ask me where I got the confidence in myself as a minister, it was at St. Joe's.*

As Bob's confidence grew, he decided to face what he saw as the thorniest problem in ministering in a well-to-do community. "How do you deal with people with power," he asks, "and at the same time preach the Gospel which, if it's not challenging, it's not the Gospel?"

People with money and influence in their professional life expect to get their way. "The Germans feel that we're hampered in our preaching," Bob Heidenreich says, referring to his clerical colleagues in the Catholic Church in Germany, "by the fact that we're dependent on the people for money. I never realized that, but you don't want to say things that upset too many people. That's one of the downsides. But people who donate to the Church," he notes, turning his attention to the upside, "are involved in the Church. The more a person is involved, the more they want to see it succeed and actually the more they want the Gospel preached. And you can't recruit people into jobs as lectors, Eucharistic ministers, or visitors of the sick without training them. And when you train, you preach the Gospel. Once they start hearing it, they understand."

....

At the end of the day, whether invested most in liturgy, Catholic education, social justice, or training parish leadership, these priests focused relentlessly on their ministry not only to, but with, the laity. Although mostly this involved direct contact with laypeople, two of the classmates, ironically, made a major contribution to the laity of the diocese by working with seminarians and priests.

After three years at St. Fabian's, Ed Upton still had no clearly defined role. "There was no school," he says. "There were two competent nuns who ran religious ed who, in a nice way, didn't want clerical interference, which was fine. Another sister visited the homebound and hospitals." Unlike his first assignment at St. Alexander's, where he had experienced a good transition, worked with a talented pastor, and was discovering his own niches, in Bridgeview Ed struggled with transition, pastor, and niche.

So when Father—later Bishop—Tom Murphy ('58), then rector of Mundelein Seminary, asked him to join the formation faculty there in 1978 to run the deacon internship program, Upton said yes. Using his own parish experiences, good and bad, he put together for seminarians entering the world of parish priesthood a road map so that they might thrive in their work with the laity.

Upton used the same approach that he had in parishes—working closely with people. He formed a committee of students and worked with formation faculty members to create a program. He developed a strong camaraderie with the formation faculty. Father—later Bishop—Jim Keleher took over as rector when the Vatican made Tom Murphy a bishop. Fathers John Canary ('69), Clete Kiley ('74), Lou Cameli ('70), Tom Rzepiela ('72), and—now Bishop—Wilton Gregory ('73) rounded out the formation team. At first Ed relied mostly on his parish experience to help him develop the deacon program. "It was training parish priests to do supervision," he says, "to help deacons reflect and make sure they've learned something about themselves so they can move better into priesthood. I picked good parishes where there'd be a priest able to spend some time with them. I always saw it as being a parish priest. I wasn't a teacher, but a parish priest to the guys."

While at Mundelein, Upton decided to take formal training in order to improve his efforts on behalf of the transitional deacons. He enrolled in Mundelein's Doctor of Ministry (D.Min.) program run by then Father Jack Shea ('67). This experience changed Ed's life because, he says, "it gave me a different perspective. What Shea did was start by having you talk about significant religious experiences and then pull out the theology or the movement of God from the experiences—that was eye-opening."

> We had been taught [in seminary] to learn theology and then push it into experience. That never made any sense to me. Shea had a new way of both looking at the validity of people's experiences and trying to help people come to the movement of God in that experience and how the Church fit. So those two years with him changed the whole way I thought.

In order to receive the D.Min. degree, students had to do a final project. Ed Upton wrote a program that developed a new approach to mentoring the newly ordained. "There was a philosophy," he notes, "that they need to tough it out, don't baby them. But we had had many difficulties in first assignments. Because it's a significant transition for people, I argued you build a series of structures to help bridge that transition."

> The first Mass was a big coronation. Six months later nobody gives a s---. So we put a mentor in that the newly ordained priest could talk to, and organized a peer group so he could put life in context with other guys going through the same thing. We had a meeting with the pastor and staff getting a newly ordained and pointed out that when the guy moves in you can't presume he knows everything; you need to sit down and give him information about your place. Don't wait until he makes a mistake and then yell at him. The image I used to use was: when you go into a parish it's a moving train. It will not stop because you're coming. But the staff can slow it down enough so you can jump on it.

....

After having spent five years developing his organizational skills at St. Joseph's, Bob Heidenreich put those skills to work during a four-year assignment as a member of the priest Personnel Board. The lessons he learned in Libertyville about the importance of professionalism proved quite important. "Here again," Bob recalls, "I was in over my head. I had no idea, initially, of how totally political the thing was." Eleven years in ministry had taught him that most parishes had no systems per se. "How did parishes work?" he asks. "How did you get a school tuition reduced? It was because you knew Father or Sister. How about the person that needed it but wasn't as friendly? That's too bad. Tell me that's just."

According to Heidenreich, the Personnel Board proved no different, in that everything depended on who you knew. So Bob made it a point to learn how personnel systems worked. He discovered that it took explicit operating procedures to make a system just. "It's not like somebody has an evil intention," he says, "but they're into a personnel system based on personal knowledge. They don't even realize they're doing it." So he worked to make the board more systematic and less political. Things slowly began to move in the right direction.

After leaving the Personnel Board in 1983, Heidenreich, while spending the next nine years as an associate at St. Edna's in Arlington Heights, also worked on the archdiocesan pastors' training program. Although it may seem ironic that he trained priests how to be pastors when he had not yet served as one himself, by this time the archdiocese had come to greatly value Bob's talents in developing systems, organizing parish groups, and professionalizing parishes. "It was amazing," he recalls. "Guys would say that they want to be a pastor. I'd say, 'Tell me why.' 'That's what we do,' they'd say, 'we become pastors.' No idea of leadership. None. That was the major thing I worked to introduce."

I see clearly what we were doing now; then it was more instinctive. We were trying to teach the people a "Mystical Body" idea of parish life. Our ecclesiology actually comes from the stuff that Reiny Hillenbrand got from the German and French monasteries. The encounter with Christ at Eucharist is an encounter with scripture and sacrament. But the third encounter

is when Christ is presented to the community and the poor are
fed and the helpless are helped. The pastor's leadership is calling
people into ministries, organizing those ministries. What they all
are is the visible manifestation of Christ in the community.

Nowhere would preaching the Mystical Body prove more diffi-cult than at St. Edna's, where a priest's sexual abuse of minors deeply divided the parish. The pastor and Bob Heidenreich made great efforts to bring healing to that traumatic situation, a story reserved for a chap-ter dedicated to these six priests' experiences facing the abuse scandal that has rocked the Church.

....

Between their first assignments and the time that each of them would eventually become pastors, Fathers Upton, Zavaski, Libera, Heiden-reich, Duris, and Ahlstrom went from being eager young rookies to veteran priests who had learned to deal with a myriad of issues in par-ish ministry. Some of the issues they wrestled with stand out as worthy of more detailed treatment. The next four chapters will treat the most significant of those: liturgy, sacraments, and preaching; relations with the laity, including social justice; youth and Catholic education; and dealing with the three archbishops who have presided over virtually their entire priesthood.

CHAPTER 8

A NEW VISION OF CHURCH
Liturgy, Sacraments, and Preaching

Bob Heidenreich sat down in the pew after the Gospel reading. He leaned forward, intent on hearing the homily. His grammar school classmate's father had died, and he was attending the funeral Mass to pay his respects. He wondered what tips he might pick up on funeral homilies from listening to his brother priest. "The homily was about the pyramids in Egypt," he says. "It had nothing to do with this guy's life, nothing to do with anything. It was meaningless. Shoot me when I do that, because these are special times that you can not only help people but also show them the consolation of God in their lives. There's grace involved in this."

Over the years, Bob's frustration with poor homilies and liturgies has prompted him to reflect on the importance of Mass and why people attend. "We can't talk people into going to church anymore because it's a mortal sin," he says, "or because they have to or because they're going to be holier people. That doesn't make any difference today with younger people."

> So I try to tell people how important Mass is to be a healthy,
> sane person and to live a good life, because there are so many
> ways that we can get off the track and not even know it.
> Sometimes we don't know it until we've come back to church the
> next week and at Mass you say, "Geez, did I screw that up." This
> young yuppie was a trader down at the Mercantile. He said, "I
> have to come to Mass. I have all these temptations. I can cheat

people. I've got to remind myself that this is not the way I want to live. It's easy for me to forget it." That's what we have to be telling people. This is why you do this.

Bob Heidenreich's stories of both the highs and the lows of people's experiences with Mass mirror those of his five classmates.

....

Tom Libera highlighted the six priests' approach to saying Mass. "This is really a philosophy," he insists, "that there should be some good news for everybody every Sunday. No matter what goes on, underneath it all there's supposed to be something good here for everybody. Now if you can help people find that, that's what it should be."

Members of the ordination class of 1969 grew up in the pre-Vatican II Church. As children, from grade school through their years together in the high school seminary at Quigley, and into their second year of college at Niles, they "heard" Mass, to use the popular expression of the day. The priest said the Mass in Latin, with his back to the congregation, in a formal ceremony during which many congregants said private prayers, such as the rosary. When the Second Vatican Council published *Sacrosanctum Concilium* (Constitution on the Sacred Liturgy) in 1963, Church fathers called for the "fully conscious and active participation" of the laity.[1] The document's publication fairly quickly led to changes in the liturgy such as priests saying Mass in the vernacular and relocating the altar with the priest standing behind it to face the people.

During their last year at Niles and throughout their time at Mundelein Seminary, therefore, the class of 1969 heard much about liturgical changes. But their actual training in that regard proved woefully insufficient. One professor, however, made a crucial difference, in terms of their ability to preach good homilies: Father John Foley, a Jesuit. "He made us write these talks," Ed Upton says. "We had to underline the main topic in red. For each paragraph, we had to underline in a different color the key theme and how it was connected to the major theme. We laughed because of the colored pencils. But, basically, that's right.

One idea and then develop it. If people leave Mass, can they at least answer the question: What the heck was the priest talking about? What was his point? If I don't know the point, they're not going to know the point."

Ready or not, then, when the class of 1969 left the seminary to begin their careers as parish priests, they arrived in the midst of an upheaval surrounding Mass and the sacraments. Parishioners were slowly becoming accustomed to the Mass being said in English, but seeing the priest facing the people still could seem shocking to some. After decades of what were universally called "sermons" on catechetical topics, parishioners now heard "homilies" actually trying to relate the scriptures of the day to their daily lives.

"My sense was that the Mass had been distant and impersonal," Upton recalls, "and having to face the people made it more personal. So the word was—I almost hate to say it anymore—relevant. We wanted to make it relevant." Upton did home Masses and small group Masses in church and tried to involve laypeople in greater planning of and participation in the liturgy. "Even at morning Mass," he says, "I invited people to stand around the altar. The emphasis was to make it personal for people because it had seemed so impersonal."

Most of the parishioners at Tom Libera's first assignment at St. Ladislaus embraced the changes in the Mass. He says, "People would come up with a new backdrop every week for the altar, putting a lot of work into the environment of the Mass. I was involved with some dialogue homilies." Not everyone, however, appreciated his efforts. "You wouldn't want that at the Polish Mass," he acknowledges. "That was traditional. You'd hear remarks like, 'We're not doing it the way we used to.' So you had a blending of tradition and openness to new things."

The African-American Catholic community where Larry Duris served found itself adapting not only to the liturgical changes wrought by the Second Vatican Council but also to alterations in black Catholic identity. Throughout the 1950s and early 1960s, the Catholic Church had focused on convert-making and Catholic education in African-American neighborhoods. Black Catholics lived their Catholicism much as white Catholics did, enlisting the aid of the Church as a spiritual, moral, and educational guide as they sought socio-economic status and success in U.S. society.

With the advent of the civil rights and subsequent black power movements in civil society—dovetailing with the period of the Second Vatican Council in the Church—the concept of African-American Catholicism underwent significant change. Key people emerged, such as Sister Thea Bowman, a Franciscan nun, who gave presentations on intercultural awareness to black Catholic audiences using prayer, Gospel preaching, storytelling, and song. She sought to combine her people's faith with their African and American roots, calling people to their rightful place and to expressing their own culture in the Mass.[2] Dominican Sister Jamie Phelps did similar work, ensuring that Gospel music made its way into black Catholic churches.[3] During the 1970s, black Church leaders founded the National Office of Black Catholics to push for enculturation in liturgy. "In Chicago," Duris says, "we had priests like Father George Clements ('57) strongly involved in that. He was the public face of black Catholic ministry."[4]

Duris remembered the joys and tensions of those days of change, recalling the first Black History Month Mass at the International Amphitheater on the South Side of Chicago, with 5,000 kids attending and Clements celebrating the Mass. "We were learning," Duris says, "from black Catholics who had the black religious tradition interwoven with their Catholic tradition." Duris recalled how tension between parishioners could be broken down by music. "We'd catch flak," he says, referring to his black parishioners, "with, 'Why are we singing these Baptist songs? I left the Baptist Church to get away from clapping and shouting.'"

There were some older, conservative people who were upset with that. Many others felt the opposite. But it was funny to watch someone protest, "Why are we doing this?" and then catch them in the middle of a great gospel song clapping and rocking. You're walking down the aisle and you catch Mrs. So and So's eye and suddenly she straightens herself up. That was great because you could laugh about it later.

Although Bill Zavaski served far from the urban area that Duris toiled in, he agreed that the changes in the Mass were overwhelmingly positive. "First of all," he says impatiently, as if it should be clear to all, "it was in English, and no longer this distant gap between us and the people. The Communion rails were gone. Christ was in the midst of us, the living Body of Christ. People sensed that and, for the most part, loved it."

If one place existed where Mass changes might find resistance, however, Zavaski feared that his home parish of St. Bartholomew's in the Lithuanian area of Waukegan would be it. "When as pastor I introduced the idea of Eucharistic ministers," he says, "none of them thought they could give the Eucharist because they weren't ordained. I conned a few of them into doing it. Gradually they felt it was a privilege that helped them grow closer to Christ. The changes were a way to help bring people together for a sense of community, which is what we're all about."

....

As these six priests grew more experienced in celebrating the sacraments, and as the initial excitement about experimentation slowed and a need developed to consolidate the many changes in the liturgy, the men of the class of 1969 put their shoulders to the wheel, as they were always wont to do. They set to work coordinating liturgical practice with their lay Catholic parishioners who had joined them on parish liturgy committees.

After a few years in which weekly liturgical themes loomed large, with the making of banners and other decorations to reflect those themes, however, these priests began to have second thoughts. "I said," Ed Upton recalls, "what are we really planning? We have a form. Let's do it well. We don't have to reinvent it every Sunday. Follow the outline. Do good music, as John Cusick ('70) said, give a homily that somebody can get something out of. We used to have meetings for hours to get a one-sentence theme for the Mass. Who cares? No one pays attention —it's gone."

Bob Heidenreich's views on the liturgy developed when he wrote his paper for the Doctor of Ministry degree at Mundelein Seminary on forming a functioning parish liturgy committee. Today he points to the strong connection between attendance at Mass and passing on the faith to one's children. As part of the follow-up to the recent Catholics Come Home program aimed at disaffected Catholics, archdiocesan leaders conducted an online survey asking respondents true or false questions about tenets of the Catholic faith. Heidenreich noticed that both those who attended Mass regularly and those who didn't knew the answers to questions such as: Is Jesus the Son of God? "The big difference," he explains, "was in belief. The people who went to Mass every week were strong in these beliefs, the others were not. Knowing the facts is not enough. How do we get people to appropriate it? Going to Mass every week has a role in helping people to appropriate it."

Larry Duris found that leading worship in the African-American community profoundly affected him over the years. "It was at Holy Cross," he says, "where worship changed my style of praying, making it more affective. In music, in prayer, and in preaching there's more dialogue. The first time some people hear 'Amen' called out they think, 'What's this?' That's great when that happens; it means you said something. There are all types of black styles, but key is a development around a word, a theme, the core messages of a song, with a particular sensitivity to the power of and the need for liberation, redemption, struggle, determination."

> People were certainly exposed to that in a public way in the '60s through the civil rights struggle. A lot of that came right out of the church doors. There weren't many black priests around, but black deacons and musicians were instrumental in helping with that. White people ministering in black Catholic communities experimented with discovering their own style: how to incorporate this without pretending to be someone you're not. People will help to train and guide you if you're open to their way of experiencing life, and vice versa. They'll let you know when you're not being yourself.

Alone among his classmates, Mike Ahlstrom had developed an

early interest in the Mass and sacraments. "I actually wound up training servers while I was at Quigley," Ahlstrom says, "and that's where I first fell in love with liturgy." At Niles, Ahlstrom coordinated the Mass for Shut-Ins that appeared on WGN-TV on Sunday mornings; at Mundelein he served as the seminary's master of ceremonies for all school-wide liturgies. And shortly after his ordination he began to work part-time at the archdiocesan Office of Divine Worship. While there, he put together a training program for ministers of care to the sick, which the archdiocese still uses today. Ahlstrom outlines key elements of that program:

> *The notion of ministry: that you are not just doing the corporal work of mercy of visiting the sick but are representing the Church. Listening skills: how to listen and show compassion and not talk at people. The psychology and theology of suffering: what do people go through emotionally and spiritually? Prayer and sacraments: how do you pray with people? Find out how they're comfortable praying, so you don't impose your way. When you actually do the ritual of giving Communion, how you do that.*

The years spent focused on the sacraments convinced Ahlstrom that welcoming people was the paramount liturgical virtue, especially as regards the potential for bringing them to the practice of the faith. He told a story from his time as pastor of St. Collette's in Rolling Meadows. "The National Conference for Gay and Lesbian Catholic Outreach," he says, "was having its national convention at a hotel in my parish. They invited Cardinal George to say Mass. He wanted Mass in a church instead of a hotel." So George asked Ahlstrom to host the Mass, warning him to expect protesters and a large media presence. "I ran it by my pastoral council and staff," he recalls. "We concluded not only could they have Mass, but we'd go out of our way to welcome them."

> *I wound up making the front page of the* Daily Herald: *"Church Extends Olive Branch to Homosexuals." It was a very powerful experience. They did a bomb sweep of the church. Nothing*

happened, but a couple families told me they were quitting the parish because of what I was doing. But four or five talked to me about how their gay children were coming back to church. One woman shared, "My neighbor told me how disgusted she was with you. I didn't have the guts to tell her that my son is gay and this is the best news I've heard, that the Catholic Church and the Cardinal are reaching out."[5]

"While the Church is not going to advocate sex outside of marriage," Ahlstrom acknowledges, "we definitely are welcoming to all gay people. They're not second-class citizens." Treating whoever walked through the doors of a Catholic church as a first-class citizen marked the approach of Ahlstrom and his classmates to sacramental practice. Motivated by this desire, they continue to work hard to develop a more professional approach to their ministry while listening to and honoring the experiences of their parishioners and treating them with compassion.

....

Bill Zavaski used to preach from the pulpit. He wrote out his homilies and read or paraphrased them, using alliteration and turning phrases. Throughout his early assignments he believed this approach worked quite well. Then he went back to Waukegan to pastor his home parish of St. Bartholomew's. "In Waukegan," he explains, "no one sat in the first 15 pews. Everybody was in the back." There was, however, one exception. "When we had the polka Mass," he says with a smile, "everybody came to the front. They had a priest who had a polka band. They did all the Mass parts and songs to polka tunes. I said, 'I should have a polka Mass every week.'"

Unfortunately for Bill, weekly Sunday Masses did not provide the pizzazz for the congregation that the occasional polka Mass clearly did. He wondered how to better reach his congregation situated in row 15 and beyond. "What happened, I'll never forget," he laughs. "One parishioner sat in the seventh pew; he was the closest. He said, 'You read homilies well. But you seem so distant from us.'" Zavaski thought long about that comment. "I'm going to put the text away," he recalls resolving. "I left the pulpit and went up and down the aisle instead. I've never gone back since to reading something. Now, I rely on the Holy Spirit a lot more because I never know what's going to happen."

....

In many ways, Bill Zavaski's move from the pulpit to the aisle symbolizes both the spirituality and pastoral sensibility out of which his and his classmates' preaching has sprung. Bob Heidenreich, for example, began preaching from the aisle when he said Mass as a resident on the West Side at Our Lady Help of Christians. Pragmatism, in part, motivated the change. He attended a workshop on preaching. "I began to realize how rotten—not rotten, but how superficially—I had been preaching over the first 15 years," he says. "Most preachers preach out of their spiritual lives. You have to get in touch with your spiritual life to preach. I began doing more of that." This, in turn, led to a desire to make a closer connection to the people, hence the move away from the pulpit.

Heidenreich's alterations in his preaching style had as much to do with theology as they did with pragmatics. As his concept of the proper role of the priest in relation to his people developed, so too did his sense of how they both could best pray the Mass. "The priest was the celebrant and the congregation was the audience," he says of the pre-Vatican II Mass, "and worship was towards Christ and God, so everything was directed towards the tabernacle. Now, Christ is the presider and the priest facilitates the involvement of the community in being people of prayer worshipping Christ around the altar."

Bob criticizes the current idea of returning the priest to a more distant, formal role and toward moving Christ, if you will, back behind the altar. "Look at the conservatives' design," he says. "They want the tabernacle returned right behind the altar. The little things they've changed, stupid things! Supposedly Eucharistic ministers can't go up and stand behind the altar now—we still do it here—and only the priests can purify the chalice."

What is this? It can be summed up in the word "ministry." The bishops are afraid of that word because it can be applied to

a bishop presiding at Confirmation as well as a Eucharistic
minister distributing Communion. And if it's a generic term,
how do you differentiate? There's something to that if all this is
the beginning of a process to devalue ordination so that ordained
ministry is on the same level as lay ministry. On the other hand,
it seems to me that if we are the Mystical Body of Christ, the
head is not the hand and the hand is not the foot and the foot is
not the knee. There are specifics of what we are called to do. Yet
this is exactly what they're worried about—that you're going to
convince everybody that they should be a minister. Well, what's
wrong with that?

....

Echoing Bob Heidenreich loudly about the importance of the spirituality of the Mass is the one true liturgist in the group, Mike Ahlstrom.
He tries each week to connect the lives of his people to the Scriptures
of the day. "I try to challenge people," Ahlstrom says, "to expand their
attitudes, to open their hearts more. Everything is a celebration of Paschal Mystery, of dying and rising. But that has to be internalized. Our
primary task is to surrender our life to God. I talk about the 12-step
program where the third step is the hardest, where you turn yourself
over to the power of God. You're letting go. You're falling into God's
hands.[6] The real purpose of liturgy is ritualizing this process of surrendering to God. It's not just ceremonies or externals. You're doing
something deeper.

"Making the spiritual connection," Ahlstrom concludes, "between Paschal Mystery and liturgy is central. I didn't completely understand that in the '70s."

....

Having spent almost his entire priesthood in the African-American
Catholic community, Larry Duris has come to understand that for
black Catholics the spirituality of the Mass focuses heavily on the
scriptures. "I look at the Word as being a living thing," he says. "I'm

trying to answer the question: what is God's Word saying to this community today?" Unique among the six classmates, Larry meets weekly with several other priests, all serving in African-American parishes, to work on homilies. "Every Tuesday," he explains, "we go over the Scriptures for Sunday for about an hour and a half. That gets you focusing early in the week. That's high priority. I want to give people a handle, a hook. Can you walk out and say: what was the clear message? At the end of Mass, without giving a second homily, I'll do a quick reminder of the theme."

Duris has worked hard to learn to preach meaningfully, listening to black preachers and reading books on preaching in the African-American community. "Some people consider themselves excellent preachers," he says. "I never have. Some say I'm very good. I've certainly gotten better. I work at it. Bad news if you don't." Larry preaches, like most of his classmates, away from the pulpit. Other than a few phrases or an occasional outline, he works without notes.

Working in the black Church affords him opportunities mostly undreamed of in white parishes. "Sometimes I'll segue into the lyrics of a song," he offers, for example, "occasionally even singing. I've even played guitar and sang. I'm 15-20 minutes. I don't do a Father Michael Pfleger ('75) 50-minute or hour-long homily. But a couple of times it's been 25. If I'm going somewhere, that's just fine with people. I've gotten where you shorten it and people are like, 'You must have been out late last night; you had nothing to give us.' I've heard people ask for more.

"Now, some folks in pink parishes," Duris says with a grin, using his unique phrase for white parishes, "couldn't imagine somebody asking us to preach longer. But that's part of the black tradition."

....

In the parishes where Ed Upton has served, the mostly white parishioners have no tradition of music during homilies and would shudder in horror at the thought of even a 20-minute talk. "I try to time it," he says, "to about seven minutes." For those seven minutes, Ed puts in hours of preparation. "The good week," he maintains, "is you start Monday to read the readings every morning. Thursday I dictate a rough draft.

Then Saturday I refine it and get ready Saturday night. I never use a text. But writing it forces discipline and thinking. The question I keep asking myself is, 'What does this Gospel mean for us today?'"

Upton has grown more cautious when preaching on controversial issues. "When I was young," he says, "we preached about open housing and Vietnam. We riled people up. Not that that was our goal, but we viewed agitating people as a good thing. Recently, with the mosque at Ground Zero in New York, I said, 'Here are issues in the context of who we are as believers.' So, not getting into a 'Get the cannons, blow them out of the water, then say I'm a prophet.' I guess I've changed."

Ed has also realized the limits of relying on personal stories to help explain the scriptures. "There's not 20 years of experience since childhood that's worthwhile," he says. For that reason, he stresses the need for priests to keep learning. "We have to continue to read novels," he says, "go to plays, read the paper, and even watch television."

....

As much as Bill Zavaski loves performing in public, he nonetheless admits, "I still get very anxious every time I have to talk on Sundays. But that's a good thing. If I ever lost that, it would be disaster. I spend time praying over the Scriptures, and then begin asking myself what would be good for my people to hear? Thoughts come and I build off of that."

Tom Libera has experimented with several styles of preaching. He used to do extensive reading and tried to cram his learning into a page from which he would paraphrase. Over time, he decided a more focused approach would yield better results. "I'll start from scratch every week and read," he says. "I introduce the Scripture in one or two sentences. Simplicity—I feel less is more in our age. I do it reverently. Don't rush. Be conscious when you might be speeding. Give people a chance to notice you as not hurrying. You've got to be there."

Libera judges his success by asking himself a couple of pointed questions. "Am I putting things in a way," he asks, "that touches people so they become a better parent or feel they're carrying Christ into their work? Am I practical enough for them to be able to take away a story about faith?"

Judging the success of their homilies remains a difficult task for these classmates even after many years of preaching the Gospel. Some of the men get quite a bit of feedback on their preaching, others not so much. "How do you know if you're good?" Ed Upton asks rhetorically. "That's a hard question. It was funny, one time a woman came up to me and said, 'That was a wonderful homily.' I wasn't trying to be a smart aleck—I said, 'What was it that you liked?' She said, 'I forgot.' She was so embarrassed.

"Honest to God," he says with exasperation, "people say something to you and the point they remembered was not the point you were trying to make. You let it go and say to yourself that God's grace works in different ways. I get very little feedback on my homilies. It's frustrating. I got more when I was first ordained because I was more radical and got them pissed off. But feedback will come back later. Someone will say, 'Do you remember what you said a month ago?' People do listen."

Larry Duris speaks bluntly to his people about his homilies. "I've told people," he says, "and more than once, that when I'm lousy, tell me. People have said, 'Thank you for trying, didn't quite hit the bull's eye today.' There are polite ways to say it."

Feedback comes without Bill Zavaski's prompting. "They're not afraid to tell you here," he says, noting that he has received glowing compliments and, on occasion, scorching criticism. One Sunday he mentioned his view that the secular press had taken a prejudicial view toward the Catholic Church in relation to the sex abuse scandal. "A guy comes up," Zavaski recalls, "and says, 'Don't be blaming the *New York Times* for the mess in this Church. It's not the *New York Times* that has caused this scandal. It's the cover-up.' Oh, they listen."

Mike Ahlstrom referenced in-homily feedback: "When you hear coughs, it's time to shut up, land the plane, and get out of here."

Some topics, meanwhile, especially those centering on sexual morality, can cause such pain and division that these priests at times tread softly, if at all, in their direction. At St. Athanasius, Tom Libera had a guest priest who once preached about in vitro fertilization as morally wrong, prompting some parishioners to walk out of Mass. The priest told Libera afterward that those who left hadn't been able to hear the moral argument. Libera explains what he thinks happened: "People heard an attack on their intention to bring life into the world, and the mind shut off and the emotions flooded out."

Libera himself shies away from preaching on abortion or birth control. But his reluctance has to do with more than conflict avoidance. "Pastorally, to talk from the pulpit to couples about the Church's sexual ethics is hard," he notes.

> *There are certain forums where you've got to be careful about what you present or at least have a warning or a forum [for discussion]. Maybe they need to hear Church teaching, but how do you say it in a way that people can hear it, that they would at least chew on it, rather than spit it out right away thinking this is just Church stuff and not what real life is about? That's a pastoral challenge. Cardinal George says there're certain things he believes and stands for, but it doesn't mean he's necessarily going to bring them upfront all the time. He asks, what's the teaching moment? That's a wise approach.*

....

The men from the class of 1969 have thought long and hard about preaching at occasions like baptisms, weddings, and funerals, and at major celebrations such as Christmas and Easter. Such moments in the Church's life invariably bring back many inactive Catholics, at least temporarily. In one common approach, the priest directly addresses these returnees, criticizing their lack of Catholic practice and admonishing them about whether they are in proper standing to receive Communion.

Tom Libera takes a different tack. "I see these special occasions as times of welcoming people," he explains, "rather than putting up barriers and hoops that you shouldn't do this or that. You have those relatively rare times when some people encounter Church or priest, so be instructive—not 'Anything goes,' but 'If we can help, we're here.' If people have come this far to the Church, especially for something like marriage—because the statistics are that fewer people are getting married in the Church—they've made some good choices already. So don't discourage that or downplay the importance of their appearing at the church doorstep."

Lapsed Catholics come home to the Church in the greatest numbers during the two most important Church feasts of the year: Christmas and Easter. These classmates have strong opinions about the don'ts and do's of preaching on those occasions. Larry Duris works to make the celebrations positive. "Hopefully, if the experience is good and people, even those who have been away a long time, feel comfortable," he says, "that's going to get them thinking about coming back. I can never understand chasing the returning prodigal son back out the door."

Mike Ahlstrom, however, does directly address infrequent returnees. "I do a two-track thing," he says, "to the folks coming back. I make sure I'm welcoming them, not just bawling them out. But I also challenge them to think whether they shouldn't come back next week. You see a lot of elbows. I don't know how much good it does, but it seems to make people think."

Looking at the situation from an entirely different angle, Bill Zavaski says, "Christmas and Easter, I'm conscious of the fact that people come to be fed."

> Whether they're here once a year, twice a year, or four times a year, I don't think about that as much as wanting to give them something that they can carry away. I have to give them something that they can hold on to because they came. I'm grateful they come. They don't have to come. It's a great thing when they're here, and that's what I celebrate.

Rites of passage in the Church—baptism, marriage, and funerals, known in some Catholic circles as "hatch, match, and dispatch"—present further opportunities and challenges for preaching to a mix of active and inactive Catholics. Because baptisms have their own built-in joy, these classmates focus on acknowledging the importance of honoring that happiness.

It is in the area of weddings where Ahlstrom and his classmates place great emphasis on the importance of preaching. Ahlstrom puts energy into premarital preparation with couples. "Prior to the wedding," he explains, "I kid with them and say, 'Sociological evidence has shown that couples that pray together have better sex. You want better sex in marriage, pray together.'"

> But I love working with couples. I'm aware that most of them rarely, if ever, go to church. Yet it's important to them to be married in church so there is some foundational faith there. I'm trying to awaken that. I say, "If you just want to celebrate your love, go to city hall. This is sacrament, Paschal Mystery." Then we talk about what that means.

During wedding Masses, Ahlstrom invites couples in the congregation to participate. "I tell the assembly ahead of time," he says, "'There's a lot of wisdom here. You know more about love and marriage than I do, so I want you to think about the secret of growing in love, and at homily time I'm going to ask you to share.' Inevitably people will share their secret of staying in love."

When it comes to preaching at weddings, Bill Zavaski does something similar to Ahlstrom. Years ago, Zavaski read a book—*Small Christian Communities*—and then met the author, Father Art Baranowski, who made a suggestion.[7] "He said," Zavaski recalls, "'Ask the couples there, what keeps them together? That's what the couple who is getting married needs to hear.'"

> So, at weddings I say, "I am the least qualified to talk to the two of you about marriage because my life is totally different. I'm always right. I can do what I want and go where I want. That's never going to happen to you again. Marriage is a very challenging vocation, and so those of you married folks who are here who are happy with your partner, before you leave this party you must tell them what keeps you together." All of a sudden everybody in the church is thinking about their own marriage, which is great. I tell them to thank God they have a partner supposed to help them grow in holiness. I love that.

"Then I tell them," Zavaski concludes, "from my lived experience there are two things to help keep a commitment: I ask God every day for help, and I surround myself with guys who are happy as priests. They have to do that with married couples who are happy, and also ask God to help them."

Although he agrees with his classmates that weddings need special attention, Ed Upton wonders if his efforts pay off when it comes to getting lapsed Catholics to return to regular attendance at Mass. "I focus on the couple that's getting married and let the chips fall where they may. My hunch is that it doesn't bring many people back. I have long since given up that these powerful words of mine will engender a conversion and they will suddenly be here every Sunday."

At no time does the need to "get it right" loom larger for these priests than when they are delivering a funeral homily. Feeling vulnerable in the face of death, people approach the Church for consolation. And many have not darkened the Church's doors for quite some time. This chapter opened with Bob Heidenreich's story of what *not* to do in a funeral homily. For these men, respecting the concerns and needs of the grieving family comes first.

In most parishes today, volunteer bereavement ministers work to help priests gather information about the deceased. Especially when the priest did not know them, these meetings provide a crucial look at the meaning of his or her life. "I had to bury a woman, 66," Bill Zavaski relates, "who died of lung cancer. My mother died of lung cancer too, so I try to equate that. I also capitalize on things that the bereavement minister put down. I do talk about how the blessed dead connect with us. They're no longer bound by their physical body. It's important for people who lose somebody they love to realize that."

"Most of the people I bury," Mike Ahlstrom admits, "I have never met. So when I go to the wake, I ask the family to tell me about the person. Were they quiet? Were they extroverted? What did they enjoy doing? In five minutes it's amazing how much you can learn about somebody. Then I take the Scripture that the family has picked for the funeral Mass and ask them: how did the deceased reflect this Scripture? I weave that into the homily. Afterwards people say, 'You must have known him all his life.' I never met him. But you ask the right questions.

"I also talk," Ahlstrom says, echoing Zavaski, "about our Catholic understanding of funerals, that it's not just a memorial. That's the Protestant idea, because they don't pray for the dead. We believe in praying for the dead; it's our way of walking with them as they leave this world and go to the next."

Ed Upton cautions against heaping too much praise on a person not well known to the homilist. "You don't want to be saying," he warns, "'Wasn't he a wonderful father?' if he was a big jerk. That's why I listen and rarely say more than they say."

If they are done well, Upton says, he has seen funerals bring people back to the regular practice of their faith. "People come back because for whatever reason they left, they now have a connection and they can talk a little bit."

Not only would Larry Duris agree with Upton's observation, he actively works to make the funeral experience inviting enough to make people want either to join the Church or return to the faith. "Funerals," he proclaims, "are a great evangelizing moment. This past year we gained more active parishioners than we lost through our funerals."

Some of what Duris does strikes a familiar note: for example, meeting with families and trying to connect the scripture with the life of the deceased. But he also asks the family during the meeting for names, addresses, and phone numbers of family members, and follows up with them after the funeral to see how they are faring after the death and to offer the parish's help.

"For a funeral at St. Ailbe's," he says, "a dozen from the parish bereavement group show up. People are greeted, ushered into the church. And then they follow up." Although the process takes a lot of time—"a funeral can blow your whole day"—for Duris it's worth it. "I couldn't have done this at Ethel's," he explains, "because we had 150 funerals a year. Here we have 30 to 40." Pulling out all the stops those 40 times has made a discernible difference. "People come back to church all the time," he says, "who say it was a funeral of their loved one that got them thinking."

....

Up until about 1965, more American Catholics went to weekly confession than received Communion at Sunday Mass. Long lines formed inside churches on Saturday afternoons, as people waited to enter the dark confessional to confess their sins, venial or mortal, to the priest seated on the other side of a veiled screen. After the Second Vatican Council, the sacrament of Penance came to be referred to as the sacrament of Reconciliation. Catholics still confessed their sins and did penance, but the theological focus shifted from *their* actions to the forgiveness of Christ. Catholics now had three options: individual confession, which could be done face-to-face *sans* the screen if the penitent so chose, communal reconciliation services with individual confessions, or at times such services with no confessions and a general absolution of the congregation.

In the last 25 years, much controversy has arisen as to whether the pre- or post-Vatican II forms of this particular sacrament best serve the Church. Proponents of the new rite argue that it allows for more reflection about serious sin on the part of Catholics, rather than just the rote listing of minor sins. Critics point out that the very name "Reconciliation" underemphasizes both the need for atonement and the seriousness of even venial sins. They worry, therefore, that Catholics no longer feel the need to confess less serious sins. That is a good thing, say some supporters of the new rite.

One thing is certain, however: The number of people using the sacrament has dramatically fallen off, enough that Father Tom Libera calls it a "sacrament on life support." Libera hears confessions on Saturday mornings at St. Athanasius. A very few attend on a regular basis. "Some days you have, especially after Easter, no one," he laments. Libera hasn't succeeded in bringing many back to the practice of the sacrament. The parish does conduct reconciliation services during Advent and Lent, but those events usually only attract crowds of between 30 and 50.

"It's great," Larry Duris teases about St. Ailbe's sparsely attended penance services, "being in a community that doesn't sin." More seriously, Duris struggled with the "why" of the decline in the sacrament's use. "Some young conservatives," he notes, "say we destroyed the sacrament. I don't think so. I wouldn't use the Saturday afternoon criteria. People don't feel a need to come weekly as if they were running through a car wash. They were glad to get away from the laundromat approach. Not many, but a few people do make appointments to go to confession, and that's significant."

While glad that Catholics have largely left behind what they saw as a superficial, rote, and overly scrupulous approach to Reconciliation, members of the class of 1969 over the decades still saw great value in the sacrament and strove to find approaches that might draw parishioners back to its perhaps less frequent but hopefully more meaningful practice. They turned to communal reconciliation services with the opportunity either for individuals to confess and receive individual absolution or for the entire congregation to receive a general absolution. This latter practice grew popular among many priests because of the huge crowds that often attended.

General absolution, however, began to cause great controversy in the Archdiocese of Chicago. Permitted, at least unofficially, for years, Cardinal Francis George admitted the benefits of the practice. "The reasons for making use of general absolution are not unpersuasive," he acknowledged in a 2001 letter to his priests, "and those talking to the question were some of our most effective pastors."[8] But canon law allows the practice only when either death is imminent—prior to a major military battle, for example—or when an insufficient number of priests are available to hear the confessions of all present. Still, George expressed in his letter a willingness to present his priests' views to the Vatican Congregation for Divine Worship. "This does not mean," he also wrote, however, "I personally believe that the conditions for the ordinary use of general absolution are met here at this time; they are not."

The Cardinal did conduct a series of meetings with his priests. Father Bill Stenzel ('75), for example, had delivered a paper at a pastors' forum on June 19, 2001. "I see [general absolution]," Stenzel said, "as an absolute pastoral necessity in order to restore a broader sense of relationship to the sacrament of Reconciliation. We get huge crowds at our services and the people coming are not radical, liberal bridge-burners; they are elderly, faithful, the backbone of the Church. They consistently attest to the significance of it in comparison to what their experiences have been in individual confession."[9] For many priests of the archdiocese, the success of the practice meant that canon law needed to change or be ignored. Cardinal George nonetheless eventually forbade further use of general absolution as a regular option in parishes.

Years later, these priests still regret that decision. Tom Libera remembered the late Father Bob McLaughlin ('66) with esteem because of his relentless efforts, when he served as rector of Holy Name Cathedral, to persuade the Cardinal to continue general absolution. "It was very pastorally courageous of him," Libera explains, "to push that. The Cardinal disagreed, but Bob spoke for a lot of people in that pastorally we've got to come up with other alternatives."

"It's unfortunate," Bob Heidenreich says, "that we can't do general absolution because that's a way people could receive forgiveness that could bring them to come to regular confession."

> If they're holding out for it to be what it used to be when we lived in a culture of guilt, people aren't going to buy that today. I'm sorry. The problem with the Vatican and bishops is that almost none of them have been in parish ministry. They work off of book ideals rather than see how you can help people the most— that's the question that's missing. It's like, "This is the only way to do the sacrament, and you better get on our bandwagon." It's not going to happen. And it's not the only way to do it.

Despite frustration with both the numbers attending the sacrament and the prohibition on general absolution, these priests expressed gratitude for the opportunity to hear people's confessions. "There are times," Tom Libera says, "when this is a moment of special grace. So I try to stay creative with the penance in that it builds off of something that they are experiencing. Make that personalized, not just three Our Fathers and two Hail Marys."

Larry Duris stressed the importance of the occasion of the celebration. "Where Reconciliation has been most significant," he says, "has been as part of renewal weekends." Duris has spent a large part of his priesthood doing retreat work. He helped conduct Christ Renews

His Parish (CRHP) retreats at both St. Lawrence and at St. Philip Neri, established Imani House in order to host retreats right in the black community, and worked as the priest on Marriage Encounter teams. "Reconciliation can make great sense," Duris says, "at those weekends."

"Some of the most powerful moments in my priesthood," Bob Heidenreich relates, "have been in hearing people's confession. It's so humbling to know how sincere and honest other people are. You get a glimpse of the goodness of their soul. Often I say, 'I wish I were as honest.' So the quantity is down, but for those who come, the quality is much better."

Heidenreich has had to wrestle with what works and doesn't work in the confessional. "I've had people," he says, "who have had abortions. My saying, 'This is against Church teaching' doesn't work. I've gotten into arguments with people about when life begins. It doesn't help. You don't convince anyone. I just tell them that while I can't make a judgment about anyone's particular motives, to have life, to give life, and to share life is one of the most positive dynamics of humanity."

So Heidenreich has developed counsel for penitents who have serious issues that arise in the confessional. "It's important for people to know," he insists, "that they're not God. Just because you see something this way now doesn't mean that that's the way it's always going to be. God has a way of writing straight with crooked lines. Ultimately it comes down to this: Can you trust God? And if you can't trust God in this, when are you going to? You and I are going to die, and we cannot trust anybody else but God at that point. So when do we start?"

....

As some of their comments have reflected, these six classmates harbor many concerns about what they refer to as the "reform of the reform," referring to the liturgical and theological pushback that began in the 1980s under Pope John Paul II and that favors what many of them consider to be pre-Vatican II ideas and practices regarding Mass and the sacraments. Another chapter will cover this division in the Church in detail, but the remarks of two members of the class of '69 in regards to the liturgy belong here.

Mike Ahlstrom's biggest concern had to do with the new translation of the Roman Missal that the Church implemented in Advent of 2011. After a long and, many believe, flawed process, the translation changed many Mass prayers and responses. The English Mass prayers that emerged in the years after Vatican II came from a philosophy of translation known as "dynamic equivalence," which sought to convey the overall meaning of the text using clear, simple, and easy to understand language. The new translation, however, relies on the theory of "formal equivalence," which attempts to translate the text as close to the original Latin as possible.[10]

Proponents of formal equivalence believe dynamic equivalence led to changes in the text that obscured its meaning. The other side objected that it is formal equivalence's very formality, so hard for ordinary people to understand, that obscures the meaning of words and phrases in the Missal. Formal equivalence won the day, however; many on the losing side (including all of the six men being followed) believe the Vatican bypassed due process—with the U.S. bishops' acquiescence —by removing the power to write the translations from the commission set up by the English-speaking bishops' conferences and giving it to translators in Rome.[11]

"We are changing," Ahlstrom laments, "the whole concept of the translation of the Mass. The principle that we've been using is that the language of the people is paramount; the liturgy should reflect the way people communicate, and now we're saying we want a literal Latin-like transliteration. It doesn't flow. It's not the way we express ourselves. Cardinal George says, 'Well, it's like the Gettysburg Address. You understand that.' Yeah, but I don't talk in the Gettysburg Address language to people or to God. God doesn't need me to talk that way."

> It's not that I'm against change. If you wanted to follow Vatican II principles and say we need a new translation, I'd be for that. But I see the principles as going back to the previous mentality. It's contradicting what the Council taught. I don't see it as a progressive change as the Cardinal implied. I see it as a retrograde, returning to what was before. So we would have our differences on that, and I'd tell him what I thought.

Behind the changes in the Missal, Ahlstrom clearly feared a return to an older theology. "This fascination with the Tridentine Mass," he says, "that's not progress; that's regression."

The Tridentine Mass was horrible. People didn't pray the Mass, they prayed at Mass. They watched the priest pray and said individual prayers, but the assembly wasn't doing anything. That makes no sense. When we turned the priest around, it was saying loud and clear it's not my Mass, it's our Mass, something we are offering together. This idea that God is in the Holy Land so we've got to face East—that's not where God is. God is in the midst of the assembly. That enrages me, to be honest.

Ahlstrom recalled exactly when that rage welled up inside him. "I did a pilgrimage with the deacons to the Holy Land," he says. "I'm saying Mass at the Church of the Holy Sepulchre in the Chapel of the Crucifixion, the spot where Jesus actually died, and I've got my back to the people."

While not a trained liturgist like Ahlstrom, Bill Zavaski shared many of his classmate's views, lamenting the onslaught of the so-called "reform of the reform." "We're dinosaurs," he says, "because the people running the thing look at liturgy differently. But liturgy is the work of the people and it's messy. Some people are more concerned about rubrics and rules.

"We're going back to that. I had one," he says, referring to an unhappy parishioner, "upset because the laypeople were going to the tabernacle to remove the Eucharist to give out Communion. These people are strange. Christ is already present in us. We just feed him to everybody."

In dealing with more conservative young associate priests coming to his parish, Zavaski has attempted to keep an open mind. "My associates are big into Eucharistic adoration, which is beautiful," he says. "We got away from it because we got into what Eucharist *does* as opposed to what it *is*. Since they know we promote what it does, maybe they have to focus on what it is. It could be a needed shift. But, we've still got to focus first on what the Eucharist *means*."

Zavaski remains ambivalent about the new Mass translation. "Change," he says, "is a life sign. If we weren't changing, we'd be dead. Maybe we have to go back to some things we had—I don't know." Zavaski has found the Mass changes painful. "But they're not major. They're all about words." Suddenly, however, anger crept into Zavaski's voice.

> *Words, words, words, I'm so sick of words. The Eucharist is still the Eucharist. The thing that disappointed me is the new translation focuses on words and not on what the Eucharist is all about. We become the living Body and Blood of Christ. We change bread and wine on the altar; we also change the assembly. We need to talk about the change in the assembly. But I'm not going to fight it. I don't use all the words exactly in the Eucharistic Prayer now. I honestly don't think I'm going to be damned to hell for that. I will try to use all the words. Put that down. I might miss a few here and there.*

....

These six priests from the class of 1969 clearly feel honored to have preached the word and celebrated the sacraments with their fellow Catholics for over 40 years. To be sure, they share some unease that the "reform of the reform" is setting back if not scuttling their lifetime efforts. Despite that anxiety, however, they remain confident that the faith, skill, and professionalism they have exercised in their sacramental ministry have touched countless lives by bringing people closer to Christ, thus reminding them that they are his body acting in the world today.

....

1. *Sacrosanctum Concilium*, Constitution on the Sacred Liturgy. Vatican II, December 4, 1963. Chapter II, paragraph 14.
2. Charlene Smith and John Feister, *Thea's Song: The Life of Thea Bowman* (Maryknoll, NY: Orbis Books, 2010).

3. Leslie Scanlon, "For Sister Jamie Phelps, Life's Joys Outweigh Struggles," in *Catholic Religious Vocation Network: Vision* (Chicago, IL: True Quest Communication, Inc., 2007).

4. Father Clements was the first African-American to graduate from Quigley Seminary. Clements served as pastor of Holy Angels on the South Side of Chicago from 1969 to 1991. He marched at Selma with Dr. King and inaugurated the One Church One Child, One Church One Addict, and One Church One Inmate programs. Clements influenced hundreds of African-Americans to convert to Catholicism.

5. Teresa Mask, "Church Extends Olive Branch to Homosexuals But Some Local Catholics Question if Compassion Implies Acceptance," in *Daily Herald* (Arlington Heights, IL: October 7, 1999).

6. The third step of Alcoholics Anonymous reads "Made a decision to turn our will and our lives over to the care of God as we understood Him." *Alcoholics Anonymous* (New York, Alcoholics Anonymous World Services, 1976), 59.

7. Art Baranowski, *Creating Small Christian Communities: A Plan for Restructuring the Parish and Renewing Catholic Life* (Cincinnati, OH: St. Anthony Messenger Press, 1988).

8. Francis Cardinal George, Letter to Priests of Chicago, as quoted in "Chicago Cardinal Cracks Down on Third Rite of Reconciliation," in *National Catholic Reporter*, August 1, 2001.

9. Judy Roberts, "Cardinal George Grapples with General Absolution," in *National Catholic Register*, August 26, 2001.

10. Rita Ferrone, "Roman Missal Crisis Timeline," in *Pray Tell: Worship, Wit and Wisdom*, April 11, 2011. http://www.praytellblog.com.

11. Rodica Stoicoiu, Ph.D., "Timeline and Translation," at website of St. Agnes Catholic Church, Shepherdstown, WV, 2011. http://www.stagnesshepherdstown.org.

CHAPTER 9

THE NAME OF THE GAME
Empowering the Laity

When Father Bob Heidenreich thinks about the Body of Christ, no abstract theological concepts spring to mind. Instead, he pictures the "nursing home angels," elderly women at Sacred Heart who every week, "come hell or high water," bring Communion to people in the nursing homes in the parish. "They could not stop doing that," he says. "It's not a burden to them. They'll say, 'Put Ann's name in the Prayer of the Faithful. She's sick.' They'll give you her whole life story. It's their ministry, as much as my ministry is to coordinate this whole thing." Heidenreich has built his priesthood on the belief that an organic relationship exists between the ministry of the priest and the layperson. "The whole idea of us being the Body of Christ," he insists, "is that Christ is present and operative in this community as much as he was in Galilee 2,000 years ago."

> *I see that happening. It doesn't happen because I was ordained a priest. No way. It only happens because all of the people come together to celebrate the Eucharist every Sunday. The role of the priest is to invoke the Holy Spirit on the gifts so they become the Body and Blood of Christ. But we all stand around the altar and do that. We have different roles in that. As we leave, we take those roles with us. That's much more of a reality today than it's ever been in the 40 years I've been a priest. That's my vision of parish.*

The six priests of the ordination class of 1969 have committed themselves to a belief that the Body of Christ is a community in which priest and laity together, in different but complementary roles, work to make the Church a sign of the Kingdom of God. Raised at the tail end of the Church era of "pay, pray and obey" that dominated priest-parishioner relations in many parishes prior to the Second Vatican Council, these men, as seminarians during and right after the Council, glimpsed the beginnings of a whole new way of working with the laity. After ordination they heartily embraced a model of collaborative ministry with laypeople. Over 45 years as priests, their experiences with the laity have brought about many joys and also some struggles, as well as some critiques of their theology and methodology, especially in the last 20 years. But these men stand united in confidence that their work has in fact helped form a cadre of active lay Catholics in Chicagoland dedicated to their Church and attempting to live out their faith in the world.

Tracing the roots of their pastoral practice regarding the laity, the men again point to their pre-diaconate retreat, given by a team of laypeople in conjunction with a priest, as the seminal moment. "I still remember it after 42 years," Mike Ahlstrom says. "Retreats we were used to had a priest preaching theory. These people talked about how they met the Lord and about their faith, which is why it was powerful." Tom Libera says the retreat "set the stage for what I hoped to experience in parishes, a new dawn of people eager to engage in their faith. That was the vision."

Even what one might term "priestly peer pressure" played its role. Ed Upton, for example, credits a diocesan *esprit de corps* for helping form his approach as a seminarian and young priest. "It came across that we were and had to remain the best," he says, "that the Chicago presbyterate has a reputation around the country for involving laypeople." Referencing some of the "observe, judge, act" programs that encouraged the laity to practice their faith in the wider community, Upton says, "It was Cana and Pre-Cana and Christian Family Movement. It was social justice. When we were ordained, that wasn't so radical. It was accepted. I take it for granted. I didn't see it being done any other way." Upton thinks it is unfortunate that the days of that *elan* have long since ended. "There is such division," he remarks. "I don't really think there's a sense of presbyterate in Chicago anymore." Still, the early lessons remain. "The theological basis" of working with the laity, Upton insists, "is that as baptized people we form a community, all sharing the responsibility for the mission of both the local and the larger community. People have to have a sense of ownership. That's what forms the Church."

The figure of Msgr. Jack Gorman ('52), appointed rector of Mundelein Seminary at the height of the Vatican Council reforms, clearly looms large in the men's memories as well; Gorman embodied for them a sea change in the Church's approach to the laity. "I remember," Mike Ahlstrom says, "Gorman saying, 'You don't know what the future is going to be. You have to be open. It's going to be full of surprises.' So we were not being ordained to become a clerical caste. We were turned off by that. In terms of Avery Dulles' five models of the Church, the first model is the hierarchical model and no, we were more the communion model."[1]

"The Vatican II documents," Bill Zavaski insists today, "were clear that we had to work with people, that they had a mission and a ministry. My task is inviting them to make the Church happen. The ecclesiology was they are the Church. I truly believe that."

Nothing confirmed this insight for Tom Libera more than his groundbreaking work with the divorced and separated, which began when a laywoman all but insisted he help her get something started. "My involvement," he says, "came both out of priests wanting to open up new ministries and also the persistent feedback from parishioners saying we've got to do something. That was an example of being led by what people were looking for, and the need was there."

....

Armed with a fresh theology of and pastoral approach to the laity, the priests had to meet the acid test: actually putting theory and ideas into practice in their daily ministry. Their attempts produced both joyful and difficult moments. The former they found mainly in encouraging lay leadership and witnessing the deepening of faith in individuals and communities. "The greatest joys," Bob Heidenreich exclaims, "are to see people turned on by their involvement in Church, people that get it. Knowing that you started the ball rolling and other people picked it up and it's not me, it's the Holy Spirit. I feel so much solidarity with people like Paul and Barnabas and the people from the Acts of the Apostles. Paul plants the seed, and then Apollos comes and builds on it. It's so neat to see that happening."

Working to strengthen the identity of Chicago's black Catholic community lifted Tom Libera's spirits. "One of the appreciations from working in a smaller, minority parish," he says, "is that people have to make a choice to want to be there. Being African-American and Catholic was something some African-Americans did not appreciate. Black Catholics needed to work with, for the most part, white leadership, who may have understood them or maybe did not. But a small group of people, staying at a particular parish year after year, generation after generation, is a wonderful lesson of what parish is about."

Mike Ahlstrom singled out watching RCIA catechumens go from hesitant beginners to dedicated Catholics as they met together for a year and received the sacraments of initiation at Easter. Better yet, for Ahlstrom, was the opportunity to train lay leaders to run RCIA. "What's a thrill," he says, "was empowering laypeople to take ownership of RCIA. I taught them the theory, but when it came to enfleshing it, they were better at it than I was, and I trusted them. It ran without me. I had no doubt when I left the parish there would be a strong catechumenate."

Ahlstrom feels even more strongly about training the permanent deacons with whom he works. "I have seen deacons take ownership," he maintains. "The priests sometimes treat them more like laity than brother clergy. That's upsetting. But to see what enthusiastic faith they have…working with the diaconate has been the best time of my whole priesthood."

Encouraging lay leadership produced tangible personal benefits for these priests. "The love that people have for their priests," Mike Ahlstrom stresses, "is overwhelming. Recently, I said Mass for the Charismatic Renewal."

I'm not a charismatic but I like to say Mass for them. Always at the end they want to have the laying on of hands and healing and they have catchers in case somebody is "slain by the Spirit." At the end of it, I said, "All of you who have had me lay hands on you, how about you lay hands on me?" I sat down in the chair and about 35 people got a hand on me and started praying for me. The next thing they were praying in tongues. It was really powerful and beautiful. I very much felt loved by these people. It wasn't like I had been personally involved in their lives, but it was obvious they had a respect and a love for me and were praying for me.

In the midst of their many efforts to instill and invigorate lay leadership, these priests take great joy in glimpsing people's spiritual lives as they change and deepen. "Over the years I've done Engaged Encounters," Ed Upton says, "and they're a lot of work. But to get couples meeting on weekends where you're on the team, it's worth it. You're moving into deeper stuff about life, about marriage."

"Experiences like CRHP (Christ Renews His Parish)," echoes Tom Libera, "have most touched me. People have the time and setting to be able to explore what their faith means and to share it. To get to that place where you can hear people reflect on the faith is very satisfying. That's what you need to do for people to change in the busy world. They might get struck by divine lightning, but otherwise we're not doing the best we can for them unless we can get them to reflect like that."

....

These priests have also delighted in seeing the power of engaged lay-people pursuing social justice efforts with them at their parishes. The Catholic Church's increased focus on social justice began with the promulgation of Pope Leo XIII's encyclical *Rerum Novarum* in 1891 and gained great momentum with the Second Vatican Council.[2] In 1971, for example, the World Synod of Bishops first published the now familiar admonition "work for social justice is a constituent element of preaching the Gospel."[3] Church leaders urged Catholics to work to change social structures that lead to poverty and other inequalities.

For the then newly ordained classmates, the bishops' focus on justice issues came not as news but as a belated confirmation of the value of the ministries in which the priests of Chicago had long been engaged with the laity. Looking back, Ed Upton praised influential priests in that regard. "Reynold Hillenbrand ('29), Jack Egan ('43), Bill Quinn ('41), George Higgins ('40)," Upton says, "and later Pat O'Malley ('57), Leo Mahon ('51), George Kane ('51)."

Larry Duris has spent his priesthood working with the African-American community on social justice issues. Soon after his ordination, Duris took classes in community organizing from the Industrial Areas Foundation founded by famed community organizer Saul Alinsky; ex-seminarian Ed Chambers ran the training program at the time. This helped Duris while at Holy Cross Parish, his second assignment, where he and parishioners worked with The Woodlawn Organization (TWO), which had previously brought the University of Chicago to the negotiating table to assist the community in building affordable housing for Woodlawn, the neighborhood that borders the university's southern edge. Later, Duris, Father Les Mollohan ('51), and others from Holy Cross organized the 65th Street Development Corporation, which rehabbed six buildings in Woodlawn.

At suburban St. Athanasius Parish in Evanston, Tom Libera notes, questions of diversity and how to be welcoming often occupy the minds of his parishioners. Some of the families in the school found a way to make an impact by bringing in the Boys Hope Girls Hope organization founded by a Jesuit priest in 1977. "They take minority students," Libera says, "who have potential but are right on the economic edge." The organization runs a family-like home in Evanston that houses students from middle school on up. Some of the students attend St. Athanasius School. If the students stay in school and stay committed to their studies, the program commits to support them through college and beyond.

Bill Zavaski's first pastorate, at his home parish of St. Bart's in Waukegan, focused him on social justice concerns when the parish went through racial change from mostly Lithuanian to mostly Hispanic. "When I got to that city," he says, "we were living in a poverty area with a lot of racial tension. Immigration was—and continues to be—big. The Church became a catalyst to help people deal with these problems. That's how we got into neighborhood organizations."

At his latest pastorate at St. James in Arlington Heights, however, the congregation is mostly white, with little poverty and few immigrants. "But that is our poverty," Zavaski says. He therefore began listening closely to the parish peace and justice committee and then preaching on social issues. "The committee," Zavaski says, "is my conscience, much to the chagrin of several parishioners."

Recently, in part because St. James' sharing parish—Misión Juan Diego, also in Arlington Heights—ministers to undocumented immigrants, Zavaski and his social justice committee have concentrated on immigration reform. Not everyone in the parish appreciates the new focus. "I've got a guy," Zavaski says, "forever finding fault with anything the committee writes. He critiques every article about immigration, health care, etc. Finally I said, 'Put the guy on the committee so that you can have some dialogue.'" Not only does Zavaski no longer shy away from controversial social issues, he appears to relish challenging the community he loves. For example, he recently invited immigration reformers walking in a pilgrimage to spend the night in the school basement, knowing that it would rile up some in his parish. About that, he grins.

Bob Heidenreich's Sacred Heart parishioners have committed to not one but two sharing parishes, one in Haiti and one on Chicago's South Side, St. Columbanus. Heidenreich expressed pride at his parish's work with Columbanus. "They feed 500 people a week," he says, "at the food pantry. They come here for a Mass; we go there for one. Some of our people tutor in their school. On our 'to do' list is a basketball game with Columbanus' teens. The school people have already done that. They called the coach and just picked up and went."

Marveling also at the efforts the parish has made in Haiti, Heidenreich focused on how one person can make a huge difference in changing the structures that keep people trapped in poverty. "Our deacon, Jerry Keenan, head of the Haiti committee for 10 years," Heidenreich says, "goes there four times a year. He told me, 'We want to do a special collection for Haiti.'"

The parish we're associated with is 140 miles from Port-au-Prince, so it was not touched by the earthquake. But 500,000 people left Port-au-Prince to return to the far-reaching areas where they grew up. This area received something like 50,000 new people right after the earthquake. Our parish received 2,000 new people.

In response, Sacred Heart raised an incredible $170,000, and Keenan sponsored two medical mission trips to the area. In the last few years he brought electricity to the parish house—the only such house in the village—and placed a satellite dish and solar panels on its roof. Villagers can at last use computers and charge their cell phones.

Heidenreich expressed awe at Keenan's successes and at the effect the efforts have had on Sacred Heart's youth. "When we got there," he says of a recent trip he made to Haiti with parish teens, "the kids were e-mailing kids at home telling them what we were doing. I came back and Sunday I was standing in back of church. Kids came in saying, 'You going next year? I want to go.' One kid said, 'I learned more going to Haiti than I learned in four years of theology at St. Ignatius.' This guy is a bit brash. If he didn't have the theology, he wouldn't know that he learned so much. But Haiti helped him to pull it together."

....

For these priests, difficulties regarding laypeople have taken two major forms: clashes with or between the laity, and battles with the hierarchy and other priests regarding lay Catholics.

Some conflicts have veered into the realm of comedy. Ed Upton laughed out loud when he recalled one of the early entertainment nights St. Alexander's hosted as a parish fundraiser. "This guy came from a great Italian family," he says. "I think he had some connections. He said, 'I'll run the gambling.'" The trouble was the gambling tables in the past had been presided over by the formidable matrons of the Altar and Rosary Society. "He said to the lady from the Altar and Rosary, 'I don't want any of them sad broads on the altar working these gambling tables. I'm bringing my own girls in.' She was furious."

Many of the conflicts Larry Duris has to deal with are tragic rather than comic. He prays, for example, for the courage to confront gun violence in his community. "At times I ask for hand-raising as part of my preaching," he says. "I don't have the guts yet to ask, 'How many people have a gun?' But they know how I feel about guns. I can count on one hand stories about somebody saving their life with a gun. I have buried more kids who were the wrong target than I can count. Shot from an alley or across the street. Whoops, wrong person. Gone. 16, 18, 20. Full of promise."

Most of their conflicts with laypeople have fallen somewhere between the extremes of comedy and tragedy. But the very fact that conflict existed at all proved quite troubling to several priests. In his current assignment at St. Athanasius, for example, Libera has felt the sting of confrontation. "We've had a few volatile things come up," he says, "and people could be somewhat demanding. With the Internet now, you can even become more intense, and word spreads like crazy quickly. So that's the downside, feeling isolated from people; they're angry at you or at the Church and you're supposed to do something about it." Libera's solution to resolve such conflicts? He decided to put all the parish stakeholders in the same room together. "The active theology," he says, "centers on this leadership night that we have once a month. You get all the people who represent ministries in the parish and they meet for the evening, conduct their work, share information. That's the vision I have: a lot of people taking very small steps that can move us forward."

Upton ran into a difficult situation involving the Catholic grade school in Orland Park that serves four parishes. During his term as executive pastor of the school, a parishioner challenged him. "This guy said," Upton recalls, "'Do you know why people are leaving the school? Do an exit interview! You'll find that they don't like that principal. So I'm going to do an interview and get you that information. Then you're going to fire the principal.' I said, 'It doesn't work that way. We have a contract.'

"It's difficult," Upton says, "when people are arrogant or focused on one thing. You're trying to keep the thing from blowing apart. Sometimes you've got a person's reputation to consider. You can't deal with that in public."

Like Libera, Upton hates conflict and prefers everybody to be happy. "That is tough for most priests," Upton reports. "We don't like confrontation. But sometimes you have to help deal with a conflict because the previous pastor ignored it—if the pastor had just talked to the person, it would have solved the problem. But many priests go passive and hope it will go away. Most priests say yes to everybody. Well, you have to say yes, but with guidelines. If people want to do something, I put it right back on them and say, 'What's its purpose?' If you can defend it, have a mission for it, fine."

At his latest pastorate at Sacred Heart in Winnetka, Bob Heidenreich has struggled to persuade his people to buy into that sense of common mission. "How do you deal," he asks, "with very talented people who have tremendous resources and contacts but are CEOs and CFOs and are used to people doing what they tell them? How do you harness all of that energy and goodwill and get folks to work together for the parish? This is one of the most generous parishes I've been at for important causes, but parish donations are declining because they don't see the parish as an important cause." Heidenreich says that a committee in the parish is confronting this issue directly.

Bill Zavaski openly admits that many problems in dealing with the laity stem from conflicts between members of the parish staff. "Working with lay staffs," he says bravely, "there's constant tension. I sometimes sit in this office saying, 'Why can't we get along?' They're well intentioned, but they get their noses out of joint. That's a tough thing." Staff members complain about colleagues, Zavaski goes on. "But I'm not about to tell somebody 50 years old how they should act, for God's sake. If you're offended, you need to talk about that directly. Don't put me in the middle."

"One of the biggest challenges," he says, "that new priests face, especially foreign-born priests, is working with women. Both of my associates, thank God, get along with women. I've had associates who have had problems working with women, and it's a disaster." So staff relationships, Zavaski maintains, "are something we have to work on. I wish the diocese could work at staff development. We ought to be talking about how we work as a team—that's a critical thing."

Like his colleagues, Zavaski dwells on the need to confront conflict head on, although it seems to run against the priestly grain to do so. The consequences of incessantly trying to please everyone can spell doom for the health of the parish, however. Zavaski has even come to see conflict as a sign of life. He recalled one controversy that led to the dismissal of two volunteers in the CCD program. The pair insisted on teaching their own curriculum, disregarding the program put together by the team. "They complained and wanted to do their own thing," says Zavaski. "They brought in the *Catechism of the Catholic Church*. Well, the kids aren't going to read that. 'But the Pope gave us this catechism,' they said. All hell broke loose because we let these two go. So a lot of fights go on between the people of God. The Church has always been like that, different attitudes and values. It makes for excitement."

Some parish conflicts would make a great comedy skit. "We don't have a narthex—a gathering space in the church," Zavaski says. "After the daily Mass the rosary ladies want to start that rosary right away."

People coming for Mass want to connect with one another afterward. There is screaming: "There'll be no talking in church so we can say the rosary." I get out there. I say, "Until we get a gathering space, everybody can talk for five minutes. Then say the rosary." They're not too pleased. There's a little tension, and every once in a while they start a little bit sooner than five minutes because they're in a hurry to get that rosary in. They give these dirty looks to people. In the sacristy I can be real loud saying, "They better not start for five minutes." That's a constant battle here—they're fighting over when they can pray. It's funny. It makes us the people of God.

Zavaski acknowledges that St. James has a well-earned reputation as a progressive parish. Faced with a division between what he calls "conservative and liberal," Zavaski knows he can't please everyone. "I respect people," he maintains, "but if you're more conservative, I would encourage you to go elsewhere because it ain't going to happen here. I do my best and work with people, encouraging them to believe that they are Church. Amen."

Mike Ahlstrom brought up a decidedly different set of concerns, having to do with conflicts that arise when dealing with the effects of Catholics who have simply walked away from the Church. Ahlstrom had an experience at St. Barbara's Parish that highlighted for him such conflicts. A 17-year-old girl wanted to have her baby baptized. She wanted the grandfather to be the godfather, but a priest at the parish said no because the grandfather didn't go to church and was living with a woman he wasn't married to. Her choice for godmother had been married outside the Church.

"The girl didn't know anybody that was a practicing Catholic," Ahlstrom exclaims, "literally knew no one that was Catholic and could stand up for the baptism. That's very common. I joke that if a couple comes to get married and tells me they're both Catholic and they go to Mass every Sunday and they're not living together, I think they're lying. That's a sad commentary."

Concerns about numbers—and dollars—have led to struggles between these parish priests and archdiocesan leadership over the best approach the Church can take to reach out to the laity. Regarding finances, Upton feels thankful, on the one hand, for the financial support he has received from his parishioners and the archdiocese. During a recent financial drive in which the archdiocese matched parish donations, St. Francis raised over 1 million dollars. Upton warns, however, that the financial numbers—not just at St. Francis but throughout the archdiocese—can mislead. At Upton's parish, for example, over 2,000 people attend Mass weekly, and clearly they contribute generously. Another 3,000 Catholics who live in the parish, however, neither attend regularly nor contribute financially. "The collections are going up," Upton admits, "but it's an older group contributing. The money in 10 years is going to go down, because those people will die off.

"The denial at the archdiocesan level," Upton says, "is just incredible."

As far as numbers are concerned, the heart of the problem for Upton is the Church's difficulty in attracting young people. "Jack Wall ('68) had a lot of success at Old St. Pat's," Upton says, "but even their numbers are down.[4] I don't seem to draw young marrieds, whether they don't have the time or just aren't interested. Not a lot of kids come to Mass. I don't know of anybody that has turned this thing around."

While unsure of the solution to the problem of declining numbers, Upton does have strong opinions on what will not work. "The answer I hear," he says, "is that they don't know the truth. If we give them the truth, they'll come." Upton doesn't believe a lack of information about Church teaching is the problem. "That's what the Church has been trying," he complains, "but if you want a different result, don't keep doing the same thing."

How a rigid focus on rules impacts lay Catholics remains a source of deep concern for Mike Ahlstrom. "The biggest issue for me," he says, "is when people are struggling with things in the Church. Some are completely alienated by the whole divorce, remarriage, annulment thing. They won't do it. They feel they've been kicked out of the Church."

Ahlstrom's struggles extend also to problems with how some of his brother priests treat laypeople. "Some insensitive priests," he admits, "have hurt people. The priest is the one person that you should trust. Ed Upton once said, 'We've got the easiest job in the world: all you need to do is be nice to people and love people.' It's amazing how often priests screw that up."

....

As what Mike Ahlstrom and others have called the "reform of the reform" movement has expanded its influence, if not its numbers, in the Catholic Church in the U.S., Vatican II-era priests have heard growing criticism of their theology and pastoral style of relating to the laity. The critique runs something like this: their generation of priests was too personal and not formal enough with laypeople, to the extent that the actual role of the priest got lost and he became just another layperson. Symptoms of this "excessive closeness" supposedly include reluctance to wear clerical garb and use the title "Father," variations from the prescribed liturgical rubrics, preaching away from the pulpit and in some cases eschewing the presider's chair for a seat in the pew, and spending too much time with the laity in homes and restaurants, all supposedly leading to an overemphasis on affirming the good qualities of the laity, along with a corresponding reluctance to confront their sinfulness. "That's why there needs to be a sense of closeness," Father Randal Kasel, a priest from the John Paul II generation, said in the May 2010 issue of *U.S. Catholic*, "but also just a little bit of distance. It's hard for priests to do, because I want people to like me. But I can't be true to myself and reject my role. What happens when you're too close to people who you also have to govern? What happens when you have to say something a little difficult or you need to correct someone?"[5]

Asked about these kinds of appraisals, some of the men from 1969 lend credence to the need to balance affirmation and confrontation, but all unequivocally rejected the notion that closeness to their people had diminished or confused their roles in the eyes of laypeople.

"The opposite is true," Mike Ahlstrom insists. "I'm not separated from the people. But I've never felt laypeople thought of me as another one of them. They have always respected the priest that I am. I'm very comfortable being called Michael or Mike. That's my name. Most people call me Father Mike. I don't care what people call me, as long as they don't call me late for supper. But I have served them better by being familiar with them than if I were up on a pedestal.

"I experienced in the '50s," Ahlstrom recalls, "what it meant for priests to be on a pedestal, to be other and separate, which was artificial. Reverence for priesthood is more authentic now, because there's awareness that I'm still a man who puts my pants on one leg at a time. In those days people never told the truth to priests. This mentality of the priest being other, it's unreal. That creates a wall and makes priesthood much less effective. You're not honest."

Nothing feels more real and less artificial to Bill Zavaski than his relationships with laypeople. "I don't feel confused about my role," he says, "and I have a very personal relationship with the people." For Zavaski, only one true example exists when it comes to discerning proper relations with the laity. "Our personal relationship with Jesus Christ," he maintains, "is most important, and we model that in every other relationship. So why would we want to dismiss personal relationships when everything is built on that relationship?" Zavaski bristles at the relatively new rubric that requires the priest to stay on the altar during the sign of peace. "I go off the altar," he asserts. "Why would you want to lose the personal impact? They know who we are. I don't understand the formality. Leaving the altar has nothing to do with diminishing the mystery of the Eucharist. How are we going to get people to come if we focus on the formalities and the liturgical rules? We have to understand the value and beauty of the Eucharist. They've got to connect what they're doing all week long with what happens in Church. We have not looked at the change that needs to take place within the body of the Church—the people. That's where the Spirit changes us into the living Body of Christ. Making it more formal isn't going to help people sense that the change must take place within them. That, to me, I don't get."

Ed Upton sees a re-emerging clericalism at the heart of the criticisms of his generation's relations with the laity. "The role of priests," Upton says, "is clear. Most parishioners see the priest as having a leadership role. His primary purpose, as best he can, is to be a believer, a person of prayer who leads the community. Most people, however, feel that the journey is one taken together. You're not leading sheep, you're leading people. Because you're a leader doesn't mean you have all the truth or right directions. You listen to people and together form a direction. So the role of the priest isn't blurred.

"I don't know of anybody here," Upton says sarcastically, "that says 'No, I'll be the priest this week.' I don't know what the critics are talking about. Do I understand my role if I wear a collar all the time? If I stay distant? If I say, 'This is the way it's going to be'? My judgment of that is it's a form of clericalism. They want an extrinsic authority as opposed to authority you get because you walk with people. But whatever authority I have, it's because people trust me."

Upton experiences more and more clericalism in gatherings with priests and seminarians. "We go to these priest meetings," he says, referring to the annual priest convocations sponsored by the archdiocese, "and everybody wears a collar. Who else is there? You're not going to the hospital for a sick call where you want access to a patient. I don't get it. At seminary they're wearing their collars to class. I know you're a seminarian—it's called Mundelein Seminary! The Cardinal said his reason was unity. If you think that builds up unity, all dressing the same way, it doesn't. That's where I stand with all that clerical stuff."

In responding to these critiques, Larry Duris said pointedly, "The criticism is nonsense, but I'm prejudiced. Each African-American community I've been in has been very affective; they look for warmth from their ministers. If people don't think you're giving that enough, they tell you. Warmth enhances the communication. I don't become any less priest or pastor." For Duris, it comes down to priests and laity having different roles in a parish, roles that in his mind are not difficult to define. "I wear my collar," he explains, "on Sundays or when we have new school parents that haven't met me yet. That easily explains who I am. I have no problem sitting in the presider's chair at Mass. Some places the celebrant sits in a pew—I think that's goofy. Sitting in the chair doesn't make me king. But if you're sitting in the chair, then you're expected to be of service to and to engage with the people. So, *vive la différence* there. The key is how you're available, open to ideas, and finally responsible without micromanaging everyone."

The elevation in 2010 of several Chicago priests to the purely honorary title of monsignor after many years of letting that custom lapse prompted Tom Libera to reflect on whether the Church is moving backward in its approach to the laity. "There's a traditional awareness," Libera acknowledges, "of Holy Orders being a special calling in the Church that confers a certain identity. But the real challenge is breaking down barriers just to stay tuned to people." For years, with Cardinal Bernardin's support, the archdiocese's priests had resisted attempts to resurrect the honorary title of monsignor in Chicago. When Cardinal Francis George changed course on this, many priests expressed concern about how the move might affect lay Catholics. Father Tom McQuaid ('79), for example, wrote a letter in the bulletin of St. Leonard's in Berwyn, where he was serving as pastor, criticizing the Cardinal's decision.[6] Libera worries about the Church's credibility. "One fellow was talking with his mother," Libera says, "who was 90. Between the excommunication of a woman who wanted to be a priest and the monsignor thing, she says to her son, 'Am I getting it wrong or is the Church going backward?'"[7]

I wasn't as direct as McQuaid, but I did mention it the week
the announcement was made. It happened to be the Gospel on
coming to the head of the table. When someone else comes, you

get knocked to the back. The Church needs to be careful about having a mechanism to honor some people, while for women and others there's none. We don't want to fall into that Gospel trap: trying to find your way up front. That's erosion of what Chicago priests stood for, for years. It looks like you're trying to build up the clerical culture; those criticisms are not off.

Memories of his early days of priesthood have made Bob Heidenreich more sanguine than his classmates about the future of priest-lay relations. "When we got ordained," he says, "how naïve and dumb we were, but we were filled with Vatican II ideals. Now young priests see some problems that were created, and they're filled with ideas. Neither one is right or is actually where the folks are.

"The process we went through," Heidenreich maintains, "is the same process that these guys will go through, and it'll change them. They won't want to be changed, but it'll change them much the same way it did us. These guys have to have relationships with people. I don't see them as immune from being changed and their ideas challenged if they're in parishes."

In responding to the second criticism leveled at their generation of priests—that their closeness to people, in addition to causing role confusion, made it hard for them to confront people's sinfulness—the men from the class of 1969 did not stand in such united opposition. "That is a legitimate criticism," Mike Ahlstrom admits, "that the pendulum went to the other extreme. Sin is very much a reality, and we do need to challenge people. In one parish, the pastor was Mr. Affirmation. We used to joke that we should have three verses of "How Great We Are," not "How Great Thou Art." It was overboard. People came to resent being challenged. So there is a correction. But the new Missal makes me uncomfortable, because it tends to be heavy on what I call 'What a worm I am' spirituality. It tends to put people down. I don't like that."

Tom Libera also searched for ways to balance affirmation and challenge. "The number of confessions I hear on Saturdays," he says, "I could fit on one hand. If that's a measure we're not preaching enough on sin, I don't know. Personality-wise I don't want to accuse people of sin." Calling people to a higher engagement, on the other hand, Libera adds, "is one way of looking at sin."

"We need," Bill Zavaski insists, "a balance. I talk about the devil. I believe the devil exists. There is evil in the world and we need to confront that and admit that we are sinful. Everything is not fine. But people aren't going to come if they're told they're evil all the time." Zavaski recently chose to preach about abortion and immigration during the same homily.

> *It was near July 4th. I said, "The things we have done to immigrants and taking a life have divided this country and both of them are sinful." I knew half that crowd was big on abortion and half was big on immigration. That's exactly why I did both issues. I said, "It's a great country, but as Catholics we have to stand up and speak about both." But I'm not going to give them that stuff all the time. People also want to come to be fed, not just told about their sinfulness. They want to know how they can grow in the image and likeness of the Risen Lord.*

While Mike Ahlstrom, Tom Libera, and Bill Zavaski acknowledged the legitimacy of the critique that their generation of priests had perhaps erred too much on the side of affirming their people's goodness and not enough on confronting their sinfulness, their other three classmates begged to differ. "Ridiculous," Larry Duris rails against the criticism, "absolutely ridiculous. Jesus taught and ate with sinners. Enough said.

"If anything," Duris insists, "as you get to know people better, you're able to confront them. What are people looking for in a priest? They're looking for a man of God, someone holy. Not pious. Someone who has a clue what they're doing, who could help and not be a hindrance. That includes someone who has the guts to challenge the parish."

"I'm not sure the Christian message," Ed Upton says, "is to call out sinfulness. It's to call out conversion. I don't know if I am the enumerator of what is sinful for people. That's arrogance. What I have to do is to call people to change." For that to happen, he believes, Church leaders must get beyond their focus on act-centered do's and don'ts to the deeper values that lie beneath the doctrines, especially in moral theology. "If those prohibitions don't make sense to people," he says, "they reject the whole package. We say as a Church you can practice birth control if you use natural family planning, but you can't take a pill to do the same thing. Does that make sense to anybody? The value is unselfishness in marriage. How do we encourage people to say pro-creativity is part of marriage? Most couples want to be generous in marriage. They don't want to be selfish. How do we encourage that as opposed to focusing on act-centered isolated things that aren't the issue? One reason people walk away is because it doesn't make sense; the teaching has to connect with their experience."

Bob Heidenreich has long thought this particular criticism comes mainly from people—often Church bureaucrats—with an ignorance of the realities of parish life. "It's an immature critique," he explains, "spoken by people who have not had any experience in parish. The people of God in the parish are just as good and just as bad as these guys. Some are very self-righteous," he continues, "like them. But others are very serving. If they're ordained and assigned to a parish," he says, referring to such critical but inexperienced seminarians, "they will find wonderful people who are there to do nothing more than to be the presence of Christ because they believe it. They need to see that. The seminary can't produce priests. It can give them the academic training, but priests are made by the people in the parish."

....

What did the ministry of the class of 1969 contribute to the life of the laity? For Tom Libera, whatever success they may have had came from their ability as priests to call the laity into more active lives as Catholics. "We have helped people see," Mike Ahlstrom agrees, "that they are the Church and the mission of Church is theirs. When people talk about the Church as 'you' or 'them,' they don't get it. They should be talking about 'us.' They say, 'You're being sued by abuse victims.' No, we're being sued. We've had success in helping people see that the Church is all of us."

His recent reading helped Bob Heidenreich put his class' efforts in perspective. "I read an article," he says, "about Vatican II written by a guy from a conservative think tank. He says the [pre-Vatican II] Church had not taught people about faith. What it did was have them memorize the shell and take part in Catholic practices that were supposed to make them Catholic."

> *He said that the changes introduced after Vatican II did not destroy the Church. The Church was going to fall apart anyway, because there was no depth to the lay spirituality we had produced. In retrospect, I say exactly. He says that the challenge of Vatican II was to call for conversion. And that's where it's succeeding. We have lay ministers who are not only theologically trained, but also have a spirituality. That's what we do in parish life. This is a new world from what it was 40 years ago.*

"There's a tension," Heidenreich explains, "between the institution and the real Church. You can't get rid of that tension. The Church couldn't exist in reality without this institution, but that's not the Church. The Church exists on a parish level.

"In some people's view," he adds, "a diocesan priest is a 'secular' priest. That's what I am. I hope I have not set myself over against laypeople. I ended up here not because of some grandiose idea I had of myself, but because this is the way grace worked in my life. This is my job just like you have a job. Why can't we just do our jobs together?"

In offering a spirited defense of the class' approach to the laity, Ed Upton attempts to put matters in historical perspective by referring to the book *A Generation of Seekers: The Spiritual Journeys of the Baby Boom Generation* by Wade Clark Roof.[8] The author emphasized that the boomer generation lived in a time of expanding choices, in particular in regards to religion. Mainline religions suddenly found themselves in competition with fundamentalism and evangelicalism on the one hand, and everything from New Age mysticism to goddess worship on the other. The boomer generation, Roof insisted, would not simply adapt the ethnic and religious traditions of their parents and grandparents. Because they both valued experience over belief and distrusted institutions, they had to be shown. Ministers of any religion, Roof insisted, had to enter into the questions people had about the old answers, not merely repeat them. By struggling together with their people, they would show that they and their religion could be trusted. Thus, Vatican II's openness to change helped keep many, if not enough, boomers in the Church. "Are the numbers down?" Upton asks. "Absolutely. Is that the result of the Council? Maybe I'm too defensive, but I don't think so. There's no question that people have a more tenuous connection with the Church. But we also have a slew of people involved. Can we build on that?

"I don't think that people would have continued with the Church that was," Upton goes on. "I also don't think educated Americans would have continued to tolerate the pastor making all the decisions in an arbitrary way. A woman on Relevant Radio recently was saying we have to go back to the reverence at Mass we exhibited before the Council. I wanted to call and say, 'Lady, what Mass did you go to?' In most parishes there was one high Mass, but there were eight low Masses. Those eight Masses," Upton says, "were populated by people who said their rosary, read the paper, didn't respond. They half genuflected, made a quick sign of the cross, and didn't know what the heck was going on. That's the reverence we're going back to? Today when people come to Mass, they know what's going on. Most respond. Many sing. They let the music touch them. I can't imagine today doing Sunday liturgy like we did 50 years ago; if we did, we'd be absolutely dead."

....

1. Avery Dulles, SJ, *Models of the Church* (Garden City, NY: Doubleday, 1974). The five models of Church are Church as Institution, as Mystical Communion, as Sacrament, as Herald, as Servant.
2. *Rerum Novarum*, Encyclical of Pope Leo XIII, On Capital and Labor, May 15, 1891.
3. *Justitia in Mundo*, World Synod of Bishops, 1971, Justice in the World, December 9, 1971.

4. Father Jack Wall served as pastor of Old St. Patrick's on the near West Side of Chicago from 1983-2007. During that time, he helped raise the number of registered parishioners from 4 to 4,000 in large part by focusing on attracting young adults and other urban professionals to the parish.
5. Christina Capecchi, "Men of the same cloth?" in *U.S. Catholic*, May, 2010, 15.
6. Father Tom McQuaid letter in St. Leonard bulletin, August 15, 2010, quoted in "Cardinal Facing Increasing Unrest in Chicago-area Parishes." http://www.ChicagoCatholicNews.com, September 6, 2010.
7. Dayna Dixon, "A Simple Wish Runs into a Buzz Saw of Bureaucracy," in *Medill Reports Chicago*, May 13, 2010. http://news.medillnorthwestern.edu.
8. Wade Clark Roof, *A Generation of Seekers: The Spiritual Journeys of the Baby Boom Generation* (San Francisco: Harper Collins, 1993).

Ordination, May 14, 1969

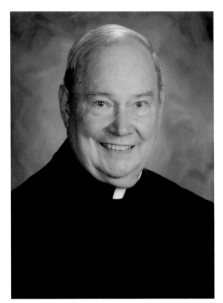

Bob Heidenreich

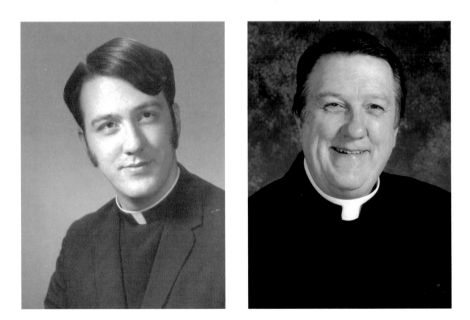

Mike Ahlstrom

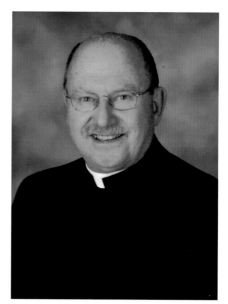

Ed Upton

Larry Duris

Tom Libera

Bill Zavaski

CHAPTER 10

PASSING ON THE FAITH
Youth and Catholic Education

During the summer of 2010, Father Bob Heidenreich accompanied the parish youth group from Sacred Heart in Winnetka to the *Niños Pequeños Hermanos* (NPH) orphanage in Cuernavaca, Mexico, then headed by Chicago's Father Phil Cleary ('79). The orphanage exists for abandoned or orphaned children or children who often end up on the streets because their parents are alcoholic or abusive.

The trip opened the eyes of the Sacred Heart youth group not only, said Bob, because the Winnetka teens saw what children in poverty must face but also because of the approach taken by the orphanage staff. "NPH brings poor kids into an environment where they will receive unconditional love," he says, "but they also have to pitch in and help run the place. After they graduate from high school, they're expected to give a year of service. Even the little kids help wash the dishes. Everybody has got roles and jobs."

> *The hope is that when these kids graduate, they'll have experienced similarities to family life. What Phil's doing is providing a vision of the way the world could be. They would have never gotten that vision if they were at the garbage dump every morning trying to eke out some food.*

What NPH is doing for Mexican orphans, Heidenreich says, the Church must do on a much larger scale for its own youth—present a view of life that challenges young people's day-to-day reality. "In an analogous sense," he says, "we have to give young people a vision of how the Church is alive and what it does in this world. It's an alternate vision, and they're going to have to say, 'Do I want to go down this road or that road?' What we can say," Bob Heidenreich insists, believing it to be the heart of the Catholic effort to pass along the faith, "is at least they have the alternate vision."

....

Any look at youth in the Catholic Church could begin with the line that anchors so many jokes: We have good news and bad news. To start with the bad news, all six of the 1969 classmates agreed that the numbers of youth attending Mass and actively involved in parishes has gone down over the course of their priesthoods. They also maintained that the reason for this decline went beyond the effectiveness or lack thereof of the Church's efforts to reach youth. Although some of their parishes still have strong Catholic schools and/or religious education (CCD) enrollments, that very fact can often obscure the reality that hundreds of other youth in their parishes attend neither. Attendance at programs for teens and young adults also has suffered.

Such problems exist, however, not only in the Catholic Church. Robert Putnam and David Campbell have outlined the decline in religious observance and identity among American adolescents of all faiths in their 2010 book *American Grace: How Religion Divides Us and Unites Us*. As late as 1968, 92% of American adolescents reported attending religious services "at least occasionally" in the previous year. By 1970, not surprisingly given the anti-authority and anti-institution mood of the times, that number dropped to 87%. But then it held at between 85 and 87% for the next 25 years. Between 1995 and 2010, however, the number of adolescents reporting at least occasional attendance fell to 75%.[1] Even more alarming, from the standpoint of organized religion, is that youth claiming no religious preference at all has risen over the last 30 years, with a huge spike since 2000. In 1965, only 7 percent of America's adolescents claimed no religious preference. This number rose to 13% by 1970, but then dropped back to 8% by 1980. It crept back up to 13% by 1995, rose to 15% by 2000, and then surged by 2008 with the percentage of youth claiming no religious preference growing to 22%.[2]

Reasons for the drop-off in both attendance and Catholic identity among adolescents remain unclear. Mike Ahlstrom says of the lower numbers, "It's a mystery. Some people say, 'It's because you changed all that stuff.' I don't think that had anything to do with it. Probably it'd be worse if we hadn't changed things. We have to experiment because I do worry about the rank and file drifting away. We have lost a generation."

The six priests of the ordination class of 1969 point to three major changes they've observed in the lives of young people that may be affecting their commitment to Catholicism: high school activity levels, technology, and, most significantly, parental influence.

Ed Upton considers today's more intense, all-encompassing high school programs as a barrier to the Church connecting with youth. "At least in suburban parishes, the high schools run everything for kids," he says. "They have very intense schedules. So I don't know that kids have changed all that much. They don't seem different, but the environment has drastically changed in terms of time pressures." Today's youth are so scheduled with activities that church events often drop right off the list, falling far behind school, sports, and other commitments.

Larry Duris has grappled with how changing modes of communication have impacted parish life. "People used to say, 'I've got to watch where my kid goes so I don't lose them,'" he notes. "Now with technology the kid doesn't have to go anywhere. He can be in his bedroom online and you can lose him." The Church is often completely absent from a young person's ever-present social media world. Duris also says that children often witness, and suffer from, their parents' overreliance on technology as well.

> We can delude ourselves into being self-sufficient. You come
> home from work and pop stuff in the microwave, get your
> remotes out, open your e-mail. Then you wonder why you're
> lonely. One person, God love him, got into computers. One night
> he's not in bed with his wife. He's in the next room. She comes to
> the door and says, "Honey?" He answers, "Yes, Dear?"

"Does it also make love to you?" She got her point across.

The influence of parents ranks as the number one cause of the young drifting away from practicing the faith in the eyes of these priests. "Part of the problem," Mike Ahlstrom says, "is that many parents don't practice the faith." Bill Zavaski provides a vivid illustration. "When I was at the high school confirmation class," he recounts, "I asked the 15 students, 'How many of you went to Mass this weekend?' Two of the 15. In '75, we would have had half. Families have changed. Our parents modeled for us." Zavaski doesn't even comment on the fact that the teens felt no need to fib to a priest about skipping Mass.

Ed Upton has thought long and hard about the significant changes in families' relationships with the Church over the last generation. "Kids tell you they're not going to Mass," he remarks, still surprised, "as if they don't get that it's a problem. They're being honest."

> *They don't see a challenge. They would self-identify as a Catholic as opposed to nothingness. But I don't know what it means for them—it's hard for us to understand because we grew up in a Catholic ghetto. The shocking thing is the drop-off in Mass attendance after eighth grade—you never see them again. How many even come back to get married? That is going down. Family support isn't there anymore. Most parents don't force their kids after eighth grade because they don't want the arguments.*

Upton finds himself wondering what role the family's ethnic customs play. He sees the religious connection stronger, for example, in Polish families than among, say, his fellow Irish, where Catholic commitment, he says, "has gone the way of the dogs. Poles have held onto it in a stronger way, perhaps because Catholicism is so connected with their culture."

Although some criticisms about parents pepper these priests' comments, Upton feels for parents who have tried to raise their children as dedicated Catholics only to see them, too, fall away from the practice of the faith. "What do you do as parents?" he questions. "I used to say to parents, if you go to Mass, your kids will go to Mass. Wrong. It doesn't always happen. There's a couple, we're great friends. They were the most active faithful church people, generous to the church, the community. They had five kids and only one goes to Mass. Another family, they had five kids. They were regular churchgoers and all their kids still go to Mass. What is the difference? Was it their peer group in high school? There's nothing that seems predictive. What I thought I knew as the truth wasn't true.

"What do you do," he asks plaintively, "to move a kid through early adulthood so they believe in the Church, they live it? Nothing seems to work universally. I don't have an answer. I wish I did."

While Tom Libera agrees that external and cultural factors no longer work to keep young people in the pews, he wonders if the solution might occur in the spiritual realm. "Is there enough spiritual hunger," he asks, "that youth will revisit—if not deepen along the way—their Catholic faith? There's more skepticism and cynicism now and that gives them pause to say, 'Church doesn't have much to offer.' If the door closes at that point, it's difficult to come back down the line. So, although we're producing good young people, whether they're going to be enough to sustain the institutions we have—that's the question."

....

Now for the good news. These six priests have made consistent efforts to address diminishing youth participation by seeking to improve youth and young adult ministry programs, and by encouraging young people to take a greater role in parish liturgies. Recently the Archdiocese of Chicago, in creating a five-year pastoral plan, conducted an online survey, the results of which highlighted the influence of teens' Mass attendance on the likelihood that they would practice their Catholicism into adulthood.[3] "The survey said," Ed Upton explains, "that the only predictor for adult practice of going to Sunday Mass was if they did so as an adolescent. It doesn't mean if they go to Sunday Mass as an adolescent they will continue to go."

What the survey did say, however, was that if people did not attend Mass as teens, they will almost certainly not do so as adults. By the age of 24, in addition, most young Catholics will have made an all but irrevocable decision as to whether they will remain active Catholics as adults.

The survey results reinforced Tom Libera's opinion about the importance of youth ministry. "If teens stay connected," he says, "there's a very good chance they'll come back. That should be sufficient justification for ministry to teenagers if we want them as adults."

Bob Heidenreich found it intriguing that attendance stood out as the key factor. "The thing that is the most important in terms of their continuing to be a practicing Catholic," he says, "is if they have been attending Mass regularly. Even if their parents make them go." That indicates that parishes should ask new questions. "Not, do we have the right systems in place? Not, do we have enough resources? Instead," he says, "we should focus on the appropriation of faith. How do you get that cyclic habit going every week?"

Attendance patterns have begun to change at St. James Parish since Bill Zavaski decided to move the sacrament of Confirmation from eighth grade to high school and to involve teens in ministries at Mass. "The archdiocese ought to try high school Confirmation," Zavaski insists. "It's the best thing we have going, because we keep those kids involved as freshmen and sophomores. It's a hook. We don't confirm them until they're juniors or seniors, so we have some time with them. Engaging kids in liturgical practices and in the community was also a big thing. We now do a high school teen Mass at 5 p.m. on Sundays. We get a lot of kids."

Zavaski has stayed close to the teens in his parish, unafraid to wade into controversial issues. "The high school kids," he says, "don't see any reason why we shouldn't have gay marriages. I had a big battle over that with them." On the other hand, he says, "a number of them were very upset when I told them I voted for Obama. They were taken aback that the priest would vote for Obama because the right had portrayed him as the big abortionist."

In the end, Zavaski remains hopeful about teens and the Church. "I'm more of an optimist than a pessimist," he says. "We've got a lot of great young people, some great peer ministers. I have great faith in them. We've got kids going on mission trips that really care and want to do something with their lives. They're bringing some hope.

"But on the other hand," Zavaski admits, "these kids are the minority. Others are moving further and further away into the secular society in which religion has no meaning for them whatsoever."

To address that reality, Mike Ahlstrom proposes the diocese implement a program for teens modeled on RCIA. "Let's create a program for them," he says, "so they can catch up with their sacraments."

Tom Libera has brought a program to St. Athanasius that would surely please Ahlstrom. Libera believes giving youth a strong formational base in Catholic practice is more crucial than ever, precisely because the older kids get, the harder it is for the Church to reach them. So he brought in the popular Life Teen model that centers on the Eucharist.[4] The program began in a parish in Mesa, Arizona, and has spread to 31 countries worldwide. "Their idea," Libera says, "is to take traditional pieces of youth ministry, social things but also times when young people discuss various topics—religious or whatever they're going through—and have a good setting for that."

> *Then the core would be a special liturgy that the teens have helped put together that really unapologetically talks about our faith and the gift that it is. In some cases we'd also have Eucharistic Adoration, which could be counter-cultural, but quiet time before the Eucharist is saying Eucharist is important to what it means to be Catholic.*

Currently, about 25 youth at St. A's regularly attend the Life Teen program. "We haven't reached critical mass on that," Libera concedes. "Why? The young people are very busy. They have other venues at Loyola or Evanston [high schools]." Attendance at the youth Mass on Sunday evening, however, has risen. "We have a lively spirit," he exclaims, "in that teen Mass. It's one of our most popular Masses."

Like Tom Libera, Larry Duris has worked to get the young connecting with one another on deeper levels. "To share aspects of life—human, faith, communal—gives them a mirror," he says. "If you never talk to someone, you have no idea what you look like. Other people are mirrors for you." To create those opportunities, St. Ailbe's hosts a myriad of programs to involve the parish's young.

> *Grade school kids are servers and we use high school kids as*
> *their mentors. Our Sunday school has as many high school*
> *assistants as we have catechists. We did a college send-off—a*
> *prayer and commissioning. We sent off 75. We've got 12 praise*
> *dancers in high school and college. We've got 15 Little Angels, the*
> *younger grammar school kids. We have the drill team—six high*
> *school and college guys who perform. We've got young adults*
> *and teens in our ushering ministry. One of the better things*
> *has been Theology on Tap.[5] I've used that as a starting point*
> *to gather young adults and then built support groups, project*
> *groups, and reflection groups.*

But Duris knows his job has only begun once he gets young people and their families to walk through the church doors. His community is plagued by a lack of good jobs, black-on-black youth violence fueled by gangs, and now two or three generations of "kids raising kids," as he phrases it. In the face of so many issues, he says, "part of the role of priests is to help families reflect on the meaning of life and what is life-giving and what is death-dealing."

Duris also purposely seeks out the youth of his parish. "When young people are on the church steps and I'm walking by," he says, "I'll introduce myself. My favorite is I walk up to a group of dudes and say, 'Gentlemen, what's happening?' It's sad. They're looking around for gentlemen. You can see in their body language they think I'm about to chase them off church property and I don't. I shake their hand and ask, 'What's your name? Good to see you.' If I get just a first name, I ask for the last name. They're confused that they weren't chased away and were addressed with respect."

According to Duris, just connecting with youth hanging around the church grounds in the African-American community can have quite an effect in neighborhoods where people often shy away from each other on the streets. "The fact that that sounds revolutionary to some people," he says, "indicates the problem we've got."

In the affluent suburb of Winnetka, at the other end of the dio-

cese from St. Ailbe's, neither resources nor energy serve as an imped-
iment to youth work. Sacred Heart Parish offers many activities for
youth, and it has a long history of having a youth minister on staff.
"But what they do," Bob Heidenreich says, "is hire a youth minister
and say, 'Take care of this.' They throw money at the problem. We're
trying intentionally now to involve a board of young people and parents to put together a program. Then it'll have some roots. We need to
ask what kind of vision do you want your children to develop in this
self-centered society where the major question is, 'What do I get?' Our
role as Church is to be on the same wavelength with parents in terms
of what that vision is, but also to reinforce it. You talk about school,
religious ed, youth ministry—that's what this is all about."

....

Parish leaders design their teen and young adult ministry programs to
keep young people connected to the Church as they grow up past their
childhood years. These programs imply, however, that these youth
have already made a connection to the parish as children, one that
Church leaders hope to sustain over time. Traditionally, parishes have
employed the Catholic school as the most popular and effective means
to form children in the faith. Over the course of their priesthood, however, the men from the class of 1969 have witnessed a steady decline
in Catholic school enrollment. Concurrently, they have seen the rise of
religious education programs—in past years known as CCD (Confraternity of Christian Doctrine)—usually held on Saturdays or Sundays
to help form Catholic children who do not attend Catholic schools.
Debates about both the relative effectiveness and the futures of both
Catholic schools and CCD have raged throughout the Catholic world
for years. While most of the six men studied here strongly support
Catholic schools, a couple have their doubts, and all of them admit that
business as usual will no longer suffice. These classmates seem more
divided over the effectiveness of CCD, but they are united in hoping
to discover creative solutions to forming the next generation of faith-
filled Catholic children.

Four of the six priests declared their unequivocal support for

Catholic education. "I'm pro-Catholic school," Larry Duris says, "because it can be us at our best, talking about the faith in a holistic way."

Tom Libera believes it crucial to continue to educate young Catholics in schools with the hope of inculcating within them a lifelong Catholic identity.

"There's no comparison," Mike Ahlstrom comments when considering the difference in effectiveness between Catholic schools and religious education or CCD in terms of passing on the faith. "Andrew Greeley ('54) did the research on that. He was a great promoter of Catholic schools." Yet Ahlstrom also acknowledges that "sometimes the CCD parents are better Mass-goers than the Catholic school parents. Why do they pay all this tuition and then don't go to church on Sunday?"

In Arlington Heights, Bill Zavaski has over 500 students enrolled in Catholic school at St. James and another 700 in CCD. "A lot of guys think a Catholic school," he says, "is a drain on the parish's economy, but there's a difference between kids in the school and in religious ed. With school kids we're walking through the halls visiting them all week. They know who we are. Kids in religious ed come for an hour and a half."

Despite the preference for schools over CCD, these four priests realize that serious obstacles stand in the way of the future of Catholic schools. "The schools are expensive," Larry Duris admits. "What's killing us are finances and personnel. We need to do some consolidating again." Recently St. Ailbe's joined 15 other South Side parishes in a pilot program looking to find new ways to market and to gain additional resources.

Bill Zavaski pointed out a particularly suburban reality. "People living in the suburbs," he says, "are not going to say it, but they don't want to invest for grade school when Catholic high schools cost them $10,000 to $12,000 a year. But people in the city make the sacrifice because the public schools are that bad."

The long-term solution to school financing, Zavaski insists, must involve a stewardship program in which the whole Catholic community of Chicago takes on responsibility for educating the next generation of Catholics. The Diocese of Wichita, Kansas, instituted such a program and over time reached a point where they now educate Catholic youth tuition-free from grade school through high school. "If we went to stewardship," Zavaski says, "with no tuition and any kid could attend, I suspect our schools would be filled and have a waiting list."

....

Ed Upton is not so sure. He could have summed up his concerns about Catholic schools as market and money. Upton's parish, St. Francis of Assisi, and three other parishes in the far southwest suburbs all feed students into a regional Catholic school. In Upton's early years at the parish, Cardinal Bernardin joined Catholic schools superintendent Elaine Schuster in asking Upton and Father Bill O'Mara ('58), the founding pastor of nearby St. Elizabeth Seton Parish, to consider opening a regional school. "We did two surveys of parents asking if they would they send their kids."

> *The survey said between 15 and 18 percent of people were interested in Catholic education and would pay for it. The survey has been accurate. So 80 percent of the people are not interested, feel they can't afford it, are happy with public education—whatever. Catholic education as we once knew it is dead. There isn't a market. Because four parishes send students to the regional school, however, it has survived. We subsidize 10 percent of the cost, and because it's regional no one complains. But costs in general are out of sight. If we didn't have four parishes, we couldn't do it. Our tuition here is relatively low, about $4,200. But, if you've got three kids, that's $12,000.*

Upton says the archdiocese needs to face economic realities. "There's this big thing about how we didn't close any schools in 2010," he says. "That's stupid. We've got schools open with 100 kids. That's not good stewardship. So I don't know the future of Catholic education."

The rising costs of Catholic schools notwithstanding, the men from 1969 are ambivalent about the ability of religious education programs to pick up the slack. "The affiliation seems not unexpectedly looser," Tom Libera says. "Some families are dedicated. Others, it's touch and go. They'll come for sacraments and disappear."

Bill Zavaski views CCD more positively. "Our religious ed program," he remarks, "has got a lot more meat to it than it had before." Despite high numbers in both the school and religious education at St. James, however, Zavaski knows that many Catholic children in his parish attend neither. "That's the scary part," he says. "We've haven't talked enough about parental responsibility for religious education. You follow your parents no matter what you say. How they live their faith life is going to influence their kids, no matter what we teach them."

Mike Ahlstrom agreed that success or failure, just like with teens, has most to do with adults. He has therefore looked for creative ways for parents to pass along the faith to their children. "We're inviting parents at St. Barbara's to come to class for adult sessions simultaneous to when the kids are meeting for CCD," he says. "I was in one parish where for kids to receive their First Communion, Confession, and Confirmation, parents had to come to six classes to learn what the sacrament was and then had to teach their children. That worked to form some friendship groups among parents that lasted beyond the sacraments."

Bill Zavaski seconds the need for parishes to involve parents. "Community catechesis," he states, "is the new religious education. You bring in families and instruct them. They work together on a project. It's teaching parents, because many parents of our kids were never trained properly. Why is Matthew Kelly writing a book like *Rediscovering Catholicism*? He's writing it for parents because they don't have the foundation for their faith in this culture. That's what we're going to have to do, because if they can't go to a Catholic school, we have to give them something more."[7]

Bob Heidenreich is frustrated by the often fractious discussions about Catholic education. He refuses to weigh in on the effectiveness of schools versus CCD programs because he thinks such debates obscure the two real issues that he sees as inexorably intertwined: parents and mission. "I don't think you can talk about Catholic education," he asserts, "without talking about the role of parents in educating their children. To talk about the institution—no matter whether it's CCD or Catholic schools—without addressing the role of parents in their kids' religious upbringing is vain and hopeless. It has no connection to reality. Then you're running institutions because you run institutions."

To make his point, Heidenreich referred to his first pastorate at St. Benedict Parish on the North Side of Chicago, which to this day maintains parish schools serving children from pre-school through high school. "I heard there," he says, "'We have to keep going. This is St. Ben's and there's history here.' But nobody ever stopped to say, 'Why are we doing this, folks?' That's not a question that people want asked."

Ed Upton also refuses to shy away from uncomfortable questions about whether the mission of Catholic schools is always crystal clear. "I'm concerned," he says, "because we get like the airline industry and just want to fill seats. Then we wake up with people who aren't Catholic and lose focus. At one Catholic high school they didn't have Mass because they didn't want to offend the non-Catholic students. What's that all about?"

Despite his concerns, Upton supports Catholic schools. "Should we have schools in the inner city?" he asks rhetorically. "Absolutely. Catholic schools should continue. But they need to be Catholic schools—not just academies for people who fill seats, but focused on Catholic life."

....

As all six of these priests near retirement age, they continued to grapple with how best to pass on the faith to the next generation, working to identify programs and methods that will keep alive the fire they feel for Christ and his Church. Whether focusing on teen and young adult ministry, Catholic schools, or religious education, these six priests continue to insist that developing strong relationships with parents—along with the youth themselves—remains the key to any successful method of reaching the young. What they've learned over time, in addition, is the need to focus those relationships more clearly on the mission and vision of Catholic Christianity, so that they pass them down, directly and indirectly, sensibly and insensibly, to the next generation of Catholics, intact and alive.

....

1. Robert D. Putnam and David E. Campbell, *American Grace: How Religion Divides and Unites Us* (New York: Simon and Schuster, 2010), 78.
2. Ibid., 101.
3. For more on the survey, see "The 2011-2016 Strategic Pastoral Plan for the Archdiocese of Chicago," 5-9 at http://www.archchicago.org.
4. Life Teen is a Catholic youth ministry organization and movement originating in the United States. It was established in 1985 at St. Timothy's Parish in Mesa, Arizona to "lead teens closer to Christ." Life Teen believes that "Eucharist-based ministry has the power to transform teens, transform parishes, and transform culture." See lifeteen.com.
5. Theology on Tap is an evangelization and catechetical speaker program for young adults. Begun in the Archdiocese of Chicago in 1981 by Father Jack Wall ('68) and then youth minister Tom James, it was run until recently by Father John Cusick ('70) and Dr. Kate DeVries, former directors of Young Adult Ministry for the Archdiocese of Chicago. The program has been offered in 48 states and seven countries. Website of Archdiocese of Chicago: Young Adult Ministry, http://www.yam.chicago.org. Father Cusick has also started Friends of Young Adult Ministry, Inc., to support ministry to young adults in the Catholic Church in America. The address is P.O. Box 617554, Chicago, IL 60661.
6. See Office of Stewardship: Catholic Diocese of Wichita at http://www.catholicdioceseofwichita.org.
7. Matthew Kelly, *Rediscovering Catholicism* (Cincinnati, OH: Beacon Publishing, 2002).

CHAPTER 11

CARDINAL SINS, CARDINAL VIRTUES
Cardinals Cody, Bernardin, and George

One of the most amazing things about the careers of the six men from the ordination class of 1969 is that they have shared only three ultimate bosses over the past 45 years: Cardinals John Cody, Joseph Bernardin, and Francis George. Pope Francis was to name a successor for Cardinal George in the fall of 2014.

While it is unusual in almost any other line of work to have had only three CEOs, so to speak, over such a long time, it is not unusual in the Archdiocese of Chicago. Chicago, as one of the most important dioceses in the country, is a "final destination" for clerics who serve in the Catholic episcopacy. The last six archbishops of Chicago have also been named to the College of Cardinals, and they usually exert a leadership role among their fellow American bishops. No archbishop of Chicago has ever been "promoted" to another diocese. When you get to Chicago, it is the end of the line…unless you are called to Rome.

In the case of Cody, Bernardin, and George, all three men were named to Chicago at a relatively young age and stayed until they either died or retired in their seventies. So each of them had a relatively long tenure in Chicago and therefore has been important in shaping the priesthoods of Mike Ahlstrom, Larry Duris, Bob Heidenreich, Tom Libera, Ed Upton, and Bill Zavaski—in decidedly different ways.

"My biggest difficulty with John Patrick Cody," Mike Ahlstrom says, "was that in the 17 years he was my archbishop, I can honestly say I never heard him say Jesus or God once, other than in a prayer he was reading."

To illustrate this stunning observation, Ahlstrom recalled attending a talk that Cody gave to his priests. On the lectern in front of the Cardinal sat a Jerusalem Bible. Cody picked up the Bible and put it on the floor, apparently without a second thought. Then he spread his elbows, leaned in, and began speaking. "Now I'm going to talk," he said, "about the Church."

If he neglected to mention the Almighty, he almost certainly dwelt on what Cody called the priests' "career" in the Church. "Any time he talked," says Ahlstrom, "it was about his Church career, about our career. I don't like that word. I did not see his faith. He believed very much in the Church as an institution, but I never saw him talking about God or about Jesus."

John Patrick Cody, born in St. Louis in 1907, entered the seminary there at the age of 13. Between his seminary training and early priestly assignments, he spent 10 years in Rome, after which he moved quickly up the ecclesiastical power ladder, including serving between 1954 and 1965 as bishop of Kansas City–St. Joseph, Missouri and archbishop of New Orleans. He arrived in Chicago in August of 1965 (Pope Paul VI named him a cardinal in 1967) with a reputation as a liberal, having advocated for racial justice while bishop of New Orleans. But Cody was seen as having been an autocrat in his dealings with the New Orleans clergy. And by the end of his first year in Chicago, it had become clear to many that he indeed would oversee the archdiocese with an autocratic style that left little room for personal warmth.

The men of the class of 1969, however, who had just begun their third year at Mundelein Seminary, greeted Cody enthusiastically during his early days. "He was initially a hero," Larry Duris remembers. "He plopped on the throne first week in August '65. By the end of September he had met with the student body about changes in the rules. That's moving fast. He freed us up from the prison." Ahlstrom tells how Cody asked students at the three seminary residence buildings on the Mundelein campus to give him ten suggestions each about how to improve the seminary. The seminarians colluded to ensure that none of the 30 suggestions overlapped, and Cody implemented 29 of the suggestions within two months. "It was a revolution overnight," says Ahlstrom. "We were repressed slaves, and Cody was Moses leading us into the Promised Land."

Cody swiftly retired Mundelein rector Mal Foley ('31), replacing him with Jack Gorman ('52), whom the class of 1969 had come to admire in their two years at Niles. "Cody had the insight to know that what was going on at Mundelein was not healthy," says Bob Heidenreich of the move.

Even Cody's controversial Project Renewal plan to invest in the black Catholic community and his "retiring" of older pastors met with approval at the seminary.[1] The class rejoiced that the Church was trying to help black Chicagoans, and the seminarians felt little sympathy for the once-powerful pastors summarily sent packing. "As young people we thought, these are old men—they should go," says Ed Upton.

....

But for all the initial euphoria around Cody's arrival, the seminarians quickly found its limits when they protested statements made by New York's Cardinal Francis Spellman in support of the Vietnam War. "As Cody was returning from the Vatican Council with Spellman," says Mike Ahlstrom, "the protest made headlines. He read us the riot act. He went from being our hero to 'Who is this man?'"

"Who is this man?" has proved a difficult question for these members of the class of 1969. To be sure, by the time they had been ordained and begun work in parish ministry, Cody's hero status had long faded. Looking back on their years under Cody, members of the class found much to critique: autocratic decision-making, an impenetrable and cold communication style, and a lack of any observable spirituality, all culminating in Cody's humiliation under the weight of a financial scandal that dominated the last two years of his life. For priests burning with enthusiasm for the sense of shared priestly ministry enkindled by the Second Vatican Council, the leadership style of their archbishop left much to be desired.

Examples of Cody's dictatorial style abound. With no consultation, he decreed that all parishes must buy the archdiocesan newspaper, *The New World*, for all their families, costing upwards of $10,000 annually, a hefty sum for any parish. Larry Duris describes how Cody once sat in an all-day meeting with the Priest Senate—supposedly his consultative body of priests—and neglected to mention that he had signed a contract committing millions in archdiocesan funds to the Catholic Television Network. When Cody called a press conference the next day to announce the contract, Duris and his fellow Priest Senate members could only shake their heads.[2] Mike Ahlstrom incurred Cody's wrath by writing an opinion piece attacking Ann Landers for declaring that sharing the cup at Communion was unsanitary. What he didn't realize was that Cody was Landers' close friend. Ahlstrom's column was torpedoed before it even appeared.

Cody's communication style with his priests ranged from distant to caustic to non-existent. "Pastors would call him, and he would never respond," says Bob Heidenreich. "Cody saw that something should be done and he did it; it didn't make any difference what other people thought." Heidenreich and Ed Upton both served on the Personnel Board which had been instituted, with Cody's approval, to improve the process of assigning priests in part by taking into consideration their wants and needs. The two men were surprised, however, that the Board saw very little of their archbishop. Cody communicated almost exclusively with Father Dick Keating ('59), who was archdiocesan vicar general and chair of the Board. "We never met with Cody," Upton says. "Keating brokered it, sending in three names, and Cody took one of those names for the most part. But he was Irish. If he didn't like you, he would remember: 'I'm not appointing him pastor.' There was animosity about the way he treated people."

Cody often left parish assignments vacant for months on end. After Cody's death in 1982, Heidenreich says, Dick Keating found in the Cardinal's nightstand a pile of status reports listing parish vacancies, none of which had been dealt with.

These very vacancies led to an embarrassing moment for Heidenreich shortly after Joseph Bernardin took over as archbishop, an incident that spoke volumes about the Personnel Board's relationship with Cody. The Board worked out of offices in Queen of Heaven Cemetery, in the Chicago suburb of Hillside. One day, early in his tenure, Bernardin called the office and spoke to Heidenreich, saying he wanted to deal with the parish appointments that Cody had left hanging. Bernardin asked Heidenreich and the other Board members to come to his office right away.

> "Archbishop, it's going to take us about 45 minutes," said Heidenreich.
> "Forty-five minutes? Aren't you downtown in this building?" asked a confused Bernardin.
> "No, your Eminence," said Heidenreich. "We're out in Hillside at the cemetery."
> "The cemetery? How did you guys get out there?" asked Bernardin.
> "It's a long story," Heidenreich told him, hesitant to inform his new archbishop that the Personnel Board had moved to the cemetery offices to get as far away from Cody as they could get.

Leave it to Larry Duris to find a silver lining in Cody's style. "Cody was ideal," Duris says, "from the standpoint of a community organizer. It's good to have an enemy to organize around."

....

After serving under Cody for just over a year, the Chicago presbyterate did just that. In an unprecedented display of clerical independence, over 1,200 Chicago priests met at McCormick Place, Chicago's massive convention hall, on October 24, 1966, to found the Association of Chicago Priests (ACP). The ACP soon became the talk of the country, with newspaper articles abounding, as well as an appearance by Father Jack Hill ('50), an early ACP leader, on NBC's *Today* show. By the end of 1966, over 40 dioceses had followed Chicago's lead and formed clergy associations. Cardinal Cody served, according to a sardonic Tom

Libera, as "one of the major recruiters." Leaders of the group, however, which still operates today—though with fewer numbers and less influence—went out of their way at the outset to say the ACP neither intended to function as a union nor was hostile to the Cardinal. In fact, Cody spoke at the McCormick Place meeting, although many priests felt his talk condescendingly belittled their new organization as unnecessary. Still, Cody attended all ACP meetings during its first year.[3]

Over time, relations between Cody and the ACP deteriorated. Cody moved to contain the ACP's influence by starting a Priest Senate, making it a formal part of the archdiocesan structure. Of this maneuver, Ed Upton says, laughing, "He tried to chop their legs off. I can admire that politically at least, but I didn't agree with it."

Relations between Cody and his priests took a turn for the worse when the Young Priests Caucus published a list of pastors that newly ordained priests and other young associates should avoid serving under. Then, on June 15, 1971, the ACP publicly censored the archbishop and his auxiliaries in a close vote of 144 to 126 for not adequately presenting their views to Rome on their desire to see a discussion of a married clergy.[4]

Two priests from the class of 1969 expressed reservations about the censure. Although most ACP members thought the auxiliary bishops hadn't spoken up on the issue, Ed Upton insists that they did indeed represent the priests' views to Rome but could not say so publicly out of a need to respect the confidentiality of the meetings. Mike Ahlstrom resigned from the ACP over the vote. "While I didn't agree with the bishops, I thought formally and publicly censuring, that's going back to medieval times," he says. "Eventually I came back." The ACP continued to act as a thorn in Cody's side, at one point writing Rome to complain about Cody's arbitrary use of authority.

Tom Libera served a term as ACP chair from 1979 to 1981. During this time, Cody spoke to him a total of once. "It wasn't cutting, but there were two sentences of exchange about the ACP. That was it. Cody wasn't at that point particularly fond of the ACP. It ran up against him a few times, so he just ignored it."

As ACP chair during Cardinal Cody's waning days as archbishop, Libera had the unenviable task of dealing with the siege of criticism about Cody's running of the archdiocese that had led to continued deterioration of the relationship between him and his priests. Then, in 1981, allegations reported in the *Chicago Sun-Times* that Cody had mingled archdiocesan funds with personal assets in order to aid a woman named Helen Dolan Wilson destroyed for most of his priests whatever respect he had retained among them. The *Sun-Times* reported that Cody had given thousands of dollars, allegedly belonging to the archdiocese, to Wilson, paid her a salary as a ghost employee, and conducted most diocesan insurance business with her son David despite the fact that he worked in St. Louis rather than Chicago. The newspaper also hinted that Cody might have had a sexual relationship with Wilson, whom he often falsely referred to as his "cousin." Only Cody's death in April of 1982 at the age of 74 prevented, in all likelihood, an indictment by the federal government and his possible removal from office by Rome.[5]

"The *Sun-Times* revelations were new territory in terms of public discourse about the Church," says Libera. "You didn't imply that cardinals had done wrong. So how do you respond as a group of priests still connected with the Cardinal yet not completely satisfied with how he was doing things? We tried to straddle that. Some people said, 'We support your role as leader but we have issues.' Others wanted a more firm critique of him."

In the end, Libera sent a letter expressing "support and compassion" for Cody on behalf of the ACP. His classmates had varying reactions.

"We were shocked," Bill Zavaski says of reading about the allegations. "I felt bad for Cody."

Bob Heidenreich remains more circumspect about the cardinal's troubles. "When he was going to be prosecuted by the feds," he says, "because of the mixing of his funds with diocesan funds, he didn't see anything wrong. He thought 'I'm the archbishop.' No, you're not the role. You're John Cody. Archbishop is your job. He didn't see that."

"When the Vatican called for an apostolic visitation of the archdiocese," Ed Upton recalls, "people lost respect. The guy was probably a crook; there wasn't a purity of character."

With the perspective of time, a number of the men from the class of 1969 acknowledge that Cody accomplished much good for the Church of Chicago. They praise his efforts in beginning the Office for Liturgy and in implementing health insurance and pensions for employees and liability insurance for parishes, in starting the Office for Peace and Justice and the Development of Ministry office. "With Project Renewal," Larry Duris says, "he began endowment funds in the inner city. Thank God. And he retired the old baron pastors, although he caught hell for that."

"When I look back on Cody," Ed Upton also concedes, "compared to where we are now, he was a lot more liberal than we gave him credit for. He poured a ton of money into the inner city, way more than we do today. The ACP wanted to do an experimental parish at Ford City. He let them. He didn't appoint rigid conservatives. His starting a capital campaign for the diocese was great. But Cody did it like a bull in a china shop. I have a little sympathy for him about the formation of the ACP. It was a huge change. As a bishop, all of sudden you have 1,200 of your priests organized—I'd be scared, too."

The public turmoil of Cody's term as archbishop could obscure the personal side of his relations with his priests, or the lack thereof. Those glimpses, however, may best explain the huge morale problem Cody left behind when he died in April of 1982. "He did appoint me as pastor," Bill Zavaski says, "but I found it strange he never called to tell me." Cody did call him at the hospital when Zavaski was recovering from cancer surgery. "I said," Zavaski recalls playfully, "'Cardinal, how do you handle these nurses poking and prodding you? How do you keep your sense of modesty? You've been in the hospital.'" Cody answered tersely, "I'll talk to you later, Father," and ended the call.

Zavaski and Ed Upton made the unpopular decision to invite Cody in 1974 to the fifth anniversary of the class' ordination. "Everyone was madder than hell," Zavaski recalls. "They made us drive him home. As we're driving, I said, 'I've never been to your house.' He said, 'Son, that's a good sign. Only those in trouble come to my house.' He did bizarre things. He called Mike Ahlstrom on Good Friday because

Mike didn't have his will signed. You'd think he'd be thinking about something religious."

Zavaski looked back with regret on Cody's final days in Chicago. "Although he was a good administrator," he says, "he was deceitful. I don't think he was very spiritual. He loved going to Rome, he loved power, and our priests wanted a spiritual leader."

Mike Ahlstrom considered Cody's personal style tragic for both the archbishop and his priests. "He was quoted," Ahlstrom remarks, "as saying, 'I have no friends. I can't have friends.' There was no rapport. 'I'm the general and you're my privates'—that's how we were treated. It wasn't a bond between the bishop as a father and priests as his sons, if you will, or a fraternity. It was a cold relationship."

....

"They felt oppressed by Cody for many reasons," Bill Zavaski says of his classmates who share the house in Michigan with him, "but felt happy with Joseph [Bernardin]." When Zavaski brought pictures of both men to put up in the house, some of his confreres didn't want him to put Cody's photo up. "He ordained us," Zavaski recalls insisting. "We've got to have his picture up." They relented but insisted he hang it in the basement. "It's a nice, finished basement," Zavaski says, laughing. "But he's in the basement. Bernardin is at the top of the stairs."

At 7:30 p.m. on August 24, 1982, Joseph Bernardin entered the sanctuary of Holy Name Cathedral to celebrate the Mass presenting him to his priests as the seventh archbishop of Chicago. (His formal installation would come a day later.) When the time came for Bernardin to deliver his homily to hundreds of assembled priests, he began with the words: "I am Joseph, your brother." The contrast in tone and style to Cody could not have been more striking.

Bernardin turned his attention to what he thought of the priests of Chicago. Admitting he knew few of them personally, he nevertheless stated boldly, "I feel that I know the priesthood of Chicago. It is more than a local reality. It is a national asset." Bernardin mentioned Chicago's role in "pioneering" programs such as the Catholic Youth Organization (CYO), Christian Family Movement (CFM), various urban ministry, social justice, liturgical, and seminary development initiatives, and the permanent diaconate program. "I think," Bernardin proclaimed, "you are a remarkable group of men. I praise you and applaud you." The archbishop then addressed his vision and plans for the archdiocese, emphasizing the need for a shared sense of ministry. Bernardin indicated his openness to working closely with the ACP, and he planned to resurrect the by then moribund Priest Senate and to begin a lay Archdiocesan Pastoral Council. In concluding his remarks, Bernardin asked the priests gathered to let go of any feelings of bitterness toward his predecessor, John Cody. "I hope that long before my name falls from the Eucharistic Prayer in the silence of death," he finished, referring to the prayer for the local bishop uttered at each Mass in his diocese, "you will know well who I am.... You will know me as a friend, fellow priest, and bishop. You will also know that I love you. For I am Joseph, your brother."[7]

Bernardin's homily triggered first relief, then joy. "He clearly distanced himself from Cody," says Ed Upton. "He captured a sense of 'I'm going to walk with you' as opposed to Cody's arrogance. He set a whole different tone, and he was well aware of that."

"There was a lot of hurt, and many of the priests felt healed," Bill Zavaski concurs, "because he was far more personable. Joseph wanted to be liked. Cody couldn't care less if anybody liked him. The great thing Bernardin did was heal the Chicago presbyterate, because it was angry and fragmented."

....

When Bernardin arrived in Chicago from Cincinnati, where he had served as archbishop from 1972-1982, he had already acquired a reputation as a politically astute progressive ecclesiastical politician, good at bringing people together to advance the work of the Church and at creating symbolic and substantive gestures designed to make people feel part of that Church. Born to Italian immigrant parents in 1928, Bernardin was ordained a priest for the diocese of Charleston, South Carolina in 1952. In 1966 he was named auxiliary bishop of Atlanta. Just 38 years old, he was the youngest bishop in the United States.

From 1968 to 1972 he served as the General Secretary of the National Council of Catholic Bishops, where he honed his ecclesiastical political skills.

On his arrival in Chicago in 1982 (Rome elevated him to the College of Cardinals in 1983), Bernardin instituted an Archdiocesan Pastoral Council; he inspired Big Shoulders, a major fundraising outreach of wealthy Catholics to aid struggling inner city Catholic schools; he worked with the Alexian Brothers to establish Bonaventure House to treat victims of AIDS; he started an annual convocation of Chicago priests, designed to boost camaraderie and morale among his presbyterate; he established an office for black Catholics. Bernardin also reached out to the ACP and supported priests when they needed to receive treatment at Guest House, the national treatment program for alcoholic priests.[8] He also demonstrated his support for young adults by hosting the annual picnic for the Theology on Tap summer speaker series in the backyard of his residence, started the first archdiocesan Mass for the divorced and separated at the Cathedral, befriended Protestant and Jewish leaders in Chicago, and put much effort into anti-pornography work. He instituted a process in the mid-1990s called "Decisions," which involved more than 8,000 Chicago Catholics at the parish level dialoguing about every aspect of the future of the archdiocese from liturgy planning to Catholic education. His tenure had its problems as well, the most pronounced of these being the onslaught of the sexual abuse crisis and the closing of over 50 parishes and schools.

Cardinal Bernardin exerted perhaps even more influence in the Catholic Church at large than he did in Chicago. As architect of the U.S. bishops' 1982 peace pastoral, *The Challenge of Peace: God's Promise and Our Response*, Bernardin's image appeared on the cover of *Time* magazine with the title "God and the Bomb."[9] The next year he articulated his consistent ethic of life, also known as "the seamless garment"—an image taken from the Gospel of John that refers to Jesus' seamless robe. He argued that abortion, euthanasia, capital punishment, militarism, and social justice all needed a consistent application of moral principles that valued the sanctity of human life.[10]

Criticized by Catholic conservatives for supposedly not stressing the importance of abortion above the other issues, Bernardin won the applause of Catholic progressives. His views dominated the U.S. Bishops' conference for almost 20 years. He launched his final national effort in 1996, shortly before he died, called the "Catholic Common Ground Initiative." Here the Cardinal sought to bring together Church leaders in dialogue to lessen the polarities and divisiveness that weakened the Church's communion.[11]

....

Members of the class of 1969 found much to like about their new archbishop and were glad when he was elevated to the status of cardinal; they appreciated his accomplishments at the archdiocesan level as well as his national and international influence in the Church. Just as important for the six men was how Bernardin went about his business. Larry Duris recalls that Bernardin agreed to attend retreats that he and then Father Wilton Gregory ('73), now Archbishop of Atlanta, organized for priests serving in African-American parishes to dialogue with the Cardinal. Bob Heidenreich praised the "Decisions" planning process. "When Bernardin died in 1996," he notes, "Cardinal George picked up on 'Decisions.' That became his blueprint."

Bernardin's efforts on the national stage also encouraged the priests of Chicago. Tom Libera saw the peace pastoral, the consistent ethic of life, and the Common Ground Initiative as successful efforts at mediation between opposing forces in both the Church and the culture. "Bernardin even entered into women's issues," Libera says, "the best he could with the little flexibility he had. He listened to them and engendered some hope without giving false hope that we're going to have women's ordination in the near future. He was in the proud tradition of the best archbishops in Chicago by breaking new ground here for the Church nationally."

Always one to appreciate political savvy, Ed Upton marveled at Bernardin's success at leading the Church in the U.S. "Bernardin really led a cabal of liberal bishops," he says, "who controlled the whole thing. And he was the conduit between the Clinton administration and the American Church. He had a vision to move the Church forward with the seamless garment and Common Ground. He tried to expand the conversation. That's all gone today. The bishops don't want to expand any conversations because they already have the truth."

Upton remembered clearly when the tide began to turn against Bernardin and the so-called "Vatican II" bishops. "He had just come out with Common Ground," Upton says. "Some cardinals had laughed at him. I was behind him in a buffet line at Mundelein. He uttered some choice words because he was so furious at those cardinals."

Upton sees Bernardin's public efforts on behalf of the American Church as a crucial part of his legacy. "He was holy and I respected that," he says, "but I liked him because he was a politician listening to people and bringing them together, developing coalitions and making something better than it was. That's good politics."

....

Indeed, the "how" as much as the "what" of Cardinal Bernardin's episcopal ministry endeared him to Chicago's priests. Over and over the men from 1969 talk about his collaborative style, which contrasted so starkly with Cody's autocratic and imperious ways. "Bernardin didn't close doors on you," Tom Libera says, "or go silent, not answering the phone." Larry Duris in fact worried that Bernardin collaborated so much that "we might never do anything because the consultation never ends."

Bill Zavaski, however, has a different take on Bernardin's seemingly endless tolerance for dialogue. "He was a genius," Zavaski exclaims. "He gave everyone the impression that people made the decisions. Well, he had everyone talk all the time, but he made the decisions. The Archdiocesan Pastoral Council would talk for months, but he got them to do what he wanted."

And at the end of the day, it was their own personal experiences with him—the likes of which they had never had with Cody—that cemented Bernardin's stature in the minds and hearts of the six priests. One thing they discovered was that he liked to have fun. Some members of the class took Bernardin out to dinner in Lake County, north of Chicago, one evening. Afterward he invited them back to his house on the grounds of Mundelein Seminary for a nightcap in the cardinal's residence on the campus. "All my life," Mike Ahlstrom admits, "I'd wanted to see the inside of that place. Well, Bernardin was like a little kid. We went up to the attic, down to the basement. Saw Cardinal Mundelein's famous nine spigot shower. He took us through the place and told us the stories. Wow—that he took the time."

Tom Libera experienced the same thoughtfulness at a more serious juncture. When three West Side parishes were merging into the newly constituted St. Martin de Porres, Libera and his priestly colleagues had spent months looking for a new worship site. Archdiocesan leaders at first had encouraged them to build a new church, but then, during a period of financial struggle, the officials had gone mum on the subject. Tension grew; Libera began calling diocesan officials looking for answers. Finally Bernardin's assistant called Libera to say that the Cardinal wanted to visit him that night.

> It's 10 p.m. before he arrives. He goes up to my room. I wonder what he's thinking. He sits down and says, "I'm going to Rome tomorrow. I know you're looking for direction. The news I have to give isn't the easiest, so I wanted to give it to you myself." He didn't say directly that we weren't going to have a new church, but it became apparent that that wasn't in the financial cards. My gosh, that he would come out to give that information. There was a fondness for that thoughtfulness. Because this guy the next day is going to be on a plane and dealing with a whole other universe of relationships.

Clearly Bernardin's personal touch, sorely lacking in their relations with John Cody, meant the world to the six priests ordained in 1969.

....

Cardinal Bernardin's final years in Chicago contained much pain, but also ultimately solace. In 1993, Steven Cook, a former seminarian in Cincinnati, accused Bernardin of sexually abusing him during the 1970s. By 1994, Cook had retracted his allegations and Bernardin eventually said Mass for his accuser and forgave him both publicly and privately. Cook died of AIDS in 1995. By then Bernardin had also been diagnosed with pancreatic cancer. His handling of these two situations only increased the respect and affection that members of the class of 1969 had for their episcopal leader. Bernardin spent months reaching out to cancer patients, even as he strove to devote himself more deeply to prayer and gradually to let go of his administrative burdens before his death in November of 1996. Loyola Press eventually published his reflections on this experience in a book, *The Gift of Peace*.[12] Tom Libera says of these final years, "Bernardin wound up being a man of deep faith who met death in a way that became an incredible pastoral ministry to people who met him. Here was an example of a priest who says by his life, 'Things aren't set in stone. You can change.' He recommitted himself as a bishop to enter more deeply into prayer and a trusting life. You lose people too soon."

Ed Upton also noticed a change in Bernardin during his final struggles. "It started with the accusation," Upton reflects, "which I'm convinced caused the cancer. The way he accepted it and talked about it was touching, human. But it wasn't maudlin. And he tried to make amends to people."

The difference between Cody and Bernardin's final years in Chicago was not lost on the priests. Mike Ahlstrom looked back on an interaction he had with Bernardin at a reception following the prayer service he celebrated with his clergy just prior to his death. The priests knew it was the last time they would see their Cardinal alive. Ahlstrom wasn't even sure if Bernardin would remember his name, given his illness and the hundreds of priests present. "At the time," he says, "I had a newly ordained associate leaving the priesthood to get married. When I approached the Cardinal, before I could open my mouth he says, 'What can we do to help this man?' Cody never would've done that. He's dying and he's worrying about how can he help one of his men. Those were his last words to me." Ahlstrom also remembered the prayer service itself. "He talked about how he was afraid to die, yet he was embracing death as a friend and wants us to embrace our crosses. I'll never forget that."

"That was the man," says Ed Upton. "He was caring, accepting, a good man." And that goodness explains why, each time the priests of Pinion walk up the stairs to their rooms, it is the picture of Cardinal Joseph Bernardin that greets them.

....

Francis George returned to his hometown of Chicago as archbishop in April of 1997. By most accounts, his reentry went poorly. Bill Zavaski remembered the "ouch" moment when George alluded to Bernardin during his opening talk to the priests of the archdiocese. "He didn't say, 'I am your brother,'" Zavaski recalls. "He said, 'I'm your neighbor.' That set the tone right there."

In his initial visits to parishes George made a habit of pointing out areas where he thought pastors had failed to toe the line in their celebration of the liturgy, such as incorrect distribution of Communion, improper altar bread, the need for retraining of deacons, the lack of kneelers in churches, and congregations that stood rather than knelt during the Eucharistic prayer. In November 1997, 43 members of the Pastor's Forum, an informal group of Chicago priests, privately wrote George complaining about issues of "style as well as substance" and referencing the nickname an unnamed priest had given the cardinal: "Francis the Corrector." George, to his great credit, defused the controversy when the letter was released to the press by his self-proclaimed defenders. Although George thanked those supporting him, he replied that he needed no defense since he had not been attacked, and he admitted that he needed to build trust with and get to know his priests, even as he asserted his right to call them to follow correct liturgical rubrics.[13]

Born in 1937 and raised on the Northwest Side of Chicago in St. Paschal Parish, George early on expressed a desire to pursue the priesthood. Denied entry to Quigley Preparatory Seminary because of a disability resulting from his having contracted polio at age 13, George entered the Missionary Oblates of Mary Immaculate instead. After his ordination in 1963, he pursued the life of the mind, earning doctorates in philosophy and theology. He served as vicar general of the Oblates in Rome from 1974 until 1986. In 1990, Pope John Paul II appointed him bishop of Yakima and then elevated him to archbishop of Portland, Oregon in 1996. Less than a year later, George became Archbishop of Chicago at age 60. The pope named him a cardinal in 1998.

Although admitting that Bernardin had been a tough act to follow, many priests' initial impressions of George were not positive. George arrived in Chicago, however, under different circumstances than did his predecessor. The profound grief Chicagoans felt at the loss of Bernardin muted George's early days. "It wasn't like after Cody," Upton explains, "where people were happy to get a new archbishop—people were sad."

For a presbyterate whose pride in the Chicago priesthood Bernardin had largely restored, their new archbishop's complaints about perceived errors and abuses, mostly liturgical in nature, stung. "He came across as the answer man," Larry Duris recalls. "Maybe that comes from his years teaching and being head of a congregation."

....

Over time, as George and his priests adjusted to one another, both positives and negatives began to emerge. George continued to implement the "Decisions" process that Bernardin had initiated. He showed strong support for Catholic schools, encouraging the Big Shoulders program and showing a reluctance to close struggling inner-city schools. He continued to host young adults from the Theology on Tap program on his lawn at their annual picnic. He insisted on implementing all norms of the Dallas Charter for the Protection of Children in response to the sexual abuse crisis in the Church. George, in addition, wrote a well-received pastoral letter on racism and championed the rights of immigrants. More recently, with the help of his vicar general, Msgr. John Canary ('69), he put together a five-year strategic pastoral plan for the archdiocese so as to leave a "Decisions"-type blueprint for his successor.

But George tended to focus too much, in the eyes of the six men from the ordination class of 1969, on moral imperatives and liturgical rules, and he did so more with a dogmatic than a pastoral approach. Initially, he meddled in minutiae these priests believed were better dealt with on the parish level. His impulsive style—sometimes described as "Speak first, think about the consequences later"—could alienate people, including his own priests. Perhaps most damaging was George's allowing an out-of-town priest who had been accused of abusing a minor to stay at his residence during a visit to Chicago, as well as his handling of the sexual abuse case of then Father Dan McCormack ('94), in which George admittedly did not follow his archdiocesan review board's recommendation to remove McCormack from ministry. (This episode will receive fuller treatment in the chapter "Unspeakable Hurt.")

But for these six priests, the biggest worry had to do with the heart of their mission as priests: carrying out the vision of the Second Vatican Council in parishes in collaboration with the laity. Would George continue to support their efforts, as Bernardin had? Or would he embrace the critique of Vatican II-era ministry that these priests mostly saw as a conservative movement gaining favor in Rome and among much of the American hierarchy? They learned that the answer was not clear cut.

"As I look at what some of the cone heads come out with," Larry Duris says, referring unflatteringly to the more conservatively strident among George's brother bishops, "he's much better than many. I'm appreciative of the stuff he's done around race; his letter on race is excellent." Mike Ahlstrom holds the most positive views of the six about George's tenure as archbishop. "He's realistic," Ahlstrom says, "about the problems we're facing. There are a lot of elephants in the room and he's not running away from them." Ahlstrom remembered his consternation when the Vatican issued in 2005 norms for seminary admission regarding men with homosexual tendencies. "The Church," the document reads, "while profoundly respecting the persons in question, cannot admit to the seminary or to Holy Orders those who practice homosexuality, present deep-seated homosexual tendencies, or support the so-called 'gay culture.' Different, however, would be the case in which one were dealing with homosexual tendencies that were only the expression of a transitory problem."[14]

Struggling with the statement, Ahlstrom wrote the Cardinal and, shortly afterwards, the two of them met. "His interpretation," as Ahlstrom recalls it, "is that if a person's being gay is more important than their faith or the priesthood, they shouldn't be in the seminary. I said, 'It'd be no different than if a straight seminarian was putting Playboy foldouts on his wall and his heterosexuality was more important than what he was doing as a priest. You wouldn't want him ordained either.'

"In no way was Cardinal George saying," Ahlstrom shares his memory of the conversation, "that people can't be admitted just because they're gay.[15] There also have been times when I've written him little epistles about other issues and he always responds. I respect him. He's a fair man. He's not going to get bad marks in my book."

Other men from the class of 1969 found the cardinal less flexible. "He's forever worried about liturgical rules," Bill Zavaski says. "He gets complaints, and he takes what people say seriously." Zavaski was plagued by one woman who wrote George about so-called "liturgical abuses" at Zavaski's parish, among them charges that too many people had access to the key to the tabernacle. George responded, asking the woman to keep him informed. Zavaski protested vehemently: "I said, 'This woman is crazy. You have given her license to keep reporting. I feel offended.' George says, 'Get your liturgical act straight and you won't have to worry about that.' My liturgical act is straight, I told him. Then she wrote him about not wanting lay Eucharistic ministers. He told her, 'That's Church law. You have to follow it.'"

George ran into opposition from many of his priests over the issue of general absolution. At the time he arrived in Chicago, many parishes, going back to the time of Cody, were conducting general absolution services, which routinely filled their churches. St. Michael in Orland Park had such an overflow crowd that the parish scheduled two services, and each had no empty pews. The Cardinal indicated he would change nothing until meeting with pastors about the issue. At the meeting, then Father Tom Ventura ('61) and the late Father Robert (Red) McLaughlin ('66), two well-respected priests who offered general absolution in their parishes, defended the practice. "You could tell George got furious," Ed Upton says. "'The Church says you can't do it'—that's his bottom line."

There was no real dialogue. It was, "I'm going to tell you what you're doing wrong and you will change." Bernardin would make efforts to bring together different viewpoints and do some synthesis. For Francis the notion of listening is, "I'll give you the time." I'll say that for him. But there was no attempt to understand the issues. If you want to have a sacrament where people feel forgiven and connected to the Church, the only way that sacrament is going to continue is if you allow these services. But in his mind we were wrong. So he forbade it.

A big part of the issue, Upton believes, has to do with George's tendency to elevate all missives from Rome to the level of unchangeable Church teaching, while undervaluing the experience of local pastoral leaders. For Upton, it makes little sense to forbid a pastoral practice such as general absolution that is filling churches, when individual confessions attract few people.

....

The issue of decision-making looms large as these priests consider Cardinal George's tenure as archbishop of Chicago. Ed Upton says, "I was on a liturgy committee. He said, 'I trust you guys. Make the decisions.' We made one; then he called an architect in and redid it. He meddles. And if he thinks something is Church teaching, he's unbendable." By way of example, Upton explained how all the pastors in the southwest suburbs and their vicar, Bishop Gorman, met about a request from the Legionaries of Christ to start a school there. "We said, 'Don't let them have the school.' Our reasoning was it'll take away kids from our existing schools and they would only cater to the rich. There were 16 pastors: Unanimous. George's response was, 'The Church says they're okay so we have to say they're okay.' The logic of the local situation made no difference."

Tom Libera feels that the role of archbishop is often a teaching or top-down one, while that of a pastor is mostly more pastoral or bottom-up. "With my beliefs about pastoral things," Libera admits, "if I had to do what bishops do, I don't think I honestly could. Cardinals have got to be teachers, representing where the Church is at. It would be nice if one became radical. You wish you had more flexibility, more dialogue over questions that they put the lid on. We can't talk about married priests or women priests."

George's leadership has changed and improved over his years in Chicago, according to several of the priests. "This sounds arrogant," Larry Duris says, "but he's learned a lot since he came home. We've learned things, too." Duris reflected that George became "smart about what he's not smart about." He pointed to the Cardinal's appointment of John Canary, Duris' classmate, in 2006 to serve as his vicar general. "He asked John to straighten up the pastoral center," Duris says, "even though he knew that he would not always hear what he'd like to hear."

George has brought in excellent people to help him run the archdiocese, says Bob Heidenreich. "A good leader doesn't have to know how to do everything," he says. "He has to know who he can get who does." At first, he notes, George didn't know how to do that, and hence he acquired the reputation for interfering. But George changed. "Bishop Ed Conway ('60) got to him," Heidenreich says, referring to the beloved late auxiliary bishop of Chicago. "Having run Catholic Charities, Conway knew that if you stick your nose into things, you're going to embarrass the person in charge. George not only listened to Conway, he talked him into being vicar general."

These classmates also came to appreciate George personally. "He's outspoken and tells you what's on his mind," Heidenreich says. "He likes to pick fights with people. I grew to like him because I'm the same. I like to give it right back." Bill Zavaski notes that George has a "good heart and soul. Every year the day after Easter I have a party for priests. He tries to come." Tom Libera has come to appreciate George's regular invitations to small groups of priests to join him on Sunday evenings at his residence for informal conversation. "Personality-wise," Larry Duris maintains, "he's more outgoing than Bernardin. I've been at things where I'm thinking, 'Francis, it's time to go. I'm trying to lock up the building.' He's there until the end."

Ed Upton, however, experienced George's shoot-from-the-hip style in an unlikely setting. When the Cardinal was presenting him with an award from the religious education office, Upton found himself taken aback. "As he's giving me the award," Upton relates, "he says, 'You're going to stop having First Reconciliation in fourth grade and move it to second grade?' I said, 'No, I'm not.' It wasn't, 'Thank you.'" Despite this, Upton sees positives in George's leadership. "He's very nice to me," he says. "He's good one-on-one. He knows people's names, goes out of his way to say hello. When guys are in the hospital, he calls them."

And George has a sensitive side, as Larry Duris discovered when a team of priests, Duris included, asked to meet with him prior to the 2008 annual priest convocation. "We wanted him to reveal a bit about his priesthood and person," Duris explains. "He reflected on how he felt hurt when he first heard the term Francis the Corrector. That's not easy to share in front of a group."

Bob Heidenreich recalled a similar moment. "When Bishop Conway died in 2004," he says, "it was a shock. The Cardinal attended an event for pastors, and he started crying when talking about Conway. I felt like crying, too. I started to see George differently. You would have never seen that from Cody because he wasn't close to anybody."

Mike Ahlstrom noticed a growing spirituality in George that has influenced his own view of ministry. "He's a man of prayer," he says. "He emphasizes the call to conversion, the need to put God at the center of everything. That comes through loud and clear. Of the three archbishops—not that Bernardin was lacking—George has got the deepest spirituality." Perhaps that's why George's portrait hangs in the prayer room in the house at Pinion. "He's not going to engage the popular imagination," Alhstrom continues, "but what he says has depth. He's not the warm fuzzy Bernardin was, but he has a good mind and spirit."

....

After his promising beginning, Cardinal John Cody soon morphed for the young men of the class of '69 into a cold, distant figure whom they viewed as an obstacle to carrying out the collaborative vision of ministry called for not only by the Council but also by Jack Gorman and the faculty at Mundelein, as well as by their mentors in summer apostolates. It is ironic that opposing Cody initially became a unifying force for many of Chicago's priests, but by the end of his tenure, weary from fighting what they saw as the good fight, the men from 1969, like many of their brother priests, felt demoralized in their efforts to advance the work of the Church. When the morale of the Chicago priesthood had about reached its lowest ebb, Joseph Bernardin arrived in Chicago proclaiming to its priests that he was "Joseph, your brother." Although none of these six priests were close to Bernardin personally, his mission to advance the work of the Council, his leadership at the local and national levels, and his compassion, especially during his public process of dying, deeply inspired them and rejuvenated their efforts to work closely with the laity to help bring about God's kingdom on earth.

For most of the men, dealing with Cardinal Francis George remains many-sided, especially set against their past efforts to relate to Cody and Bernardin. Over time, however, most of these classmates have developed a deeper respect and appreciation for George. If the Cardinal has not acted in outspoken advocacy of their view of the mandates of the Second Vatican Council, often interpreting it, they say, from a rule-bound, top-down point of view, neither has he attempted to dismantle all they have accomplished and simply turn the Church clock, as it were, backwards. George's emphasis on a God-centered conversion of hearts has inspired certain members of the class, and most have found him very likable. Perhaps due to their higher positions on the ladder of Church leadership as they have aged, or perhaps as a function of the maturity that often comes with such experience, the men from the class of 1969 have come to appreciate the Cardinal in all his complexity. So, while George today is neither villain nor hero to these men, as Cody and Bernardin were, he is something else: real.

....

1. Edward R. Kantowicz, "The Beginning and the End of an Era: George William Mundelein and John Patrick Cody in Chicago" in Ellen Skerrett, Edward R. Kantowicz, and Steven M. Avella, *Catholicism: Chicago Style* (Chicago: Loyola University Press, 1993), 131, 133. See also Charles Dahm, *Power and Authority in the Catholic Church: Cardinal Cody in Chicago* (Notre Dame, IN: University of Notre Dame Press, 1981).
2. Dahm, 219.
3. Margery Frisbie, *An Alley in Chicago: The Ministry of a City Priest* (Kansas City, MO: Sheed and Ward, 1991), 209-218. See also, Dahm, 28-33.
4. Richard Philbrick, "Cody is Censured by Priests Group." *Chicago Tribune (1963-Current file): ProQuest Historical Newspapers: Chicago Tribune* (1849-1988). June 16, 1971.
5. William Clements, George Mustain, Roy Larson, "Federal Grand Jury Probes Cardinal Cody Use of Church Funds: Investigation Centers on Gifts to Friend" in *Chicago Sun-Times*, September 10, 1981. See also John Conroy, "Cardinal Sins," in *Chicago Reader*, June 4, 1987.
6. Tom Libera to Cody, September 10, 1981 in ACP, *Upturn*, October, 1981, 1.
7. "I Am Joseph Your Brother," Bishop Bernardin's homily for the evening prayer service on the eve of his installation as the seventh Archbishop of Chicago, August 24, 1982, AAC
8. Opened in Michigan in 1956, Guest House is a nonprofit charitable organization dedicated to the treatment of Catholic priests, deacons, brothers, seminarians and (since 1994) women religious with alcoholism, other chemical dependencies, and related problems. For men's treatment, call 1-800-634-4155. For women's treatment, call 1-800-626-6910.
9. National Conference of Catholic Bishops, *The Challenge of Peace: God's Promise and Our Response: A Pastoral Letter on War and Peace*, May 3, 1983 (Washington, DC: United States Conference of Catholic Bishops, Inc., 1983). See also "God and the Bomb," cover of *Time*, November 29, 1982.
10. Joseph Cardinal Bernardin, "A Consistent Ethic of Life: An American-Catholic Dialogue." Gannon Lecture, Fordham University, December 6, 1983. AAC

11. Joseph Cardinal Bernardin, "Faithful and Hopeful: The Catholic Common Ground Project." Address, October 24, 1996. AAC. The initiative continues today out of Catholic Theological Union in Chicago. See the website http://www.catholiccommonground.org.

12. Joseph Cardinal Bernardin, *The Gift of Peace: Personal reflections by Joseph Cardinal Bernardin* (Chicago, Loyola Press, 1997).

13. Pam Belluck, "Priests' Missive Reveals Tensions in Chicago Archdiocese" in *New York Times*, November 14, 1997.

14. *Instruction Concerning the Criteria for the Discernment of Vocations with regard to Persons with Homosexual Tendencies in view of their Admission to the Seminary and to Holy Orders.* Congregation for Catholic Education, November 4, 2005.

15. Paragraph Two from *Statement of Cardinal Francis George, O.M.I regarding the Instruction from the Holy See Concerning the Criteria for the Discernment of Vocations with Regard to Persons with Homosexual Tendencies in View of Their Admission to the Seminary and to Holy Orders.* November 29, 2005. The document is a timely help to those responsible for the preparation of priestly candidates in the Latin Catholic Church. It speaks of affective maturity as a requirement for exercising the spiritual fatherhood essential to the priestly vocation. The document therefore encourages special consideration of those candidates for ordained priesthood whose personal identity includes homosexual tendencies. While every person is to be respected, men cannot be admitted to Holy Orders who 1) practice homosexuality; 2) have "deeply rooted" homosexual tendencies; or 3) support the so-called "gay culture." In other words, if one's self-identification as a "gay man" is the most important component of a man's personality, he is not a candidate for Holy Orders. In all cases, the final decision about a candidate's calling is the responsibility of the seminary rector and the ordaining bishop, whose prudent judgment the Church relies upon.

PART III

LEADERSHIP AND WISDOM

CHAPTER 12

AT THE HELM
Pastoring

"Unbelievable" might best describe the reaction Father Larry Duris experienced when he became pastor of St. Lawrence Parish on the Southeast Side of Chicago in 1976, only seven years after his ordination. The pastor at the time, Father Ray Kubas ('51), resigned from the priesthood and Duris applied for the job. Shortly thereafter Father Dick Keating ('53), the vicar general, offered him the position. "I guess arrogantly," Larry says now, "I thought I was ready."

Duris found himself quickly disabused of this notion when he encountered his associate pastor, who had already stayed beyond the maximum term of seven years for an associate, had outlasted two pastors, and had made it clear to Larry that he had expected to be named pastor and had no intention of leaving the parish. Although the man had at one time served energetically as a parish priest, by all accounts that Larry received, in recent years the associate had become difficult to work with.

Aware of the fact that the archdiocese was trying unsuccessfully to move the associate, Duris raised the issue with Keating. "I don't know where I got the nerve," he says. "I was much more an introvert than I am now. But I said, 'What's going to happen with him?' He said, 'We're working on it.' So I said, 'I will do my best to work with him. But it's obvious to me that he thinks he should be pastor. If we can't communicate and he's not gone by the end of September, I will resign Lawrence. Does that sound fair?' Keating said, 'Okay, that's fair.' I wrote that down. He said, 'When do you want to start?' I said, 'It's

Tuesday. With what he might be up to, the sooner the better. I'll move in Friday.'"

Meanwhile, the associate asked to meet with Duris and tried to talk him out of taking the parish. "He said," Larry remembers, "'You've got an excellent reputation and are concerned about justice issues, especially within the Church. This isn't the way you would do something; I know you're not going to take it.' He went from there to veiled threats. I ended with, 'I'll be coming over tomorrow morning with my bags. What time will you be in?' 'I don't know when I'll be in,' he said. 'I presume the keys are in the rectory,' I told him. 'You don't have them with you?' He didn't answer. I then knew that physically getting into the place would be challenge number one."

The next morning Duris could find neither associate nor key, so he called the parish deacon, who let him into the rectory. The associate was reportedly so furious when he learned Duris had made his way inside that over the next month he spent only four nights there. "There was no communication," Duris says, laughing. "As I put my key in the door, I can see through the frosted glass window he's running out the other door. We made Mass schedules by note. My first week there I wrote, 'You've got the 5 p.m. Mass, but I'll talk at all three Masses.' After I gave the homily at the five, I stayed for the rest of the liturgy. At the sign of peace, I'm shaking hands and he is, too. He says to me, 'For you, the sword of Christ.' I'm thinking, 'This is just him.'"

Others didn't take the associate's veiled threat during the handshake of peace so lightly. While attending the priesthood ordination at Mundelein Seminary the following week, many of Larry's colleagues offered him congratulations on becoming the youngest pastor in the archdiocese. Others, however, questioned his sanity for agreeing to serve with the associate. When Duris mentioned the "sword of Christ" story, he noticed looks of real concern among his friends. "The next morning," he remembers, "about 7 a.m., I get a phone call: 'Larry, this is Dick Keating. How are you?' 'I'm fine.' 'No, really, how are you?' 'I'm fine.' 'Physically are you fine? I heard about the sword of Christ. Cody will be calling later today. He wants to see him.'"

The associate had been trying to meet with Cody for ages. Two days later he meets with Cody. Come the transfer date, I hear rattling of boxes. He moves out. He was assigned to another parish, but he never showed up and eventually drifted out of ministry. On his deathbed, a few years ago, he reconciled. Francis George was good with him. It was a bizarre beginning. I didn't realize how tense that was until after he moved out. Then I thought, boy, it feels so different in here now.

....

Cardinal Cody named Bill Zavaski pastor of his home parish of St. Bartholomew's in Waukegan in 1979. Between 1986 and 1990, Cardinal Bernardin appointed Mike Ahlstrom, Bob Heidenreich, Tom Libera, and Ed Upton as pastors, Ahlstrom at St Collette's in Rolling Meadows, Libera at Resurrection on the West Side, Heidenreich at St. Benedict's on the North Side, and Upton to Orland Park to open the brand-new parish of St. Francis of Assisi.

Although their transitions to their first pastorates did not contain quite the drama that Larry Duris' did, each of these priests did feel quickly taken by surprise in different ways when they became pastors. A review of these early surprises is in order, therefore, before the chapter turns to examine each individual priest's career as a pastor.

In Bill Zavaski's case, the sense of surprise had to do with the fact that Cody had selected him as pastor of St. Bart's, his family's home parish. He had applied for the job, but only as a formality to let the Personnel Board know he'd like to be a pastor one day. "But when Father John Kuzinskas ('52) left," Zavaski adds, "they called me because nobody wanted to go to Waukegan. That's why I ended up back home. I wanted to tell the vicar general that I had written this letter but that I didn't mean it. It was traumatic." Zavaski agreed to relearn Lithuanian—he had studied it in grade school at St. Bart's—because so many of the people knew the language. This task symbolized for Zavaski the greater responsibility that being a pastor entailed. "It's like night and day," he reflects. "Associates get a freedom to go where they want. Pastor is a different ballgame. All of a sudden you're responsible for all of them."

Mike Ahlstrom's surprise had to do with quickly noticing that parishioners related to him much differently than when he had served as an associate. "I was objectified," he recalls. "You hear women say, 'Don't treat me as an object.' I understood in my head what they meant, but I didn't really appreciate it until I felt I had been objectified because I was the pastor, the authority, the one where the buck stopped. People would become very angry with me. It took me a couple of years to figure out they weren't really angry at me—they didn't know me. They were angry at the pastor, because I stood for something that they disagreed with, whereas as an associate I could have a disagreement over an idea and it was no big deal. I remember one guy telling me, 'The archdiocese has sent us three pastors. All of them were terrible. You're the worst.' I thought, geez, what did I do to deserve that?" Aware that any transition takes at least a year, it took Ahlstrom a full two and a half years to feel comfortable in the role.

Returning to work in the African-American community as pastor of Resurrection Parish, Tom Libera felt racial tensions in a way vastly different from his days as an associate at St. Eulalia's. A white staff member managed the property; a black group was meeting in the basement of the school using the kitchen. "The staff person's comment was," Libera recalls, "'You don't belong down here,' and the group's feedback was, 'You're dispossessing us of our place.'" Libera worked to sensitize the staff member and to help her keep her credibility, while listening to the hurt experienced by the group. He remembers deciding, "I'm not going to fire someone over this incident," but he knew discontent remained. "People might not have agreed with my way of dealing with it, but they stuck it out. Actually, some friendships developed out of that," he recalls, "which was generous of people to not turn and walk away."

When Bob Heidenreich took over as pastor at St. Benedict's in 1991, he was astonished to have to confront a conflict born of generational differences. The outgoing pastor had earlier served at Ben's as an associate in the 1950s; when he returned as pastor in the 1980s he had found a very different situation. The parish schools—St. Ben's still has its own high school in addition to a grade school—had become expensive and more complex. The neighborhood demographic had shifted from working class to white collar and young upwardly mobile families, people who expected to engage in consultation in determining the parish's direction. "You didn't need to have that style in the '50s," Heidenreich comments, "but you needed to have it in the '80s and '90s, and he had no idea about that." A conflict of loyalties had broken out and continued to simmer between the older and newer families in the parish.

"When as a new pastor you move into a situation like that," Heidenreich points out, "you're a moving target. You've got to fix this like right now. The newer families felt like they had no entrée into anything. So, we kept on reaching out to the younger families. The older people, some of them to this day will have nothing to do with me because I wasn't going to take their advice. Too bad."

Ed Upton also stumbled upon a startling discovery shortly after he began his new assignment in Orland Park. With neither a church nor a rectory to live in, he clearly needed to do significant fundraising to create a parish infrastructure from scratch. Upton decided to ask a well-off couple who had volunteered to help with publicity for the new parish for $25,000. He set up a dinner with them to discuss the possible donation. Because the couple knew the reason for the meal and because, as Upton put it, "There was a bit of braggadocio about how many promotions the husband had had," he felt confident. "I made the request," he says, "and they just lit into me—I mean lit into me."

> "The church you're building is too extravagant. No one likes it.
> And to ask us for $25,000!" That shook me to the foundation.
> If you don't want to give, why not just say, "Ed, we can't do it."
> But I got a lecturette saying, "We know your people and building
> better than you do."

Upton called the building committee together and asked, "Are we on board with this? I can't go forward if people are ambivalent." The people quickly reassured him. "They were like, 'What are you talking about?'" he says. "'Of course we are.'"

After surviving their first surprises as new pastors, members of the class of 1969 began to realize the enormity of their new responsibilities. At first the job seemed overwhelming, but over time they negotiated successfully the role of pastor by putting into practice the practical lessons they had learned about parish ministry over what by now had been many, many years of seminary training and priestly experience.

....

The archdiocese founded St. Colette's Parish in middle-class northwest suburban Rolling Meadows in 1957. Called upon to introduce the changes in the Church envisioned by the Second Vatican Council, the founding pastor resisted. When the parish's second pastor took over, parishioners who had complained about the Council not being implemented at Colette's initially had great hope. The new pastor, for example, began a parish council. When the pastor and the parish council clashed, however, he fired the entire council. "His ideas were progressive," Mike Ahlstrom says of his predecessor, "yet he had a hard time implementing them." So when Ahlstrom arrived as pastor in 1989 eager to make the changes of the Council real at Colette's, the people remained skeptical, to say the least.

Before his appointment, Mike had believed in the adage, "Don't make any major changes the first year." But when he learned that the previous pastor personally answered the doorbell and phone after 4 p.m., he hired parish teenagers for the job. When he found out parishioners couldn't take photographs in church during weddings, he reversed the policy. And when he discovered the parish had no RCIA program, he started one. Ahlstrom also restarted the parish council.

But more important than the "what" of his new pastorate was the "how." "I believed strongly in consensus," he says, "as a decision-making model. At first they didn't believe me when I said, 'We're going to make decisions together; I'm not going to dictate. It's not what I want; it's what *we* want and what's best for *us.*'" Mike had an early opportunity to prove he meant business about consensus. Kneelers in the church had been collapsing. Floor tiles routinely came up. Pews had begun to fall apart. Because of his liturgy background, Ahlstrom suggested the parish use the need for a new floor and new pews as a reason to renovate the church. Ahlstrom had a grand design in mind for the church's remodeling, one he had seen work elsewhere.

> I wanted the altar at one end of the church and the ambo for Scripture at the other end and the seating facing in an oval shape almost like a football stadium, so that no matter where you sat in church, there would be no back-of-church. Nobody would be more than five or six rows from the action, and people could see each other and relate as an assembly where God is in our midst, rather than everybody like an audience looking up at the altar.

But Ahlstrom's renovation committee thought the plan would likely constitute too radical a change for people. They thought that simply moving the altar closer to the people and fanning the seating around them would be enough change. So Mike and the committee decided to build models of each plan to present to the parish. For the next four weeks in lieu of a homily, they instructed Mass-goers on the "whys" of sacred space and worship, and on the implications any change would have on the way the church looked.

"I asked people to meet in small groups," Ahlstrom recalls, "and talk about these two plans for the four weeks. The other decision was how we were going to pay for this. We were blessed with a large campus of 20 acres. I said, 'We can sell land or have a capital campaign.' So they had to reach a consensus on which design they wanted and how to pay for it."

Sixty-five small groups met for four weeks in an astounding experiment in Church democracy. The decisions were made by consensus, which to Ahlstrom meant much more than a simple up or down vote. "I talked about how we listen," he says. "You listen to each person without speaking. After they have all spoken then you go around the circle again to see if anybody has altered their thinking in light of what they heard, and then you discuss. But you listen to everybody in the group first." His plans provoked quite a reaction from some of his clerical colleagues. "Everybody told me that I was nuts," Mike remembers. "They said, 'Just tell them what you're going to do. You're the pastor.'"

Ahlstrom told them, "No, I believe that this is how decisions should be made, and I believe in the wisdom of the Holy Spirit to direct all of this."

Sister Mary Benet McKinney, the Benedictine who literally wrote the book on discernment and consensus building, came to direct the final meeting.[1] Representatives from the 65 small groups gathered to see if a consensus had emerged. Indeed one had. "It was clear," Ahlstrom says, "my idea was too radical. That was rejected by 90 percent of the people. They have to pray there. It's not my church, it's their church. Ten percent of the people didn't want anything changed except repairs. But 80 percent liked the less radical plan of bringing the altar out closer to the people and fanning the pews around, which was progress." The people also decided to sell land rather than conduct a capital campaign. "It was a very different process," Mike recollects with justifiable pride, "than, 'Tell us what you want, Father, and we'll do it.'"

When Ahlstrom discovered to his surprise that the 1990 census showed that Hispanics made up 12 percent of the Rolling Meadows population, he knew his consensus model of leadership would again need to be put to the test. First, however, he immersed himself in learning about the Hispanics living in his parish. The city of Rolling Meadows had made the forward-thinking decision that their police, fire fighters, and city workers would all take Spanish lessons, and city officials invited Mike to join them. The majority of the town's Hispanics lived in a complex with 250 apartments. Because 50 percent of the suburb's police calls about crime came from there, the city set up a police district right in the complex. The police refused to cooperate with immigration officials on deportations, and they set up a room where children from the complex could study in quiet. They sponsored English as a Second Language (ESL) classes and enlisted a physician and dentist to volunteer their time. After a few years, calls to the police from that complex numbered no more than anywhere else in Rolling Meadows, bringing the suburb national recognition.

Ahlstrom wished to replicate the city's welcoming approach to Hispanics at St. Colette's. He wanted to start a Spanish Mass, but he didn't believe in forcing the issue. "I used a similar method," he says, referring to the church remodeling, "in that I preached about it for several weeks and did bulletin articles. I reminded them of their parents and grandparents who came from Europe and were ministered to in their language at the Polish and German and Italian churches. I said, 'The last thing you change when you learn a new language is your prayers. They want to learn English, but they want to pray in Spanish.'"

After weeks of meetings, Ahlstrom asked whether a consensus had developed to change the noon Mass to a Spanish Mass. "Ten percent," he recalls, "were opposed, 90 percent said we must minister to Hispanics in their language, and 80 percent said change the noon Mass to Spanish. So to anybody that objected, I said, 'The people have spoken. The Holy Spirit has spoken.' There were people that tried to bar the doors and prevent people from coming to the first Spanish Mass. But others in the parish escorted those who objected away."

Ahlstrom says today that if the parish vote had been 80 percent opposed to a Spanish Mass he might have decided to resign back then. Instead he gradually learned Spanish, appreciating people's tolerance along the way. "One Latino parishioner," he says, "who saw me stumbling through Spanish said, 'We need Hispanic priests.' He wound up going in the seminary, and I was his spiritual director. Benji (Benjamin Arevalos Lupercio) was ordained in 2009. Up to then, I had encouraged men to go to the seminary, but none got ordained. Finally, indirectly, because of my lousy Spanish, I inspired someone to become a priest."

When he left St. Colette's, Mike was appointed by Cardinal George to take over the office for the archdiocese's more than 875 permanent deacons and to serve as part-time spiritual director for seminarians at Mundelein, while residing at St. Barbara's in Brookfield." I kept my foot in the parish," he says. "I also got a little bit of the seminary, and I still love working with the deacons."

As director of the Office for the Diaconate since 2002, Ahlstrom tries to serve as a pastor for the largest group of deacons in any diocese in the U.S. today. In doing so, he has found most challenging the personnel issues that range from priest-deacon and lay-deacon struggles to negotiating how properly to involve deacons' wives in diaconal ministry. "If a deacon and a pastor get on a collision course," he says, "I can sit down with them and work things out. Or if it isn't going to work out, we'll find another assignment for the deacon." As for the deacon's wives, he says, "The women are a very important part of the community. But Cardinal George once sent me a newspaper article with the headline 'Six local men and their wives ordained deacons.' He said, 'That's why you don't use the term 'deacon couple.' Well, there is no one model. In some couples the wife says, 'That's his vocation. Leave me be.' The other extreme is couples joined at the hip in ministry. In between there are women who say, 'I've got my ministry; he has his ministry. Occasionally we do something together.' All three models are legitimate. There is some tension."

There are also tensions in progressive parishes where active lay leaders question the need for diaconal ministry. But in most parishes today, according to Ahlstrom, people and priests greatly appreciate deacons. In negotiating conflicts regarding deacons, Mike Ahlstrom has striven to avoid dictating solutions and has instead thrived on bringing people together to resolve issues and plan for the future. The heart of his leadership style, he insists, "is introducing consensus building as a decision-making process and trying to instill that in people."

....

Having spent the better part of eight years running the pastor training program for the archdiocese before he took on his own first pastorate, Bob Heidenreich arrived at St. Benedict's Parish determined to put into action what he had learned about challenging entrenched relationships and outmoded ways of conducting parish life. As noted, the pastor Heidenreich followed had earlier served at St. Ben's and had maintained friendships with those who were now the older families of the parish. "Those were the people," he says, "who decisions were being made for." So Bob began the process of getting younger families involved in the parish by restarting the long-dormant parish council and adding young people to the finance committee. He also inaugurated the popular parish retreat program Christ Renews His Parish. People began to sense that the parish had finally started becoming more inclusive.

Eventually Heidenreich led a long but ultimately successful effort to raise a million dollars to renovate the church. "People could see," he recalls, "that things were different. Until that time I was walking on eggs." When the newly ordained Father Jason Malave ('97) arrived, says Heidenreich, "he brought a lot of life and credibility to the younger folks." Bob asked the young priest to take charge of the church renovation: "Boom, it happened and happened well. Thank God for Jason. Once the church was renovated, it was like a magnet for the young adults moving into the parish."

The two priests cemented this development by starting a Sunday night 6:30 p.m. Mass for young adults, co-hosted by several parishes in the area. But it was important, Heidenreich understood, not to exclude the older people. When the parish began an outdoor block party as a fundraiser, tensions arose. "When we started Ben Fest," he remembers, "these older ladies would run little games of chance. It was not needed to make money, but it was a good way to include them so they felt part of this. The younger folks running Ben Fest at first were like, 'We don't need these older ladies.' No," Bob recalls disagreeing, "it ties in a whole other segment of the community. And that's how it got to be a whole parish venture."

By the middle of his term, Heidenreich heartily enjoyed life at Ben's. "I would actually look forward to parish council meetings," he says, "because there were great people that you could depend on to work together and come up with great ideas. It was fun reaching out and getting the young adults involved."

Bob also worked hard as pastor to mentor newly ordained priests, among them Malave, who would eventually himself become pastor of the same parish. "It was very good but challenging working with Jason," he says. "We have a mutual respect with one another." Efforts to train young priests as effective ministers, however, have not always gone smoothly. One young associate "was very conservative," he says. "I hope I presented another way of doing Church. If nothing else, I didn't roll over and play dead, but neither did I try to change him or pick fights."

There was one exception, however. "Priests have ministerial expense accounts," Heidenreich explains. "He went out and bought a cope (a long, enveloping ecclesiastical vestment). Well, at St. Ben's we've got copes coming out of our kazoo. I told him, 'We don't need this. I'm not paying for your personal thing.' I wanted him to know that buying that stuff was not going to be helpful in priesthood."

> *Some of the priests now look on their role as only spiritual and sacramental. It's a modern version of the gas station. They tank people up, but they don't get involved with them socially. But, especially in Chicago, I can't see that that's going to work. Because in not just the Anglo community but also in the Hispanic and the Polish communities, there's so much involvement among the people by priests. They expect that. We had this theology and ecclesiology of the people as the Body of Christ, and people bought into it. Some of the guys from different cultures and even our culture don't get it. A guy that says, "I'm just here to take care of your sacraments and why aren't you going to confession?"—I don't think this is going to work. I think there's going to be trouble in Dodge City.*

Given his concerns, Heidenreich has attempted to lead both by example and by putting the young priests assigned to his parishes into practical ministerial situations where they must learn to work directly with their people.

Heidenreich began his second pastorate—at Sacred Heart Parish in Winnetka—with a mixture of confidence and trepidation. The previous pastor, according to Heidenreich, "had a pastoral style described by many as 'strategic helplessness.' When they had to raise money or needed to form a new ministry, he'd say, 'I can't think of how to do this.' People would say, 'Father, do this. Can I help?' He knew exactly what he wanted to do," Bob claims, "he just waited until the right person said it. But that pastoral style—laissez faire—presumes that everybody knows what to do and you don't need any direction or focusing. It's not true."

The primary challenge for Heidenreich in Winnetka remained to get educated, wealthy, talented parishioners to form a community working together to help others. "My style of leadership," he says, "is a coaching style. One style is where you tell everybody what to do. Another is that strategic helplessness. The style that I developed is to work with people."

Bob always continued to try to coach the parish into greater unity of purpose. As one example, he tells the story of how he had to confront a situation where parishioners invariably asked a deacon born and raised in the parish to conduct weddings in lieu of the newly ordained associate, an African priest from Tanzania, Father Avitus Kiguta ('06). "One of the reasons we have to change the process here," he says, "is because Avitus, who is starting his fifth year here, has had only three weddings. By the time I was ordained five years, I couldn't even tell you how many weddings I had. Things should have changed a long time ago."

Kiguta, meanwhile, has also received challenges from Heidenreich to prove that the parish comes first. "When he first came," Heidenreich recalls, "I asked him to be in charge of the liturgy. He said, 'That's the last thing I want to do.' I said, 'That's your job.' He'll tell you now he's learned so much from that assignment."

Heidenreich has come to believe priests must understand the change in the role of pastor over the last 40-plus years in order to operate out of a sound and effective theology of Church. "The pastor went from a spiritual head whose big administrative task was signing checks and passing out report cards," he says, "to a manager of parishes that suddenly had finance and parish councils, liturgy and outreach committees. I've been critical of some of the men who were my pastors. But it wasn't their fault. The tools that we've developed—and we now have some expertise—are more sophisticated than they were in those days. I don't know if I'm a pioneer in this or not, but I feel like I am."

For Bob Heidenreich, the changes in pastors' roles emanate from a theology of the Church being the Mystical Body of Christ. "Our parish system," he insists, "is built on that image. That's why the Eucharist is so important. Christ is present not just as we celebrate the Eucharist in the Word and in the reception of Communion, but also as we go out into the community, and that's the way staffs need to be structured." He credits theologian Jack Shea ('67), who long directed the Doctor of Ministry program for the archdiocese before leaving the priesthood, with training scores of pastors how to take Mystical Body theology and apply it in a systemic way to bring changes to dysfunctional ways of living parish life.[2] "I've applied that in parishes ever since," he claims.

"I told Jack Shea that the Doctorate of Ministry has shaped this diocese more than anything. It was equal to the founding of Mundelein Seminary."

....

Larry Duris served as pastor of St. Lawrence's Parish from 1976 to 1991. When appointed, he became, at just over 30 years old, the youngest pastor then serving in the archdiocese. Larry brought tremendous creativity to the task. He sought to discover and implement ways to bring his people together to reflect on their lives and then to act in service toward one another and the larger community. But, initially, the new young pastor at St. Lawrence, who had already had to endure being threatened by his associate before he had even moved into the rectory, seemed to find little respite from some seemingly irrational people.

Duris found that first year particularly challenging. He knew the previous pastor had planned to get married. What he didn't realize until he arrived on May 8 was that the former priest intended to marry the parish school's principal, an Adrian Dominican nun. So Larry's first task involved finding a new principal. He hired another Adrian Dominican, whom he describes as an excellent educator but poor on public relations: "She came in with an agenda to fix the school overnight, and she shot herself in the foot."

Her school board, for example, decided to pressure parents into coming to parent meetings by fining them $5 if they didn't attend. But they also decided to combine school parent meetings with the regular meetings of the women's and men's groups, and those groups charged a $2 admission fee. So school parents who attended meetings to avoid paying a fine ended up paying anyway. "People wanted to know," Larry says, "why the fees." At a parent meeting, he explained the board's policy, despite thinking it was foolish. When he asked members of the board to defend the policy, none of them, including the principal, would do so.

By Christmas, to make matters worse, the principal had fired two faculty members. "This is not going to wash," Duris told her. "You're sinking yourself and what you're trying to do." At the contentious faculty meeting that followed, the principal again refused to defend her decision. "She stood in the back of the hall," he remembers. "I asked her to come to the front and she would not. I was ready to kill her."

Eventually Larry brought in Sister Mary Benet McKinney, the Benedictine sister well versed in the art of negotiation, to help him run a school board meeting. By this time, half of the six-member board remained supportive of their new principal, but half wanted her to go. "When Mary Benet gets there," he says, "the opposition won't let her speak. Finally, she did. The meeting after that almost got physical. They were sitting at opposite ends of the table, and one side started crawling across the table toward the other side."

Duris eventually dissolved the hopelessly deadlocked school board. Disgruntled board members promptly sued him. By then, he had planned a well-earned vacation with Ed Upton to Florida. "I'm out finally on the beach," Larry, still incredulous, remembers, "and the lady running the place we're staying at comes out and says, 'There's a call for you from Cardinal Cody.' Cody had heard about the court thing with the school board. But it never went anywhere. The opposition didn't realize how much it was going to cost them.

"Then," Duris says in a masterful bit of understatement, "the parish calmed down." After the first year, Larry hired Curtis Arthur, an African-American, as principal. Arthur remained for 12 years and worked with Larry to increase enrollment from 300 to 500 students. Duris also brought in Father Tom McQuaid ('79) as an associate pastor and BVM Sister Katherine Hinshe as a pastoral associate. They made deliberate attempts to revive the flagging spirit of the parish. "The two previous years, the pastor had closed the church down stone-cold in the winter," he says. "Drained the pipes. They had Mass in the basement of the school in a chapel. It was like this is the beginning of the end." Duris thought differently. "Once I got there," he says, "we redecorated the church in time for the 100th anniversary. I tried to do some new creative things. We were one of the first churches to do revivals. We did some stuff around black enculturation."

Long frustrated by the need for African-Americans to travel far out of their neighborhoods to attend retreats, Duris worked with Mc-

Quaid and Hinshe to find an alternative. St. Lawrence's convent seemed the perfect place to open a new retreat center right in the neighborhood. At the time six women religious rented space there, and they felt they were being evicted from their home. Eventually, to Duris' relief, the women found another place and moved out.

Work soon began to convert the space into the Imani House Retreat Center. The word *Imani* is Swahili for faith or belief. "Tom and Katherine hit on 12 pastors, money parishes," Larry recalls, "and asked them to donate $100 a month for a year to give us seed money." The parish not only held its own retreats at Imani House, but neighboring parishes, CRHP retreats, and even Worldwide Marriage Encounter began renting the house. At last, life at the parish seemed to have come together for Duris.

In 1991, however, after 15 years at St. Lawrence, Duris found himself assigned to take over as pastor for the legendary Father Les Mollohan ('51) at St. Philip Neri in the once tony South Shore neighborhood of Chicago. (For part of that time, he served simultaneously in the same role at Our Lady of Peace Parish.) Although his transition was nowhere near as turbulent as his entrance into St. Lawrence had proved to be, Larry nevertheless encountered a serious issue at St. Philip Neri that had to do with attitude and money.

"Neri had a reputation among some people," Duris says, "that this wasn't just a parish. This was St. Philip Neri, the crown jewel among black parishes." That attitude, however, no longer reflected the increasingly harsh economic realities of the parish. Eventually Duris and the people of Neri adjusted to one another as they worked together to address the new economic situation of the parish.

Over time, Duris began to experience success in improving parish programs. "Part of the thrust at Neri," he says, "was working at evangelization and building up the worshipping and educational communities." The fortunes of the school improved during his tenure. Enrollment grew from 300 to over 400 students. Weekly Mass attendance rose to almost 400 a week, and Larry strengthened the leadership of the parish council, in part by recruiting young adults.

In 2009, the archdiocese appointed Duris pastor of St. Ailbe's Parish, also on the South Side, where he presently serves. The transition to Ailbe's came as a relief compared to his beginnings at both Lawrence and Neri. Part of what made his initial months at Ailbe's easier, of course, was that Duris had now practiced his craft for 40 years. It also helped that Father John Breslin ('85), the previous pastor, had made great strides in creating an active parish. To provide a sense of life at Ailbe's, Duris pointed to a recent parish bulletin, a vehicle he says he uses not only for information but for formation as well. Almost 20 pages long, it contains information about a prayer breakfast, the parish revival, both the Catholic men's and women's retreats, the health and wellness ministry, an upcoming health fair, and Theology on Tap, the noted young adult speaker program.

Duris recently created a parish council, ensuring that people in their 20s and 30s made up three of its members. He praises, too, the strength of the parish bereavement ministry, which maintains a team to assist families in grief. Similarly, over 70 people serve as greeters and ushers, working in teams of six at each Sunday Mass. "When you come in from the parking lot," Larry explains, "you'll be greeted three times before you get inside the door." But he remains most impressed with the Men's Ministry group, which took over a Protestant church's food pantry that was shutting down. "We're feeding 200-250 families a week."

Despite Duris' success at St. Ailbe's, problems remain, one of them the reaction to immigrants from Africa who have moved into the parish. "African-Americans can do what whites have done," Duris admits. "What's the classic line in a parish that's becoming multicultural? 'We don't mind them being here—if they come to our stuff and act like us, they're welcome.' With never a thought to what do I need to change. That's a challenge." Larry has worked to remind his people that many of them have had their own experiences of feeling tolerated at best as minorities in the Church.

One of the satisfactions for Duris of serving as the longest "lifer" in the African-American community has been mentoring younger priests. He has relished the opportunity during over 35 years of pastoring to have had many young associates, as well as seminarians, serve under his leadership. "As I'm becoming a dinosaur," he says, "having younger guys has been refreshing and a challenge. I've tried to push each guy to be present to and involved with all the ministries initially, so they have a general feel of what ministry is like at the place. The second piece is, 'Where do you want to take the lead as the key staff person?'"

As part of the mentoring process, Duris insists on at least bi-weekly meetings with his associates. "Besides the nuts and bolts stuff," he says, "it's important to share what are the gut issues about me, about the place. Because we can as priests delude ourselves into thinking we're not like the rest of men."

Overall, Larry Duris thinks he has done a good job creating healthy rectories. "I try to create a community," he maintains, "with a sense that it's our house." His work in parishes, ironically enough, has mirrored what he has accomplished on a smaller scale in his rectories: creating communities that get at the "gut issues" in prayer and reflection, and then working together in service to grapple as Christians with those real-life issues.

....

When Tom Libera arrived on the West Side of Chicago to become pastor of Resurrection Parish in 1986, he met a relatively unique situation. The priests of the neighboring two parishes and he would share a residence and together begin a long-term consultation about the future of the Catholic presence in the area. The priests lived at St. Thomas Aquinas, where Father Mike Reardon ('76) was the pastor. The retired pastor at Resurrection, Father Frank Phelan ('40), remained very much involved. And at St. Mel's, just to the east, Father Greg Rom ('75) was pastor and Father Larry McBrady ('71) a resident. "It was a good mix of guys," Tom recalls. "It wasn't being cast out alone. Along the way, as we began to combine parishes, we worked as a team. I ultimately wound up as the single pastor there after the combining was completed."

After arriving at Resurrection, Libera found himself contradicting friends from white parishes who told him that the area was dangerous and nothing much happened in the parish. Actually, the three small congregations, each ranging from just over 100 to 300 parishioners, had much going on. "There was a job referral service," he explains, "a food pantry, and a clothing store."

> *There was a community organization with headquarters at St. Thomas. We had sharing parishes that would help out with the food. You had three busy schools going and three bingos. The schools functioned without people feeling threatened. People know how to navigate around neighborhoods. We didn't have much direct connection with gangs. The annual grant that we got from the diocese was sufficient. We were never in dire straits.*

The neighborhood struggled with poverty but was not a monolith in that regard. The west end of the parish, for example, which bordered the suburb of Oak Park, remained middle class for some time. "As you went east towards St. Mel, however," Tom says, "you had more gangs and drugs. You had to deal with blight, vacant lots, and efforts with government money to refurbish apartments." Even in that struggle, the parish took a role, staying alert to the area's bad landlords.

The gradual consolidation of the three separate parishes into one faith community took almost seven years to complete. Libera remembered the initial resistance, with people from each of the parishes in theory accepting the need to work together but speaking vociferously about the importance of having the worship space at their own parish. When he and his confreres started the popular Christ Renews His Parish (CRHP) retreats across parish lines, resistance started to melt. CRHP brings together women and men on single-gender weekends to give personal witness to their faith. The retreats had the effect of allowing members of the three distinct parishes to get to know one another. "Some leaders, especially the deacons," Tom recalls, "were active wisdom people who could see that we had to come together."

As a move toward further unity, parish leaders held a naming contest for the new parish. They named it St. Martin de Porres, after the Dominican brother (1579-1639) who devoted his life to working among the poor. De Porres, who came from a Spanish noble father and an African slave mother, is the patron saint of interracial harmony.

Having chosen a name, the congregation needed to agree upon a site. As noted previously, initially Cardinal Bernardin indicated a willingness to build a new church on the site of the old Resurrection Church. Economic distress caused him to change course, and the archdiocese decided to renovate the existing church at St. Thomas Aquinas. (The Jesuits eventually built the new Christ the King High School on the site where Resurrection Church had stood. "So there's a resurrection story," Libera rejoices, "at that site.")

Until the archdiocese had made the final decision on the site, priests held Mass at St. Mel's. "I remember," Tom says, "after a closing ceremony the entire congregation walked over from St. Mel's to Thomas Aquinas and had the first official Mass there."

Previously, Libera discovered an artifact he hoped might serve as a symbol of unity for the new parish. "I was at a religious goods store," he says, "on Archer Avenue. Here is a bronze copy of the original of an upper torso picture of Martin de Porres holding out a hand of welcome and a piece of bread in the other hand. This was just what we needed to crystallize our identity." Tom bought the piece and commissioned the well-known Polish-born Chicago sculptor Jerzy Kenar to create the stand for it. "We had it right by the door," he says proudly, "to welcome people as they came into the new church. We also had a baptismal font that came from Mel's. The floor was a mosaic that was already there at Aquinas. Some of the marble came from Resurrection. So there were parts of all three churches."

For years, Libera remained and other priests rotated in to assist him. Eventually, while still pastor, he had to close one of the three school sites. But the fact that the Catholic Church did not abandon the neighborhood meant much to him. He is convinced that a big reason the archdiocese stayed in the area had to do with a West Side group of priests who met on a regular basis. "There was a sense," he says, "of us wanting to show we have a presence here. When we moved to Aquinas, in fact, we put up an electric sign that said 'St. Martin de Porres Catholic Church.' That stamped that we weren't going anywhere."

After a sabbatical at a Christian Brothers' center for spiritual renewal in Santa Fe, New Mexico and a brief period as administrator of Our Lady of the Woods Parish in the southwest suburbs, Libera was asked by the Personnel Board to take the pastorate at St. Athanasius in Evanston in 1998. Having spent most of his priesthood in either

Polish-American or African-American parishes, the request to run the fairly well-to-do suburban parish came as a surprise. "By that point," he nonetheless acknowledges, "I had already characterized my ministry assignments as a football. You toss it down on the ground and it bounces in different directions, a little unpredictably. I didn't have an attitude of 'It's got to be this place.' You roll with it, and there'll be good things there."

Libera arrived in Evanston to find a parish bustling with activity. Over one thousand families had registered as parishioners. He built upon that foundation. The school, after having dipped into the low 200s, now has over 365 students enrolled. Another 165 children participate in the weekend CCD religious education program. St. A's, as it is known, has a sharing parish in the inner city, St. Agnes of Bohemia, and also has a hardworking liturgy committee. Tom takes pride in the youth ministry program for teenagers. The numbers attending weekly Mass, though, are relatively low. The strongest involvement has come from the school. "There's very good leadership there," he says, "a hardworking school board. A lot of wheels go round to keep things going: room parents, volunteers for the fundraiser, the Angel Ball. A lot of parents coach."

Despite the myriad of parish activities, Libera has concerns about parish unity. "This place," Libera says, echoing Heidenreich's comments about Sacred Heart, "is highly organized, but it's self-organized." Parishioners tend to invest in their own area of concern without thinking through how their group or activity impacts the rest of the parish. "There are times when you have to make some hard decisions in a place like this and stick by them and be fair," he says. "The expectations are high."

Libera knows that he must bring the various parish ministries together to create a sense of unity around a parish-wide vision, so he has reinstituted the process he began five years ago of having all the parish leadership groups conduct their meetings on one night directly before the parish council meeting. In addition, he has brought Father Tom Sweetser to the parish to conduct his Parish Evaluation Project (PEP). The idea behind PEP is to get leadership to look ahead so that they're working together on things that matter.

As Tom Libera looked at his own role in bringing people togeth-er, he knows that the outgoing, charismatic style of leadership that's characteristic of some of his colleagues has not been his strong suit. "My leadership style," he says, "is working behind the scenes. One of the teams I worked with back when we were doing retreats for the separated and divorced gave me a plaque that read, 'The quiet quarter-back.' There's probably a lot to that. The contribution I would hope to make would be encouraging people, being present, and seeing things starting to brew that need to be dealt with sooner rather than later."

....

"It all depends," Bill Zavaski says regarding the job of being a pastor, "on who you follow." To him, nothing mattered more in the transition process to a new pastorate than who had most recently occupied the position. He came to this opinion honestly, having served as pastor of three parishes: St. Bartholomew in Waukegan, his home parish, from 1979-1990; Transfiguration in north suburban Wauconda, from 1990-1995; and St. James in Arlington Heights since 1995. In the first in-stance, Bill succeeded a parish legend; in the second, the parish could not wait to see the previous pastor go; and in his current pastorate, he replaced a popular but later disgraced pastor.

"I got my home parish of 400 families," Zavaski recalls of his first pastorate, "and John Kuzinskas ('52), whom I replaced, was my hero. He took care of the place very well. He fixed it up physically and fi-nancially—it was a financial disaster before he got there. Like my own family, John's family was from there, so they loved him. I just capital-ized on his good work."

Even Kuzinskas had his limitations, of course. When Zavaski in-vestigated what changes in the Mass Kuzinskas had instituted in the wake of the Second Vatican Council, by then 14 years past, he found that little had occurred. "For all his goodness," he says, "liturgy was not John's forte." Even that worked to Bill's ultimate advantage. "I came in with these 'radical' ideas," he reports. "For example, they had never had Eucharistic ministers and lectors."

Eventually the people of St. Bart's loved the changes Bill instituted, but not at first. Since the parishioners had had minimal experience with liturgical reforms, they worried that he would change too much too fast—they weren't used to anyone spending time with liturgy, working on music, or trying to get them to participate. Once again, the fact that his mother had helped so many people in the parish, especially the Lithuanian immigrants, made it easier for Zavaski—the hometown boy now made priest—to forge ahead with new ideas. He recalls his decision to repaint the church's statues. "I painted all 14 one color," he says, "flesh tone. They couldn't take that. 'Father, the statues, they look like statues.' I said, 'That's what they are.' But the people related to them like they were real people, putting notes under their statue."

Zavaski had inherited from Kuzinskas a small Lithuanian/Lithuanian-American parish situated in a blue-collar town that had similar little ethnic parishes dotting its map: German, Polish, Irish, Slovenian. "We had people," he recalls, "born in this country who grew up in the parish like my parents. Then you had the immigrants that came in the '50s." The parish, on the one hand, could not afford a paid staff. "I had to handle everything by myself," he explains, "until I got two permanent deacons and two or three volunteers. We worked as a team to move the parish forward, so I didn't find myself totally alone. You need to have a group of people that you can feed ideas off of and be creative with."

On the other hand, despite the parish's financial difficulties, parishioners kept their own private parish bank account unbeknownst to the archdiocese. "They would never tell downtown," Bill admits, "but they put money in the bank. The Lithuanians didn't trust Cody. A finance committee watched that money. If I needed anything I'd say, 'The roof is leaking.' I collected $80,000 in six weeks to pay for the roof. They were very loyal to the parish."

Fairly early in his tenure, a conversation with an immigrant parishioner helped Zavaski realize that changes far beyond the liturgical lay in store for the parish. "He said," Bill recalls, "'Father, you'll have to learn Lithuanian first, but then you'll have to learn Spanish.'" Both Hispanics and African-Americans had begun moving into St. Bart's boundaries. Although eventually most of his white ethnic parishioners physically moved out of the parish, many returned every Sunday for Mass. "Some never left," Zavaski says. "My dad and my step-mom never left the neighborhood. But our Hispanic population kept growing." So, after relearning enough Lithuanian to say Mass in that language, Bill indeed had to learn to say Mass in Spanish. "By the time I left," he says, "we had Mass in English, Lithuanian, and Spanish. The Lithuanian at 10 a.m. was the least attended—55 people plus a choir of 20 people. But our choir was absolutely magnificent. Then I had two Masses in English and one in Spanish."

Zavaski began attempting to unite the communities that now made up the parish by celebrating one liturgy using the three different languages during Holy Week. It took time before the practice gained acceptance. "There was a lot of prejudice and tension," he concedes. "Some of the original parishioners did not like the newer Lithuanian immigrants and vice versa. The originals didn't like the Mexicans. I tried to bring them all together."

As living in the area became problematic due to rising crime rates—Bill got robbed twice and bought his first dog—the parish had to adjust. With 100 students left in the school, he met with nearby pastors also facing enrollment declines and developed a consolidation plan that included turning St. Bart's school building into a retreat and social center. "We had a celebration," he recalls with humor of the final send-off for the school, "with people hugging the building goodbye."

The problem is, I forgot to tell the people to stop hugging. We hugged it for about three minutes and went downstairs for the party. The people in the back of the building did not get the word. After 25 minutes they said, "When can we stop hugging the building?"

Zavaski also met with neighborhood leaders and began Southside Neighbors Allied for Progress, a community organization founded to address social ills in a changing area. Although guiding the parish through neighborhood change did not come easily to him, the fact that he hailed from the parish allowed change to take place with a minimum of hostility and a maximum of grace.

Sandwiched between two pastorates in which he followed a beloved figure, Zavaski arrived in 1990 at Transfiguration Parish in the northwest suburb of Wauconda to replace a pastor with a more problematic reputation. As dean of the cluster of parishes that included both St. Bart's and Transfiguration, Bill had read many letters of complaint about the outgoing pastor. "He put his foot in his mouth," he says incredulously, "on a regular basis. He held no meetings, nothing. He was forever going and shutting the heat off in the school. The steps to the rectory were falling apart." Bishop John Vlasny ('61), the vicar for the local vicariate, made a pastoral visit to the parish. Vlasny later told Zavaski that the pastor had refused to let him speak to any of the parishioners.

When the pastor finally left, relieved parishioners of Transfiguration placed a sign in front of the church reading, "Under New Management." "After this guy," Zavaski says, "I thought: all I have to do is smile. I met with parish leadership and said, 'I'm not changing anything for six months.' People said, 'Please, change something. Don't wait.'" Bill gave his parishioners what they wanted, beginning by encouraging them to believe that Transfiguration was their parish. "People didn't think they could participate," he explains. "There was nothing."

So we enhanced the liturgy, started the parish council, gave them something to think about in the homily. They never had that before. They took ownership and became excited about being Church. I didn't do much. You make people feel part of the process. They get committed when you invite them.

Zavaski knew his efforts had begun to pay off when a group of parishioners decided to renovate the rectory, steps and all. "They were that excited," he recalls gratefully, "about having somebody who wanted people around. I had five happy years there."

Bill found his term at Transfiguration shortened when archdiocesan leaders asked him in 1995 to return to the parish of his first assignment, St. James in Arlington Heights, to replace the enormously popular Father Peter Bowman ('55), who had just received an appointment to moderate the curia for the archdiocese. "I didn't want to go," Zavaski insists. "I loved Wauconda. I knew I was replacing Peter, who walked on water. But I figured that Pete had everything under control. But God gets even. The first thing they hand me is a 10-year plan in which we're supposed to build a new school. I was so mad."

But the parish had grown from 2,000 to 4,000 families in the 19 years since Bill had left in 1976. It took 10 years to build, but the school, whose enrollment reached a peak of 900 (it stands at about 500 now), eventually got built. "Now we want to build a new church," he says wearily, "but I'll be dead by the time we get to that point. I want that on record. I'll be dead. I'm not building a new church. That fight is going to be really something."

With the exception of learning about the school building project, Zavaski didn't mind following Bowman. "Pete was a wonderful, well-loved administrator," he reflects, "who never said no to anybody. He developed a wonderful staff. This had been my first assignment so I still had good relationships with many of the people." (Later in his pastorate, however, Bill had to deal with the blow to the parish of the archdiocese removing Bowman from ministry due to an accusation of sexual misconduct with a minor. This is covered in the chapter "Scandal.")

Unlike at Transfiguration, parishioners at St. James already had a strong sense of Church. Social activities were long established; the parish belonged to United Power for Action and Justice, a Cook County community organization working on health care, housing, and other complex issues. In short, Zavaski's job, as he saw it, was to build on Bowman's success. He began a St. Vincent de Paul Society and a peace and justice committee, and the parish began offering shelter and food to the homeless once each week through the PADS organization.[3]

Given his own personal emphasis on spirituality, Bill attempted to deepen the spiritual life of the parish. Noticing that some parents with children in the school or CCD did not attend Mass, for example, he responded by making parents the chief educators for their children's sacramental preparation for First Reconciliation and Eucharist. "We're using this strategic planning," he explains, "that John Canary ('69) has done for the archdiocese." The plan noted that getting parents involved in their children's sacramental prep encourages the whole family to commit more fully to attending Mass. "We want to train parents," Zavaski insists, "to be coaches for their children's faith formation."

Aware that only half of the 4,000 registered families attend Mass regularly, Bill's staff has also initiated a program to bring non-attendees back into parish life. "We think we're crowded on Sundays," Zavaski maintains, "but if they all came—they come on Christmas and Easter—we could not physically handle them. There's a disconnect. We have a lot of evangelization work to do."

> One attempt is a neighborhood ministry project where we have active parishioners visit people in their area to give them a more personal Catholic face. We've broken up the parish into sections like a ward map and tried to find a block captain for each section. There was genius in the Democratic Party machine.

As people get to know one another, invitations to attend St. James for Mass follow. Bill Zavaski continues to find ways to carry the message of the importance of faith to those parishioners for whom religious activity has dwindled or disappeared. Recently, for example, he had people turn their cell phones on during his homily and text friends to say that they were at Mass praying for them.

....

When the archdiocesan personnel board asked Ed Upton to found a new parish—St. Francis of Assisi—in the southwest suburb of Orland Park in 1990, they left him to fend for himself. "They said there is no public building for Mass," Upton recalls, "no one has to become part of the parish because everybody can be grandfathered into their current parish, and there's no rectory to live in, but go ahead."

Upton quickly rented 2,200 square feet of space in a shopping mall storefront and began celebrating Mass, initially to crowds of about 200 people. Two priest friends—Fathers Brian Fisher ('79) and John Hall ('80)—accompanied him to scrounge through a warehouse containing items from closed churches in search of religious articles with which to adorn the storefront and turn it into a small chapel. After the first year, a regional Catholic grade school serving four local parishes in the area opened, and Ed began to celebrate Mass there, as well as in the mall. Once temporary arrangements proved tolerable, he started the more arduous task of planning for the building of a church and the major fundraising drive to make it possible.

What Upton learned in the process of attracting people and encouraging them to commit to a new parish flies in the face of what he hears from some young priests today. In reaction to what they see as too much focus on personality by Vatican II-era clergy, many priests now stress the role rather than the person of the priest. In starting a parish from scratch, though, Ed realized that "people respond to the person," not to abstractions or roles. "As the pastor," he says, "you must embody the mission of the parish. If you do, they go with you. So it is personal."

Putting his personal leadership skills to work, Upton sought out advice on fundraising and building a church. He recalled his classmate Father John Canary warning him not to begin fundraising only then to have a fight with parishioners about the building. "That made sense," Ed says. "So we had town hall meetings and put up the architect's drawings so that people had a sense of what the church would look like. People really liked it." Canary also recommended using key themes as a reference point. "The first one," Upton says, "was it should look like a church. What does that mean? It's usually people's image of the church they grew up in. So we have a bell tower, a peaked roof. Things that you can tell, unless you're a complete dolt, that it's a church."

> Secondly, we want it to communicate the mission statement, make sure that it's a place of welcome. There's no concrete in the front. Bricks soften it so that people feel a sense of welcome. There are flowers as people come up to church. We built the narthex round because square angles are harsh; round is inviting. It had to be conducive to liturgy.

"Those were the principles we used," Ed explains. "I didn't know anybody, so the committee ended up being anybody who volunteered. It worked out; people are satisfied and happy."

In order for the building plans to take real shape, however, Upton needed funds. "The toughest thing," he admits, "was asking for money. You hire a company and what they tell you—there's no secret—is you just have to ask for it. To come close to your goal, you ask for way more than you think you'll get. I knocked on people's doors who I barely knew saying, 'Would you give $50,000?' Same thing anywhere: A third give generously, a third give moderately, and a third give nothing. No matter what you do, that bottom third won't give. We tried everything."

The importance of a church structure and funds to build it with notwithstanding, Ed also realized the necessity of the parish acquiring its own identity. "On the South Side," Upton acknowledges from long experience, "parishes have an identity. How do you create that identity? How do you get people to say they belong to a community? That was the challenge." Aware that people no longer simply attended the nearest parish but that rather they shopped for their places of worship, he worked to create a good liturgical and communal experience for those browsing at his church. He received much inadvertent help in that regard from a nearby parish, where people were voting with their feet right out the door. "People didn't like the inflexible stewardship there," Ed admits, "that was based on lots of requirements. So when we started, the floodgates opened. People were willing to come for a sense of community and ownership."

Upton worked quickly to capitalize on his growing numbers. "In an older parish," he says, "if the place gets a difficult pastor, people have some loyalty because the parish has been there for a while, so they will stick with it because of the history. But here, there was nothing to be loyal to. So you try to build up in people a sense of responsibility.

"Without my intending it," he admits, "the storefront gave St. Francis of Assisi a cutesy identity. People would call it St. Walgreen's or Our Lady of the Mall." To help cement people's new loyalty and establish parish identity, Upton hired Father Stan Sloan, an Omaha artist, to create an image of St. Francis that was put on all parish materials.

Upton's efforts to form a new Church community did not always go smoothly. Some people looked askance at the storefront chapel, for example, and refused to have their babies baptized there. Others, to his amazement, told him they would refrain from contributing financially to the parish until he had built a proper church. "How do you think I'm going to build a church?" he would ask, rhetorically lowering the boom on the freeloaders. "You want to say to them, whose names I still remember, when they come to have their grandma buried, 'Now you want us—you didn't give a darn dime when we built it.' But I hold my tongue."

Offsetting unpleasant moments were the myriad of people who gave St. Francis Parish a chance. Few of Upton's new parishioners knew one another; many had just moved to the subdivisions being built in the neighborhood. But most seemed ready for a new experience of Church.

Over the course of 20 years, Upton and the community of St. Francis have built a thriving parish with over 3,000 registered parishioners and a weekly collection averaging $28,000. A perusal of a typical parish bulletin reveals a wealth of activities pointing to a rich tapestry of parish life. The parish Lenten mission and a CRHP retreat for men highlight a recent 16-page bulletin, which also contains information on the local Catholic school, CCD, liturgy commission, RCIA, choirs, Catholic Charities committee, St. Vincent de Paul, a senior citizens' group, Alcoholics Anonymous meetings, Marian Movement, a youth group, service projects, and an Easter food drive for the poor.

Despite Upton's unquestionable success, he remains anything but complacent about his parish. "St. Francis is so alive and vibrant," he says, "that people don't notice how many are *not* here on a regular basis. We confirmed 200 kids in March. We're lucky to have 50 of them on Sundays. We've registered 3,300 families, but the number coming to church has continued to decline."

> *The decline is rampant—which we don't want to look at. The people that come to Mass every Sunday, it's about 25 percent; about 40 percent come a few times over the course of the year. I've learned that people are very focused on their children. At the sacramental ages they're very active but then they move on to high school activities. So to them the parish is a set of activities, not a life principle, and they move on. You start to see them come back after the kids are gone.*

Ed has also noticed a significant decrease in the number of couples coming to church to celebrate their 25th anniversaries at Mass.

"There really is a shift," he says. "I'm in a quandary."

Attempting to resolve the dilemma of dropping church attendance, Upton commented on the pluses and minuses of the cultural change in how people look at the larger Church. "People have a sense of helping others," he asserts, "a tremendous sense of charity. They ask themselves if they are being decent folks. For example, are they helping the poor? It's more a generic sense of being good. There truly is also a sense of the transcendent. People do believe in afterlife, in the presence of God, and in prayer."

Ed has no rose-colored glasses, however, when reflecting on the negative side of the cultural change. "Mass and the Church for most people," he says, "are on the same level as Boy Scouts, Brownies, and Little League. The Church is nice to be a part of but..." To counter this attitude, he believes the principle of attraction works better than promotion or coercion. "We try to do a decent liturgy," he says, "a decent homily, work through the kids to have stuff for families, because telling them you're going to go to hell if you don't go to Mass is useless. People make their moral decisions themselves. We are in a voluntary church. That's how people view it. I don't know any way but to continue to invite people, to welcome, to encourage their participation, and to provide opportunities for them to grow. We have to learn to live with that voluntary culture. To go back and say here are the rules, here's what you have to follow isn't going to have a darn bit of influence."

It is pastors like Ed Upton and his five classmates, on the front lines of the Church ministering to people in real-life situations, who most often have to make decisions about how to address controversial issues in the Church. "I'm into the wide boat," he explains, "with a lot of flexibility. Rather than say this is the way it's going to be or you're out, our generation has been good at applying the principles of our faith to individual situations. Francis George has said, 'People are going to be influenced by outside sources: why not have them influenced by the Church?' That's a pretty good thought."

1. Mary Benet McKinney, OSB, *Sharing Wisdom: A Process for Group Decision Making* (Valencia, CA: Tabor Publishing, 1987).
2. Mundelein Seminary confers the Doctor of Ministry (D.Min.) degree on post-graduate students in pastoral ministry.
3. PADS is Public Action to Deliver Shelter, an independent not-for-profit corporation that sponsors homeless shelters in Chicagoland and other areas of the United States.

CHAPTER 13

DISCORDANT VOICES
A Divided Church

Divisions in the contemporary Catholic Church in the United States are not difficult to observe. Three members of the ordination class of 1969 offer up stories that illustrate these differences in living color.

"Where I see the split," Mike Ahlstrom says, "is between the priests on the one hand and the deacons and laity on the other." A few years ago he was given an assignment to teach a crash course in Vatican II to both permanent diaconate candidates and those training for lay ministry. After lecturing, Ahlstrom split his class into 10 small groups, asking each to reach a consensus on three items they would put on the agenda should a Vatican III occur in their lifetimes. "With no prompting on my part," Ahlstrom recalls, "9 of the 10 groups came up with revisiting *Humanae Vitae*, the role of women in the Church—including ordination—and optional versus obligatory celibacy for priests. The deacons and laypeople were on the same wavelength."

Shortly thereafter, Ahlstrom taught a course to seminarians on parish liturgy. Given the then recent controversy in Chicago over general absolution, Ahlstrom broached the topic, saying to the men, "The Pope is against it. It's not allowed. But as men who are going to be priests, you should understand why some pastors think this is a good thing." "The seminarians were horrified that I would even bring it up," he recalls. "I thought I was going to be tried for heresy. I see a collision course on ministry and theology between the men being ordained priests and the men and women coming through the diaconate and lay ministry programs."

Tom Libera took part in a local archdiocesan process that he saw as exemplifying the best of Vatican II methods, only to see it dismantled for a time. He served on the Catholic Campaign for Human Development's (CCHD) recommendation committee for Chicago. Founded in 1969, CCHD is the domestic anti-poverty, social justice program of the U.S. Catholic bishops, designed to empower the poor by addressing the root causes of poverty in America. Funded by an annual collection taken up across the country, it gives grants to community-controlled, self-help organizations.[1] The local committee, consisting of about 35 members, mostly laypeople, reviews applications for grants from local organizations that apply, visits the finalists on site, and then votes on recommendations for which groups to fund. In 2009, CCHD came under attack by a coalition of pro-life groups—and even from a few U.S. bishops—for supposedly funding organizations that promoted activities opposed to Catholic teaching. Although the bishops have, as a group, strenuously denied such charges, several dioceses, including Chicago, changed the process for picking which organizations to fund by eliminating the selection committees and putting the grant choices solely in the hands of the program directors and bishops. A small number of dioceses, in addition, have even pulled out of the annual CCHD collection.[2]

For Libera, the process of committee members meeting with community organizations and discerning which groups CCHD should fund served as a model of collaborative ministry. "The diocese wanted to be cautious," Libera says, "but in the process lost 35 people who were on its side." Thankfully, when a new local CCHD director took over, she reinstated the site visits by committee. Libera also regretted the actions of those dioceses that pulled out of the campaign. "These groups," he says, "have small budgets. The Catholic Church is making an important contribution to their success. It's a step backwards."

And then there's Ed Upton's perspective on the gap between the pastoral perspectives of front-line parish ministers such as pastors and those of diocesan officials and bishops. As dean of his southwest suburban deanery, Upton at times has received complaints from unhappy Catholics in parishes. Recently the Respect Life office forwarded a missive from a woman decrying her pastor. His offense? "A woman gave a reflection on Mother's Day," Upton says, "and talked on how happy she was with her child. She mentioned she had had the child through *in vitro* fertilization." Two archdiocesan officials subsequently contacted Upton about the complaint. One suggested sending the pastor of the parish in question several articles on in vitro fertilization. The person insisted, Upton recalls, "'that we have to educate people, including pastors, that this kind of unorthodox comment should not be tolerated.' The other official complained, 'You can't talk about Mother's Day, a secular holiday, at Mass.' I'm thinking: Jesus, I must be in the wrong world. If you don't talk about mothers on Mother's Day, the congregation's crazy."

> *About in vitro fertilization, you have people who want to have children. If they're convinced it's morally acceptable, is it so awful that I would preach you can't do that? If you ask most Catholics, they'd say, "Aren't we supposed to encourage people to have children?" Maybe I'm missing something. They're not taking somebody else's sperm and egg and implanting it. They're not having the child to sell it; that's a different movie. Circumstances change the action. The bishops—sometimes I wonder if they live in the real world. They don't live in my world.*

Upton and the pastor invited archdiocesan officials to give a talk at the parish. For Upton, indicating the priority he places on pastoral concerns, timing was crucial. The talk would be far removed from the time of the controversy, he explains, "so as not to embarrass the woman."

....

The six priests being followed here believe the U.S. Catholic Church of the 21st century faces divisions on at least three distinct though related battlegrounds: generational differences, ideologies, and pastoral practices. Changes in the Catholic priesthood—also generational, ideological, and pastoral—have contributed to and reflect these divisions in the American Church. The 2012 book *Same Call, Different Men:*

The Evolution of the Priesthood since Vatican II, published by Liturgical Press, outlined some of those shifts in a remarkable sociological survey of American priests. The book examines multiple cohorts of priests, including the Vatican II group of priests ordained between 1964 and 1977 and the group of millennials ordained after 1992. Sixty-seven percent of priests now in their 60s—thus most likely to have been ordained between 1964 and 1977—fell into either the "progressive" or "somewhat progressive" category in their vision of priestly identity, while the almost identical percentage—68 percent—of priests in their 30s landed in the "traditional" or "somewhat traditional" category.[3] Following this trend, 78 percent of Vatican II-era priests want open discussion on the importance of lay ministry. For the millennial cohort, the percentage drops to 65 percent.[4] Eighty-nine percent of Vatican II-era priests agree the Church should allow women greater participation in lay ministries; for millennials, the numbers drop again to 65 percent. Finally, only 61 percent of Vatican II-era clergy agree that ordination conferred a "permanent character" which made them essentially different from the laity, while 88 percent of millennial-era priests agree with that statement.[5]

Great divergence of views clearly exists between the generations. Millennials, for example, often criticize Vatican II-era priests for over-emphasizing internal Church reform at the expense of the Church's efforts to confront American culture. These men from the class of '69, however, disagree, pointing to areas where they stand united against elements of that culture: immigration reform, pro-life, reducing gun violence, anti-capital punishment, and others. Bill Zavaski, for his part, has taken on youth in his parish on same-sex marriage: "Most of our confirmation group," he reports, "doesn't think anything's wrong with gay marriage. 'Why not? They have rights,' they say. I tell them, 'They have rights, but don't call it marriage. It contradicts the definition of marriage.'" Regardless, many younger priests today see the efforts of their elders as too little, and too focused on "liberal" aspects of Church teaching.

Tom Libera has experienced contempt from the millennial generation. "A young guy characterized us as demons," he says. "'You had your day, and we'll wait for you to move out.'" On the other hand,

Libera has also seen young clergy grow and change, such as one traditionally minded young priest who initially would invariably respond, "We can't do that," to requests from parishioners. His pastor showed him ways to make practical pastoral adjustments that the young priest credits with helping him learn to work with people.

Mike Ahlstrom tempered his concerns about generational conflicts with memories of his own early days in priesthood. "One pastor says, 'The new guys—their heart isn't in it,'" Ahlstrom remarks, "I wouldn't be so harsh. It takes a while to get seasoned. When I started out, I was judgmental whenever people weren't thinking the way I thought—what was the matter with them? It took me time to fall in love with and accept people for who they were."

Ahlstrom does worry, however, about foreign-born priests coming into U.S. ministry, saying, "We're not doing a good job of integrating priests from other cultures into American culture. There is a difference in ecclesiology as well as pastoral aspects of how you do ministry." He points to one possible but small-scale solution: "I belong to a priest prayer support group, and we started as intergenerational. More recently we have become international: Polish and Mexican."

One clear concern emerges from the men from 1969. They all observe that, in a multitude of settings, some younger priests feel most comfortable when keeping their distance from their parishioners. Bill Zavaski, who has mentored the newly ordained, worries about how this plays out in relationships. "The new ones are good," he says, "but there is distance."

> They don't want to engage in people's lives as much. They find
> it harder to work with people. It's easier if Father makes the
> decisions. Some want to go back to the '50s. The scariest part is
> that they never lived in the '50s.

Zavaski has also noticed a pronounced reluctance on the part of millennial clergy to work with the ecumenical ministerial association in Arlington Heights. "They will have nothing to do with them," Zavaski says. "Maybe it's because John Paul II kept saying, 'We have the truth,' and Francis George was big into that. I buy the truth, but to me the truth is a person. Pope Benedict said that Jesus of Nazareth is the law. I quote Benedict on that," he says, laughing, "so I'm safe."

Ed Upton, who has also supervised the newly ordained, goes even further than Zavaski, fearing that some young priests have moved past traditionalism into a rampant clericalism—yet another form of distancing themselves from the non-ordained. "I saw some young guys at Mundelein," he reports, "for a strategic planning meeting. Holy good God, they're parading around in cassocks and collars and it's 95 degrees in the middle of summer. I don't get it. Maybe they have a better identity," he surmises, "or they're just more pious. It seems self-aggrandizing: 'We dress differently; we are essentially different; we are not only different, we're better.' Even that phrase, 'essential difference,' has been misunderstood. It's a scholastic word," Upton explains, "that says when you're ordained, you change as a person; we say the same thing with baptism. So it's not this clerical thing that 'I'm higher.' The thing that upsets me about the cassocks or collars is what it says about relationships: that you're a special caste. In our day we worked to say you come out of the people and you're with them, and now we're going backwards. I just don't buy it."

In mentoring younger priests, Upton has noticed, in addition to clericalism, a not unrelated problem. "As a pastor," he remarks, "you have to be able to organize and lead people. Many of them don't have that ability. They tend to be one-on-one oriented, and fine there. But ask them to organize something, they almost seem paralyzed. That worries me more than even the theology. When I say organize, I mean take a group of people, have an idea, get it going, and let it run by it-self. Visiting hospitals as a priest is important. But if you get a group of people—my pastoral associate, she's got 40 people, mostly women, who bring Communion to the sick and reflect on their experience. She does the whole thing: recruits, trains, organizes, evaluates. I haven't had an associate who can do that. There's nothing wrong with visiting the hospital, but if you've got a parish to run, then you've got a community to develop."

Despite their frustrations, these classmates challenge themselves to understand younger priests as well as the influences that have shaped their attitudes. "I'm afraid priests being ordained today aren't immersed in the Catholic culture," says Bob Heidenreich. "We were so much a part of the Church, serving Mass every day, working in the rectory from age 13. We were wet behind the ears, but we knew what ministry was and how to take care of people because we saw the priests doing that. I'm not sure with guys today that there's a transfer like that."

"Young people have grown up in the secular world," Ed Upton speculates, "and found it wanting. They're looking for values that are more stable, whereas we always lived in the Church world. We've never had to deal with a pagan environment. Most of us wanted to change the world and to make the Church better. The young seminarians today come to priesthood out of a personal graced religious experience; for example, perhaps they were at World Youth Day. Their call to priesthood has nothing to do with transforming the world. It's personal piety—not to change society but to grow themselves. So they're caught up in things like Eucharistic Adoration and following the rules at Mass."

Tom Libera has slowly come to appreciate, if not agree with, that world view. "It's powerful," he notes, "to look at the world young people come out of and ask what is missing that they're looking for? It's different from when you came out of a Catholic neighborhood like we did," he says. "People in seminary today come out of a world where whatever you want, it's okay—your truth is yours and wonderful, but it's not mine. It's not surprising that they want to tap into the more established part of Church tradition. We might be the same way if we grew up when they did."

....

Battles over theology and ideology rage not only among clergy but also among laity, the American bishops, and Church authorities in Rome. Clashing views fan the flames of debate over the future of the Church in the U.S., often leading to a glaring lack of civility, not to mention unity. "There is a growing conservative influence," Bill Zavaski says, "among some parishioners. I find them mean-spirited. That was not the intent when we were opening up the doors and windows. I'm re-reading the Vatican documents. They don't contain anything wrong. They make a lot of sense about who we are as Church. It's all scripturally founded. I'm very comfortable in what I believe in."

Zavaski, however, does not shrink from examining possible past mistakes. "We discounted some things that maybe we shouldn't have," he says. "The classic example is John Paul II bringing back formal Adoration of the Blessed Sacrament. For me, I always believed what St. Paul recognized: that Christ is present within us. 'It is no longer I who live but Christ Jesus that lives in me,' so I don't need to go to the tabernacle to connect with Christ. But there has been a shift in that theology, so some people want adoration. I don't have a problem if you spend time in front of the Blessed Sacrament, but that practice wouldn't enhance my spiritual life. I believe Christ is present in the Eucharist, certainly, but he's most present within us."

Some good, however, has come from the renewal of the practice, according to Zavaski. "Perhaps people doing adoration," he surmises, "have more respect for the Eucharist. Some people here say, 'I'll take care of the wine.' It's not wine. So we have lost a sense of reverence. We have to be more respectful of the Precious Blood—we are consuming Christ."

But the younger generations' fondness for some traditional Catholic practices makes Zavaski scratch his head. "Why in God's name would you want to have priests return to turning their back to you at the altar?" he says. "It's bizarre that people who never lived pre-Vatican II think that's the way things should be. You don't need bells rung if the consecration is in English. The reason we had bells was that the Mass was in Latin and people didn't even know what was happening. But I like the sound of bells—so ring bells, I don't care."

Nevertheless, Zavaski refuses to shy away from one core message: that the people of God *are* the Church and are called to have a voice in the Church and in the world. "Church leadership," he complains, "at times doesn't want to have that voice spoken. It's easier for authority if you don't question. For example, I don't see why we can't have women priests. St. Paul said there's no male or female. We're all one in Christ. They don't bring that up when they talk about women priests."

His biggest concern about the hierarchy, however, has to do with the growing lack of civility that, in his mind, obscures Catholicism's central message. "The conservative element," Zavaski says, "is becoming nastier. Some aren't respectful. They hated Bernardin's Common Ground Initiative—look at all those cardinals who were so nasty about it. Of course some liberals are mean-spirited, too. There is always a tension. Somewhere in the middle is the truth. We can get so wrapped up in non-essentials. We have to focus on the essential thing: a personal relationship with Jesus, making a commitment to follow him to the best of my ability. That was central in the early Church."

Larry Duris has less ambivalence than Zavaski. "We didn't harangue on birth control," he says, "because we sensed people didn't believe it. I don't. But none of us were ever soft on abortion. Bernardin's seamless garment made immense sense. Some right-wing people want to save the unborn but are trampling to death things to help them once they're here." Duris acknowledged the contempt with which some Catholics—clergy included—view him and his more progressive colleagues. "We hear, 'You guys destroyed the Church,'" he says. "When anyone says Vatican II was an enemy of the Church, I ask, what in it was counter to the Gospel message?

"But every age has," Duris says, "in building something up, also trampled on some gardens." Take the sacrament of Reconciliation, where the frequency of going to personal confession has greatly diminished over the last 50 years. In Duris' view, the quality of confessions has actually improved because of the education people have received as to its meaning. "Our generation," he says, "did a pendulum swing from Reconciliation being a car wash. We did catechesis. The sacrament has a power greater than it used to when it was: 'Step in the box, press the button, and get a quick shower.'"

Despite the critiques, overall Duris remains optimistic, saying: "Maybe I'm Mary Poppins or in denial—nobody will destroy the sandcastle I built as this elephant comes down the beach." If anything, he thinks the Church has barely scratched the surface in implementing the ideals of the Council. "When people say, 'Let's scrap Vatican II,' I say, 'You haven't even opened the book to see what it says!'"

"One criticism," Duris bristles, "was that we blurred the lines between laity and clergy. We did better than that—we got rid of the lines altogether. I'm glad we did."

Two very different philosophical understandings, Ed Upton says, lie beneath most of the ideological divisions in today's Church. One is from classical philosophy, claiming that humans can understand the essence of things and then everything else will follow from there. Upton claims that notion simply does not ring true. He gives a far greater role to people's actual lived experience as they seek to live out the values that the church teaches.

Upton explained what this disagreement can look like in parish life. "The Church says: 'We have the truth.' We do have truth, but when it resides in human beings that truth has to have some flex. To say absolutely no one can practice artificial birth control because it's a mortal sin and is always wrong, for example, doesn't ring true to most people's experience. But they—and I—still hold that there's a value to having a procreative marriage."

Early in his priesthood, Upton faced questions from parishioners about Church teaching on birth control. "But in the last 25 years I don't think I've ever had a person ask. They've made up their own mind. I don't think it's even an issue for people. That's why there aren't many talks on sexuality from the pulpit, because most priests aren't comfortable with the classicist interpretation—as opposed to a relational interpretation—of moral teaching. I'm not sure about younger priests or the hierarchy, but that's where most of us would be today."

Upton remains skeptical about the approach of bishops and theologians who advocate for better instruction or catechesis as a solution to divisions in the Church. "I'm not sure that information is the problem," he says, "or the answer. People have fundamental differences with the Church. For example, in every religion, the core is women. Many women find it offensive in this American culture when the Church says they can't be priests, not because of their talents but only because they are female. Many women today—even if they come to Church—keep their distance. Moms don't encourage their sons to be priests partly because their daughters can't be.

"Most Catholics," Upton says, switching gears, "don't believe abortion is a good thing. But some feel that there can be situations when it is a moral option. When they hear that a conversation can't even be had, they dismiss the teaching. Sexual ethics are similar. When you still teach that any sexual thought or act outside of marriage is a mortal sin, you make sense to few human beings. People make up their own mind, because the only thing that makes sense to people is what's persuasive. The argument from authority is dead."

Upton has worried that a "take it or leave it" approach, an insistence that only one way of looking at Church teaching exists, has begun to make the "unattainable perfect" the enemy of the "attainable good" and thus is driving people away from the Church. He supported, for example, the Catholic Health Association (CHA) and the Leadership Conference of Women Religious (LCWR) when they came out in favor of the Affordable Care Act, despite the fact that the U.S. bishops opposed the bill. Upton thought the two Catholic groups had made the correct moral judgment that the law would help poor women have the resources they needed to make it more likely that they would carry their children to term. "The LCWR and the CHA said the health care bill is not the best," Upton points out, "but it's going to help poor women have medical care. The bishops who think more open-mindedly on this issue are hiding under rocks. It's the herd mentality—the pack is staying together."

During the debate on health care reform, Bill Zavaski's advocacy riled up people enough that archdiocesan leaders insisted on a halt to his efforts. Zavaski had published in the parish bulletin the pro-reform views of Network, a Catholic social justice lobbying group formed by American nuns back in the progressive heyday of 1971. Sister Simone Campbell, Network's executive director, had supported Obama's health care bill at a critical time and attended the bill signing when it became law in 2010. "I belong to Network," Zavaski explains. "I love these nuns, but we're Republican out here in Arlington Heights. I'm one of the few Democrats." So when he published Network's views and preached on them, the resulting uproar led archdiocesan leaders who heard about it to deem it overly partisan. "Oh God, they got mad," Zavaski recalls with a smile.

Struggling to understand these ideological tensions within the Church, Tom Libera has begun to read more traditional material, like the journal *First Things*. Most parishioners he encounters, however, don't fit into neat categories such as liberal/conservative or progressive/traditional. "[University of Chicago religious historian] Martin Marty talked about that," Libera says, "in terms of abortion. Two groups, each about 10 percent of the population, are on these two cliffs shooting cannons at each other. In the valley you've got 80 percent of the people trying to make sense of things, and occasionally these cannonballs get dropped on them. But most people don't have a pure position one way or the other."

Accordingly, Libera has maintained that it is imperative to find forums where people can discuss their concerns about what the Church teaches and, more importantly, why. "It is strange in a country where we have freedom of expression that a Catholic who wants to speak about women's ordination has to do it in a Methodist Church. Can't we say there might not be agreement right now, but is exclusion of those with a different opinion the only way we can operate? It's nice when you can have some discussions along these lines in parishes. But you'd find people who relish those moments when they can call somebody out, saying, 'This isn't what the bishops say you should be doing.'"

More than his five colleagues, Bob Heidenreich has attempted to bridge the gap between progressive and traditional Catholics, both by admitting some mistakes were made in the early implementation of Vatican II and by acknowledging that both groups have a common purpose—catechesis—even as they have employed different strategies to achieve it. "It's too simple to say," he says, "that the conservatives want to change the Church back to what it was before Vatican II. There are some people that want to do that, but not everyone. What I see is we keep on trying to catechize people. If we understand the challenge of Vatican II—the ongoing conversion of people—we're on the right track."

Heidenreich has spent not inconsiderable time reevaluating what he sees as mistakes made in the implementation of Vatican II. "The initial decoration of churches after Vatican II was atrocious," he concedes. "St. Ben's Church was just painted beige. When we formed a committee and my associate Jason Malave ('97) worked with them, they brought out these beautiful baroque curlicues and highlighted them. That was a symbol for me that things had been too black and white. Back then, you were liberal or conservative. You either went along with Vatican II or you didn't. You either worshipped in Latin or English. You sang cool songs with a guitar or you didn't. And we lost some beauty and depth.

"I remember," Heidenreich says, "thinking so negatively of Opus Dei and being upset with Cardinal George because he gave St. Mary of the Angels Parish to Opus Dei priests.[6] When I was doing the pre-pastor workshops, their priest came. He was in a collar all the time but was a nice guy. He had this ecclesiology, though, that everything had to go through him." Instead of critiquing the priest, however, Heidenreich tried to show him how Vatican II theology and methodology could help him run his parish by involving laypeople and relieving pressure on himself. "But a year later he broke down because he was trying to do it all," Heidenreich reports.

In the past, Opus Dei members in his various parishes had confronted Heidenreich about the "liberal" way he did things. At Sacred Heart, however, they simply ask how they can help the parish. "I don't know if I've changed or they've changed," he says.

To some extent, Mike Ahlstrom concurs with Heidenreich on the need for self-criticism and getting past labels. "We all need to be critiqued," he says. "Nobody has got the thing perfect." But Ahlstrom's still wrestling with the reality of a divided Church. Some things do come down to ideology, and the divide can be difficult to bridge. He uses the recent new translation for the Mass as an example. "If the bishops from 50 years ago were bishops today," he says, "they would have rejected the new liturgical translation as unacceptable. There's a different climate today. That causes tension. I love the tradition of the Church, but that tradition is not Mass in Latin with the priest facing the wall. Tradition is alive and evolving.

"I would hate that we become a rigid Church," Ahlstrom concludes, "where if you don't like the rules, you're out. You want to bring people to conversion—that's an area where Cardinal George has been very good. We're here to convert our hearts. So is there room for critique? Yes. We've got a lot to teach each other."

....

When these six priests talk about the divisions in the Catholic Church, it becomes apparent that questions of how people get treated and how ministry actually gets carried out in parishes—a pastoral approach—often weigh more heavily on them than the generational or ideological content that makes up those disputes.

Referring again to a priest who had preached at St. Athanasius about Church teaching against in vitro fertilization, Tom Libera says, emphasizing the need for a pastoral response: "I hadn't been sensitive that if you're going to have discussions on means of fertilization, the best place to handle that is in a voluntary forum, not from the pulpit. It's just too much to handle emotionally. I don't feel comfortable in not saying anything, but the trick is finding a forum where you can open up discussion."

Libera remains unconvinced, in addition, that the Church's doctrine is essential in initially helping to form people in their faith. To him, experience in the practice of the faith leads to an appreciation of doctrine, not the other way around. "We pretend," he says, "it has always been doctrine first in the western Church. It's more complicated than that. You're part of the Church community; you enter into its life, and maybe eventually you go into deeper study and listen to what the doctrine, such as the Creed, is saying."

It is practices that form believers. "Perpetual adoration, chaplet, or rosary," Libera says, "can work. Others are into yoga or meditation and blend modern spiritual practices with their faith. A few years ago we got feedback from parents not familiar with Christmas carols. We started during Advent teaching carols to the families. If this is what was needed, let's put that in."

Ed Upton also has emphasized the importance of responding to needs as a way of organizing parish ministry. "We learned in the Doctor of Ministry program," he says, "how to organize. Larry Gorman ('58) taught this course using Jerry Egan's ('65) stuff.[7] You always have to ask the question: What needs are you trying to meet and what are the target groups involved? Just because it's a good idea doesn't count. Francis George said throw information at people and that will solve it. It's not that simple. It's complicated; it's a matter of appropriation."

For Upton, these differences in pastoral approaches have decidedly ideological roots. "Those are fundamental fights," he says, "between liberals and conservatives. When Cardinal George first got here, he had a great line. A reporter asked him about women's ordination and he gave an answer, and she came back and asked the question again. Finally he said, 'I think we have a question of epistemological dissonance.' Well, that's right. We look at things and think in a different way. I don't believe in these absolute absolutes. People can have the same values and make a different practical decision."

Father Robert Barron ('86), a Chicago priest and well-known theologian, creator of the *Catholicism* video series and now the rector of Mundelein Seminary, addressed the philosophical underpinnings of these two approaches to ministry in his book *Bridging the Great Divide: Musings of a Post-Liberal, Post-Conservative Evangelical Catholic*.[8] In advocating a Catholicism both "radically liberal and radically conservative," Barron made a distinction, using terms coined by the philosopher Soren Kierkegaard, between "religiousness A" and "religiousness B," in which "A" was characterized by an approach that begins with people's lived personal experiences of transcendence and mystery and moves toward God and specifically Christian content. "B" starts with that God and content, particularly the cross, allowing it to reconfigure human experience.[9] In making the distinction, Barron agreed with Upton that tensions between the two approaches to ministry form "the ground for significant disagreements today in pastoral practice, ecclesial attitudes toward the culture, and methods of evangelization."[10] Here their viewpoints diverge, as Barron, while recognizing the validity and even necessity of both approaches, clearly favors an increasing focus on religiousness "B," from belief in God and the cross, whereas Upton and his classmates prefer approach "A" that moves from experience to faith.

"I would not discount lived experience," Bill Zavaski says. "That's very important in our theological development. Yes, God came first. But if it wasn't for people struggling to understand what is happening to them, where would we be? With couples getting married, God could tell them they have to stay together. But *how* are they going to do it? Other couples who have struggled with the commitment—they've got to be the ones to share that. When you come into a parish, you've got to respect lived experience."

Ed Upton's years in ministry have led him to a blunt observation:

"A lot of this dogmatic stuff, people don't care. They want to be a good person, raise their family with values, be part of a Church community, keep their kids from doing drugs like their fathers did, have a sense of sharing and altruism to help other people."

Both Bob Heidenreich and Larry Duris continue to look to Vatican II for inspiration to help them aid their parishioners to live out, in a specifically Christian context, the values Upton mentions. They clearly believe the Council has provided the underpinnings for a primarily pastoral approach to parish ministry that has led and can lead people to Christ. "Our excitement and zeal," Duris says, "and love affair with God and each other is what's going to do it. Our holiness —spelled with a W—moves us toward wholeness and integrity." For that holiness to happen, priests must involve themselves deeply in the lives of their people. "If you want to be a priest," Heidenreich stresses, "you must have an intimate loving relationship with your wife—that is, with the people you serve. You can't be cold. You have to be able to be like the father of a family: to put food on the table for your children, to educate them."

> We do that by becoming the Body of Christ and internalizing
> that. Before the Council, we just put people through steps.
> Now look at our catechesis. You can't have a baby baptized
> or a couple married unless you go through a pre-baptism or
> pre-Cana class. Is that a hoop to jump through? No. We're
> committed to that because Vatican II was about looking at our
> lives as disciples of Jesus.

Heidenreich then raised the supremely pastoral question of how to place that possibility of deeper conversion continually in front of people. His answer contained an interesting balance between religiousness "A," meeting people where they're at and responding to their needs, and religiousness "B," challenging them to let the Scriptures and the Eucharist change their lives. He thinks the central element to help people's ongoing conversion is weekly attendance at Sunday Mass. "One thing we lost as a culture," he laments, "but we have to struggle to regain—and this is maybe a mistake made—was we've told people it's okay if you don't go to Sunday Mass. We've become very Protestant. But, to tell people it's a mortal sin or they're going to go to hell if they don't go to Mass—Church teaching or not—has little or no effect today. People don't believe that anymore, so we need to say to them, 'This is what you can get out of this.'"

> *Sunday Mass has to be practiced all the time because that's where you can develop spirituality. How central the Eucharist is to our belief—that's what separates us from Protestants. Some people don't understand that. They're good people, but could be even better if they listened to the Gospels at Sunday Eucharist. It makes a difference in your life. How? It gives you ability to cope with life from a different viewpoint. That doesn't come automatically. It only comes when you start seeing things in a different way.*

"People serious about their lives need to be challenged," Heidenreich says, "and there's nothing more challenging than the Gospels. You don't get that just because they pour water over your head and you make First Communion. You get it because you're at Mass allowing stuff to get into your heart, saying, 'I never thought of it that way.' That's what we have to tell people."

....

1. Catholic Campaign for Human Development, 2012. United States Conference of Catholic Bishops, October 23, 2012. http://www.usccb.org/about/catholic-campaign-for-human-development.
2. Robert J. McClory, "The Fight Over Fighting Poverty: CCHD and the Push for Reform," in *U.S. Catholic*: July 2010 (Vol. 75, No. 7), 12-17.
3. Mary L. Gautier, Paul M. Perl, and Rev. Stephen J. Fichter, *Same Call, Different Men: the Evolution of the Priesthood since Vatican II* (Collegeville, MN: Liturgical Press, 2012), 32.
4. Ibid., 83.
5. Ibid., 87.
6. According to their website, Opus Dei is a Catholic institution founded "to help people turn their work and daily activities into occasions for growing closer to God, for serving others, and for improving society."

Opus Dei, 2012, www.opusdei.org/. The organization has received considerable criticism. See John L. Allen, Jr., *Opus Dei: An Objective Look Behind the Myths and Reality of the Most Controversial Force in the Catholic Church* (New York: Doubleday, 2005).

7. This reference is to Rev. Gerard Egan, Professor Emeritus of Psychology and Organizational Studies at Loyola University of Chicago and author of *The Skilled Helper: A Problem-Management and Opportunity-Development Approach to Helping* (Belmont, CA: Brooks/Cole Cengage Learning, 2010 latest edition). Father Larry Gorman taught theology, initiated the permanent deacon program in Chicago, and was a well-regarded mentor of many priests, encouraging them to work closely with the laity.

8. Robert Barron, *Bridging the Great Divide: Musings of a Post-Liberal, Post-Conservative Evangelical Catholic* (Lanham, MD: Sheed and Ward, 2004).

9. Ibid., 12.

10. Ibid., 16.

CHAPTER 14

UNSPEAKABLE HURT
The Sexual Abuse Scandal

Ed Upton decided to address the sexual abuse scandal directly from the pulpit at St. Francis Parish. "I said," Upton recalls, "not just 'I'm sorry' but 'I'm as angry as you, particularly with the bishops.' Naming the problem publicly, not trying to defend the Church, was helpful to people. And while it was national and international, for most people it was local."

In the back of church after Mass that Sunday, Upton, to his great surprise, found out just how local. "I had at least three people," he says, "come up to me who had been abused as children."

> One instance was a woman whom a priest in Ireland had abused. When she told her mother, she was beaten and told to shut up and, "How dare you say that about a priest?" The second was a man whose mother and the priest were alcoholic. They'd drink and the priest would abuse the boy. He had never told anybody in his entire life. This priest married him and his wife because he was a family friend. The priest had since died. The people who came to me had kept that inside for so long. I had thought victims were trying to get money—why would they wait so long to talk? But from those people I learned you can't talk about it. It changed my consciousness: the first thing is to protect children.

These revelations taught Upton how little he knew about the

problem. He felt some measure of relief, however, knowing that his homily had helped some parishioners to open up.

Like Upton, his classmates responded to the abuse crisis by insisting on discussion at the parish level. Bob Heidenreich asked the vicar general, along with the head of the archdiocesan Office for Protection of Children and Youth, to discuss the archdiocese's response to the scandal with Sacred Heart parishioners. "A few days after that," Heidenreich notes, echoing Upton, "this guy I never heard of wants to see me. He said, 'I have to tell you I was abused as a kid by a priest. It wasn't here and he's dead now, but I had to tell somebody.'"

In response to his preaching and his writing about the scandal in the parish bulletin, several parishioners at St. Ailbe's shared with Larry Duris their experiences of priests abusing them right in the parish in the 1970s and again, by another priest, in the 1990s. When told of such instances, Duris listened and encouraged. "You invite people to talk," he says. "You let them teach you. In the process, they teach themselves. Some say you never get over it. I can see that. But I still believe, no matter what, you can move from victim to survivor to thriver."

When Mike Ahlstrom hosted an open forum in 2002 at St. Collette's in Rolling Meadows at the time the U.S. bishops were passing the Charter for the Protection of Children, he received both affirmation and a challenge. "I was a bit scared," he recalls. "People told me I was opening Pandora's box, but I'm glad I did it. I was honest with people that I was horrified and shocked by what happened—not that somebody could have abused children, but that it was so widespread, 4 percent of the clergy. We call the priest 'Father.' You're supposed to be able to trust your father; it's like a spiritual incest. I was also upset that the Church had not done a better job of protecting victims."

After providing an opportunity for people to vent and ask questions, Ahlstrom's parishioners gave him a standing ovation. "But someone challenged me," Ahlstrom says, "saying, 'You should talk to the teens.' I was more scared to talk to them than to their parents, because they were at or still near the ages of the victims. But I found them less condemning than their parents—not that they were okay with it."

Always sensitive to the potential emotional impact of pronouncements from the pulpit, Tom Libera wrote a bulletin article at St. Athanasius in Evanston about the scandal. He recalls the gist of what he wrote: "You hoped that the new norms would have taken care of the scandal, but this is more like a long-term convalescence that's going to last beyond my lifetime. Yet people still have a faith," Libera adds. "They've somehow adjusted to the realities of the harm done and, at least on a local level, the Church is still something they want."

For Larry Duris, the point in all the discussions, regardless of the forum, is to rebuild trust. "We need to reclaim what we at least said we had," he says, "that we were a place that protected the young and vulnerable. In many of our ministries we do that in an awesome way. It hurts that this certainty has been taken away, at least in the public domain. But when you stain a part of the rug, the rug is stained."

....

For three members of the class of 1969, trying to address the scandal has included dealing directly with priests or deacons whom the archdiocese has ultimately removed from ministry. As director of the office for deacons, Mike Ahlstrom has needed to act when people accuse deacons of abuse. "I meet with the accuser," Ahlstrom explains, "and then with the deacon, and listen. Leah McCluskey, the head of the Child Abuse Investigation and Review Office, does the brunt of it—the verbatim of the victim and the cleric." If the allegations prove credible, Ahlstrom has helped to remove the deacon from ministry. At times deacons are wrongly accused. "When that is established," Ahlstrom says, "I can be more supportive. I try to be supportive anyway. People who have been removed from ministry, I'm not their enemy."

Bob Heidenreich dealt with a priest who later became known as a notorious pedophile. Assigned to St. Edna's in Arlington Heights as an associate from 1981 to 1983, then Father Robert Mayer ('64) had long served as a lightning rod for controversy in virtually every parish in which he had served. Accused of playing favorites, especially with youth, the charismatic Mayer, an excellent preacher, built up loyalists and detractors. While at St. Edna's, Mayer allegedly exposed himself and tried to remove the bathing suits of boys on a trip to Fox Lake in northern Illinois. Eventually one of the boys' mothers filed a civil lawsuit, which the archdiocese settled out of court. Although the archdiocese did not remove Mayer from ministry at the time and the lawsuit remained out of the public eye, rumors ran wild at the parish. In 1987, the mother wrote a book about the series of incidents.[1]

The archdiocese in 1983 assigned a new pastor, Father John Hurley ('56), and a new associate, Heidenreich, to replace the controversial Mayer, whom they assigned to St. Stephen's in Des Plaines. "Mayer did not have any intentions of moving out," Heidenreich recounts. "He was popular. People said, 'You're going to defame someone who is working with our kids! Nobody else works with our kids.' We had to deal with that crowd. But the other crowd wanted to get rid of him." Father Dick Keating ('59), then the vicar general, resolved the impasse. "He said to Mayer, 'If I have to hire a moving company,'" Heidenreich recalls, "'and come myself to move you out, you're going. And you don't want me to move you out.' So he left."

Assigned to unite the community at Edna's, Hurley and Heidenreich held emergency meetings starting just three days after their arrival to diffuse the contentious situation. Fifty to 100 people attended these meetings. The priests met with the half who wanted Mayer to stay and with the half who wanted him gone. The second group was triumphant. "It was a mess," Heidenreich says. "It took three or four years for things to settle down. John Hurley did so much to try to help heal the people whose kids were abused. He was one of the great priests I served with. He dealt with them straightforwardly and addressed their issues. But, again, all of that was before Bernardin had begun to put in structures. Now it's clear that kids were abused and Mayer was a pedophile, but it was very murky in those days."

Some 22 years later, in 2005, near the end of his term as pastor of St. Benedict's, Heidenreich had to be the bearer of bad news about a popular priest. By this time, the murkiness was long gone, and Heidenreich, then the dean of the local deanery, informed parishioners at Queen of Angels, a parish just north of St. Ben's, that the archdiocese had removed pastor Father William O'Brien ('73) due to an alleged incidence of abuse of a minor in O'Brien's past, before his time at Queen's. "Those poor people were saying, 'We're sure Father Bill will be back in a couple of weeks,'" Heidenreich says. "I didn't think so. But

I couldn't say that."

Bill Zavaski has found himself in the unfortunate position of having to confront the scandal at three different parishes. "Abuse," Zavaski says with hard-earned wisdom, "absolutely destroys the parish." Zavaski's first brush with the scandal came at his first pastorate when the archdiocese removed the associate pastor at St. Bartholomew's in Waukegan. "The guy was very suspicious," Zavaski says, recalling the unpopular priest, "so people were not too upset."

But when his associate at Transfiguration Parish in Wauconda, Father James Ray ('75), was accused of abusing a minor at a previous parish in the early 1980s, Zavaski described it as "horrific. I didn't know Jim was accused until three months after I was assigned. And then I was supposed to be the guy's supervisor." Eventually the archdiocese removed Ray from ministry. "I was devastated," Zavaski says. "Jim and I were friends. We'd done variety shows together. I knew his family. It was like your brother had been accused."

Zavaski's shock and hurt mirrored that of Transfiguration Parish. "Father Jim was well loved," he says. "It divided the parish. I'll never forget the day I had to read this letter to the people. They were absolutely stunned, walking out of church crying. One little mentally disabled girl said, 'Father, who died?' It is like an absolute death. She'd captured the essence." When investigators arrived at the parish asking questions, both parents and the school principal inevitably began wondering if Ray had abused any children in the parish. "Parents panicked," Zavaski remembers, "because he was constantly focused on kids. Parents had loved that about him. I didn't think it was abnormal. But once I found out about the allegation, I realized that he had very few classmates visit him. He didn't have many adult friends."

When Zavaski returned as pastor in 1996 to St. James in Arlington Heights, the scene of his first assignment, he succeeded Father Peter Bowman ('55), considered at the time one of the most successful and gifted pastors in the archdiocese. Having worked with Bowman first at St. James and later when both priests served as deans in Lake County deaneries, Zavaski knew him well. During the parish's 100th anniversary celebration in 2002, Cardinal George informed Zavaski of an allegation against Bowman: a claim that he had abused a minor 45 years previously. "We were devastated," Zavaski recalls, the pain still on his face and in his voice. "He walked on water. Our parish center was named after him. It was very painful for this parish to walk through that crisis when he was removed. We had 800 people come to the first meeting on this—800 people."

Parishioners felt so angry that many attacked the messenger and blamed Zavaski for Bowman's removal. To this day, many of them refuse to believe the allegation. As for Bowman, Zavaski says he "could not comprehend the hurt people experienced. Peter never came back except to attend a few funerals. For months people were upset. We had three meetings to lay out the facts. People reacted both ways: 'It can't be true' and 'This is credible evidence.' Eventually the meetings got down to 400. The staff fell apart, beside themselves. Peter had hired them; he loved them. They could not comprehend this."

For four years after Bowman's removal from ministry, the parish kept the name "Bowman Center" on the parish center and, for much longer, Bowman remained listed as pastor emeritus in the parish bulletin. In 2006, however, when Chicago police arrested Father Dan McCormack ('94) on sexual misconduct charges, the parish council advised Zavaski to remove Bowman's name from the center. "Peter's name was public again," Zavaski says. "It came from the council, not from me. But there were still weeks of hate mail: 'How could you do this to Peter?' I didn't do it to Peter.

"But when we removed the name," Zavaski adds as a note of consolation amidst the vitriol he suffered, "I got one letter from a victim's mother that thanked me that he would no longer be honored after what he had done to children."

Informing Bowman of the parish's decision tore at Zavaski's heart. "When we had to change the name," he says, "before I made that public, I had to go talk to him. God, I was sick to my stomach. He was gracious. He said, 'Bill, I'm surprised you didn't do it sooner.' I felt terrible. He respected what the people said because that's the type of guy Pete was."

Finally things calmed down at St. James, although Cardinal George did ask Zavaski to remove Bowman's name as pastor emeritus. "I'd kept that pastor emeritus on," Zavaski says, "because there was no incidence of misconduct at St. James, and I've had so much trouble with that name." For example, some people still call the center the Bowman Center. "I'm slowly trying to let that die down," Zavaski says. [Bowman died in April 2011.]

....

In response to the sexual abuse crisis, the U.S. bishops established in 2002 the Charter for the Protection of Children and Young People. Priests sign a pledge not to be alone with minors as one component of the charter. While these six classmates understand the need for the pledge from both a legal and safety standpoint, they not only mourn the loss of more innocent times but also worry that younger priests have become reticent about working with youth. "The norms and codes of conduct," Tom Libera maintains, "are positive in that now you do know what the boundaries are, so misinterpretations are less likely. But even though nothing untoward ever happened at St. A's, trips with youth are not considered good practice anymore. Yet I still need to be close to the young people and spend time with them."

Larry Duris understands that, when it comes to ministry with youth, times have changed. "When I was at Lawrence and Holy Cross," he explains, "we used Pinion [the house in Michigan owned jointly by several priests] for youth retreats. But I wouldn't touch that now. I don't want to be a cold fish, but those days are over, because unfortunately priests are just so suspect.

"I don't think I'm gun-shy," Duris insists, "but it's different now when you're standing in the vestibule after Mass and little kids come up and wrap themselves around your leg. You're aware. Anyone who wanted to could go home from church and say I hugged them the wrong way. There are stories about a couple of accused priests who were exonerated, but it was after three or four years in court. It beat the life out of them. Yet you've got to remain warm and real."

As a young priest, Ed Upton used to drive three or four teenage boys from the parish to Holy Name Cathedral during Holy Week to pick up the oils for the Triduum liturgy. Afterwards they would stop for pizza. "I would never do that now," he says with sadness, "but those kids, it's amazing, many of them have moved to this parish and they talk about that as a good, positive thing."

Bill Zavaski has cherished memories of bringing young families, friends, and parishioners to Pinion to enjoy the beach. "We'd take kids up on retreats," Zavaski says. "I babysat five kids one weekend. That would never happen today. Ever!"

Mike Ahlstrom, for one, has refused to hold back on appropriate priestly contact with youth. "I've heard a few guys say," he reports on conversations with colleagues, "that they're afraid to work with young people. Cardinal Bernardin told us when this scandal first was coming out, 'Don't overdo this. You still have to be a warm human being.' I'm as affectionate with children as ever. But I'm not taking them behind a closed door. At the Spanish Mass, for example, I invite kids to get a hug from Padre at the greeting of peace. They run up to the altar. That hasn't stopped."

"I understand the restrictions," Bob Heidenreich admits, "and it's probably legally the right thing." He recalled a story, however, that for him exemplified how at times the new norms bump into common sense. "At St. Ben's one night," he says, "the weather changed. It started snowing. The kid working phones didn't have a coat or boots. I said, 'I'll drive you home. Call your mother and tell her.' Later, a friend said, 'You can't be in a car alone with a minor. She has to call her mother or you have to put her in a cab.'"

Bill Zavaski shared a similar story. Recuperating at Pinion from prostate cancer surgery, he mentioned on the phone to Ahlstrom that he needed to hire someone to cut the grass because he wasn't feeling up to it. "Mike's on the phone," Zavaski says, "screaming at me, 'No kids!' It's sad because of the sins of some that we have to have these restrictions on everybody."

....

Parish priests function administratively much like mid-level management, responsible for much but exercising little ultimate authority outside their immediate sphere when it comes to the workings of their "company." The six men from '69 being followed here, then, have had to look on and hope for the best from their superiors—the bishops—as the news media have reported on the shocking extent of the problem of clerical sexual abuse. In the main, these priests give their own local ordinaries good marks on their handling of the crisis while simultaneously criticizing the U.S. hierarchy, as well as Pope Benedict XVI. In both cases, however, some exceptions apply.

All six priests, for example, praised Cardinal Joseph Bernardin's handling of the crisis. Larry Duris remembered Bernardin moving strongly on the issue by calling a meeting of vicars and deans back in 1987 or 1988. Bernardin had asked archdiocesan attorney Jim Serritella to address the group. "Serritella talked," Duris recalls, "about the monster coming over the hill, and it was prophetic. Boy, what he said came to be in spades. He said it would not only bite our butts in Chicago but it was a looming national and international crisis."

Duris' respect for Bernardin grew in the early 1990s when he removed 20 priests from ministry based on credible allegations: "What I found frightening among some clergy," Duris remarks, "was the denial: 'Look what they're doing to us,' and being clueless about where people in the pews were. I also remember Bernardin telling us he was frustrated with the East Coast hierarchy; he was pushing to have the bishops' conference adopt the protocol he had put in place in Chicago [the U.S. bishops finally adopted a similar protocol at their Dallas meeting in 2002], and was being told by people like New York's Cardinal John O'Connor and Boston's Cardinal Bernard Law that the problem was a Midwest one—their clergy didn't do stuff like that."[2]

The classmates also gave both Bernardin and his successor Cardinal Francis George credit for quietly meeting with victims personally and for establishing and institutionalizing archdiocesan structures—including an expectation that all church employees and volunteers receive awareness training regarding sexual abuse—to ensure both proper care for victims and a thorough investigation of new accusations. "We've got one of the best programs in the country," Bob Heidenreich says. "My German friends were very impressed. That didn't happen by accident."

"The Church will pick up the tab," Mike Ahlstrom explains, "for counseling for anyone victimized by an employee of the archdiocese."

The archdiocesan record in Chicago, however, certainly has not been perfect. Early on, like many other ordinaries, Bernardin sent credibly accused priests to therapy and eventually returned them to ministry. "I remember the psychologist saying to Jim Ray that he could go back to work," Bill Zavaski says. "That's what they believed then. It just doesn't work."

Larry Duris defended that early practice, insisting that Bernardin and others acted in good faith on the expertise available to them at the time. "In Chicago," Duris says, "one of the first guys pulled went into hospital treatment and had a full year of aftercare and then counseling for years. Eventually was sent back to ministry. There's no way to explain today how people saw it back then. But it was true that psychiatrists and psychologists claimed you could get better. Now the professional stance is that there is no cure."

One case of misconduct in Chicago has aroused particular ire because Cardinal George admittedly mishandled the situation. Police arrested then Father Daniel McCormack ('94) in 2006 for sexually abusing young boys. McCormack was sentenced to prison in 2007. (Chicago police had earlier questioned and then released McCormack in 2005.) As details of the archdiocesan response to complaints against McCormack came to light, it became clear that George had not taken his own review board's advice to remove McCormack from ministry as early as the fall of 2005, and that further abuse of young boys by Mc-Cormack took place between then and the time of his arrest in 2006.[3]

"There was a breakdown," Mike Ahlstrom says, "in the communication system. It wasn't handled right and George admitted it wasn't handled right. But overall, the cardinal has been very forthright on this issue."

Ed Upton, however, has not excused George. In fact, he resigned from the Association of Chicago Priests (ACP) when they issued a statement in support of the cardinal in the midst of the McCormack crisis. Referring to George, Upton says, "He has no credibility on the issue."

While many of his five classmates mentioned their anger at the U.S. Church hierarchy and at the Vatican response to the sexual abuse crisis, none spoke as freely as did Upton. "I read on the Internet the *Boston Globe* documents," he recalls, "released in the Archdiocese of

Boston. That got me infuriated. There was one letter in particular that Boston sent to another diocese saying something like, 'Father so and so wants to minister. He has our permission and will not be a cause of concern to your diocese.' They had a whole dossier on the guy. It was awful."

Upton believes that, while abusers have met punishment from the Church, those bishops who covered up the problem have gotten away with it. "None of them yet," he says, "have been held accountable for mismanagement. It's a feudal system."

Although bishops hold their titles for life, Upton proposes an easy solution if the Church wants to address episcopal malfeasance. "You fire a bishop," he explains, "by saying you're still a bishop but you can't run a diocese. Simple. But we don't do that. They're not accountable to anybody but the pope, and up until recently Pope Benedict didn't think it was such a big deal." Upton acknowledged that the current Archbishop of Dublin, Diarmuid Martin, had encouraged Irish bishops who were implicated in that country's abuse scandal to resign, but beyond that he has seen little real remorse or responsibility. "It certainly has affected my morale," he laments. "It's hard to have confidence in the hierarchy of our Church."

Upton's good friend Bill Zavaski sees the bishops' handling of the abuse crisis somewhat differently. "People are all upset about the bishops protecting their priests," he points out, "but there is a father-son relationship between bishops and their priests. I'm not saying the priests shouldn't have been removed, but it's not surprising that bishops tried to help their men. Sexual abusers have an illness. We thought it could be controlled like alcoholism, but it can't be. The bishops got screwed—it was the psychologists who told them that those priests could go back to work."

....

The sexual abuse crisis has hit home most deeply on the personal level for these six men of the class of 1969. "Shameful, embarrassing, horrific, unconscionable," the words poured out of Larry Duris. "It's a sign of what can happen when you bury your head in the sand, very much a wake-up call. A part of that is about ego, but there's a flipside that reveals our fragility, our vulnerability, and how quickly we can move to a delusion of invincibility. It's very humbling. For anyone into the lively sport of Catholic-bashing, we just painted a target on our chest and said here are the arrows."

Bob Heidenreich shares Duris' sense of the magnitude of the Church's sin. "It's a total abuse of trust," he exclaims, "Total! It has done irreparable harm to who we are as Church. If I was an ordinary citizen, I'd think, how can I believe these people when so many of the leaders covered this over? I don't think about the scandal often, but it's been very difficult for me personally. Maybe it's good. I'm not as naïve."

Duris' and Heidenreich's classmates expressed everything from sorrow, astonishment, and compassion for victims as well as for accused priests to a desire that the Church refocus humbly on the person of Christ. "Some of the priests removed," Bill Zavaski comments, "are like your brothers. The average person says, 'You've got to talk about this.' But it's like someone in your own family, something you don't want to talk about."

Perhaps it is not surprising, given his introverted nature, that Tom Libera's remarks on the subject contained much food for thought. "What's changed in me?" he asks.

> It's opened up the possibility that we as a Church have to learn we were blind or arrogant. Those are spiritual struggles, not theoretical, but at the core of what Christ was getting at when he talked about turning away from sin and being faithful to the Gospel. We've got to work harder to get back to that core. It's hard to be optimistic, but if Christ has called you, then it's in this life with all its complications and struggle.

One complication the abuse scandal has created for these priests has been a changing public image of the priesthood. "I heard somebody tell a story," Mike Ahlstrom says, "that a stranger came up to them and said, 'How many kids did you abuse today, Father?'" Larry Duris added that wearing a collar in public can be different than it used to be. "I walked out of the rectory to go to the garage at Neri," he recalls, "and two ladies are walking down the street. One says, 'Are you a Catholic priest?' I say, 'Yes.' She says, 'I'm going to keep my boy away from you.' Whump. I've had a couple of those. But I'm not paranoid or afraid of wearing a collar. I'm not ashamed of who I am."

Perhaps revealing the depth of their vulnerability, the six priests gave contradictory comments about whether the archdiocese had removed any of their classmates for sexual abuse. While Mike Ahlstrom reported that two classmates had credible accusations made against them, others indicated that only one had been accused, and Bill Zavaski said, "We haven't had any classmates removed." The fact that it remains unclear who has committed abuse in even their own class speaks to the difficulty these men have talking about the scandal on a personal level.

Tom Libera shed some light on this reticence by focusing on the fact that, because some priests have been falsely accused, it is difficult to know if priests are getting a fair shake. "Part of the morale piece," he maintains, "is that some priests have been made vulnerable in accusation. One strike and you're out. Or you're put in suspended animation for a long time before something is resolved. By that point, you can never get back to where you were. So there's a hope among priests for more due process.

"On the other hand," Libera admits, most cases prove credible. "You can see the anguish that victims are going through. You want these things nipped in the bud."

Referring to his parishioners, Bill Zavaski made some comments that might apply to him and his classmates as well. "Has it shaken people's faith?" he asks rhetorically. "Yes. But I don't think it's going to destroy their faith. Francis George wrote this woman who kept writing him letters about Peter Bowman, saying something like, 'It's important for you to remember that good people sometimes do bad things.' And they do."

Mike Ahlstrom focuses on the effect the sins of their colleagues have had on other priests. "We've also been victimized by our brothers," he says, "who've ruined trust. While I did feel angry about it, I'm not bound up by that. I lived with a priest, though, who was pounding his fists on the table with rage over how the acts of others were affecting him. While upset, I didn't feel the need to pound my fists. You don't let something like that ruin you; I'm not."

For Ed Upton, however, the cover-up of the scandal has loomed so large that it has forced him to rethink his view of the role of the Church when faced with a misconduct charge of any kind made by the laity. Upton recalled an incident with a seminarian back when he ran the deacon program at Mundelein Seminary. "He had gotten into something that was not sexual misbehavior," he says, "but actual fights at the parish. It became clear to me—15 years later—that my instinct was to protect him. At the time it didn't dawn on me. It was like, I'm the deacon director and my job is to take care of him. I have learned that my instincts were wrong. It was, 'Let's not cause scandal to the Church. We'll help the person that got hurt, but we'll do it internally.' We sent the seminarian to get tested and counseling. It appeared to be an isolated incident. But the real point was my instinct was to protect the Church's reputation—don't let this get out, and only secondarily to take care of the victim. It's unfortunate, that culture of clericalism. It's so ingrained I didn't even know it. This sexual abuse crisis has made me much more sensitive today about it."

....

Differences of opinion arose amongst the classmates as to whether the Church had moved past the clerical sexual abuse scandal or whether its effects would remain at the center of its life for years to come. "I don't think," Mike Ahlstrom says, "most priests are stuck in it. The vast majority are past it. The proof in the pudding for laypeople was when the media was hottest and heaviest, we were having our Catholic fundraising campaign and it was our most successful. If people were that upset, they wouldn't be pledging money. The majority recognized that there're rotten apples in the barrel. They don't stop eating apples."

Bob Heidenreich considered such a viewpoint overly optimistic or, at the least, premature. "When we were in Germany in May of 2010," he says, recounting his visit with auxiliary bishop and classmate Frank Kane, "this stuff was starting to break there. What strikes me is how naïve they were. One said to me, 'We're going to get beyond this;

things will be back the way they were.' Kane told them, 'This is not going away in our lifetimes.' And it's not just because lawyers are making tons of money on it. This is a horrendous problem.

"A positive thing, however," Heidenreich concludes, "is that many of us priests feel we're committed to making up for it."

Alone among his classmates, Ed Upton sought to answer the question of why priests engaged in abuse. "We kept people in the seminary immature," he says. "The bulk of abuse came from people trained in the old seminary and then pushed into a whole new world of the Church and the United States. When the external boundaries fell away, they had built up nothing inside. It's not homosexuality; it's immaturity. So to the extent that the seminary now is going back to having more externals—rules and wearing collars, for example—it appears to be going back to a system that will reinforce gross immaturity rather than allow people to develop in a more adult manner."

What has the Church learned from the scandal? Tom Libera wondered. "Protecting priests has had awful consequences," he says. "We're taking our lumps for that as an institution." Libera worried about the Church having had both Pope Benedict and the U.S. hierarchy severely criticized for their response to the scandal. Although good might come out of such scrutiny in the long run, he says, "I don't know how that can be a short-term or even a mid-term positive. How does this scandal inspire people to be faithful to the Lord or find models they can follow?

"The situation," Libera notes, "calls for transparency. Responses have been more direct recently than in the past. And even though it might not be acknowledged, we have come up with models of how institutions can work at spotting abuse. It's a contribution we're making painfully."

....

1. Hilary Styles (pseudonym), *Assault on Innocence* (Albuquerque, NM: Band K Publishers, 1987).

2. Duris' references are to John Cardinal O'Connor, then archbishop of New York, and Bernard Cardinal Law, then archbishop of Boston. "Dallas" refers to the Charter for the Protection of Children and Young People, United States Conference of Catholic Bishops, June 2002, old.usccb.org/ocyp/charter.shtml.

3. Michelle Martin, "Cardinal George resists Pressure to Resign," *Catholic Herald*, March 10, 2006.

CHAPTER 15

INTERIOR LIVES
Prayer

....

When the new priests of the Archdiocese of Chicago's ordination class of 1969 strode into their first parishes in the summer after ordination, they arrived as men of action. Flying the banner of the Second Vatican Council, they quickly set about getting things done for—and with—the people of God. Personal prayer took a back seat to public prayer, and the breviaries they were supposed to pray thrice daily sat unused on rectory bookshelves, as the young associates ran from one parish activity to another. Experience, ever a reliable teacher, however, quickly led them to acknowledge that—invigorating as it might be—parish ministry was exhausting work. They quickly learned that accompanying people through crises and tragedies, while maintaining a celibate commitment, required a deep reservoir of personal strength, energy, and compassion. These men needed a deeper relationship with God.

....

"I had not put Christ at the center," says Bill Zavaski.

Visiting the Mundelein retreat house one day during the early 1980s, Zavaski was asked by the director, Msgr. Harry Koenig ('32), if he would do a retreat for priests. "I'd had two martinis," says Bill, "and thought I could conquer the world, so I said yes. Later I said, 'What am I going to do?' It was a rude awakening because my spiritual life was pretty barren." Bill says he was happy and active as a priest. He believed in the Eucharist. But he didn't have a deep, intimate relationship with

God. When he gave the retreat, he led with his weakness. "I'm one of the worst people here," he explained to the priests. They talked about how they all needed to grow in the spiritual life. It was the first retreat he would give on prayer, but not the last.

Zavaski found he could preach about prayer, but would he actually practice what he had preached? It turned out that he needed another lightning bolt. This one involved not a martini but a pole vaulter, the star of a story he was reading, written by Jesuit author Mark Link. As Bill tells it, the young man in the story had been the world's greatest pole vaulter as well as the trampoline champion of the U.S.

> *The day he broke the world's pole vaulting record he broke his back on the trampoline exercising and couldn't move a single part of his body except his eyes and his mouth. No one then heard of this guy for five years when they brought him out at an athletic event. He said, "I pray to God that you never experience the pain and loss and suffering and dependence that I have to live with every day, unless that's what it takes for you to put Jesus Christ in the center of your life."*

The story not only moved Zavaski, it haunted him. "I had not put Jesus at the center," he says. "I was the center of my life, and I was happy. But when I heard this guy's story, it was such a powerful experience that I started to read and reflect about relationships."

Over time, Bill turned to other contemporary spiritual writers: Oblate Father Ronald Rolheiser, Franciscan Father Richard Rohr, M. Scott Peck.[1] William Reiser's *Drawn to the Divine* hit him the hardest: Reiser described the 12 characteristics of a committed disciple, among them a sense of community and of mission, being a loved sinner, freedom, trust, compassion, a willingness to learn.[2] "That became the focus of my life," says Zavaski. "I felt myself growing closer to Christ." Several women religious in his community told him they could see "a real difference" in him.

"I couldn't tell," he says now, "but other people could sense something that had not been there before. That was reassuring." A stunning Lithuanian wood crucifix, with Jesus bent doubled over, hangs from

Zavaski's office wall at St. James, symbolizing his commitment to keeping Christ at the forefront of his life. "The older you get," Bill says, "the more you get in tune with prayer. You know you're getting close to the end."

He even blew the dust off his breviary. "I never prayed it for years," he says, "because I didn't know how. It wasn't until seminarians were living with me in Waukegan that I started using it because they could help me figure it out." Now he makes a concerted effort to spend a solid hour each morning in prayer. "I couldn't live without it today," he says. "I talk to God about my life, about the will of the Father. I spend the bulk of my time on what does God expect me to say to the people in light of the Scriptures. My dream is to instill in them a love for the Eucharist."

Wondering how his parishioners, particularly those married with children, could possibly pray for an hour, Zavaski bought a dog to complicate his life so he could better relate to his people. "When I got the dog, I had to adjust," he says, "because previous to that I lived like a monk. I'd get up early, say Mass, spend my hour in prayer. My walks with the dog became prayer time."

Zavaski—and, to a man, his five classmates—speaks about the transforming effect of praying with people at the hour of death. He recalls being at the bedside of a former priest who lay dying in the hospital. His wife had invited close friends and family for the sacrament of the sick. "Everybody was there praying," he recalls. "Jim knew he was going; we knew he was going. There was a lot of faith." Years later, when the man's son, John, turned 21, his mother called the important men in his life together, including Bill. "Most kids want to go to the bar," he says. Instead the men engaged in a ritual of prayer. "Eight men talked about how John was part of their life, how they loved him," he says, clearly still touched. "Once in a while you have a beautiful moment."

The support Bill gets from other priests is crucial. He has met with the same priest prayer group monthly for more than 20 years; it purposely includes a mix of older and younger priests and two newly ordained, one Polish and one Hispanic. They meet, have dinner, discuss the challenges they face in ministry. "We talk about how we feel God is operating in our lives," Zavaski explains. The group functions as an antidote to priestly self-pity. "If a younger priest complains about a strict pastor or a bad rectory, for example," he says, "John Hurley ('56) tells his story and everybody shuts up. He had the three worst pastors in the diocese for his first three assignments. The first one was bad, the second one was even worse, and the third assignment, the pastor was just awful."

Worrying that priests ordained today lack the depth of connection that he enjoys with other priests, especially classmates he's known for 50 years, Zavaski fears that many young priests have no one to talk to. "These guys start after college and come to Mundelein for just four years. They're not together long, so they don't have that bond. And it can show in their ministry. They're unhappy or get depressed. So the prayer group is very important." So is the Michigan house, Pinion, where the priests say morning prayer together. "With Carp [Mike Ahlstrom's nickname] it's not until about 11:00," Bill laughs, "but it's still morning prayer. You go in our prayer room and the breviaries are lined up. When we go on vacation, we pray together." Bill Zavaski has come to see that praying with other priests is not a luxury, but a necessity.

....

"If any cross comes my way today, I embrace that cross," says Mike Ahlstrom.

Mike experienced no lightning bolts, no martini-prompted about-face in his prayer life. But he did have to change. At first, he says, he took "the heresy of action" to an extreme in his priesthood. "As a young priest, I was guilty of always doing something else. I prayed at liturgy, but I did not take the time for personal prayer that I take now."

What began to turn the tide for Ahlstrom was a sabbatical he took after finishing his term as pastor at St. Collette's. He discovered within himself a desire for solitude. "I wanted to spend time alone," he recalls. "I don't think I'd ever been alone for more than 24 hours in my life. I went to Mexico for two weeks of solitude." After that, still on sabbatical, Mike enrolled in a program called Rediscovering the Sabbath, in which participants wrote their own autobiographies. He took up the autobiography project in four parts: family of origin, adult story, sexual story, and spiritual story. During week one, he discussed it with a psychologist. In week two, group members shared their stories with one another. The process invigorated and focused Ahlstrom's spiritual life, he says.

After the sabbatical, Cardinal Francis George assigned Ahlstrom to take over the ongoing formation program for the archdiocese's permanent deacons, along with working part time as a spiritual director at Mundelein Seminary. These assignments only increased his urgency to deepen his own spiritual life. He began studying contemporary spiritual writers, remembering in particular a presentation Richard Rohr and Ronald Rolheiser did on adult Christianity and the second half of life.[3] "They say," Mike explains, "you don't reach the second half of life spiritually until 60. Usually it's when you get a slap in the face and something difficult happens. For the male, the first half is the road of ascent. You go to school and compete with other students academically, in sports, and dating girls. You start a career and compete for job advancement. Priests want to be pastors. Everything is upward mobility. When you finally get to the second half," he continues, "you realize success doesn't mean anything, so you spend the rest of your life letting go of it all and becoming old fools for Christ—wisdom people." Ahlstrom has noticed this shift among his classmates. "We have grown," he says. "In the early years we didn't even say grace when we ate together. Now we do Morning Prayer when we're up at our house in Michigan, and we always pray before meals."

Mike provided a remarkably detailed and practical glimpse into his prayer life each day. "I am not a morning person," he admits. "I struggle to wake up."

> But the first thing I do is I take a little hand cross that's on my bed stand, kiss it, and make the sign of the cross with it. As I do that, I say if any cross comes my way today, I embrace that cross. If I meet people that have their crosses, help me bear their cross. I bless myself and I pray God the Father, Abba, my daddy; Jesus my brother; Holy Spirit, I need you to get me through this day. When I'm still in this wake-up phase, I ask the question: Lord, what do you want me to do today? I listen and think God gives

me a pep talk and helps me focus. It's not that I hear words; it's
an awareness. That's how I get centered. Then I go off to Mass.
If I don't have Mass, I do Morning Prayer out of the Liturgy
of the Hours. At night, I kiss the cross and say: For the crosses
I've encountered today, mine or others, I embrace and kiss this.
I come up with five things to say thank you for. That affects
my attitude because it's accenting the positive. When you've
got more to be grateful for, you're open to more good things
happening.

"If I'm doing something difficult," Ahlstrom continues, "I'll pray before that. I'll take the telephone and hold it to my heart before I talk to somebody I'm not looking forward to calling and make a little prayer: Lord, help me get my ego out of the way. It's a four-second prayer, but it centers me. I always pray when I eat, no matter where I am or who I'm with. If it's a hot dog stand, I'll say a prayer." Mike's constancy in prayer, he says, has led him to become comfortable praying with others. As a young priest, Ahlstrom never thought of saying a prayer with people unless they asked him. "Now I would never think of meeting with people," he says, "without saying a prayer. My closest friend in the world, Cynthia Hernandez Kolski," Ahlstrom says, pointing to a picture of her on the table in his office, "died six months ago. I met her and her husband Phil 30 years ago doing Engaged Encounter weekends and then became close with them and their kids. She encouraged me: 'Write a prayer for so and so.' Or with friends going through a hard time—'Call them and say a prayer.' Now I have people calling me, 'How about saying a prayer?' Cindy's son lives in California. I check in with him every week. He always says, 'Uncle Mike, let's say a prayer.' I pray much more often."

A particular form of contemplative prayer, ironically, has increased Ahlstrom's comfort level when praying with others. "I thought *lectio divina* was something monks did in a monastery or up on a mountain," he says, "until I learned what it was."

Now as part of my night prayer I take the Scripture for the next
day. I read it. That's the first step: the lectio. *The second step is*

the meditatio: *What does this mean? Who am I, where are the people I'll be preaching to in this story? The* oratio *is you talk to God and, more importantly, listen: What are you trying to tell me, Lord? Then the* contemplatio *is you sit with God. No words. You turn off the mind. You don't think or imagine. You're not alert but you're not asleep. That's when God goes to work emptying out the garbage and grace comes in.*

Mike's attitude toward prayer has come full circle: "I used to think of it as a duty. Now it's a delight. If anything, I'm upset I don't have more time to pray." Greater attention to his own spiritual life has led him to realize how valuable a rich prayer life can be, especially for those involved in the busy world of pastoral ministry. He has thus worked hard to encourage the seminarians and deacons he supervises to pray and attend retreats. "Every human being should have a spiritual director," he says. He has found that 19 times out of 20 when deacons run into trouble, they don't have a spiritual director. Alarmed to find that the number of deacons making their annual retreats has declined recently, he has committed himself to hounding them about it. "People deserve you at your best," he says. "If you won't do it for yourself, do it for the people."

Ahlstrom has learned that when he steps into a crisis as a priest, what speaks loudest is not his words but his presence. "It is not what I say—they're not going to remember that. If they remember anything, it's that I prayed with them." He recalls a day as pastor of St. Collette's when a friend in the parish lost his father. The family had gathered. Like many families, they coped with the death by fighting with one another. "They called me and said, 'Michael, you better get over here and be prepared for the worst. They're all screaming.' Over to the house I go. Everybody is fine. I said, 'Where's this crisis?' We shared memories, prayed, and planned the funeral. I left. Later I called. 'You don't know what a difference you made,' they told me. 'What are you talking about? I didn't do a thing.' 'When you walked in, everything changed.' 'But I didn't say anything,' I said. They said, 'You didn't have to. You were there.'"

....

"I'm not as pious as others," says Ed Upton.

Many laypeople evaluate themselves quite harshly if asked to report on their prayer lives. It's instructive to learn that priests, too, can indulge in this practice. Upton, on the one hand, can explain when and how his spiritual life improved. During the 1980s, when he served on the faculty of Mundelein Seminary, Upton worked with colleagues Fathers Lou Cameli ('70) and John Canary ('69), who both stressed the importance of consistent prayer. He took it to heart. Since then, Ed says, "I try every morning to take 45 minutes of quiet time to center myself, whether it's reading the Gospel for the day or saying a morning prayer or reflecting on a book." At St. Francis of Assisi Parish, which Upton founded, it is no coincidence that every single meeting begins with prayer—not a speedy Our Father, but a prayerful reading of the next Sunday's Gospel. "You're always connecting the meeting to Sunday," says Upton, who, as an attendee at many meetings, has opportunities all week to let the Gospel do its work on him.

On the other hand, he can rattle off what he sees as his deficiencies. He admits he is not as pious as others. "Some priests say Mass every day," says Upton. "I don't." Some days his prayer time slips away, and he's currently lacking a spiritual director. "That's probably why I'm angry at times," he says half-kiddingly. "It is a loss. You think you're fine, but getting with somebody else moves you back on track." And staying on track is important to Ed because, he says, "It's easy to get caught up in self-stuff. Prayer is the connector to keep you human."

Public and private prayers play different roles. "Celebrating Mass publicly gives me energy," Upton says, "whereas private prayer gives me focus." He loves to preach, but he knows that to be effective he must first discern for himself what the Scriptures mean. "The Gospel about the Good Samaritan," he says, for example, "asks: what does it mean to be a neighbor? It's too simple to say everybody is my neighbor. I thought about walking downtown where people ask for money. Every time you go by, you should feel guilty. Sometimes you can't respond; sometimes you should; sometimes it's enabling if you do. But it's a question you have to keep asking yourself."

When it comes to sick call visits, again Ed is quick to note his perceived shortcomings. "Somebody commented once," he recalls,

"'I'm tired of the sick call clichés.' I thought, Christ, I'm a walking cliché. Cliché is all I know." Cliché, however, is the polar opposite of the thoughtfulness with which Upton approaches a hospital room. Sensitive to the drawbacks of performing rituals before making himself aware of where people are at with their illness or with the Church, he has learned to tread carefully. "My first instinct in a hospital," he maintains, "is not to pray but to see who this person is. I'm afraid if I start talking, I'll shut them down. If somebody hasn't been to Church in 30 years, they may just want to talk."

Ed acknowledged that some priests have a different approach that stresses simply anointing anyone who's Catholic—as he puts it, "Just get people oiled up." The master of this style, Upton claims, was Father Ed Fitzgerald ('40), who took over as chaplain at Mercy Hospital when he left his post as Dean of Students at Mundelein Seminary. "Fitz never slept," Upton recalls with a smile. "He walked the halls of the seminary and later the hospital 24 hours a day. Larry Duris was in Mercy for a nosebleed one time. They put him under to cauterize it. He wakes up at 2 a.m., and there is Fitz anointing him. Larry yells, 'What the heck is this?'"

"Most of the time," Upton says, "what's important is people are afraid—can you reassure them that their life wasn't that awful, that there's a loving God and they can be at peace? It's being with people in prayer, an accompanying prayer, as opposed to just saying a prayer."

....

"I'm usually out in the roar of things," says Tom Libera.

In reflecting on his personal prayer life over the course of his priesthood, Tom Libera lapsed into a prolonged silence. "I've never done enough of it," he eventually says. "Conversation with God takes place through the day, but being one who sits down at a particular time never took hold. That's one reason I look forward to going to New Melleray [a Trappist monastery in Dubuque, Iowa] on retreat, because it puts you into that rhythm. I say I want to take that rhythm home with me, but it doesn't usually last too long." As laypeople often do, Tom appears to be measuring himself with a prayer yardstick sure to find him wanting. He brings up the Scripture passage of Elijah listening for the voice of God. "Elijah's at the mouth of the cave," he says, "waiting for God to come in the earthquake and all that noise, and then finally God's in the gentle breeze. I'm out in the roar of things rather than spending quiet time waiting for the Lord." Neither does he pray the breviary, but he does use *A Book of Hours*, a volume of prayers featuring Thomas Merton's material that contains reflections for dawn, day, dusk, and dark.[4] "I'm, in effect, using his reflections," Libera says, "in place of the traditional Office."[5]

Like Ed Upton, Tom has created a culture of scriptural prayer at his parish—with himself as its chief beneficiary, he claims. All parish meetings begin with the Gospel for the coming Sunday, so some days Libera reflects on the reading two or three times. He also stresses the importance of prayer groups but then claims that he has not participated in one lately. Yet he then mentions two parish groups with whom he still prays weekly. "Three of us," he says, "go over the Scripture for the week. Another group meets every Tuesday using Mark Link's books."

Although convinced of his deficiencies in the practice of private prayer, Libera does see the day-to-day work of ministry as a prayer of sorts. "I'm aware, not as an excuse," he says, "that there are spiritualities that put everyone in a box of devotional time in Church. That doesn't work for everyone. I'm reading Karen Armstrong's books on God. She was asked the question: how do you pray? She found that studying in the library, scholarship, was her way of delving into the faith. Spirituality can be being a parent giving of himself or herself. You're at beck and call of what that child needs. You might not even think about Jesus the whole day. Yet you're doing the work of Jesus.

"We are embodied incarnated creatures here," Tom insists, "so the work of it is trying to build a better world—a better kingdom. Prayer helps us ask how being Catholic can become an ongoing awareness. Here, when street people come in for help, for example, we don't put them through a church service, but we give them a handout plus a simple prayer. We also keep the church open during the day—you see people stopping."

Although grateful for Karen Armstrong's insight that daily life and ministry can serve as a prayer, Libera admits that prayer needs to reach a deeper level that requires significant blocks of time. Looking toward retirement, he hopes to spend more time doing spiritual direction and less on administration. He is keenly aware, however, of the need to practice what he preaches. "I've had spiritual directors in the past, but I don't have one now," he says. "Part of my retirement plan is to get one, but I haven't acted on it."

When reflecting on moments of deep prayer, Tom, like his classmates, spoke of ministry to the sick, but with an assuredness that was lacking when the spotlight shined, as it were, on him. "When I'm called to the hospital," Libera reveals, "in the car I'm starting to pray. I won't turn on the radio."

> *It's a few minutes to get there, and I want to get into being an instrument. If the person is conscious, they hope the Church can give them something. How do you attend to them? I ask people: Who else loves this person, who would be here if they could? Get them naming them to fill that room up. I'm trying to tap into the person's goodness. If I'm here for nothing else, it's to be of assistance. What is prayer about other than a way of bringing people together in a situation beyond their control? They want to acknowledge that—and that prayer can change you however God wants it to work.*

"As years go on," Tom Libera adds, "I'm more appreciative of anointing. I want to connect with everybody there, especially that person, that this is their moment. How can this reinforce a person's faith? I try to get out of the way for what I hope will be a positive experience for them."

....

"You might not want prayer to change you, but it will," says Bob Heidenreich.

As a young priest, Heidenreich looked askance at traditional private prayer practices such as reciting the Office daily. "Back in 1969," he recalls, "we didn't have much use for the breviary. One of my classmates had to leave his breviary sitting out in his room because the pastor would check his ribbons to make sure he was on the right page—so he had to change his ribbons every day." The younger Heidenreich would also roll out of bed just 10 minutes before having to say morning Mass. Fifteen-plus years into his priesthood, however, Bob got a spiritual director who pushed the importance of daily private prayer. "Almost without fail since," Heidenreich says, "I'm up an hour ahead of Mass. I read the readings for the day and some commentaries. I realized that without letting Christ challenge me in prayer, I can't preach."

Bob has even embraced the once-neglected breviary. "I heard a lay woman say," he explains, "and I agree, 'The Office of Readings is the greatest, even though I read it over and over.' In fact, I've even been praying the breviary in German to get my German skills up. I bought a program on my laptop so I don't have to carry the book around." When the priests at Pinion began praying the Office together on days off, Heidenreich supported the practice. "We say Morning Prayer," he says, laughing, "as soon as we get Mike Ahlstrom out of bed."

> I figured out that if you're serious about this, you have to spend
> an hour in prayer every day. And the Office, which was not
> one of my favorite things when we started, causes your mind
> to wander. You think it's a distraction but then you remember
> to visit so and so and why don't you try this approach with this
> guy. People that are all wet—all of a sudden I get these ideas
> that maybe there's something to them. Where did those ideas
> come from? Prayer's healthy. It's something that I can't at this
> point stop. Don't want to, because without that it's absolutely
> right that this would be just another job.

Bob's deepened spirituality has cut both ways with parishioners. Many, on the one hand, have told him he says Mass too slowly. "It's this thing," he says, "about their time is precious. That's exactly the point. Whose time is it, anyway? But I understand because my time is precious, too. I'm sorry, though. If they want a 15-minute Mass, they'll have to go elsewhere." Other parishioners, however, seem drawn to Heidenreich's spiritual presence. "Saying Mass here at Sacred Heart is different," he admits. "When you approach the words of institution, babies stop crying. There's a hush. When you preach, you feel that people are with you."

Heidenreich's prayer life always connects to the people he serves. Nowhere is this proven truer than in his poignant recollection of a sick call visit. "When I was in Libertyville," he says, "I was called to the hospital. This guy was going to die that day or the next. His whole family was there, his wife and their girls and son, all circling the bed and holding his hand. What a way to go—having your family in love hand you off to God! Then I got to thinking: Who is going to be standing around my bed?" That story and that question point to the fact that, for Bob Heidenreich, prayer—private or public—ultimately has to do with intimacy. Perhaps that explains why he has spent most of the last 25 years involved in prayer groups: first a priest prayer group for 10 years that prayed the Office together. For the last 20 years he's prayed with a group consisting of lay couples and himself. "We do a meal, prayer, then we hold hands, putting intentions forth," he says. "That's after our sharing. The sharing is asking: God, what are you doing here? This group has had illnesses; kids have gotten married; parents have died. Being part of that on an ordinary life level has helped me a lot. One of the deficits of being celibate," he says, "is that in marriage—I realize it's not true in all marriages—there's an intimacy that is so natural. Even older couples who don't engage in sex the way they used to share this intimacy, which priests miss. My theory is that a similar intimacy comes about in prayer. As I listen to our group, it's not only about what they want individually. You see that the couples have had lots of dialogue about issues we discuss. And it's changed them. And if you engage in prayer, it'll change you. You might not want it to, but it will. That's what true prayer does because of intimacy."

....

"There are moments where getting started in prayer is hell," says Larry Duris.

"I'm better with communal prayer than private," says Duris. At times when other priests choose solitude, he thrives on companionship. Take homily preparation, for example. Every Tuesday, Larry meets with nearby priests to reflect on the Scriptures for the coming Sunday.[6] "We ask," he says, "what do they say to us and to our people in our relationship with God?" Likewise the breviary. "I don't think it's any surprise," he says as if it's a foregone conclusion, "that our class and era didn't see the book as a value. But I've done it since I was pastor at Neri with Bishop Joe Perry ('75 for archdiocese of Milwaukee) and Tom Belanger ('06). Bill Sheridan ('54) didn't join us because he came out of a different era—they'd turn on the football game and read the Office while finishing off a cold one."

Finding models or mentors in prayer? Duris discovered them in a group setting as well, having participated in a monthly priest prayer group for over 25 years. "We spend time in private prayer between 5 and 6 p.m., have a drink together, and prepare dinner," he says. "Then we review our ministry and spiritual journey for the past month." Initially all the group's members served in African-American or Hispanic ministry, but over time the group expanded to include priests with a wide range of ministries.[7] "Maybe that's why it has worked," Duris surmises. "And we've made it a priority. After the first meeting I came home saying, 'I guess I'm not crazy. I'm not the only one experiencing life this way.'"

Duris admits, however, that group prayer has its limits, as does the belief that ministry itself is prayer. "I should carve out more time in private prayer," he concedes, "because I can deceive myself into thinking my whole life is a prayer. That's crap. My whole life is not a prayer. It should be, but it's not. I've got a long way to go, but I'm getting better."

"It's the old 'You run until you run out of steam,'" he continues. "Then you say: 'Why isn't this working?' I'm a lousy meditator. I'm a fidget. I don't spend an hour in contemplation every day. I'm not willing to discipline myself." Similarly, Duris does not see a spiritual director on a regular basis. "Should have, should still," he says cryptically. "Maybe I'm afraid. What of? It's the old letting go struggle, the Augustine in me: Lord, make me holy but not yet."

Real holiness for Larry means that his prayer must always reconnect him to the community, not as someone above it but as a part of it. He's not of the school that thinks a priest's prayers count for more than a layperson's. "Do I feel an obligation to pray for the community? Yes. Do I say to God tons of words about that? No. But do I pray for this parish every day? Yes. My obligation is to ask God's blessing on this parish and the community it's called to serve." Duris nudges his people toward retreats: Marriage Encounter, Emmaus, CRHP, the parish council's planning retreat. "Creating experiences of shared prayer is demanding, but I'm comfortable with that." Duris gets as much as he gives from the parish when it comes to prayer: The African-American community has transformed his prayer life. "There's a holistic sense of God in affective aspects such as gospel music," he says. "Love the spirituals."

Larry has come to see the value of his presence as a priest when he prays with the sick and dying. "It's powerful when you can help people face those next big steps from death to eternal life—the individual—and then bring their loved ones along. It's usually easier for the person making the journey than for those accompanying them. I can't remember the last person I had a death talk with who was angry with God or saying, 'Why me?'

"A few times," Duris admits, laughing, "I got chased away. The person sees the collar and says, 'No, no. Get the hell out of here. I'm not ready to see you yet.' But more often than not in the final journey the person is more resigned, ready and wanting to talk about it—it's wonderful. You've been allowed to step on holy ground. It's humbling. I don't deserve this privilege."

Families accompanying the dying, however, can prove problematic. "Here's a classic," Duris says. "People call for a priest for an elderly man. I come over and he's in the bedroom. I go in and they slam the door behind me. I open it and say, 'No, no. I want you all to come in, we're going to do this together.' That's powerful." Larry recalls another situation:

> My friend's father-in-law was dying. The family members were in denial. "Daddy, you're going to be fine. In a few days you'll be out. We just bought you a brand-new car parked outside." He couldn't even get out of bed. Finally he says, "I need to talk to Father Larry. You all get out of here." They interpret this

*as he needs to go to Confession. He did that, too. But he says,
"Help me. I know I'm not leaving this room. I'll never even
see the car, let alone get behind the wheel. I just want to say
goodbye to them and they won't let me. Can you help me so
they'll let me say goodbye?" They were mad at me when I had
the conversation with them. Hopping mad. "How is he supposed
to get well?" But it was good in the end that they said their
goodbyes.*

Larry Duris has struck a balance between the joy and the challenge that he thinks prayer should provide. "I tell people," he says, "that prayer should be fun. Then I ask myself: is it fun for me? At times it is. Other times it's a challenge. It should be both, like any real conversation. If conversation with people you love is always easy, then it's surface—no gut talk. If it's real, there are moments where getting started in prayer is hell, where I hide from God as he calls me. Or I say to myself, if I do all this stuff he'll think I did enough. But if prayer is like a love affair, you can never have enough of it."

....

The exhausting work of committed parish ministry, the struggle to live a healthy spiritual life, the withering reaction to their theology and pastoral practice by some in both the hierarchy and a younger generation of priests—all these factors contributed to the classmates' decisions to make the practice of praying a central reality of their lives. Perhaps, in addition, as Mike Ahlstrom has indicated, as the first half of their spiritual lives was ending and as archdiocesan leaders had long since placed each of them in positions of respect and authority, the time had come to begin not only to reflect more deeply on the meaning of their ministry but also to find a source of nourishment that would best support the second half of their priesthood.

Nowhere did that need become more apparent than in these men's efforts to accompany their parishioners and family members as they confronted sickness and death. Their ability to respond in these moments, they realized more and more, required them to connect with

God so they could truly stand present in the sacred space between life and death, between this world and the next. This insight underscores the focus of their renewed lives of prayer: their people. As new priests, these classmates showed little interest in personal piety for its own sake, and even now, just short of their retirement, their motivation has never changed even as their prayer lives have deepened. If in the early years of their ministry they stood guilty, as Mike Ahlstrom noted, of the "heresy of action," their choosing to enter into a life of greater prayer in no way symbolized a repudiation of ministerial action. Rather, prayer provided an intimacy with the Lord, as Bob Heidenreich said, that allowed them to remain fed with the Spirit and to continue carrying out their mission as priests: ministering to and with their people out of the vision provided by the Second Vatican Council. Prayer has given these six priests the focus and energy necessary to continue to take action in the service of the Gospel and the kingdom of God.

....

1. For more see www.ignatianspirituality.com; www.ronrolheiser.com; cac.org/richard-rohr; www.mscottpeck.com.
2. William Reiser, *Drawn to the Divine: A Spirituality of Revelation* (Notre Dame, IN: Ave Maria Press, 1987).
3. Richard Rohr, Ronald Rolheiser, Edwina Gateley, *Loving the Two Halves of Life: the Further Journey*. A DVD series from the Center for Action and Contemplation from their January 2011 conference.
4. Thomas Merton, Kathleen Deignan (editor), *A Book of Hours* (Notre Dame, IN: Ave Maria Press, 2007).
5. For more on the Trappist monk Thomas Merton, see www.thomas-mertoncenter.org.
6. Andrew Smith ('09) then at St. Ailbe's and Bob Gilbert ('98), Tom Belanger ('06), and Mel Hermanns, OFM, then pastors at nearby St. Joachim's, St. Philip Neri, and Our Lady Gate of Heaven.
7. Current members include Fischer, Bishop John Manz ('71), who is, as Duris jokes, "a conehead now," Kevin Hayes ('77), Kevin Feeney ('77), Greg Rom ('75), who is pastor of St. Felicitas, and Tom Tivy ('62), who has recently retired.

CHAPTER 16

INTERIOR LIVES
Celibacy

....

"I will be honest," Mike Ahlstrom says. "Celibacy was never easy for me. I got interested in priesthood in junior high, talking with Jack Crosby ('52), my parish priest and hero." At the time, Ahlstrom broached the subject of celibacy with his mentor: "He said, 'You're not thinking of getting married, are you?'" Thirteen years old, Ahlstrom's response consisted of one word: no. "Well then," Crosby summarily responded, "celibacy is not a problem."

But as soon as puberty hit, Ahlstrom experienced conflict. "Each year," he says, "I felt more attracted not just to sex but to the whole notion of love and marriage. But I also felt more attracted to priesthood—and celibacy was part and parcel of priesthood. So I took it as, this is my instinct as a male, but the calling to priesthood is higher. But I struggled with it."

"We were taught from the old book," Larry Duris explains. "It was a given that people thought priesthood equals celibacy." But the early 1960s brought the Second Vatican Council with its winds of change blowing through the Church. "We didn't buy that celibacy can't change," Duris says, "but I don't know that anybody went into it with the thought that in the near future this will surely change. I don't think we were that naïve."

Bob Heidenreich, however, thought exactly that. "Before we were ordained sub-deacons," he recalls, "we had to sign a promise of celibacy. A classmate and I agreed that signing it wasn't a problem because this was for sure going to change in the next three or four years."

These stories reveal a seminary and Church culture that assumed priestly celibacy as a way of life and yet denied the difficulties of living it. Even the prospect of changes in the discipline led to vastly different reactions among these seminarians, precisely because, early on, it seemed that no one shared his inner thoughts about celibacy with anyone else.

Once they were ordained, however, that began to change because the six men being followed here realized that the only way to negotiate celibacy successfully was to focus on strong friendships with their parishioners, with one another, and with God.

....

Reflecting on his seminary training on celibacy, Larry Duris is succinct. "Bad," he insists tersely. "Our formation came out of the old-Church bag. Those areas of your life were never addressed at all. What we were taught was just 'No.'" Larry traces this approach all the way back to high school. "George McKenna ('44) was our freshman spiritual director at Quigley," he remarks. "He's talking and I'm trying to figure out what the heck he's talking about—oh, this is supposed to be about sex. But he was so uncomfortable and roundabout." In Duris' second year of spiritual direction, one of the sessions dealt with sexuality. "'Even if you're riding the bus,'" Duris remembers hearing, "'and you get an erection, that's a mortal sin.'" Duris recalls receiving that lesson with a grin: "If that's the case, I'm not going to get upset. I'm doomed already because I probably had an erection that morning on the Skokie 97 bus as it was bouncing over the railroad tracks."

....

Others in the class of '69, however, took such admonitions seriously. "I was open with my spiritual directors," Mike Ahlstrom says, "but they weren't prepared to help me accept my sexuality. It was like sex was from the devil and celibacy was from God."

With the arrival of Father Jack Gorman ('52) as rector of Mundelein in the fall of 1965, the seminarians finally began taking baby steps toward open discussions about celibacy. Human sexuality was presented on a spiritual level rather than as simply a list of do's and don'ts. Ahlstrom noted the change that fall. "I finally had a spiritual director—Jesuit Father Leo McKenna—after eight years of struggling," Mike says, "who helped me accept myself. I had a lot of guilt, and being 50 percent Irish, that'll do it. He helped relieve me of that. I learned from him that being celibate does not mean being without human love, although not the same way as a married person. That is what finally enabled me to say yes to Holy Orders and to celibacy." McKenna, however, remained the exception. For the most part, the class of 1969 had to negotiate matters of celibacy on their own as they prepared to enter the real world of parish ministry.

....

The "real world" that the class of 1969 moved into after ordination to the priesthood was the culture of the late 1960s, which included the sexual revolution. Even the Catholic culture the men had all grown up in experienced rapid change during this time. The common view of celibacy shifted fairly quickly. In previous decades, most Catholics had held their priests in high regard, often precisely because of their commitment to sexual abstinence for God's sake. As the 1960s wore on, however, society came to regard priestly celibacy with incomprehension or ridiculed the idea that anyone could live without physical sexual expression. Even within the Church, calls for the elimination of mandatory celibacy abounded; many priests and vowed religious left the priesthood or religious life to pursue marriage.

The men of the ordination class of 1969, therefore, found themselves catapulted into personal tumult in regards to their celibate commitment. "After Vatican II," Tom Libera recalls, "a so-called 'third way' was discussed, in terms of whether there could be some sexual expression in a celibate life. Some of my friends were potentially headed in that direction. But you learned from experience. At what point do you start losing your integrity in a relationship? Do you have to go through a crisis of where is a friendship going and how you are going to physically respond to it?"

Some years after ordination, Tom began a friendship with a woman religious that forced him—and her—to struggle with the meaning of celibacy. "The working norm we came up with," Libera says, "in terms of how you behave with each other was: Would the parishioners be comfortable with this? Would they understand? It's very simple in a way, not that it was easy, but that was a norm that really fit in the sense that it related back to what was your calling and identity. Our choice was to continue our friendship, even as it had to be reshaped and pulled back. I don't know if I ever imagined being in these sort of dilemmas, but they were there. What you realize out of that is you're not going to be a perfect specimen."

> You're not going to be able to say you've gone through life and never strayed or been imperfect. At times you had to talk to a spiritual director to sort that out; we went into counseling. There was a little stumbling around, figuring out what choices you're going to make, what is a way of integrity. You're—my gosh— almost wishing to get old where, supposedly, sexual urges go away. I don't think it quite works that way.

Libera learned from that experience that he had to apply to himself what he had taught others. "When you say God forgives," he says, "God gives you another chance, God knows you're vulnerable—that idea of starting over is real. The learning was to be human and appreciate what some people's struggles are from the inside, not excusing them but having sympathy for someone who does sexual violations in the sense of 'What was the drive that they had to deal with but couldn't?'

"There are people," Tom acknowledges, "who have those same temptations who do say no. Going through those times, I wished for the option of marriage—I would've probably pursued it if it was there." But such an option wasn't—and isn't—available to Catholic priests.

"Having gone through struggles helps," he insists. "If a new relationship developed, I'd have more experience. Someone described it as your red zone. When you get fatigued or vulnerable, do you recognize it and bring it into conversation with the person? I can't guarantee that would work, but I'd have the perspective of wanting to remain who I am."

Larry Duris learned to pay attention to the emotional undercurrents in relationships. "Being honest with yourself," he says, "is number one. Priest craft has its dangers. You can be deceived into thinking you're something you're not, out of people's fear of confronting you. I look back at some relationships going in an unhealthy direction to see how I got there. At times it was my fault. Flirting—that's shameful to admit. Talk about learning the hard way. It was a bumpy ride."

Larry remains grateful for those who have helped him negotiate the bumpiness. He recalled with gratitude the retreat he attended before his diaconate ordination conducted by then Father Pete Shannon ('53) and a group of laypeople. "They gave us insight," he notes, "on how they looked at celibacy, and how they expected intimacy from us." Other experiences helped, too. "I worked with Marriage Encounter for 15 years," he says. "Being a team priest, I became close friends with couples. Priests on the Marriage Encounter retreat deal with sexuality as part of their own reflection that they give to the couples on retreat. That's healthy.

"In later years," Duris recalls, "we reflected at the Pinion house as the sexual abuse thing developed. I talked with Ed Upton and other guys about dynamics that we had never addressed before."

> *Looking back, we were immature in terms of being in touch with feelings and sexual identity and how you live that out as a celibate. I'm a ghetto kid. I went to Catholic school and I've been institutionalized since I was 18 living in seminaries and parishes. That colors it. I have to be frank—if you're looking to draw up a list of who to send a person to talk to on how to do celibacy, you might not want to put me on the list. Or maybe you do—because people who think it's simple may have it all wrong.*

....

One big obstacle regarding celibacy was that, while these men felt called to the priesthood, celibacy—at least initially—was seen by them as neither a calling nor a gift from God but rather as a discipline and a cross. Ed Upton states unequivocally, "I never felt called to celibacy—no." Upton commented on remarks that Cardinal George has made indicating that first a man must be called to celibacy and only out of those so called comes the pool of candidates for priesthood. "I don't know where he gets that," Ed says incredulously. "I never heard anyone say that but him." George's view may have arisen in reaction to the sexual abuse crisis, from a desire to ensure that men ordained as priests could in fact live a celibate life. The problem for the six men being followed here, however, is that such a view severely limits the number of candidates for the seminary to those very few males who believe God has called them not only to priesthood but to celibacy as well. Such an understanding of the role of celibacy in the priesthood would probably have disqualified all six of them and, it is safe to say, the vast majority of their colleagues.

Upton nonetheless does see value in the discipline of celibacy in its ability to keep him pointed toward the mission of the Church. "Part of celibacy," he says, "has been fidelity to the work. There's no mistress taking my time away. Not even a mistress of vacations, of money, or anything else. Celibacy is primarily about commitment to your people and to the Church. That's your focus."

Ed makes a distinction between celibacy and pure chastity. "Few people," he maintains, "are perfectly chaste. The question is: If you are at times unchaste, does it rise to such a level that it's taking your whole direction of dedication away? That's the key. Whether at times someone masturbates, I don't think that's relevant. He's a big God—if he really cares about that, then we're in big trouble. Yes, if that begins to take over or if someone has a girlfriend or is going to the gambling boats all the time, that's a different movie."

....

Unlike his classmates, Bill Zavaski has found little personal struggle in living a celibate life. "I know some priests can't live up to that commitment," he says. "But I, fortunately through the grace of God, got a guardian angel that looks out for me. It's never been a bother. I'm focused on my ministry, and that keeps me going. I've never fallen from that commitment."

Some of Zavaski's lay friends, however, have had trouble believing him. "I remember telling this one guy that I haven't ever had a sexual relationship," Bill says, laughing. "He said, 'You mean you've never done it?' 'No.' 'I don't get it. How can you live?' He was a riot. He just could not figure this out."

For Zavaski, the issue hasn't been that he doesn't experience loneliness but rather that he has discovered ways to overcome it. "I sometimes miss having my own family," he admits. "But I regard the people in this parish as my family. I've never felt without a family."

Zavaski's relative ease in living celibately has not meant that problems don't occasionally arise. "Once in a while," he confides, "somebody comes on to you. You sense that quick when somebody wants to go after you physically. You've got to set boundaries. I once had this poor lonely single person dying for physical affection, and it's sad. But you have to say no. You can tell right away. You don't have to be a rocket scientist to figure that out."

Nevertheless, living celibately has opened the door for Bill to have healthy friendships with men and, especially, women. "The great thing about being a celibate," he notes, "is that men aren't jealous because they know I have no sexual intentions with their partners, so I can have great relationships with them." To illustrate his point, he told a story: "There was a morning TV show in New York that asked people to write letters about their favorite clergyperson. My friend's husband had died unexpectedly on Christmas Eve. I had spent time with the family after Christmas. She wrote a letter about how I had encouraged her. The show called: 'We'd like to fly you to New York to talk about your being a Roman Catholic priest.' They did bring up celibacy. 'Do you ever get lonely?' they asked. 'Everybody gets lonely,' I said. 'I don't dwell on it. I've lived with it for over 40 years. I feel comfortable.'"

....

Like Zavaski, Bob Heidenreich has had to negotiate relationships with women to ensure they remain proper. Concentrating on what the title "Father" represents has worked best for him in that regard. "I was having dinner with this gal who's a bit younger than me, at her request," Heidenreich says. "I was close to the family when I was in their parish. Her husband had died, so this is a new relationship between us; it's not the same. At first I thought: What's going on? But the reason she wanted to see me was to ask my advice about dating. I'm thinking: It isn't about dating me? But she said, 'I needed to talk to somebody I can trust.' That brought me back to the 'Father' thing. I think I naturally give off this image of myself as priest. I don't even know it. I get warnings that something could happen with a woman, but I have such a sense of myself as 'Father' that it just doesn't seem appropriate."

That image of priest as Father has guided Bob more than any other in terms of relating celibacy to priesthood. "If there's a criterion for priesthood," he says, "the person must be able to be a good father of a family—like the prodigal father in the Gospels. Celibacy is neutral. It can be healthy or unhealthy. What's more important is learning the lessons of intimacy and fatherhood. Of course, it's easier for me at age 67. I still see beautiful women and they're nice to look at. But psychologically it's like they're babies, kids.

"If you look at the Body of Christ," he explains, "and at the role of the priest as a father, it changes the whole complex to how I can be the image of Christ for people. What do I have to give up, what do I have to extend in my life? Where's my generosity, my forgiveness? That's why the image of father is connected to celibacy."

....

Mike Ahlstrom never felt called to celibacy. "I felt called to priesthood," he says, "and celibacy was part of priesthood. But I never found an attraction to the celibate way of life. But as a celibate, I see myself as able to give everything to serve the people of God."

Celibacy has become easier for Mike as he has deepened his prayer life. He uses a famous story from *Report to Greco* by Nikos Kazantzakis to make his point.[1] "You spend the first half of life spiritually fighting the devil, and you hope to win," he says. "In the second half you've worn out the devil and he leaves you alone. Then you realize you're fighting God, and you hope to lose. I'm wrestling with God now. I want him to win, and he is. In that sense it's easier. You're a lot more with God. It's a better place to be."

....

In considering the efforts of these six classmates to come to terms with the realities of celibate life, it is impossible not to notice the focus on the need for friendship and intimacy. Balancing friendships—with God, brother priests, and laity—appears to have allowed them to live as happily and wholly as the general population, if not more so. In a countercultural comment, Tom Libera discusses the importance of friendship. "There's a line of thought," he begins, "which would not be popular in our culture, coming out of the Greek philosophers, that the deepest human experiences were in friendship, not sexual expression—that was almost a side piece."

> *Our culture has completely discarded the possibility that the deepest and richest parts of life are in friendship. And while sexual expression has its place, it is not the central piece as you look at a whole life. You find that in the Christian tradition, but to sell it now you won't get too far. But it speaks to where many people are, because not everyone can be sexually active—that opportunity is not going to be there for many people, at least at points in their lives. So are there ways to fulfill your life other than being sexual?*

Mike Ahlstrom shares a similar point of view. "I don't think you should go through life," he says, "without human intimacy. Our society doesn't understand this because people identify intimacy with genital activity. But the celibate is called to integrate his or her sexuality into celibacy, not to become isolated, living independent of intimacy."

For most of these men, as important as friendships with lay men and women have become, their connections to other priests have proved crucial in different ways. For one thing, priests have to live with one another in rectories. Having lived through the troubles of dysfunctional rectories, these six men have worked to transform their rectories into healthy, normal environments. Although many parishioners don't believe it to be the case, for example, most priests now cook for themselves. "Virtually no rectory has cooks anymore," Larry Duris says. "But most Catholics think we still do. It happened again last week at the grocery store." A parishioner with a look of disbelief asked Larry what he was doing there. Duris replied quickly, "Shoplifting! No, I'm shopping. What do you think I'm doing?" The parishioner couldn't let it go: "But the cook does the shopping." "The cook," Duris replied with exasperation, "*is* doing the shopping." The point for these men is precisely to get away from such stereotypes and create a normal home. The house many of them own together in Michigan, Pinion, also has become, according to Ed Upton, "a way to have a supportive community to broker celibacy."

The camaraderie provided by Pinion, healthy rectories, and both priest and lay friendships have clearly aided these priests' attempts, as Ed Upton says, to "broker" celibacy. But going to a deeper level, and sharing with others the difficulties of living out their promise of celibacy, has proven more challenging. They recognize, however, the need to talk about them to at least one other person. "A priest friend and I both have friendships with women," Bob Heidenreich says. "We talk about that."

"There's a distance I can go with my prayer group," Larry Duris adds, "and a couple personal friends where I can go more deeply, like Upton. That's necessary." For Mike Ahlstrom, the ability to live celibately—and healthily—comes down to the need to love and to be loved. "The Lord has put people in my life," he says, "men and women, who have loved me. I say to the seminarians, if you cannot experience human intimacy, you have no business becoming a priest. That's part of your spirituality. If you want a close relationship with God, you must be able to experience a close relationship with people."

Switching gears to emphasize another aspect of intimacy, Ahlstrom remarks, "Part of what helped me is definitely prayer. Some things are only possible with God's help."

You don't do it on your own. The degree to which I thought celibacy was my personal project was the degree to which I suffered with it. When I could turn it over to God—it's like somebody going through the 12-step program that I love. I'm not an alcoholic, but I love the spirituality: There's a higher power that will help you, and the third step is surrendering to that power.[2] I say, "Lord, I can't be a celibate without you. I need you." The image of Jesus as a celibate helps: "If you could do it, and you're every bit as much a man as I am, then you can help me to do it."

....

Having ministered during an era when the value of priestly celibacy has come under severe scrutiny, these classmates have long considered both whether celibacy ought to be mandatory for parish priests and whether the discipline had helped or hindered them in their ministry. On the first question, the men from 1969 all favored optional rather than mandatory celibacy.

Larry Duris says that the celibacy requirement is already changing. He pointed to the Vatican's welcoming of scores of married priests from the Anglican Church into the Catholic priesthood. Nonetheless, he himself has given up thoughts of marriage. "Part of me," he admits, "would love to have kids, to have the relationship that is marriage. But I don't even fantasize. I've talked about how if the celibacy requirement suddenly changed, we older priests would have a moral obligation not to marry, having lived as bachelors and as our own boss for so long. We'd be a nightmare as husbands."

Although also demurring about marriage for himself, Mike Ahlstrom supports the idea of a married priesthood, but he expressed concern that even should marriage be opened to all Catholic priests, celibacy should also remain a cherished choice available to the clergy. "Jesus was celibate," Ahlstrom says. "Paul was celibate. In no way would I want it to be like with Protestant clergy. There you're considered weird if you're not married. Celibacy is a charism we need in the Church."

Ed Upton expressed similar ambivalence. "I don't see a lot of sense," he says, "in the insistence on celibacy for the whole priesthood. Maybe a priest being married would strain a marriage, but lots of people work long hours. Some of the priests don't work as long as many people do with a family. I suppose there's been a mystique about celibacy, a sense of trust because you don't have a wife to tell secrets to. But that mystique is gone because of the abuse stuff."

The more personal question of whether, at the end of the day, celibacy had proved a help or a hindrance to these six priests got a varied response. "It's a mixed bag," Tom Libera remarks. When his mom and two aunts became ill, he made the time to care for them, and saw how celibacy allowed him to be stretched. "After the three of them died," he says, "it occurred to me, 'You're as free as you're going to get. You're healthy. You've got a calling that fits. You're grateful to be able to work with people. Now you're free to be that person.' I found out this doesn't mean that you automatically become Mother Teresa, or that you take up that full freedom."

Larry Duris remembered a talk the late Cardinal Bernardin had given on celibacy. "He said that the first half of his priesthood," Duris recalls, "it was a discipline, not a gift. But he later moved into seeing it the other way." For Duris, too, celibacy began as discipline but "maybe it's a gift now."

Contrasting his life with those of his male lay friends led Bob Heidenreich to concentrate on celibacy's practical aspects. "As I progressed in priesthood," he explains, "I started to understand the utilitarian purpose of celibacy, especially as some of my lay classmates were involved in service occupations. One is a health administrator, another is a doctor. There was tension in their families because they didn't take enough time to spend with the kids.

"The downside of celibacy," Heidenreich admits conversely, "is that I'm probably a workaholic. I might do better if I had a family I loved who would demand my time, too."

For Ed Upton, determining whether celibacy helped or hindered is not his call. "It's hard to say," he admits. "You almost have to ask the people a priest serves."

Do you understand people's problems as a celibate? In some
ways you do and in some you don't. Some problems are human
problems. Some are unique in relationships. But if you're a jerk,
married or celibate, you're still a jerk. If you're a decent person,
married or celibate, you can connect to people even if you don't
fully understand them.

At the end of the day, all six priests insist they would and in fact do recommend not just priesthood but celibate priesthood to Catholic youth today. "I hope people would have as happy a life as I've had," Ed Upton says.

Ever the optimist, Bill Zavaski raved about his life as a celibate priest. "I wouldn't trade my life for the world," he insists. "It's a wonderful lifestyle, but not everybody is called to it. Our culture thinks celibacy is crazy. Society is so into physical sex it's incredible, as if you can't live without it. We celibate priests are countercultural in that sense. Jesus said we must become fools for Christ's sake."

While less effusive than Zavaski, Mike Ahlstrom also "absolutely" recommends the celibate priesthood. "Celibacy was a cross I was willing to embrace as part of priesthood," he says. "But you do have to embrace it, not take it on with a negative attitude or hope that it'll change. If you do that, you're headed for disaster. I embrace celibacy out of love for the people of God and the Lord. Some seminarians talk about the 'gift' of celibacy. I would never use that term. I would use 'cross.' But cross is part of the spiritual life. Without it you ain't going to make it. Only through the cross can you find salvation."

....

On September 13, 2012, Mundelein Seminary honored Father Bill Zavaski at its fall fundraiser with the "In Service of One Another" Catholic Humanitarian Award named after the late Cardinal Joseph Bernardin. Although he did not speak directly about celibacy, Zavaski's comments to the seminarians who were present, working tables as waiters, provides a summary statement about how the six men from the ordination class of 1969 have negotiated celibacy and how the next generation of priests might follow their example.

Zavaski asked the seminarians to focus on three relationships. First, he exhorted them truly to love their people in the parishes they serve. "The Church is," he insisted, "the People of God. All of us work together to build up the Kingdom of God."

Second, he encouraged the seminarians to develop strong bonds with their classmates and other priests. He acknowledged that this was difficult in today's seminary environment where men come from all over the world and spend usually just four short years together, a far cry from the 12 years he and his confreres spent literally growing up together in the seminary. Still, Zavaski stressed that these men's effectiveness as celibate priests would be largely tied to their ability to forge close friendships with other priests.

Finally, Zavaski talked to the seminarians about how developing a deep personal relationship with Jesus Christ helped him realize that he is never truly alone and can handle anything. His comments could and would have been seconded by any of his five classmates.

....

1. Nikos Kazantzakis, *Report to Greco* (New York: Simon and Schuster, 1961), 222.
2. For more on the 12 steps and 12-step spirituality, see *Alcoholics Anonymous* (New York: Alcoholics Anonymous World Services, Inc., 1976).

CHAPTER 17

LEGACY
A Church Changed Forever

....

Should anyone aim to evaluate their era of parish priesthood, these six priests from the ordination class of 1969 being followed here would urge them to pay attention to the remarkable period of change and even revolution in which they first trained and then ministered. "If there's a consistent thing in our seminary and priesthood, it's been to be in the midst of change," says Bob Heidenreich. "We had one foot in the old Church and another foot in the new. Our legacy has been to take the best from both, refine it in our personal lives, and then share it with others."

"We were—and are—devoted to building up a Church of laity and clergy," says Ed Upton, "to taking Church teaching and punching it through cultural barriers in order to touch people's spirits, starting in the rapidly changing culture begun in the '60s. In a time of tremendous upheaval, we were able to penetrate that and say that living a life of faith, in the Church, can still make sense and enable you to live in this crazy world. Our legacy is that we love the Church."

As these men stand on the brink of retirement, they do what is customary at such a juncture: look backward, at their legacy, and forward, at the contributions they still want to make to the Church in which they have invested their entire lives. Their legacy, personally and as a class, is inextricably tied to the vision of the Second Vatican Council, which opened when they were just a year out of high school and which remains at the heart of their priesthood. All six of them—Mike Ahlstrom, Larry Duris, Bob Heidenreich, Tom Libera,

Ed Upton, and Bill Zavaski—remain hopeful and pray that both the new pope and a new archbishop will further the vision of that great council.

....

Bill Zavaski has not a shred of doubt about what his class has contributed to the life of the Church: They helped people experience God's grace by taking on the implementation of the reforms of Vatican II, about which Zavaski retains great enthusiasm and for which he will brook no apology. "We were excited about engaging people in ministry and believing what those Council documents said," he says, "that the Church is the people of God; it's not just the priests. We were all part of the Body of Christ. That's one of the best things we did. That was our mission. We have done a good job."

Mike Ahlstrom sees the fruits of this work in the altered attitudes and actions of the people with whom the classmates have worked over the decades. "We've broadened people's horizons as to what their faith is," he says. "There is less racism than before 1969. There is more awareness of a preferential option for the poor, of the ethical demands of the Eucharist, of the responsibility for social justice. We've helped people know that there's a God who loves them and how to get in touch with that God, who's calling them to build his kingdom.

"We also brought priesthood off the pedestal," Ahlstrom continues, "to where priests are close and real to people. And people never lost respect for priesthood, but they actually discovered, by getting to know us at a deeper level, what priesthood is. I can't think of a more exciting time to live."

Although some might view them as pioneers, the men are quick to acknowledge their debt to the priests and the laypeople who modeled for them both the spirit and the strategy of effective ministry. "We come into this standing on other people's shoulders," says Larry Duris simply. "We've influenced people by passing along what we've been taught by pastors and priests we served with," says Bob Heidenreich, "and even more so by families in parishes."

The six men have come to rely on three key practices to see them through their 40-plus years of ministry: steadfastness, flexibility, and unity. Tom Libera pointed to the persistence of the class: "We contributed hard-working guys who went into some difficult parish assignments that enhanced the Church in Chicago. I've found strength and inspiration from the relative intactness of the class. You have a strong core of guys still working in the field. That's one of our legacies: we've stuck with it."

Libera considers his own perseverance in priesthood: "I'm still at it, not done yet," he says. "I'm basically happy. It's amazing how that calling could have stayed alive all those years."

Precisely because the ground of the Church has continually shifted under their feet, these men have learned to deal with unpredictability by developing an ever greater flexibility and reliance on the grace of God. "You realize about things that have happened," Ed Upton reflects, "that you never could have anticipated them. I hope I've been open to God's grace to move into those moments. Sometimes you are surprised that you were part of such graced moments. Regretfully, it is also true that sometimes you find that you inhibited the movement of the Spirit. But I do believe that we're moving on a path with God to better be human, better be Christian, and to trust that journey."

When he gets discouraged about the Church's many struggles and failings, Tom Libera has found consolation in an unlikely place: the archdiocesan directory,[1] which helps him take the long view. "There's a section listing parishes or schools that have closed and the year," he explains. "This list goes back into the late 1800s. At that time the Church is exploding with newness, but even then there were circumstances where places closed. That gives you a perspective. Don't get too nervous if things start diminishing. Maybe we'll be back to storefronts. So let's take a risk and run a storefront!"

....

That they stuck with priesthood during a time when so many other priests left also speaks to the strong ties the classmates formed, which still sustain them today. "We survived a traumatic time when you look at the incredible changes that took place over the last 50 years," says

Bill Zavaski. "But it was fun, too. I've loved every minute of it. I don't want to stop. Part of it is our Pinion house. The bond we have, it's been incredible. Most priests don't have that."

"A class," Tom Libera reflects, "is a cluster of real human identity that you appreciate as time goes on. The theme song for our class—'Moon River,' a very optimistic song—characterizes the times we lived in and tapped into our hope for the future. I suspect if you ask the guys in the class, they would still sing that song with both fond memory and real engagement."

The classmates' slim catalogue of potential regrets brings to mind the line from another song, "My Way": "Regrets, I've had a few, but then again, too few to mention."

"Did I make mistakes?" Ed Upton asks. "Oh yeah. But you can't redo it. I don't know if it's arrogant, but I don't think I'd change much. If I go tomorrow, I have absolutely no regrets."

"I don't know if I would change anything," says Bill Zavaski, before admitting that the Church should not have jettisoned some of its traditional devotions. He cautions, "I'm not for making us into the pietistic people that we were before, but some of those things were valuable and beautiful."

Mike Ahlstrom gently reproaches himself. "I should have gotten into evangelizing sooner," he says. "As I look at the numbers who have become less active in their faith, I've woken up to the need for evangelization. We could have done that sooner or better, so we wouldn't have the attrition rate we've experienced."

These men, while clearly not unaware of their fallibility, nonetheless stand behind their accomplishments, even while knowing full well that many priests ordained in the last 20-plus years view their legacy less than favorably. "The two generations of priests behind us, their first judgment is pretty negative," Ed Upton says. "They say we haven't been strict enough."

Tom Libera suggested, however, that those rendering such a judgment are not only harsh, but lacking in understanding of historical context. "The ideals of Vatican II said that the Church could only survive engaging a new age," Libera says, "by figuring out how to be modest, instead of saying you're forbidden to discuss things."

"Take choosing a godparent," Mike Ahlstrom explains, by way of example.

If you can't find one married in the Church, what do you do? Godparents should be role models on living a Catholic life. But if you don't know anyone like that, take the best people you can. Hope to form them. Don't say they can't do it. You wind up with people walking away, not coming back. That's intolerable. You're going to destroy the Church.

"I don't want a parish," he says, "with 80 people because we've alienated 95 percent of the others."

The men do not appear preoccupied with what their parishioners or others will say about them after they retire. The introvert of the group was uncomfortable with the notion that people would think about him at all. "I'd like to leave," says Tom Libera, "with people having a deeper faith and a sense that everything is running right in the parish. If I then fade out of the picture, that would fit my personality. You make the contribution, knowing you will miss some signals, but you try to encourage people and not get in their way. You're saying this is all beyond your control. You're inviting God to do it. We help a bit as local agents, but I don't need to have a classroom named after me." He seemed moved, however, by the fact that parishioners at St. Eulalia's had indeed named their community room for Msgr. Bill Quinn ('41), Libera's former pastor there. "He's still remembered." Libera says. "Isn't it something that people wanted to do that?"

Bob Heidenreich considered how younger priests might assess what he had endeavored to pass on to them when they served as newly ordained priests under him. He recalled how one of his priest friends from Germany, as part of the German project, was visiting a Chicago parish where one of Heidenreich's former associates, Father Jason Malave ('97), was pastor. "The priest comes back and says, 'Malave said he learned so much from you,'" says Heidenreich. "Like the priests who were my mentors when I was young, I'm passing what I learned along. It's great to see how it's worked well in some people's lives."

Larry Duris simply hoped people knew that he stood with them.

"The phrase: 'He was my priest' or 'my pastor,'" he says, "is one way it would be put in the black community. When people say that with warmth, they're not talking about who the archbishop appointed but that I was there for them—that I helped them walk on their journey to God and with God and didn't get in the way." Duris echoed Libera with that last phrase, revealing the humility that underlies each of these men's self-appraisals. "My purpose is to love people," Mike Ahlstrom reflects, "and let them know there's a God who loves them. That would be central to what I would hope people would say about me."

"If they could say," says Bill Zavaski, "that Father Bill taught us the most important thing in life was to have a relationship with Jesus as our best friend, that would be great."

....

Not one of these classmates appears headed for a life of full-time golf or a move to the Sunbelt any time soon. Although they look forward to escaping a pastor's endless administrative onslaught, they each expressed an interest in continuing to minister to the Church of Chicago. And, if anything, their passion for ministry appears as strong as it was on their ordination day.

"I'm the oldest unretired priest on the South or West Side," Larry Duris admits about his tenure in the African-American Catholic community. Bob Heidenreich put Duris' longevity in perspective, referring to him as "the living history." Preserving and passing on that history has grown increasingly important to Duris as he approaches retirement, especially as the number of "lifers," archdiocesan priests who spend the bulk of their ministry in the black community, has dwindled. "There're hardly any of us anymore," he laments. Duris wants to prevent the history of black Catholics in Chicago from being lost. "I want to be available to Church communities to help people tell their stories," he says. "To have a vision of the future, you have to have a sense of where we've come from, how we got to this point, and where that helps to lead us."

Mike Ahlstrom wants to facilitate dialogue between lay ministers, deacons, and priests. "Actually I'm already involved," he says, "and

Bob [Heidenreich] is too, with an initiative to reach out to international priests to listen to their experiences, frustrations, and hopes. We want to help them understand American culture, the American Church, what a deacon is, what a lay minister is, because many of them have no concept." When his days at Sacred Heart come to an end, Heidenreich wants to continue to work on the exchange program with German priests.

"I'd hope that I'd rediscover parts of priesthood," Tom Libera concludes, "that have been buried in administration, that there's a rediscovery of passion."

This enthusiasm for ministry springs from deep and sturdy roots for each of these men. "The foundation of the Christmas homily," Ed Upton insists, "is that the darkness does not win. The light is more powerful. I truly believe that faith is the powerful element you need in order not to get overcome by negative forces. Faith keeps me going. So does the response you get when people feel touched by ministry and you see you have had an impact."

"What has sustained me," Bill Zavaski says, "is that people have accepted me. I feel affirmed and able to help people grow spiritually because I'm committed to following Jesus." He pointed to one retired priest, Father George Kane ('51), now in his 80s. "He's a great model," Zavaski insists. "He's running groups, giving talks, still filled with excitement."

Larry Duris too spoke of Kane, recalling a meeting they had both attended: "Kane's saying, 'This is crap. What the bishops need....' He's turning red talking. I want to be passionate like that." Duris grows reflective: "What happens at the ambo, at the table—word and sacrament—still touches people. We help to connect them to that. It's also a great support when people say, 'I'll never forget what you did for us at my mother's funeral.' Even people who have drifted away, they run into you, and it clicks into something significant from their past."

Mike Ahlstrom gives credit where he feels it is due. "It's the grace of God," he explains, "communicated through people who keep the passion alive. If I start to get dull, I'm challenged, whether it's by classmates or lay friends. They're not going to allow it."

....

The passion Ahlstrom alludes to emerges with spirit and fire in regards to the future of the Church when these six priests respond to the popular Catholic game of finishing the sentence, "If I were Pope long enough to make just one pronouncement, I would...."

"General absolution," Ed Upton exclaims succinctly. "You're all forgiven. Start over."

Three of the men think the Church's sexual ethic needs reappraisal because, as Larry Duris explains it, the legislative model of do's and don'ts no longer works. Tackling the question of sexuality will be problematic, Bob Heidenreich admitted. "But it's a fundamental piece," he insists, "that alienates people and keeps them from Church. And it does have to do with women's ordination."

Tom Libera proposes the Pope ask Jesus in prayer, "Do you now want women ordained?"

Mike Ahlstrom suggested a series of dialogues between so-called progressive and conservative Catholics in order, as he put it, "to put an end to the thinking of them vs. us. We don't arrive at truth by pronouncement but by listening and consensus building."

Bill Zavaski would take things even further. "I'd have the local people elect the bishops," he says. "That's what we did in the early Church. The Vatican has kept choosing guys of the same mindset, so let's change that."

Zavaski remains confident about the Church's future once his generation has passed on. "The Church has been around 2,000 years," he says. "Look at what it's gone through and survived. Jesus said that nothing will tear down his kingdom. The Holy Spirit will take care of things just fine."

....

From many teachers—their families, priests from seminary and parish assignments, laypeople in parishes—these six priests from the class of 1969 learned that to serve the Church and help build the kingdom of God on earth, they must carefully tend relationships. But their primary impetus for making relationships the focal point of their ministry was the vision of Church inspired by the Second Vatican Council, the

watershed event that defined their years in the seminary. "The implementation of the Council," Ed Upton says, "has been the central theme
of our 45 years. Jack Gorman ('52) said we're going to create a new,
different, and better Church out of the Council—not out of our heads,
but out of the Council. People ask me what the Council has meant to
me. I answer: Trying to build a Church of laypeople—it's been my life."

....

1. *Archdiocese of Chicago Directory 2012* (Chicago: New World Publications, 2012).

CONCLUSION

Six priests ordained for the Archdiocese of Chicago in 1969 and now at or near their retirement from full-time ministry, who have told their story here in their own words, have had the remarkable experience of serving through three eras of the Catholic Church in the U.S. in one lifetime. They spent their childhoods and their early seminary years in the post-war Catholic Church of Latin Masses and weekly Confessions. The Second Vatican Council, which met during the middle of their seminary training, set off reverberations that fueled the priestly work of these men for the next quarter century, in what is often called the Vatican II era of the Church. Then, beginning in the late 1980s when Pope John Paul II's pontificate had taken firm root, these priests experienced the "reform of the reform," that liturgical and theological critique lasting at least through the election of Pope Francis, in which they felt from some traditional Catholics a relentless pushback against the perceived inadequacies of Vatican II-era theology and ministry. What did these men accomplish across these three eras, and what difference did it make?

To answer that question, it has been necessary to examine their time as priests in its proper historical context. As boys, these six future priests experienced a world different from that of their parents' childhood. Although they still lived in Catholic neighborhoods, where the parish served as not only the spiritual but also the educational and social center of their lives, their neighborhoods were becoming less immigrant and less ethnic. English, rather than a foreign language, was for most of them the language they heard on the streets and playgrounds.

And although "pray, pay, and obey" still had meaning in their parishes, where the pastor reigned supreme, some laity had begun to replace that phrase with the Catholic Action slogan: "observe, judge, act." Catholics had arrived financially and politically in Chicago, running local politics and labor unions and making inroads in business. The Catholic Church in America, due in no small part to Archbishop of Chicago Cardinal George Mundelein, was setting its stamp on American life, proving to WASP America that Catholics could indeed be fully Catholic and fully American. These boys were part of what historian Steven Avella called "This Confident Church," referring to the era of the Church in Chicago just prior to the Second Vatican Council.[1]

Upon entering high school at Quigley, these six young men encountered a whole new Catholic world, one that extended far beyond the boundaries of just their own parish. They met classmates from every area of the city, some of whom would journey through seminary with them all the way to priesthood. Then, during their two short years at the new Niles campus, they saw their worlds turned upside down. Even before Cardinal Albert Meyer headed to the Second Vatican Council, which would introduce use of the vernacular at Mass, he had begun to focus on race, labor relations, and laypersons' roles in the Church. Msgr. Eugene Lyons ('42), the rector at Niles, then began loosening the strictures of the seminary Rule and bringing in speakers to talk about issues facing the Church and society. Faculty members admitted they didn't have all the answers and entered into dialogue with students, treating them, to the seminarians' great surprise, as thinking adults.

What a shock, then, to enter Mundelein Seminary in the fall of 1963 where Msgr. Malachy Foley ('31) made it clear from day one that seminarians were to be seen not heard, and where the worldwide excitement from the Council in Rome was all but ignored. Nothing symbolized this close-minded environment better than the nonchalant way seminary officials treated the most significant event not only in Catholic America but in the whole country—the assassination of President John F. Kennedy. At this point, members of the class began to rebel against authority at Mundelein because that authority refused to give rational explanations for policies and decisions. Told simply

that whatever seminary authorities said was "God's will," they no longer believed it. Never again would these men buy that argument from
authority, whether from pastor, bishop, or pope. When Catholics who
never lived through those times wax nostalgic about the good old days
of seminary life, the men from 1969 can barely contain their incredu-
lity because, as one of them put it so crudely yet succinctly, "the old
seminary sucked."

Imagine their relief and even joy, then, when in the winter of
1965, Msgr. John Gorman ('52) took over as rector of Mundelein Seminary. Under Gorman, the seminary changed its formation program,
its liturgies, its academic program—and faculty. He introduced, partly
due to the insistence of seminarians from the ordination class of 1969,
summer apostolates and a six-month diaconate internship in urban
parishes, at last making Mundelein a true professional graduate school.
Gorman believed that dialogue about how to make the Church—and
seminary—a better sign of the Kingdom of God would teach seminarians to lead parishes where thinking Catholic adults would buy in
and become active members. The focus became pastoral—training the
men to treat people with respect so they could advance the Gospel
message as men, Christians, and priests, in that order.

Their rector's commitment to this approach culminated in his
support for a retreat, just prior to the class' diaconate ordination, given
by a community of laypeople who shared their faith stories and expectations for their priests. Such a retreat was unheard of then and would
be unlikely to be repeated today. Yet the six priests from 1969 refer
back to that retreat as the event that encouraged them, more than any
other, to take the plunge and say yes to priesthood.

As they readied themselves for ordination, they had experienced
in the seminary different models of priestly leadership, best symbolized by their two rectors at Mundelein: Msgrs. Mal Foley and Jack Gorman. Foley personified a leadership style that was cold, authoritarian,
and, not only unpastoral, but ironically, anti-intellectual as well. All
seminary rules, procedures, policies, and dictates—and by extension
all of the Church's as well—were indisputably God's will, to be accepted
whether understood or not. The six men met these claims with impa-
tience and then rebellion, embodying a changing world that increas-

ingly refused to accept the status quo and demanded to understand the "why" behind every pronouncement. To continue to proclaim Christ in this era would require the Church to persuade, to explain why its teachings and practices made sense, to respond to questions its members were now raising about their Church. At the major seminary, no one grasped this more clearly than Msgr. John Gorman, Foley's successor.

The class of 1969 clearly began their priestly ministry during a time of tremendous social upheaval in both the Church and the country. Ed Upton pointed to the book *A Generation of Seekers: the Spiritual Journeys of the Baby Boom Generation* by Wade Clark Roof[2] as a reminder of what his class—and that whole generation of religious leaders—had to face upon embarking on priestly ministry. Roof stresses that the baby boom generation lived in a time of increasing choices as regards to religion. They would adopt neither the ethnic and religious traditions of their parents nor the doctrines of any religious institution unless ministers took seriously the questions they had about the old answers of the faith. By struggling together with their people, ministers would show that they and their religion could be trusted.

The point, according to Upton, was that Vatican II's openness to change helped keep many of the boomer generation in the Church. Had they ministered in the top-down authoritarian way that previous generations had (and that some still call for), they would have been, Upton insists, dead in the water. But some in the Church today suggest that Vatican II-era priests turned the Church in on itself and away from the great task of proclaiming Christ by falling in love with collaboration, dialogue, and listening. This argument seems to ignore the key insight of Roof's work: that in the era of the civil rights and women's movements, the protests against the Vietnam war, the insistence on free speech, and the reaction against *Humanae Vitae* from American Catholics, the Church had to engage in honest dialogue with its members and with non-Catholics or risk becoming an irrelevant relic stuck in the past. Dialogue didn't turn the Church in on itself. It allowed it to reexamine itself so that it might again turn outward to speak to a rapidly changing world in a voice the world could hear.

....

So, what did Fathers Mike Ahlstrom, Larry Duris, Bob Heidenreich, Tom Libera, Ed Upton, and Bill Zavaski accomplish? Over time, as these priests attempted to carry out the vision of the Second Vatican Council, they helped to transform many parishes into active, thriving faith communities. They started and strengthened parish councils, finance councils, liturgy teams, Christ Renews His Parish retreats, Eucharistic ministry teams, social justice and RCIA programs, and more. And, yes, they experimented. They tried dialogue homilies, home Masses, and once, one of them almost witnessed a wedding in the forest preserves. Shared ministry with religious and laity, bringing the priests into professional and social contact with women, became the norm. Together with these lay and religious parish leaders, they worked to improve Catholic schools, transform religious education programs, invigorate Sunday Mass, and form base communities that shared faith on a deep personal level. These men also took on the important task of mentoring the newly ordained priests assigned to their parishes. By the time these priests of 1969 became pastors, they had helped to remake the face of parish life in Chicago. Committed to the Vatican II theology that the Church was the people of God, these men bet their lives on developing across the archdiocese a cadre of intelligent, active, and committed lay leaders, dedicated to living out the Gospel in their parishes, workplaces, and communities. The rise of lay leadership never threatened their own sense of themselves or their roles as priests. Firm in their knowledge and understanding both of who they were and what their ministry should entail, they carried out, to the best of their ability, the vision of Vatican II.

....

What difference did the accomplishments and hard work of these six men make to the life of the Church? What legacy did the members of the class of 1969, and the era of Catholic clergy that they represent, leave to the Church of Chicago and by extension to the wider American Church? In elucidating themes of their priesthood, it seems most appropriate to return to the four characteristics Msgr. John Gorman—now a retired auxiliary bishop of Chicago—hoped for these men as they finished their seminary training. Gorman wanted his protégés to be competent ministers of the Gospel, to exercise responsible freedom, to value relationships, and to develop healthy and holy interior lives.

As much of the Catholic community moved into the middle class, seeking higher education and joining the ranks of professionals, they sought a role in operating their parishes; they desired prepared, intelligent homilies and good music at Mass. And they began to look for greater professionalism from their clergy. The priests studied here earned advanced degrees and certificates in liturgy, counseling, ministry, and community organization. Ed Upton's building of not only the church but the new parish of St. Francis of Assisi in Orland Park serves as one good example of the need for professional expertise. Upton had to raise funds, run meetings, broker factions with differing ideas about the design of the church, and keep people united around the long-term goal when setbacks inevitably occurred. Later, when the idea of opening a Catholic school in the area surfaced, a survey Upton had conducted showed that a school could survive only if four area parishes contributed to it. He also learned, however, that most Catholic parents preferred a strong weekend religious education program to a traditional Catholic school. By doing needs-based analysis, Upton successfully helped to launch both.

Bob Heidenreich, meanwhile, helped transform the archdiocesan Priests' Personnel Board from a political bastion based on "who you know" to a professional office balancing the needs of priests with those of the diocese. He then spent years running the pastors' training program of the diocese, working to ensure that prospective pastors' talents actually fit the parishes they had applied to lead.

All six of these priests passed on to lay leaders the lessons they had learned about a more competent Church, encouraging them to get training in scripture, liturgy, community organizing, and social justice, and thus leaving a legacy today in many parishes of capable and skillful Church leadership.

Msgr. Gorman also wanted his priests to be capable of exercising "responsible freedom." His study of psychology persuaded him that the strict life imposed on seminarians—and to a very real extent also on lay Catholics prior to the Council—tended to produce either compliance or, for some, rebellion, as opposed to maturity. For Catholics freely to embrace the truth and value of Catholic teaching and practice, priests needed creatively to engage laypeople's real questions about their Church. Recall Tom Libera hearing the relentless requests from a divorced female parishioner to start a program for divorced Catholics. For Mike Ahlstrom, responsible freedom meant employing a method of decision-making as a pastor that was undreamed of in previous generations. He insisted on a participatory, consensus model of Church governance—putting both the church renovation and the question of starting a Spanish Mass to a vote of his parish.

Increasingly, these priests found themselves in the difficult position of being on the front lines of debates about theology and Church policy that personally impacted their people. Precisely because these parishioners also seemed to be exercising a responsible freedom, the men ordained in 1969, not always publicly, began to support them in their efforts to have the Church reexamine the strictures against artificial birth control within marriage and the prohibition on divorced and remarried Catholics receiving Communion. Listening to their people, these priests stayed in dialogue and often stood with them. The men thought their people's arguments made sense and believed reasoned conversation would help keep people in the Church.

Of the four hopes Gorman expressed for his priests, the men from the class of 1969 perhaps most fully embraced the counsel to value relationships. As they grew close to their people, these six men became part of the communities they served. Being one of the people was, for them, neither an abdication of leadership nor a matter of losing their priestly identity but rather a carefully chosen method of priestly leadership. They reached back and reclaimed Msgr. Reynold Hillenbrand's focus on the Church as a Mystical Body in which an organic relationship existed between a priest and his people. And these priests learned that they could better challenge those people when necessary—for example, in the area of race relations—if first they had made a strong connection with them and made it clear that they loved them. They had not failed to heed the lesson Ed Upton's mother had taught him:

acknowledge the sin, but love and welcome the sinner.

These six priests also saw an opportunity to develop ties of intimacy that would bring their people close not only to them, but to the Church and to the Lord. Bill Zavaski showed special sensitivity to families in grief. Recall how much time he spent with the family at St. James who suffered multiple losses from a car accident. As a boy, he watched his mom help new immigrants adjust to life at St. Bart's in Waukegan, and saw their gratitude. Then, during college, when she died, he received support from many quarters. All this convinced Zavaski early on that loyalty, friendship, and relationships should mean most to a priest. It also reminded him that life was short. By far the most extroverted of the six, Zavaski believes deeply in celebrating life with his people. While some might criticize this as overly social and lacking in piety, he has learned that making friendships with parishioners allows priests easier access when tragedy inevitably strikes their people's lives.

For Larry Duris, intimacy between priest and people must extend to the whole community. Duris came to high school in search of himself and a community where he could make his many dreams—teacher, musician, social worker—come alive. Perhaps that explains why he chose to immerse himself for a lifetime in the Southeast Side African-American Catholic community. He enjoys letting people know that he and the Church value their presence. Immersion in the community mattered enough that Duris spent weeks living in an abandoned building so that no one could burn it down before it could be rehabbed. He also ran down the street to hold the body of a murdered friend. St. Ailbe's Parish is awash in groups—greeters, choirs, bereavement groups, and youth groups—highlighting the value Duris places on communal relations.

Msgr. Gorman stressed one final aspect of priesthood: the development of the interior life. Unlike the other three themes, this area took quite some time before it arrived on the "A" list for these classmates. As they grew closer to people, they gradually realized that meeting the demands of living a celibate life did not come automatically; they would have to work at it. These men also pled guilty to what Mike Ahlstrom called the "heresy of action." They prayed, to be sure, but initially rarely took sufficient time for or even realized the necessity of placing prayer at the very center of their lives. As their years in priestly ministry progressed, however, this changed. A number of factors led to that change, chief among them the growing ideological division in the Church and the clerical—and episcopal—sexual abuse scandal.

Particularly after the pontificate of Pope John Paul II had taken shape, members of the class of 1969 began to hear growing criticism—often from much younger priests—of their ministry. When Cardinal Francis George arrived in 1997 to succeed their beloved archbishop, Cardinal Joseph Bernardin, and it became clear that George had a more nuanced if not critical view of the Vatican II era than Bernardin, these six priests began to feel taken to task, as if Church hierarchy and young priests had decided to call into question their life's work. The critiques tended to claim that these priests had become too close to their people, especially in the liturgy, and had lost the sense of otherness necessary to delineate a clear role for the priesthood, to confront sinfulness, and to defend Church teaching. While these six priests admit making mistakes, particularly early in their priesthoods, overall they reject most of this critique. They ran active parishes, often with thousands of parishioners attending Sunday Mass and hundreds of children in their schools and religious education programs. When they—especially Bob Heidenreich—compared that to almost empty European parishes, where by and large diocesan priests had not become as close to their people or as dedicated to implementing Vatican II on the parish level, they saw that their approach had indeed produced considerable success. Nor did they observe new conservative Catholics filling churches. In fact, they often heard from them, much to their astonishment, how the Church would be better off with a purer but smaller group of true believers. The criticism, nevertheless, stung. Half kiddingly but with a touch of sadness, several of the priests referred to themselves during the interviews as "dinosaurs." The sense that their work had come under an often mean-spirited scrutiny helped turn the men more deeply toward the interior life of prayer.

If this critique affected the spirits of these six men from the class of 1969, the sexual abuse scandal turned them upside down. Dealing with the scandal meant addressing it honestly with parishioners, coming to terms with the fact that fellow priests they knew had abused children, and facing the increased scrutiny and at times ridicule of an increasingly skeptical and mistrusting public. Each man also had to face the fact that the Church hierarchy both nationally and in Rome—and to some extent, even in Chicago—had failed miserably to protect children. Even after the USCCB had passed the Dallas Charter for the Protection of Children and Young People, some bishops had failed to follow the charter, not reporting some abuse cases and not following recommendations of the review boards the Charter had set up.

These men faced this tragedy as they had so many things—honestly and publicly. By so doing, they mitigated in some small part the absolute devastation, as Bill Zavaski put it, that the scandal wreaked upon their parishes, especially parishes where a priest had in fact abused minors. These men openly criticized their own hierarchy where they thought it necessary, speaking and writing of their own hurt and anger. In so doing, they allowed room for parishioners to approach them and open up enough to admit, many for the first times in their lives, that they had suffered sexual abuse, sometimes by a priest. These interactions convinced them of the need for the Church to become both more transparent and more humble going forward. As Ed Upton so honestly noted, it also forced them to confront a problem endemic to all organizations: the tendency to place self-protection over the demands of justice. Listening to their people's suffering changed their hearts; it snuffed out their instinct to put their brother priests and the institutional Church first and caused them to put the needs of children before anything else.

Growing criticism of their priesthood, the horror of the sexual abuse scandal, not to mention the many challenges of daily living on the front lines of leadership in the Church, have all challenged these six priests in their attempts to remain happy, healthy, and spiritually fit. In strengthening their interior lives so as to better negotiate the vicissitudes of a celibate priesthood, these priests have come to appreciate the importance of prayer and of friendships with classmates and other clergy and their many good lay friends. Pinion, the house that many members of the class share, stands as a visible sign of the value they place on class friendships. Prayer groups, both priest and lay, also testify to the importance of intimate friendships in helping them cope with life's struggles. As Bill Zavaski recently told today's Mundelein seminarians, if they nurture three relationships—with Christ, their people, and each other—they will be happy priests indeed. Perhaps Bob Heidenreich put the importance of prayer best when he noted that Christ must first challenge him in prayer in order for him to have anything real to say at Sunday Mass.

....

In June of 2013, four of the six priests retired: Ed Upton, Bill Zavaski, Tom Libera, and Mike Ahlstrom. Bob Heidenreich retired in June of 2014. For the time being, Larry Duris soldiers on. These six priests from the class of '69 feel remarkably happy about their lives as Catholic priests. The theme of change dominated the lives and ministry of these men. To a man, they loved living through the great era of change that the Second Vatican Council triggered. And while some admit their efforts at evangelization could have proven stronger or that they undervalued traditional practices such as Eucharistic Adoration, in the main they stand unrepentant about trying to build a Church centered on properly formed laypeople open to the message of God's love for his people. When critics say to Ed Upton that the main thing people learned from this approach is that God loves them, he responds: "What's wrong with that?" He and his classmates see Catholics today as less racist, more open to the poor, more involved in social justice, and much more likely to take on responsibility not only for the life of the parish and larger Church but also for their neighbors in general. They believe that their leadership played at least some small role in that transformation, and for that they are grateful.

Change not only has come to personify the priestly careers of these men, it also preoccupies their thoughts of the future. In a group interview conducted late in 2010, the men imagined what concerns they might address if they could play "pope for a day." Tom Libera, Bob Heidenreich, and Larry Duris would address the role of women in the Church; Ed Upton would permit the return of general absolution; Bill Zavaski called for the election of bishops by the people; and Mike

Ahlstrom suggested ongoing dialogue between so-called progressives and traditionalists in the Church. None expressed much hope that the then current pope, Benedict XVI, or any pope in the near future would likely focus on any of their "dinosaur" issues.

Dinosaurs or not, these men have stressed throughout their priesthoods that without a greater pastoral sensibility that includes an embrace of real conversation with the laity and the secular culture, the promulgation of policy or doctrine is a waste of time. They continue to insist that only people who know they are loved and respected are likely to listen to, much less engage, the Church and its teaching and practice. The surprising election of Pope Francis in March of 2013, therefore—followed by his refreshing call for dialogue on issues such as social justice, women's leadership in the Church, divorce and remarriage, and pastoral sensitivity in the treatment of gays and lesbians—could not help but give them hope that the theology of ministry from their much maligned Vatican II era may yet come back into its own. Such an unexpected development would happily postpone the extinction of—and perhaps bring new life to—the ideas and practices that these six good priests from the Chicago ordination class of 1969 have in these pages so honestly, bravely, and generously discussed.

....

1. Steven M. Avella, *This Confident Church: Catholic Leadership and Life in Chicago*, 1940-1965 (Notre Dame, IN: University of Notre Dame Press, 1992).
2. Wade Clark Roof, *A Generation of Seekers: The Spiritual Journeys of the Baby Boom Generation* (San Francisco: Harper Collins, 1993).

AFTERWORD

The idea for this book dawned shortly after the death of a priest. On January 24, 2005, Father Bob "Red" McLaughlin, a Chicago priest ordained in 1966, died suddenly of a heart attack in Florida while playing golf. Red was a vibrant, thoughtful, funny—and also pugnacious—priest, and an unrepentant Catholic progressive of the Vatican II era. He was also a dear friend to my wife Cathy and me, and we grieved him deeply—and still do. Having spent 10 years in the seminary system of Chicago in my youth, I knew many priests, most of whom had been ordained in the 1960s or early '70s. While some Catholics have found the Church of the mid-'70s to early '80s—the era I came of age in—lacking in evangelical fervor, I surely found myself aflame with a spirit of excitement about the Church and its ministry when being formed by its priests. When Red died, it dawned on me that before too long this generation of priests would pass on.

Some years after that, visiting with another friend, Father John Canary, a Chicago priest from the class of 1969, I told him that I had struggled to continue to feel comfortable in a Church that seemed to be rejecting much of what I had learned from our generation of Catholic leaders, clerical and lay. As only a great friend could, John said something like, "If you try to leave the Church, I will come and get you and bring you back." What a marvelous example of pastoral ministry. Afterward, reflecting again on Red and the priests I'd come to respect, I decided I wanted to tell their story or, better yet, become the vehicle through which some of them could share their incredible journey as Catholic priests who've lived through three distinct periods of American Catholic history: the pre-Vatican II, Vatican II, and post-Vatican II eras.

After much thought, I decided to do extensive interviews with a number of priests to ask about their lives in the pre-Vatican II Church, to inquire about the impact of the Vatican Council on their lives and ministry, and finally to invite them to reflect on their response to the criticism of their era of priestly ministry by some in the Church. But the key question remained: whom to ask? Eventually it came to me that examining the lives of men from the same class might prove illuminating to and also help to structure the narrative. Ordination classes were important to priests of that era; they provided a sense of corporate identity. So much so that in the book, I identify Chicago priests by ordination class by listing their class in parenthesis the first time I introduce them in each chapter. For example: Bob McLaughlin ('66). I decided I wanted to choose a class with which I had some familiarity, and I chose the class of 1969.

There was no magic to this choice, although two things influenced it. First, I wanted a class that would likely be retired by the time this work got published, because I suspected that priests anticipating retirement might be more honest in their reflections. Second, I knew two priests from the class, Ed Upton and Bob Heidenreich, and I believed they might take to the project and agree to give their candid thoughts. Father Canary, another member of the class, agreed to help me pick other candidates who might agree to be interviewed. After initial meetings with several priests, Upton and Heidenreich did indeed agree, as did four others. Three priests declined to do the interviews—one, if there is such a thing, from an excess of humility. The other four priests interviewed here—Mike Ahlstrom, Larry Duris, Tom Libera, and Bill Zavaski—I did not know, although I had heard of them.

I began to interview these priests individually in their offices or rectories in March of 2010. I recorded the interviews, meeting with each priest either five or six times, the interviews averaging one and a half to two hours each.[1] The final interview, the only group interview I conducted, took place on December 23, 2010. For those who might be prompted to ask why it took so long to publish the manuscript, I can only plead a combination of thoroughness, a full-time job, and the fact that Cathy and I have been nearing the end of the intensive phase of raising two great children.

This book, as much as possible, uses the words of the six priests themselves. Letting them take the lead in telling their stories seemed the best way to communicate their lives from the inside out. A word on how I used the transcripts is in order. Mostly, anything in quotes came right off the recordings. Three exceptions, however, bear noting. First, I made slight changes in quotes to improve grammar, sentence structure, etc. without changing their meaning. Second, at times I combined quotes from different places in the interviews. Third, the priests made some minor changes to the transcripts after being presented with their quotes for review.

In writing this book I have, needless to say, incurred many obligations. First, I must thank John Treanor, the Vice Chancellor for Archives and Records at the Archdiocese of Chicago, for permission to work in the archives. No one was more helpful in navigating those archives than Julie Satzik, a former assistant research archivist there. Meg Hall also provided me with help on a recent visit. I also am indebted to Msgr. Dennis Lyle ('91), then rector of Mundelein Seminary, and to the academic dean there, Father Thomas Baima ('80), for permission to do research in their library, as well as to the library director, Lorraine Olley, for her help in locating materials relevant to the six priests' years of study at the seminary. Thanks also go to Paula Kamen, the executive director of Transcription Professionals, who agreed to transcribe the interviews. I must also most sincerely thank in that regard Gina Marie Brady, who took on the difficult task of actually transcribing 36 interviews, and without whose superb assistance I never would have completed this work. Tom McGrath, Terry Cahill, and Ted Rosean all read parts or all of the manuscript and offered valuable insights. McGrath, in addition, along with Joe Durepos, provided much help in teaching me the process of putting together a manuscript of this sort. Several friends guided me personally in navigating how to write a book while also working and raising a family. These include Rita Rogan, Tom O'Neill, and Bob Adams. Msgr. John Canary deserves special thanks for helping me discern who might best serve as spokesmen from his class. I can't express enough appreciation to Bishop John Gorman ('52), whose influence on this class was so palpable in my interviews that I simply had to interview him as well. He not only agreed, but spent a thoroughly enjoyable couple of hours with me candidly sharing his memories of the class of '69.

It should go without saying how much I owe to Fathers Mike Ahlstrom, Larry Duris, Bob Heidenreich, Tom Libera, Ed Upton, and Bill Zavaski. Unfailingly gracious, remarkably candid, and, at times, touchingly personal, these men have done a great service to the Catholic Church by opening a window on what the day-to-day lives of parish priests look like over 40-plus years and three distinct periods. How privileged I felt to spend a great deal of time listening to their stories, often laughing out loud, and occasionally shedding a tear as they revealed to me the depth of their love for the Church, the people of God, and also for one another.

Greg Pierce of ACTA Publications agreed readily to publish the book through its new imprint, In Extenso Press, and has been an enthusiastic supporter and a skilled editor. What a thrill to have one of the preeminent publishers of books on the American—and Chicago—Catholic Church firmly in my corner. I could not have placed this work in better hands. I also wish to thank the book's excellent typesetter, Patricia Lynch, as well as Caitlyn Schmid for her expert proofreading.

Lastly, I would be remiss if I did not thank my wife, Catherine O'Connell-Cahill, who served as another key editor on this book. Cathy has worked as an editor at *U.S. Catholic* magazine for 35 years and knows the insides and outs of both editing and the American Church. When I asked her to consider editing this work, she insisted—in the interest of marital harmony—that I not comment on any of her edits in progress, but that I wait until she finished a chapter to view it whole. I—mostly—complied, and the result is a better book and a stronger marriage. In the end, she agreed because she believed so deeply that the story needed to be told and that I was indeed the one who should tell it. My gratitude is endless.

....

1. The interviews with Mike Ahlstrom took place on March 16, May 5, June 8, June 30, September 21, and October 6, 2010. The interviews with Larry Duris took place on March 23, May 11, July 7, September 8, September 29, and October 13, 2010. The interviews with Bob Heidenreich took place on April 14, June 1, June 29, September 7, October 5, and November 1, 2010. The interviews with Tom Libera took place on March 16, April 13, May 4, June 9, July 13, and September 14, 2010. The interviews with Ed Upton took place on March 25, April 22, May 13, June 5, July 14, and September 16, 2010. The interviews with Bill Zavaski took place on April 21, May 19, June 18, July 20, and September 22, 2010.

Index

ALSO AVAILABLE

THE MESSAGE: CATHOLIC/ECUMENICAL EDITION
Translated by Eugene Peterson
with Deuterocanonical Writings by William Griffin
This faith-filled paraphrase of the Bible in contemporary idiomatic American English is first and foremost a reader's Bible, bringing the Scriptures alive by transforming the words in a way people can understand what God is trying to say to us today. 1984 pages, paperback and hardcover

AN IRREPRESSIBLE HOPE
Notes from Chicago Catholics
Edited by Claire Bushey; Illustrations by Franklin McMahon
In this slim volume of stories, essays, poems, and passionate personal pleas, more than thirty Chicago Catholics reveal their hopes for the church they love—sometimes ardently, sometimes painfully, but always faithfully. 84 pages, paperback

CHURCH, CHICAGO STYLE
William L. Droel
Church, Chicago-Style examines the unique legacy of the Catholic Church in Chicago, and profiles well-known church leaders, including Russell Barta; Msgr. John Egan; Father Dennis Geaney, OSA; Monsignor George Higgins; Ed Marciniak; and Mary Irene Zotti. 128 pages, paperback

ACTS OF RECOVERY
The Story of One Man's Ongoing Healing from Sexual Abuse by a Priest
Michael D. Hoffman
One man's story, told honestly and bravely, of healing after sexually abused as a child by a trusted family friend, a priest serving in the Archdiocese of Chicago. Through trying to understand and reconcile the trauma he experienced, the author focuses on what he calls his twelve "acts of recovery." 96 pages, paperback

UNFINISHED PENTECOST
Vatican II and the Altered Lives of Those Who Witnessed It
Ken Trainor
The story of the Second Vatican Council and its aftermath is told through the eyes of men and women religious—those who, as students in Rome, witnessed that remarkable turning point and whose subsequent lives were strongly influenced by the shock waves that continue to reverberate. 332 pages, paperback

WITNESSES TO RACISM
Personal Experiences of Racial Injustice
Edited by Lois Prebil, osf
Here are heartfelt testimonies by members of the Archdiocese of Chicago about their own experiences with racial injustice, all driving home the message that racism can only be dealt with if we get to know one another in honest, deep, and ongoing relationships. 80 pages, paperback

ACTA PUBLICATIONS
800-397-2282 • www.actapublications.com